Austria
in the
European
Union

Contemporary Austrian Studies

Sponsored by the University of New Orleans and Universität Innsbruck

Publication of this volume has been made possible through a generous grant from the Austrian Ministry of Foreign Affairs through the Austrian Cultural Forum in New York. The Bank Gutmann AG in Vienna, the University of Innsbruck, and Metropolitan College of the University of New Orleans have also provided financial support. All pictures in this volume are courtesy of Harald Hofmeister and *Die Presse* photo archives (Vienna).

Contemporary
Austrian Studies
Volume 10

Austria
in the
European
Union

Günter Bischof
Anton Pelinka
Michael Gehler
editors

Transaction Publishers
New Brunswick (U.S.A.) and London (U.K.)

Fourth printing 2009

Library of Congress Catalog Number: 2001056880
ISBN: 978-0-7658-0899-8
Printed in the United States of America

Library of Congress Cataloging-in-Publication Data

Austria in the European Union / Giinter Bischof, Anton Pelinka, and Michael Gehler, editors.
    p. cm.—(Contemporary Austrian studies ; v. 10)
    Includes bibliographical references.
    ISBN: 0-7658-0899-4 (pbk. : alk. paper)
        1. European Union—Austria. I. Bischof, Giinter, 1953- II. Pelinka, Anton, 1941- III. Gehler, Michael. IV. Series. II. Title.

HC240.25.A9A953 2001
337.40436—dc21   2001056880

Table of Contents

III. DOMESTIC POLITICS PERSPECTIVES

NONTOPICAL ESSAY

FORUM: World War II Crimes against Jews in Austria and Their Prosecution in Austrian Courts after the War

REVIEW ESSAYS

BOOK REVIEWS

ANNUAL REVIEW

LIST OF AUTHORS

Preface

Contemporary Austrian Studies (CAS) after Ten Years

Academic journals can be ephemeral projects. The publishers' rule of thumb is the "three-year-rule." If it is still alive after three years, you can count your blessings. After that the new journal actually has a fair chance of survival. To make it beyond this three-year-mark is a small victory. By this standard, to make it to the ten-year mark can be considered a considerable success. We are quite pleased to have reached this point with our journal and still be in business. This is all the more astounding since our resources have always been scarce—budgets have been shoestring and had to be cobbled together from year to year. Against all odds, we have been making it.

Our *editorial philosophy* was laid out in vol. I (pp. 1-3). We have sought to further the study of modern Austria with *"an international and comprehensive interdisciplinary approach."* We also asserted the need for a field of Austrian Studies separate from German Studies and devoted *CAS* "to a self-confident assertion of separate Austrian identity vis-à-vis Germany." In the past ten years the shadow of Germany over Austria has in fact waned (while the shadow of the European Union has waxed). Austria's identity has become less "Austrian" and more European. We wanted to promote Austrian Studies abroad and particularly in the English-speaking world. Our goal of "combining all social sciences" in our interdisciplinary approach has been vigorously pursued. The vast majority of essays published in these first ten *CAS* volumes has been in the fields of contemporary history and political science/and political culture, with economics/economic history and society/social change following as distant cousins. We have not succeeded in our aim to cover the field of international and constitutional law.

Our *chronological framework* to devote equal space to all periods of post-Habsburg Austrian history has also not been fully realized. Scant attention has been paid to the interwar period, the field of contemporary history that was almost exclusively the focus of Austrian *Zeitgeschichte-forschung* prior to the 1980's. We will attempt to correct that in vol. XI, which will be devoted to a reassessment of the Dollfuss/Schuschnigg years (1934-38). The bulk of essays published in *CAS* concentrated on postwar Austria (the Second Republic) and World War II. More recent contemporary history has received the lion's share of our attention. Here we follow the Anglo-American tradition of "contemporary history" that does not shy away from giving only yesterday's events academic attention and not leave it exclusively to the journalists to provide first interpretations of recent history. Such *"presentism"* would be considered unscholarly in such a journal were it published in Austria. We think we can fill an important void. As it were, with our postwar focus we have anticipated a trend in international contemporary history research as both the prestigious Munich *Vierteljahrshefte für Zeitgeschichte* and London *Journal of Contemporary History* have explicitly shifted their focus on the post-World War II period. With the coming of the 21st century, contemporary historical research is increasingly concentrating on the second half of the 20th century.

The current volume bolsters this *presentist focus*. We think Austria's relationship with the European Union—from its solid beginning in 1995 to its more rocky recent state—deserves the full attention of scholars from all fields. Scholars are called upon to provide paradigms to help the larger public understand recent events and their deeper historical taproots.

The following statistical portrait of the chronological distribution of the essays published in the first ten *CAS* volumes buttress the picture of our foci (see next page).

The majority of our essays have concentrated on the "long fifties" and the Kreisky years of "social-liberal consensus" (E. Hanisch - M. Gehler). Yet the realignment of Austrian politics and the rise of Haiderism since 1983/86 have received almost equal attention. If we had any "pet peeves", they probably were Austria's historical memory of World War II and its contribution to postwar Austrian identity, the economic reconstruction of the country after the war (Marshall Plan!), the towering political figures of Chancellors Bruno Kreisky and Franz Vranitzky and their devotion to active diplomacy and to salvaging the country's celebrated welfare state and social peace (against all odds), as well as the antics of Jörg Haider and his political movement. Austria's accession to the European Union, its role in it, as well as the difficult reassessment of its "permanent" neutrality—the country's major international realignment in the late 20th century—have obviously caught our historical attention, too. We have looked at some of these events and trends from a comparative European/American perspective but hope to do even more in that direction.

Table 1: A Statistical Survey of CAS Essays and Their Chronological Distribution

	1918-1938	1938-1945	1945-1983	1984-2000
HISTORY				
Historiography Essay				1
Historiography Roundtables				2
Political	2	5	5	
Diplomatic/International			11	2
Economic			11	2
Intellectual	1			
Memory			12	1
Identity		2	1	
Women	1	3	3	
Intelligence		2	3	
POLITICAL SCIENCE				
Domestic/Political Culture			11	17
Foreign Relations/International		2		9
European Union				6
REVIEW ESSAYS				12
BOOK REVIEWS				51
SURVEYS OF AUSTRIAN POLITICS				10
INTRODUCTIONS				21
TOTAL NUMBER OF MANUSCRIPTS				190

We are particularly proud of *CAS*'s book reviewing culture. Here major intellectual trends can be followed and preoccupations in Austrian studies intimately traced. With a major historiographical and oft-cited programmatic essay by Thomas Angerer (vol. III), two dynamic "Historiography Roundtables" (on John Boyer's work in vol. VI, and Gerald Stourzh definitive state treaty history in vol. IX), 12 extensive review essays and 51 book reviews, the pages of *CAS* have become home to lively intellectual debates and solid scholarly discourse. If we follow a model here it is the combative reviewing culture of the *New York Review of Books*, or the measured reviews of the *Atlantic Monthly*.

To readers living outside Austria who do not have the opportunity to follow Austrian events on a daily basis, we have tried to provide a service with our "annual reviews of politics." These surveys constitute a running commentary on major political events and election results.

In toto our editorial staff has handled an astounding 190 manuscripts published over the past ten years (not counting the ones rejected). We would like to thank our staff for their sterling and unselfish contribution in the production of photo-ready copy of ten *CAS* volumes – usually finished in the last minute on a wing and a prayer and with deadlines stretched to the max. Our changing staff has always risen to the occasion and made up with enthusiasm and dedication what we were lacking in manpower and financial security. By the end of each volume's production cycle they always managed to deliver a copy-edited and type-set manuscript to our publisher of ten years, Transaction Publishers of Rutgers University in New Jersey. Ellen Palli in Innsbruck and Dean Robert ("Bobby") Dupont have been present since the creation and deserve our deepest appreciation. Ellen has been Anton Pelinka's right hand from the beginning and has produced the photo-ready copy of 4 of the volumes. Bobby's budgetary genius has found ways on the UNO side of helping to finance the volumes, when all other sources ran dry. Gordon "Nick" Mueller at UNO and Erich Thöni and Franz Mathis at the University of Innsbruck, the coordinators of the friendship treaty between these two universities and the executive editors of *CAS*, have helped Bobby in this endeavor of insuring financial survival.

Next to Ellen Palli, Gloria Alvares, Allison Duvernay Watling and Judy Nides at UNO prepared photo-ready copy of the rest of the volumes. Our talented copy-editing staff did yeo(wo)man work. Melanie McKay, Jennifer Shimek and Irene Brameshuber-Ziegler surprised many an Austrian contributor when they rendered their "*Engleutsch*" ("Austro-English") into literate and readable prose overnight. Not only are they masters of the English language but willy-nilly they have also become experts in the *Chicago Manual of Style*. We recruited our editorial assistants amongst the University of Innsbruck students who have been coming year after year to study in the UNO History Department. Rainer Fadinger, Irene Brameshuber, Gerald Steinacher, Günther Walder, Martin Kofler, Daniela Kundmann, Daniela Jäger, and Elisabeth Wagner have spent untold hours with organizational tasks, correspondence with contributors and book publishers (handling review copies) and keying in copy-editors' corrections on the computer. Without their contributions, the timely submission of volumes would not have been possible. Some have become budding historians in their own right and contributed to *CAS* (Kofler in vol.VIII) – a small triumph in encouraging and *internationalizing* historical talent in Austria.

Rainer Nick and Reinhold Gärtner of the University of Innsbruck's Political Science Department have faithfully gathered the data and delivered the annual surveys of Austrian politics.

We thank our financial supporters for making the publication of these volumes possible. Next to the Universities of New Orleans' and Innsbruck's regular financial backing, the Austrian Foreign Ministry's Cultural Department (then under Peter Marboe) gave us a five-year grant to help launch *CAS*. Through the Austrian Cultural Institute (now Austrian Cultural Forum) in New York the Foreign Ministry is still subsidizing publication of *CAS* by buying a set number of volumes annually for worldwide distribution to Austrian libraries. At the ACI Ernst Aichinger and Peter Mikl were instrumental in helping us secure and administer this official government support; ACI-directors Wolfgang Waldner and Christoph Thun-Hohenstein benevolently have encouraged the project. The Bank Guttmann AG in Vienna has been our only regular corporate sponsor. We would like to thank Anton Fink, one of its directors, for his astute sense of the need for philanthropy of scholar-ship; he has helped us secure this sponsorship year after year.

At Transaction Publishers, director Mary Curtis and publisher Irving Louis Horwitz have been congenial and supportive partners in publishing and marketing *CAS*. With their "flagship" *CAS*, they have made Transaction one of the premier publishers of Austrian studies in the United States. Their staff has provided much needed support in directing the manuscript through the final publication process. Anne Schneider has been the editor responsible for *CAS* in recent years. Alicija Garbie has helped time and again with marketing the volumes.

Last but not least we would like to thank our international advisory board who has helped review manuscripts and books, pick volume topics, and guarantee the scholarly integrity of *CAS*. The distribution of our board members over the years has been from

AUSTRIA

University of Innsbruck
Max Preglau (Sociology)
Rolf Steininger (History)

University of Salzburg
Ingrid Bauer (History)
Ernst Hanisch (History)
Reinhold Wagnleitner (History)

University of Graz
Siegfried Beer (History)
Konrad Ginther (Law)
Manfred Prisching (Sociology)

University of Linz
Wilhelm Kohler (Economics)

University of Vienna
Felix Butschek (Economics)
Peter Gerlich (Political Science)
Hanspeter Neuhold (Law)
Helga Nowotny (Social Sciences)
Sonja Puntscher Riekmann (Political Science)
Oliver Rathkolb (History)
Sieglinde Rosenberger (Political Science)
Dieter Stiefel (History)
Gerald Stourzh (History)
Ruth Wodak (Linguistics)

CANADA
Hans-Gerog Betz (Political Science)
Robert Keyserlingk (History)
Franz Szabo (History)

FRANCE
Jacques LeRider (History)
Michael Pollak (History)

GERMANY
Dietmut Majer (Law)
Margareta Mommsen (Political Science)

ITALY
Mario Caciagli (Political Science)

UNITED KINGDOM
Kurt Richard Luther (Political Science)
Peter Pulzer (Political Science)

UNITED STATES
Evan Burr Bukey (History)
Gary Cohen (History)
Wolfgang Danspeckgruber (Political Science)
Michael Huelshoff (Political Science)
David Good (History)
Robert Jordan (Political Science)
Radomir Luza (History)
Andrei Markovits (Political Science)
Sybil Milton (History)
Richard Mitten (History)
Bruce Pauley (History)
Richard Rudolph (History)

May we be able to provide such a *resumé* at the twenty-year mark as well!

May 2001

Günter Bischof
University of New Orleans

Anton Pelinka
University of Innsbruck

TOPICAL ESSAY

Introduction

When *Contemporary Austrian Studies* published its first volume in 1993, its topic was dedicated to "Austria in the New Europe." Already in 1989 Austria had applied for EU-membership, and in 1993 the negotiations were just getting started. This step was seen as the direct result of a new European context: The East-West-conflict was over; the European Community no longer belonged to one side in a bipolar bloc system; and the EU, as a consequence of the Maastricht-Treaty, decided to deepen and widen its character by introducing the European Monetary Union and a Common Foreign and Security policy.

Austria joined the EU in 1995—together with Sweden and Finland. This step was legitimized by a plebiscite which demonstrated that a very significant majority of Austrians was in favor of this membership in the "New Europe." Since then Austria has experienced high and low points in its relationship with the EU: Its presidency in 1998 gave the young member the feeling to be—at last—fully accepted into the Union; the bilateral measures, however, with which Austria's European partners boycotted the ÖVP-FPÖ coalition government in 2000, demonstrated that EU-membership is not so much an end than a beginning—the beginning of learning to live in a new and ever changing political environment.

The experiences of the first years of Austrian EU-membership are the topic of this volume. It is a "first assessment," a first evaluation. It is an analysis not so much of clear-cut effects but more of an ongoing process.

Heinrich Neisser, Jean Monnet-Professor of political science at the University of Innsbruck, discusses the most important questions the European Union will have to answer in the future, most prominently the role of a European Charter for Fundamental Rights. Neisser, who represented Austria at the convention held to prepare this charter, provides the theoretical background for such an agreement. In December 2000, it was accepted at the European Council in Nice, however only in its "lighter" version as an non-binding political statement. Some principal aspects have to be considered regarding this charta: first, the possible conflict between the Council of Europe and its Convention of Human Rights; and, second, the conflict between the anti-federalist sentiments (most prominently articulated in the United Kingdom and in Denmark, but also—rather surprisingly—in the Irish referendum of June 2001) and the development towards further political unification, entailed by a charter.

Thomas Angerer, professor of history at the University of Vienna, provides the historical background to this volume's topic: Austria's foreign policy in the interwar period. After 1918, Austria had to get acquainted with its new role as a smaller European state. The context of regionalization and globalization already defined the field in which the First Republic had to shape its international standing. Angerer argues that globalization generally weakens smaller states while regionalization provides opportunities to escape dependencies. What was later to become "*glocalization*" (in Euro-speak)—the decline of the nation state in favor of global and regional levels—was also a challenge to the First Republic and the authoritarian regime. Limited by great power interests (French, Italian, German) and anti-Habsburg fears of the other successor states, Austria's foreign policy was not yet able to develop the "leverage of the weak," which the Second Republic would successfully apply (see Günter Bischof, *Austria in the First Cold War, 1945 – 1955*, Basing-stoke, 1999).

Jacques Le Rider, professor at the École Pratique des Hautes Études in Paris, describes the motives and effects of the measures (or "sanctions") which the governments of the fourteen other EU-members used to boycott the ÖVP-FPÖ coalition between February and September 2000. Especially the French government, supported by French public opinion, regarded the Freedom Party's access to the government of an EU-member state as a breach of the values forming the basis for French "Republicanism" and European integration. This conflict expresses the lack of a common understanding of the "European Value System." The crisis between Austria and its European partners could be an incentive to restart the debate about such a system.

Sonja Puntscher Riekmann and Johannes Pollak of the Austrian Academy of Sciences discuss another aspect which became important during the period of the "sanctions": the conflict of interest between small and big countries. This conflict is reflected in the debate about the future structure (constitution?) of the EU: Is the "sovereign" of the—future—Union the "European people" or is it the conference of (still sovereign) nation states? Indirectly, this conflict played an important role when public opinion in Austria (and in other smaller EU-member states, especially in Denmark) interpreted the "sanctions" as the result of a "directorate" of the big members over the small members.

Michael Huelshoff, professor of political science at the University of New Orleans, presents a comparative evaluation of the German and the Austrian EU-presidencies. With the Austrian presidency of the EU-Council in the second half of 1998, one of the three new members presided over the EU's main decision-making body for the first time. With the German presidency, which followed in the first half of 1999, one of the founding members of the EU took over the lead. Huelshoff argues that the classical tug-of-war between Commission and Council did not play a significant role during both presidencies. Huelshoff stresses the importance of short-term domestic and international factors which influence the impact of each a presidency. Thus, for example, the German elections overshadowed the Austrian presidency and the Kosovo-conflict and the NATO-strikes against Serbia significantly influenced the German presidency.

Hans-Georg Betz, professor of political science at York University (Ontario), and Walter Manoschek, professor of political science at the University of Vienna, analyze the FPÖ from two different perspectives. Both assume a comparative stance, stressing specifically Austrian features. Betz, however, argues that the decisively deviant quality of post-1945 Austria—consociationalism, social partnership, power sharing—provided for the FPÖ's rise and the "Haider phenomenon." Manoschek, on the other hand, claims that Austria's ambivalent attitude towards its Nazi-past, represented especially by the Freedom Party and its predecessors, is the main reason for Austria's deviation from the (West-) European mainstream. Betz tends to look at the Freedom Party as an overall European phenomenon—a rightist protest movement or a populist phenomenon—while Manoschek perceives the FPÖ as a specifically Austrian party with particularly Austrian characteristics. For Betz, the FPÖ successfully denies Austrian peculiarities; for Manoschek, the FPÖ embodies Austrian peculiarities. The Betz – Manoschek debate does not represent a conflict between irreconcilable positions; it is an academic discourse which confronts different sides of the same reality. The debate should be seen as an instrument that can draw a more complex picture of contemporary Austrian politics.

Gerda Falkner of the Max Planck-Institute in Cologne analyzed an important policy aspect: the possible "withering away" of the Austrian welfare state as a consequence of Austria's EU-membership. As long as the EU does not develop its own social policy and create a "European Social Union," Austria—like all the other member states—is in full control of its own social agenda. The EU is not responsible—at least not directly—for any changes in the social policy performance. This could, of course, change quickly: The more important the federal aspects of the Union become, the more probable an impact of European decisions on the welfare systems of its members will be.

Michael Gehler, professor of contemporary history at the University of Innsbruck, underlines the more general aspects of the "sanctions" against the Schüssel/Riess-Passer government. Domestic motives played an important role, especially in Belgium, France, and Germany. Other members, like Denmark, had their reservations regarding the diplomatic boycott—also due to domestic reasons. There was no consistent policy within the EU 14. And there is no proof for a decisive "conspiracy" of the Socialist International. On the other side, the crisis of the German CDU was decisive for the absence of mediation in transnational party cooperation and for the lack of political support of the ÖVP-FPÖ government. In addition, the differences within the EU 14 were created at least as much by the conflict between "big" and "small" states as by the conflict between "left" and "right" parties.

Richard Mitten's Nontopical essay, a historiography forum and reviews complete this volume.

Anton Pelinka and *Michael Gehler*

Innsbruck June 2001

Austrian President Thomas Klestil signs the ratification instrument of the treaty of Austrian accession to the European Union on 22 November 1994; Chancellor Franz Vranitzky is sitting next to him. Standing in the back (from left to right) are Herbert Schambeck, President of the *Bundesrat* (2nd chamber), Vice-Chancellor Erhard Busek, Heinz Fischer, President of the *Nationalrat* (1st chamber), Brigitte Ederer, State Secretary for EU-issues, and Foreign Minister Alois Mock. (photo Harald Hofmeister, *Die Presse*)

I. A FIRST ASSESSMENT

The European Union and Fundamental Rights

Heinrich Neisser

On the Road to a Political Union

With the accession to the European Union on 1 January 1995 Austria has become a member of a political community. Since the Treaty of Maastricht, which came into force on 1 November 1993, European integration has moved from a merely economic dimension to an extensive political unification. The three *pillars* of the European Union are the supranational Economic Monetary Union, the intergovernmental Common Foreign and Security Policy, and the Cooperation of the Interior and Justice, which, since the Treaty of Amsterdam, is officially referred to as Police and Judicial Cooperation in Criminal Matters. The Union's task is to "organize, in a manner demonstrating consistency and solidarity, relations between the member states and between their peoples . ... [D]ecisions are taken as openly as possible and as closely as possible to the citizen." (Article 1, Treaty on European Union).

The Treaty of Maastricht marks a new stage in the European unification process. Unification no longer implies only a strong convergence of the European states, but also a better protection of the rights and interests of the member states' citizens. One important measure in that context has been the introduction of a Union citizenship, which is related to the nationality of a member state and provides certain rights: the right to freely move and reside within the territory of the member states, the right to vote at elections of the European Parliament, and the right to petition. While a general debate on democracy aspects like legitimacy and representation is going on throughout the Union, the construction of a political union moved the European citizen increasingly into the center of the discussions on further developments of the European unification process. The ratification procedure of the Treaty of Maastricht has clearly shown that the European citizens do not want to be passive spectators of the continent's unification any longer. Despite his personal commitment, French President François Mitterand only received a very narrow majority favoring the creation of a political union.[1] In Denmark, the referendum had to be repeated before the Danish people would support a shift towards a political union.[2] The German Constitutional Court decided that every step towards a further development of the European Union required a parliamentary-democratic legitimacy in the member states.[3] Austria legitimated its decision to join the Union with a democratic decision: In the referendum of 12 June 1994 almost two thirds of the Austrian voters voted for the accession to the European Union as it was laid down in the Treaty of Maastricht.

The growing relevance of a democratically legitimated unification process has an impact on the position of the citizens in the member states. They have increasingly moved into the focus of political life and need to play an active part. The discussion on fundamental rights in the European Union has reflected this development.

The Development of Fundamental Rights
in the European Community

The European Court of Justice (ECJ) in Luxembourg played an active part in the development of European fundamental rights. The initial concept of European integration focused on economic unification, which was determined by the four freedoms, i.e. freedom of movement, capital, goods, and services. Apparently there was no need for a general charter on fundamental rights. However, the ECJ quickly pointed out that fundamental rights would have to be considered for the European Community. In the late 1960s, the Court had already derived the fundamental rights in its jurisdiction from general community law, ruling that these were the basic principles of Community law. These principles were developed by comparing the member states' system of fundamental rights and their international treaties, referring in particular to the European Convention on Human Rights (ECHR), which had been ratified by all the member states of the European Community.[4] However, the European Court of Justice could not directly apply the ECHR since it was not a system of fundamental rights but only a source of guidelines for matters concerning fundamental rights: "Similarly, international treaties for the protection of human rights on which the Member States have collaborated or of which they are signatories, can supply guidelines which should be followed within the framework of Community law."[5]

Consequently, the ECJ put the fundamental principle of human rights into concrete terms by recognizing individual fundamental rights in several court decisions. In particular it accepted the right to equal treatment,[6] the right to non-discrimination,[7] the freedom of religion and belief,[8] the right to privacy,[9] and the right to the respect of family life.[10] Together with the ECJ as a fundamental rights authority, the European Court also tried to act as a driving force in fundamental rights affairs. In the 1970s, for example, the European Parliament introduced the human rights problem into the dialogue with Third World countries and strongly condemned the violation of human rights. In 1977 the European Court issued a declaration on the political principles of the definition of fundamental rights, which was accepted by the European Council and the European Commission and was signed by the presidents of the three institutions in Luxembourg.

The Treaty of Amsterdam

The Treaty of Amsterdam gave a new dimension to the debate on fundamental rights in the European Union. Even though that treaty did not comprise an extensive codification of the fundamental freedoms and human rights, it introduced substantial changes, partly as a continuation of the Treaty of Maastricht. For the first time, Article 6 Section 1 of the Treaty on the European Union contains a catalog of principles which mentions the respect for human rights and fundamental freedoms, along with the principles of liberty, democracy, and the rule of law. These principles are the basis of the ECJ when controlling actions of the Community institutions in the fields of the Community Treaty and the third pillar of the Treaty of Maastricht; they are also a prerequisite to an application for membership (Article 49 Treaty on European Union).

As a result of the Treaty of Amsterdam, the violation of the above mentioned basic principles can now be sanctioned. Upon suspicion of a serious and persistent breach of these principles by a member state, the Council, composed of the heads of state and government, meets and acts by unanimity on a proposal by one third of the member states or the Commission. After obtaining the assent of the European Parliament, it then affirms the existence of such a serious and persistent breach. On the grounds of that ruling, the Council, acting by a qualified majority, may impose sanctions. These sanctions do not allow an exclusion of the member state in question. However, certain rights deriving from the Treaty may be suspended, including the voting rights of the government representative of that member state in the Council.

The Treaty of Nice includes the provision that the Council may direct recommendations towards a member state which is clearly running the risk of a serious breach of the principles laid down in Article 6 Section 1 in the Treaty on European Union. Such a measure requires a substantial proposal of one third of the member states, the European Parliament and the European Commission. Before that decision, which requires a 4/5 majority, the member state in question has to be heard; the Council can also ask independent experts to submit a report on the situation in the particular member state within a reasonable period of time.

Furthermore it needs to be stressed that Article 6 Section 2 of the Treaty on European Union conforms with the European Convention on Human Rights: "The European Union shall respect fundamental rights, as guaranteed by the European Convention for the Protection of Human Rights and Fundamental Freedoms signed in Rome on 4 November 1950 and as they result from the constitutional traditions common to the Member States, as general principles of community law."

Article 13 of the Treaty on establishing the European Community is of particular importance, too. The European Council, acting unanimously on a proposal from the Commission and consulting the European Parliament, may take appropriate action to combat discrimination based on sex, racial or ethnic origin, religion or belief, disability, age, or sexual orientation. So far, the Council has made use of this authority in two directives.[11]

Briefly, the fundamental rights situation resulting from the Treaty of Amsterdam is the following:

- The respect for human rights and fundamental freedoms is a basic principle that may lead to sanctions in case of a serious and persistent breach. It is a precondition for the accession of new candidates.
- Discrimination is protected in primary law (i.e. the law established in the treaties) and secondary legislation (Article 13 of the Treaty on establishing the European Community and relevant guidelines).
- The system of fundamental rights established by the ECHR has to be respected and is a guideline in the Union's fundamental rights policy and practice.

- The fundamental rights exercised in the jurisdiction of the ECJ are by fact part of the fundamental rights *acquis* of the EU because it can be assumed that the ECJ will not revoke its jurisdiction.

A Charter of Fundamental Rights
for the European Union

The Treaty of Amsterdam introduced a new phase in the Union's fundamental rights policy. In discussions throughout the European Union it was often emphasized that these fundamental rights would constitute a necessary measure for the strengthening of a European identity and the development of a European constitution. The popular proposal that the European Union should sign the ECHR, and thus apply to the Union's institutions and organs the binding fundamental rights decided upon by the Council of Europe in 1950, was declined by the ECJ in Luxembourg. In a 1996 report, following a petition of April 1994, the court found that the EU had no authority to join the ECHR nor was it authorized to make rules in the field of human rights or to conclude relevant international treaties. The member states never reached an agreement on a potential amendment of their EU treaties, which would have laid down a basis for joining the ECHR.

This problem provoked the idea of developing a charter of fundamental rights for the Union itself. The charter would aim to emphasize the character of the European Union as a community of rules and values. In particular Germany, which held the presidency of the Council in the first six months of 1999, supported this idea. At the Cologne European Council on 3/4 June 1999 the green light was given for an ambitious and extensive fundamental rights project. The European Council assigned the task to draft a charter of fundamental rights. For that purpose a specific body was created, including fifteen personal representatives of the heads of state and government of the fifteen member states, thirty representatives of the national parliaments, sixteen representatives of the European Parliament and one representative of the European Commission. The ECJ and the Council of Europe were granted observer status. In the history of European integration the implementation of such a body was a real novelty. For the first time the preparation for a decision was transferred to an institution that received its legitimacy from both the institutions of the member states (government and parliament) and the European Union (European Parliament).

The Cologne European Council entrusted this commission with the task to present a draft charter of fundamental rights "in due time for the European Council in December 2000"[12] so that it could be solemnly proclaimed at the Nice summit under French EU presidency. Then, the question "if and how the charter could be integrated into the treaties"[13] would be reviewed. The task included only a mandate to draft an analysis of the fundamental rights at the time.

It took the Convention of Fundamental Rights, as the commission called itself, nine months to carry out this task. The discussion procedure was established at the informal Tampere summit in October 1999. The meetings of the Convention members took place in Brussels, alternating between the facilities of the European Parliament and the Council. The sessions were open to the public. The presidency was responsible for the draft texts and consisted of one chairman elected by the Convention and three vice-chairmen, representing the three groups the Convention was composed of (representatives of the heads of state and government, the national parliaments, and the European Parliament). In the debates all the official languages of the European Union were allowed. The hearings of the Non Governmental Organizations and the applicant countries were of particular importance. The decision making process followed the consensus proceedings, i.e. the presidency determined a consent ability; no votes were taken.

The Convention of Fundamental Rights accomplished the task with which it had been entrusted by the Cologne European Council. On 2 October 2000, after intense debates that had been going on for months, it presented a draft charter with fifty-four articles, which can be considered a genuine system of fundamental rights of the European Union. In many respects the result is a compromise of quite dissenting opinions within the Convention. However, it is the first analysis of fundamental rights relevant to the European Union. The draft also proposes to establish new fundamental rights, for example in the fields of asylum, protection of personal data, and good governance.

The charter was solemnly proclaimed at the Nice summit in December 2000. It is a political proclamation but no legally binding document.

Fundamental Rights Guaranteed by the Charter

The Charter of Fundamental Rights contains a systematic synopsis of the Union's *acquis* of fundamental rights. These rights are divided into six sections that form a typology of fundamental rights. For the first time, a single text sets out the whole range of classic civil rights, liberties, and social rights. Therefore, the charter not only contains rights that protect the individual against intrusions by the state, but also provides the citizen with the right to certain services rendered by the state. The following is a short overview of the Charter of Fundamental Rights:

The preamble of the charter emphasizes the fact that the enjoyment of these rights entails "responsibilities and duties with regard to other persons, to the human community and to future generations."

The first section of the charter is dedicated to human dignity. Article 1 provides that "human dignity is inviolable. It must be respected and protected." The protection of human dignity is not only a specific fundamental right, but also a basic norm of the Charter of Fundamental Rights in general. The respect of human dignity is a decisive principle for all matters, but in particular for the social fundamental rights.

The second section is about civil rights and liberties. They are the hard core of the classic fundamental rights and include for example the right to liberty and security, the respect for private life and family life, the freedom of conscience and religion, the freedom of speech, the freedom of assembly and association, the right to education, the freedom to conduct a business, the right to property, and the right to asylum.

Another section deals with the core concern of equality. The principle that every individual is equal before the law has been interpreted by the modern fundamental rights policy particularly as a principle of non-discrimination. Any discrimination on the following grounds shall be prohibited: sex, race, color, ethnic or social origins, genetic features, language, religion or belief, opinion—political or otherwise—, minority membership, property, birth, disability, age, or sexual orientation. This section of the charter guarantees equality between men and women; cultural, religious, and linguistic diversity; the rights of the child and of the elderly; and the integration of people with disabilities. It has already been stated that the link between classic and social fundamental rights is a specific characteristic of the charter.

Chapter IV is called "Solidarity." It contains the traditional rights of employees, such as the right to information and consultation with the employer, the right to collective action (including the right to strike), protection in the event of unjustified dismissal, the right to fair and just working conditions. This chapter also establishes the responsibilities of the European Union to guarantee a system of social security and social assistance and to ensure health care, environmental and consumer protection.

Chapter V is dedicated to the citizens' rights. According to the Treaty of Maastricht every citizen of the member state is granted, in addition to the national citizenship, the citizenship of the Union, which guarantees concrete rights listed in the Treaty establishing the European Community. These rights have been incorporated into the charter, and one important fundamental right was added: "Every person has the right to have his or her affairs handled impartially, fairly and within a reasonable time by the institutions and bodies of the Union." The right to good governance includes the right to compensation if the organs or servants of the Union cause any damage in the performance of their duties. The citizens' rights of the Union, already valid, are now part of the charter as well. These include the right to vote and to stand as a candidate at elections to the European Parliament and at municipal elections, the right to petition, the right to report cases of maladministration to the ombudsman, and the right to diplomatic and consular protection in such countries in which a member state is not presented.

Chapter VI contains the guarantee of judicial rights. Most of these rights originate in the ECHR, including the right to an effective remedy and to a fair trial, the right to defense, the presumption of innocence, and others.

The final chapter stresses that the provisions of the charter apply to the institutions and bodies of the Union and to the member states only when they implement Union law. The charter does not establish new powers or tasks for the Union. The meaning and scope of the rights laid down by the Convention shall be the same as those of the rights guaranteed in the ECHR.

The Charter: A Contribution to the Constitutionalization Process in the European Union

The ongoing discussions about the EU-Charter aroused many expectations. The committed supporters of a European constitution consider it an important progress in the development of such a constitution. The debates about a European constitution are quite controversial. Opponents of the idea stress the fact that the term *constitution* is tied to the state. Since the European Union is no nation, it cannot act as a constituent force. This position requires further analysis. In a supranational organization power is exercised as well. This process takes place within the framework of a system of fundamental rights and principles agreed upon by the member states. Thus the European constitution is a contractual constitution. The incorporation of a Charter of Fundamental Rights into the treaties, i.e. into the constitutional system of the Union and the Community, is an important measure because it defines the relationship between the European citizens and the institutions of the European Union from a new, qualitative perspective. Thus the integration of the charter into primary law is a further step in the constitutionalization process of the Union and the Community.

Future Perspectives of the Fundamental Rights Policy of the European Union

With the solemn proclamation of the Charter of Fundamental Rights on the eve of the Nice summit in December 2000 the EU gained a new political declaration on fundamental rights. However, this declaration is not legally binding, and future debate will focus on this aspect. At the Nice summit no commitment was made in that respect. In a declaration concluding the conference on the future of the Union a timetable was proposed: In 2001 the Swedish and Belgian presidency (Sweden in the first half, Belgium in the second half of 2001) will initiate an extensive debate with all groups of interest (representatives of politics, business, academia, civil society) in cooperation with the European Commission and the European Parliament. In December 2001 the European Council will agree on a declaration establishing the appropriate measures for this debate, which will include the discussion of the status of the charter. At a governmental conference in 2004 the content of that discussion will be debated with regard to necessary treaty amendments.

In any case, the EU-Charter has already created a new awareness of fundamental rights within the European Union. In view of the increasing economic globalization the legal protection of fundamental rights in Europe is an important goal. This process limits the public power of the institutions of the European Union. Fundamental rights are also rightly considered an expression of an objective system of values that is valid for the both the European Community and the political system of the member states. They are a fundamental element of the European identity.

Notes

1. In the French referendum 51.2 % of the voters decided in favor of the Maastricht Treaty; 48.8 % were against it.

2. In the first referendum of June 1992 50.7 % of the Danish people voted against the Maastricht Treaty; 49.3 % were in favor of it. The second referendum of May 1993 brought a majority for Maastricht: 56.8 % versus 43.2 %.

3. Bundesverfassungsgericht, ruling of 12 October 1993 (Maastricht), BVerfGE 89, 155.

4. The ECHR is a basic human rights document in Europe. It is a multilateral international treaty, elaborated by the Council of Europe. The ECHR was adopted in November 1950.

5. Case 4/73, Nold AG v. Commission of the European Communities, ECR 491, para. 13 (1974).

6. Case Casagrande, ECR 773 (1974).

7. Case Defrenne v. Sabena, ECR 455 (1976).

8. Case Prais, ECR 1598, 1599 (1976).

9. Case National Panasonic, ECR 2033, 2056 ff. (1980).

10. Case Commission v. Germany, ECR 1263 (1989).

11. These directives must be implemented by the member states.

12. Final declaration of the Summit of Cologne 3/4 June 1999.

13. Final declaration of the Summit of Cologne 3/4 June 1999.

II. FOREIGN POLICY PERSPECTIVES

Regionalization and Globalization in Austrian Foreign Policy since 1918[1]

Thomas Angerer

Introduction

Modern Austria is a small, federal state. As a small state it is relatively weak and dependent. Regionalization and globalization tend to weaken it further and make it more dependent as connections between states intensify and state borders matter less and less.[2] This is even more so as Austria has a federal structure. It is composed of nine provinces which enjoy considerable autonomy and are interested in increasing this autonomy through transborder initiatives that would further regionalize them on a substate level. In Austria, regionalization therefore puts the state under pressure from above and below. On the other hand, Austria can take particular advantage from regionalization and globalization alike. After all, forming regional groups to coordinate or pool resources with other states (small and/or big) is a classic small-state-strategy against dependence, isolation, or discrimination. Conversely, globalization can be a resort against discrimination by regional blocks which exclude the state in question. Finally, regionalization on the substate level opens new opportunities to further state interests when strong federal traditions count more than the weakened sovereignties of small states. Thus, in Austria, regionalization and globalization are both the source of dependencies and the remedy against them.

This particular ambivalence of regionalization and globalization for small, federal states is the first hypothesis of this paper. The other hypothesis I want to present is less general in character and more specifically drawn from the Austrian case: If regionalization and globalization affect how, and how well, states are able to affirm themselves in international and transnational relations, the perceived vices and virtues of regionalization and globalization will also depend on the strength of a state's identity, i.e. its effective determination to affirm itself. It makes a difference whether a state has the support of its people and shows a spontaneous will for autonomy, or whether its very existence is subject to controversy; it also matters whether a state's will for autonomy has tradition or whether it is a recent, more precarious achievement.

In this respect, Austria is a particular case. During long periods of its existence, its identity was weak, if not radically put into question. A leftover of the defeated and dissolved Habsburg empire, Austria didn't want to be a small, independent state after World War I, and it took decades and repeated crises to adapt itself to its new existence.[3] Conversely, after the reestablishment of its independence at the end of World War II, and even more so after the end of Allied occupation ten years later, Austria showed particular eagerness to maintain its newly appreciated autonomy. As a consequence—and that is the main thesis of this paper—troubles with its own identity deeply affected Austria's attitudes towards regionalization and globalization, at least until very recently.

One more word on regionalization and globalization in general. International relations experts distinguish these two concepts from *internationalization*, whether on the regional or global level. Whereas internationalization "refers to a process of intensifying connections between national domains," globalization "refers to processes whereby social relations acquire relatively distanceless and borderless qualities," making the world become "a single place;"[4] by analogy, the same would be true for suprastate regionalization. However, the processes of *internationalization*, *globalization*, and *suprastate regionalization* mix in practice.[5] Their differences are in fact more gradual than radical. Historically, regionalization and globalization largely grew out of internationalization. It would therefore be anachronistic to insist on their different denomination when dealing—as this paper does—with the entire period since 1918. I therefore prefer a larger definition of regionalization and globalization, including internationalization on a respectively regional and global level.

Of course, this larger definition does not preclude distinctions between the various forms of regionalization or globalization, ranging from loose cooperation to supranational integration. On the contrary, it is easier to see what these related phenomena have in common by first putting them under the same, large umbrella before differentiating them. As an example, I will insist on the difference between purely

intergovernmental cooperation and cooperation with strong supranational elements as this differentiation is necessary to understand Austria's
opposite attitudes towards the corresponding types of regionalization in
Western Europe during most of the period after World War II.

Finally, when studying the Austrian example, one can turn into an
advantage what at first sight seems rather problematic: the analysis of
substate and suprastate regionalization in the same context, without even
separating the two more clearly in terminology (by speaking, for
example, of integration rather than suprastate regionalization). When
several Austrian provinces started to make their own foreign policy and
tried to separate in the early 1920s or when they began to cooperate with
transborder regions in the 1980s, what did these developments have in
common with Austrian attempts on the federal level such as to unite
with Germany in 1918/19 or to find arrangements with the European
Communities without membership during the 1960s? Does the concept
of regionalization not generalize excessively and create unnecessary
confusion? I leave it to the reader to judge in the light of the results of
this paper. My own experience was the following: While the concept of
regionalization may indeed tend to overgeneralize, it may nevertheless
be more suitable to the Austrian case than to others. The reason is
simple but most important—for much of the period since 1918, not only
Austria's identity, but its very statehood was precarious. Over time,
various concepts of Austrian politics tried either to dispose of or to hold
onto statehood much more than it would have been imaginable in similar
countries. In Austria, therefore, movements towards substate or
suprastate regionalization often turn out to have more in common than
expected.

I shall proceed chronologically and analyze the roles of regiona-
lization(s) and globalization(s) in Austrian foreign policy in two stages:
one, the period of Austria's first existence as a small state (1918 – 1938)
and its annexation by Germany (1938 – 1945); two, the period since the
reestablishment of its independence in 1945.

1. Regionalization as Remedy for the "Problem of Austria"? (1918 – 1945)

Modern Austria is a by-product of the dissolution of the Habsburg
monarchy and the ensuing peace treaties. At the end of World War I, the
German speaking regions of the monarchy declared themselves an
independent republic. Yet this Republic of German-Austria *(Republik*

Deutschösterreich), as it originally named itself, suffered fundamental problems of identity and considered its existence purely transitional.

The new Austria had hardly anything in common with the old one. The break of identity had been radical.[6] To begin with, there was no Austrian republican tradition. Austria had been a monarchy and, what was more, had been unthinkable without the monarchy as a constituent and integrative factor of the state. There was no small state tradition either. Austria had been an empire, a great power, with German Austrians in the leading positions. German Austrians thus felt amputated and humiliated at the end of World War I. At least the elites thought in what was called *post-imperial* categories; they could hardly imagine living in a small state which they considered insignificant by definition.[7] That the state was poor made things even worse. While the Habsburg monarchy had been a largely self-sufficient economic entity, the viability of its German speaking fragments seemed in question as they heavily depended on imports of basic goods. Finally, there was no Austrian national identity. Austria had been a multi-national state, with a Slavic majority; Hungary formed a proper state in the Austro-Hungarian federation during the last half century of the monarchy's existence. As citizens, German Austrians had been loyal to the monarchy and the empire, which granted them a privileged position. Their national feelings, however, like those of the Czechs, Poles, and the other peoples of the monarchy, had developed on a substate level. The national feelings of the German Austrians, therefore, turned towards the Germans in Germany for reasons of common language and—as German nationalism concluded—common culture (in fact German Austrian cultural identity was more complex and irreducible to national terms).[8]

In contrast to the historical Austrian provinces with their strong traditions of individual substate identities,[9] Germany provided a more promising state identity than Austria could offer after the collapse of both the monarchy and the empire. Germany was supposed to remain a great power and to become a modern nation state which would include German Austrians and give them a priviledged, federal, position on the model of Bavaria. Unification with Germany would resolve Austria's economic problems and direct those Austrian workers that were tempted by Bolchevism towards German nationalism. Last but not least, it would provide Austrian Social democrats, then the leading political force—shortly followed by the Christian Socials—with a more secure position in power by allowing them to join their strong fellows in Germany and preventing once and for all any resurrection of old, traditionalist Austria.

Thus, the Republic of German Austria immediately declared itself part of the newly constituted Weimar Republic.[10]

For reasons of balance of power, the victors of World War I denied German Austria to unite with Germany and even forced it to drop the prefix "German" from its name.[11] However, "the Austrian question" or "the problem of Austria"—i.e. how to assure the new country's existence and how to make it accept its identity—remained unsolved. Note that identity problems were rampant on the provincial level as well. The Treaty of St. Germain notably allocated South Tyrol to Italy, thereby dividing a province with a strong historical identity. To reunite their province, Tyrolians proposed to separate from both Austria and Italy and to form a single, neutral entity. Whereas the southern provinces of Carinthia and Styria had major border conflicts with newly constituted Yugoslavia, and the most western province, Vorarlberg, voted to unite with Switzerland. In short, there were serious signs of decomposition in the new state. Due to the lack of an accepted state identity historic provincial identities regained all their importance and individual provinces were tempted to conduct their own foreign policies. Yet, tendencies to *regionalize foreign policy* and to divide the Austrian question into individual substate questions, in other words to *regionalize the Austrian problem on the provincial level*, were rapidly stopped by their respective lack of success.

On the federal level various options existed and most had the familiar pattern of regionalization. The reason is simple. The "Austrian question" was never seen isolately. In the views of the contemporaries, the "Austrian question" either formed part of the "German question," or the "Danubian question," or the "Central European question," or the "European question" – or all of them. In other words, on contemporary "mental maps"[12] the Austrian question was spontaneously regionalized. As we will see, the way in which this was done prefigured the options for resolving the problem. The Danubian and the European reading of the Austrian question excluded German answers. Conversely, Germanizing the Austrian problem precluded Danubian and European formulas; and the same was true for Central European concepts *(Mitteleuropa)*. It goes without saying that behind the conflicting concepts were conflicting interests, with revisionism and anti-revisionism being the most important. Interesting enough, regionalization could serve one as well as the other.

In most minds the Austrian question continued to be identified with the so-called *Anschluss* question: Austria's temptation to unite with

Germany and Germany's disposition to keep its doors to Austria open.[13] Although the Treaties of Versailles and St. Germain, the Geneva protocols of 1922, and the Lausanne protocols of 1932 all prohibited the *Anschluss*, Austria politically, economically, and legislatively aligned itself to Germany, which in its turn heavily supported the Austrian *Anschluss* movement.[14] In the early 1920s, after Allied protests, the federal government was at pains to stop a campaign of provincial referendums about a union with Germany.[15] In 1931, Germany and Austria agreed on a customs union project (the so-called Curtius–Schober plan), which they abandoned only under severe Allied pressure.[16] Whereas a customs union would have meant *suprastate regionalization as a substitute for state union*, the *Anschluss* would have meant *substate regionalization in compensation for state union* as Austria was supposed to maintain a strong, federal identity within Great Germany.

Union with Germany was the most popular proposition for solving the Austrian question, but it held no monopoly. As we have seen, Austria's identity problem was complex and, in principle, allowed for other solutions as well. If there were alternative ways to become self-confident again—economically "viable," politically consistent, "great" in one form or another—they seemed worth trying. This attitude was especially strong among Christian Socials who cultivated old Austrian traditions including an anti-national state conception and a catholic universalism incompatible with integral nationalism. They also felt uneasy with Germany's record of modernization and anti-Austrian sentiment (neither the *Kulturkampf*, nor the conflict between Great Austrians and Great Germans in 1848/49, neither Sadowa nor the repeated humiliations during World War I were forgotten).[17]

Thus the immediate counterpart to the Great German solution was the Great Austrian one. It encompassed two types of restauration: on the one side, the restauration of the Austrian empire in a renewed form of a federalization along the various lines of imperial reform models vainly discussed during the last decades of the monarchy; on the other side, the restauration of the Austrian-led Holy Roman Empire according to the model of the defeated Great Austrian plans of 1848/49, i.e. including the whole Habsburg monarchy (not only its German speaking territories). This Austrian variant of imperial romanticism *(Reichsromantik)* played an important role well into the 1930s.[18] In terms of regionalization, one could speak of *imperial regionalism as an alternative to integral nationalism*. Though its chances were poor because of decisive opposition both within and without the country, the Great Austrian idea figured prominently in the minds of Austrian Catholics. It was often not far behind two of the other regionalist propositions to solve the Austrian problem.

For one, there were different forms of Danubian projects reaching from trade and finance cooperation to customs unions and even more far-reaching schemes of economic federation.[19] They essentially tended to maintain or recreate the economic unity of the region formerly covered by the Habsburg monarchy. Originally, then, Danubian plans looked for *economic instead of imperial regionalism*. Yet, they soon got a second meaning as economic cooperation plans sponsored by the League of Nations and private initiatives, such as the European Customs Union *(Union douanière européenne)* with its Austrian committee, rapidly turned from global to European and, further, to even smaller regionalist patterns.[20] This pattern can be described as *regionalization instead of globalization*, with the *Danubian pattern of regionalization* being *one of the first steps to more comprehensive schemes* which we shall elaborate on in a moment.

The Danubian option was attractive from the beginning and was seriously opposed by *Anschluss* partisans. Its implementation was supposed to revive Austrian economy and thereby reduce the partly panic-driven appeal of union with Germany. For precisely this reason Danubian schemes were welcome to and repeatedly sponsored by France, with the Tardieu plan of 1932 as the most prominent one.[21] However, there were deep reservations among other Danubian states which feared a renewed tutelage by Austria. Austria, in its turn, showed resentment of being treated as one successor state among others. Furthermore, France and the members of the Little Entente tended to give Danubian plans an anti-German spin which was unacceptable for Austria. Last but not least, Germany and Italy did their best to sabotage any attempts to exclude them from solutions of the Austrian problem. Thus, no Danubian plan could ever be implemented.

There was a second, similar pattern of regionalization destined to provide an alternative to Great Germany and Great Austria: *Mitteleuropa* (Central Europe). In fact, it squared the circle by sub-stituting both Great Germany and Great Austria, economically uniting the regions formerly covered by the two empires, and extending even more to the East and South-East if possible. Of course, plans for *Mitteleuropa* had a controversial tradition which went back to the nineteenth century and received an imperialist twist well before World War I.[22] Be it despite or because of this, these plans continued to nourish the imagination of many economists and politicians from the region and even led to the creation of important institutions such as the *Mitteleuropäischer Wirtschaftstag* (created by the Austrian Julius Meinl).[23] The big difference to the Danubian plans was that Germany was in—and that by its sheer economic power it was bound to dominate the region under construction. Needless to say that this was unacceptable to France and unwelcome to several of the countries immediately concerned.

Finally, there was a third, even bolder, pattern for regionalization: Europe. The two most echoed initiatives were the Paneuropean movement and the Briand plan. Both presented ambitious, if somewhat incoherent, schemes of cooperation which need no further explanation here.[24] Note, however, their specific Austrian implications. As presented by Coudenhove-Kalergi, Paneurope would have been the "ideal solution" for the Austrian problem as, among other things, it amounted to "union with the successor states and with Germany." It would have taken place in the framework of the existing European order, i.e. with the possible consent of the otherwise reluctant victorious or defeated powers. Finally, it included the promise that Vienna would become the centre of Europe, i.e. that Austria would obtain—as Paneurope's most recent historian put it—"a surrogate of the lost great power status."[25]

Paneurope had full support of Austrian officials but was not expected to be put into practice in the near future. There are even indications that the utopian aspect of Paneurope was one of the reasons why Chancellor Ignaz Seipel, along with other important leaders, welcomed this model. For Seipel would neither sacrifice Great German nor Great Austrian options to any European construction as long as anti-revisionist powers dominated the European scene.[26] As a consequence, Austria later showed strong reservations against Briand's plan for a European Union which was accused of building on "a peace of injustices."[27] In fact, Austria played an active role in the custums union project with Germany which was as much an Austrian than a "German alternative"[28] to the Briand plan: a first step to *Mitteleuropa*, as opposed to a (pan-)european Union.

In short, regionalization was never an aim in itself but an economic and political instrument. Like others, Austria wanted *regionalization à la carte*. Preferences could change, of course, and they dramatically did so after the Nazis took power in Germany.

Whereas Austrian Christian Socials and Social Democrats dropped their demand for *Anschluss* for the time being, Austrian Nazis, with the help of Nazi Germany, began to terrorize the country. The political conflict escalated rapidly and, in 1933/34, it not only provoked a break in Austria's internal and external politics but also a far-reaching reassessment of the country's identity.[29] Providing the last "German" stronghold against Nazism, Austria and its independence from Germany obtained new significance. Official discourse now presented German Austrians as the better Germans and Austria as the better Germany. The small-state inferiority complex was compensated by an ideology of ethical, cultural, and political superiority, which basically meant that the new Austria stepped in the traditions of the old. These included the idea of a defensive mission against barbarism, with Nazi Germans slipping into the historical role of the Muslim Turcs, and, most importantly, the view that Austrian identity transcended German dimensions. Austria was presented as the holder of a European mission by virtue of its great, transnational past; it was not simply German, it was "German-European."[30]

It was hoped that the partial Europeanization of Austrian identity would counterbalance the continued stress on Austria's German identity in the official self-presentation. Whereas national references had largely predominated before, *(suprastate) regional references*—e.g. Europe, the Occident—now held entry in the modern Austrian identity discourse. Regionalization neither became dominant nor exclusive. It nevertheless expressed a defensive reorientation sometimes underestimated by an Austrian historiography obsessed with Austrian nation building and easily scandalized by the reluctance of pre-war Austrians to follow the already existing, but then still isolated, herolds of an Austrian nation, separate from the German nation (Ernst-Karl Winter, Alfred Klahr[31]). The trouble was that while combating Nazism and fostering a new state identity Chancellor Engelbert Dollfuss (who was to fall victim to a failed Nazi coup in July 1934 and was succeeded by Kurt Schuschnigg) also combated Social Democrats and destroyed democracy.[32] The popular basis of the new, dictatorial (some say semi-fascist) regime therefore remained small, and consequently its new discourse on Austrian identity was hardly convincing.

Whereas regionalization with Germany—be it within Great Germany or *Mitteleuropa*—was put on hold, regionalization with Danubian Europe had become both more urgent and more difficult. The great crisis and mounting protectionism on all sides effectively distroyed what had been left from the economic unity of the Danubian area after the collapse of the Habsburg empire.[33] Cooperation with Italy and Hungary (intensified by the Rome protocols, 17 March 1934) could hardly limit the damage and brought more political tutelage than *economic regionalization*. Coudenhove-Kalergi's Paneurope vehemently took Austria's side against Nazi Germany and found strong support in the Austrian government, but it had largely lost its international influence (especially its basis in Germany). More importantly, repeated efforts for *regionalizing security* proved difficult as well. Neither within nor outside of the framework of the League of Nations was it possible to unite the main interested parties in a regional security pact which would have effectively guaranteed Austria's territorial integrity and political sovereignty.[34]

In an international environment of mounting tension Austria found itself more and more isolated. It partly gave in to Germany by signing an agreement in July 1936 which brought Austria a formal recognition of its independence but at the same time forced it back on an exclusively "German path." Thus, regionalization schemes other than German ones were practically blocked, and German regionalization effectively began with the insertion of German nationalists into the Austrian government. In March 1938 the Austrian government resigned under the pressure of German ultimatums and Nazi revolts within the country. German troops went in and a few days later Germany formally annexed Austria.[35]

Austria's annexation by Germany did not lead to the form of *German regionalization* expected by most *Anschluss* partisans. Austria was not integrated as a substate entity nor were the historic provinces respected. Instead, the country was deprived of its federal administrative unity, including its name, and was divided into new provinces directly ruled from Berlin. In fact, this amounted to *de-regionalization* and *centralization*. Vienna, at least politically, was downgraded to a provincial city.[36]

At least until the beginning of the war most contemporaries considered Austria's annexation by Germany as definitive. It seemed to resolve once and for all the "Austrian question" in a "national," German, way. Even opponents of the Nazi regime (most of them in exile or in concentration camps) generally considered the "small Austrian" chapter of history as closed for good. Socialists wanted a Socialist revolution but maintained the idea of Great Germany. Catholics, who opposed both the Nazi regime and Austria's union with Germany, advocated a Danubian federation, if not the outright restauration of the Habsburg monarchy. *Suprastate regionalization* therefore, continued to occupy the thoughts of those minority (ex-)Austrians who still believed in the existence of an "Austrian question." This was equally true for those socialists who had second thoughts and began to advocate the reestablishment of Austria's independence in a united, Socialist Europe. Only Communists posed the problem in purely "Austrian national" terms and asked for the reestablishment of the country's pre-annexation independence.[37]

Yet perspectives changed with the turning of the war. Popular discontent as well as Allied propaganda leaned towards Austria's separation from Germany. Whereas the British would have strongly favored Danubian schemes, the Soviets were strictly opposed. Only minimum consent was reached at the Moscow Conference in late 1943: the return to the *status quo ante*, i.e. the reestablishment of Austria's independence. Even before German capitulation and Austria's complete occupation by the four Allies, a committee of representatives from the newly constituted Socialist, Popular (in succession of the Christian Socialists), and Communist parties declared Austrian independence on 27 April 1945.[38]

2. The Long Path to Regionalization in a Globalizing World (1945 – 2000)

Like the Great Austrian period, the Great German period had ended in war and defeat. Among the differences was that in 1945 Germany had lost its attraction and Austrians could agree on an alternative. Though Austria's problems between 1918 and 1938 were far from being forgotten, living in a small, independent state at least meant living in peace. Unanimously, Austria wanted to give it a second try and to learn from the errors which had led to failure in the first run. The exact nature of these errors continued to be disputed for decades. However, there was consensus to return to democracy, to oppose Communism, to create a new, cooperative culture of conflict among the main political forces, and to hold on to the regained Austrian state. Yet, Austrian identity had to be redefined. In this process, regionalization played a new, if somewhat paradoxical, role.

From the outset, regionalization was high on the agenda, escpecially on the substate level. As the country was divided into four zones of Allied occupation and the Soviet Union under suspicion of planning to install a puppet regime in Vienna, the former provinces were the natural points of departure for the internal recognition of the provisional federal government. *Re-regionalization on the substate level* was therefore both a prerequisite and an essential part of returning to pre-*Anschluss* Austria.[39] It represented legitimate continuity and therefore helped to rebuild identity.

On the suprastate level, regionalization was of more programmatic importance (which is still underestimated). There were two aspects to this. On the one side, the leading representatives of the new state had to answer the question of what the Austrian identity was under the new circumstances. They had to find other than pragmatic reasons for welcoming the separation from Germany and the return to a state which for many had made no sense during its earlier existence. The options were limited. Defining the state's identity as German Austrian had led to the call for unification with Germany. Efforts to counterbalance the German element of definition by a European one and to promote a "German-European" identity had proved non-resistent to the magnetic power of a strong Germany within a weak Europe. As a consequence, if Austria wanted to distance itself from Germany for good, the German reference in the Austrian identity discourse had to be totally relinquished. The remaining reference was still no national but a regional one: Europe.

The idea that Austria, by virtue of its multinational past, was not German but European in essence goes back to the late 1920s (especially the *Österreichische Aktion*) and was the basis for an identity discourse that wanted to prove the existence of an Austrian nation in its own right.[40] The existence of an Austrian nation was precisely what the newly elected, conservative chancellor of the republic, Leopold Figl, emphasized in his first governmental address. To the question of what Austrian identity consisted of his answer was simple: "Austria is Europe." Thus public discourse began to de-Germanize Austrian identity by Europeanizing it. In other words, *the way from de-nationalization to re-nationalization went through regionalization.* Most importantly, this was also acceptable to the majority of Austrians who welcomed the separation from Germany but continued to have reservations against the idea of forming a separate Austrian nation. After all, Europe included Germany as well.

Regionalization of national identity also *compensated Austria for being a small state.* Because of its European past, it was destined to have a Europen future, which meant a great mission for the small state. According to old Austrian tradition this was presented as a peace mission; it essentially consisted of holding the balance in Europe and mediating between East and West. The national program of European Austria therefore was an international one as well, and even more so because Europe, at the time, was a general catchword for the hopes of a peaceful future. To unify the continent in order to prevent a new conflict and to reduce Europe's dependence on the United States and the

Soviet Union were ideas not less attractive in Austria than elsewhere on the continent in the aftermath of World War II. They already build on various traditions within Austria, including the Paneuropean movement. The European idea succeeded the Great Austrian and the Great German ideas as well as nationalism and imperialism in both its Austrian and German forms.

Interestingly enough, *traditional internationalism of global ambitions* still existed, especially among Socialists. Catholic universalism, which continued to play an important role, was not exclusively European either. However, the dominance of the non-European superpowers (the Soviet Union being considered non-European) rapidly focused the hopes on Europe. *Regionalization* as a way back to autonomy from the superpowers got more and more profile and became an *alternative to globalization* which had lost its traditional image of being essentially the Europeanization of the world.

The sense of urgency was particulary strong in Austria as the superpowers were occupying the country. Though it involved all the Great Four (Russians, Americans, British, and French), Allied occupation rapidly proved to be an "East-West occupation" with the demarcation line going right through the country, including its capital Vienna.[41] Mounting tensions between East and West raised fears about the unity of the country and the progress of Allied negotiations ending the occupation. Since Austria, contrary to Germany, had no chance to survive if divided, the cold war threatened not only the recovery of its full sovereignty but also its very existence—not to speak of Austria's evoked hopes to become again a key communicator between Eastern and Western Europe. European cooperation on a continental scale seemed the best way out of this situation. Thus, European *regionalization* was called for *to put an end to Austria's existential fears as well as to Allied occupation* and, furthermore, *to create the necessary conditions under which Austria could develop its newly defined identity.*

The division of the continent crossed these plans and, as a consequence, dramatically altered Austria's perspectives of regionali-zation and identity building. European regionalization became an option for the West only and was intimately related to the globalizing conflict between the superpowers. This put Austria in a difficult situation. On the one hand, Austria needed Western help, economically, politically, and militarily; it also welcomed the West's efforts to strengthen itself by divers forms of regionalization. On the other side, Western regionalization went further than Austria could go and pushed the country into a delicate, peripheral position.

Against Soviet protests, Austria—already a member of the General Agreement of Tariffs and Trade (GATT)—participated in the Marshall plan and became a founding member of the Organiziation of European Economic Cooperation (OEEC), joining later the European Payments Union.[42] As a liberal democracy on the edge of Western Europe, Austria took interest in the Council of Europe; as a coal importing and steel exporting country it was directly concerned by the European Coal and Steel Community (ECSC). However, when sending official observers to the two organizations respectively in 1952 and 1953, the Austrian government had reached, in its own words, "the limits of the possible."[43] If Austria became a full member in one of these organizations—not to speak of NATO with which cooperation went far but remained secret[44]—it would have to fear Soviet measures of retortion including the division of the country and the indefinitive prolongation of Allied occupation. Austrian priorities were clear: integrity and sovereignty went before integration.[45]

The regionalizing states, of course, had their own priorities and did not wait for Austria. When they passed from purely intergovernmental to supranational cooperation by creating the ECSC, Austria had to confront the particularly exclusive nature of this new form of regionalization.[46] As a non-member Austria was discriminated against on the ECSC market and was excluded from decisions which were vital for the country. Facing demands for individual arrangements, the Community was in a position to fix unilaterally the terms of negotiations and remained keen to draw a clear line between insiders and outsiders. Austria rightfully expected the same experience with the European Economic Community (EEC) and was among those countries which deeply resented the 1958 failure of negotiations, on a Great Free Trade Area covering all OEEC member states. It accused the Community members of *dis*integrating the OEEC, of unilaterally breaking with a functioning, comprehensive regional cooperation by creating another one which excluded Austria along with a number of other countries.[47]

Meanwhile, the terms of the debate had changed with Austria recovering full sovereignty in 1955. The conditions had been, among others, to refrain from any political or economic union with Germany (Article 4, Austrian State Treaty, 15 May 1955) and—in response to a Soviet demand—to observe neutrality (constitutional law of 26 October 1955).[48] While these provisions and close Soviet observation did not prevent Austria from joining the U.N. and the Council of Europe within a year, they were later presented as prohibiting Austria from joining the European Communities.[49] In this context, *global politics continued to put limits on Austria's participation in Western European regionalization.*

However, this is only part of the story. Austria seriously considered candidacy for ECSC membership in October 1956 with the obvious future perspective to join the Common Market, then under negotiation. Apprehension about possible Soviet retaliation was only one of the reasons behind the final decision not to ask for entry negotiations. Other, equally prominent reasons were protectionism and the will of the main political forces, especially the Social Democrats, to retain power over important branches of the largely nationalized economy. This was a key element of the neo-corporatist culture of conflict developed in the Second Republic, the specific Austrian form of Social Partnership *(Sozialpartnerschaft).*[50] As the continued debate in the late 1950s and 1960s showed,[51] *non-regionalization on a supranational pattern was as much an internal political opportunity as an external constraint of political globalization.*

So-called full sovereignty—not shared with supranational authorities and symbolized by neutrality—became an axiom of Austrian politics.[52] However, formal and real sovereignty soon became very different things. This was particulary true in the economic field as Austria increasingly depended on trade with the Federal Republic of Germany.[53] Western Germany, of course, was an important member of the European Communities, and the question was whether Austria's hypothetical accession would diversify or simply intensify its German dependence. Critics (including Austria's foreign minister and future chancellor Bruno Kreisky) even feared a new sort of *Anschluss.*[54] The terms of the debate were set as early as 1953/54 when French officials internally discussed a possible rapprochement of Austria with the ECSC.[55] Arguments continued until Austria's accession to the European Union forty years later. Their political significance, however, changed over time. In the late 1950s and 1960s, Austria's nation-building was still full in process.[56] Under these circumstances, non-membership in the European Communities, along with neutrality, became important factors in distinguishing Austria from Germany.

Discrimination by the Common Market nevertheless continued to create problems for Austria's economy. Thus the quest for trade arrangements with Brussels remained high on the agenda of Austrian politics.

In order to strengthen its position, Austria united with other outsiders and engaged in *alternative Western European regionalization as a first step to comprehensive Western European regionalization on a free trade basis*. For this purpose it participated in the creation of the European Free Trade Area (EFTA) in 1959/60. Austria intended to use EFTA as a common platform for renewed negotiations with the European Communities. Yet, the British bid for full EEC membership divided EFTA almost as soon as it was created and made negotiations for non-applicants even more difficult as long as EEC enlargement remained an unresolved issue. It therefore took Austria another decade to reach (along with other European neutrals) a series of agreements with Brussels.[57] They were concluded in 1972 and allowed for extensive free trade in industrial (not agricultural) goods. Equally important was that they did not intervene in Austria's liberty of trade with third parties—in particular the Soviet Union and East European coun-tries—and that they did not involve any cooperation on the supranational level.[58]

Thus, while intensifying its *Western European regionalization by loose political cooperation* (accession to the Council of Europe) and *by trade liberalization* (creation of EFTA, free trade accords with EEC and ESCE), Austria continued to refuse regionalization by supranational cooperation as developed in the European Communities. In other words, Austria remained true to *selective regionalization* in Western Europe. Most significantly, this left room for initiatives of regionalization in other directions, including parts of Eastern Europe.

In the late 1950s and during the 1960s, Austria developed a Central European—or, as it was alternatively called, Danubian—policy which was essentially aimed at its East European neighbours (Hungary, Czechoslovakia, Yugoslavia) but also included the other successor states of the Danubian monarchy (Poland and Rumania). The long term objective was to draw Central Europe out of the cold war and to get rid of the Soviets—the official language called for the creation of "a region free from Great power influences."[59] This could have been the first step towards the unified Europe, so much hoped for after the war. The medium term objectives were *regional détente* and the liberalization of the Soviet-style regimes in Austria's Eastern neigh-bours. This would allow the progressive diffusion of Western political ideas. For reasons of opportunity, Austria concentrated on a "cultural foreign policy" using the legacies of the common historical past of the region to renew cultural and intellectual ties and to permit Eastern intellectuals, writers, and others to get Western contacts via neutral Austria.

Cultural regionalization was to create *the basis for future political regionalization*, and *Central European regionalization* was to provide *a future complement to Western European regionalization*. As Austria belonged to both Western and Central Europe and could use its neutral status, it held a privileged position which allowed it to assume an instrumental role in the process. This evoked flattering memories of Austria's leading position in Danubian Europe and revived the traditional idea of Austria serving as a bridge between East and West. Most importantly, Austria's Central European policy was conceived as *small states regionalism* and was presented as undangerous by definition. It particularly excluded Germany, or at least reserved her only a limited, peripheral role. Though Germany was perfectly Danubian and traditionally saw itself as part of *Mitteleuropa*, it was less welcome because it clearly had a big power potential despite the actual division of the country. As Germany's marginalization was key to the success of the initiative, Austria also used this form of regionalization to give a signal of political and cultural autonomy in contrast to its heavy economic dependence on the Federal Republic of Germany. However, the ongoing confusion over the term *Mitteleuropa* continued to evoke memories of German great power politics.

During the 1980s, the idea of *Mitteleuropa* again played a significant role in Austrian foreign policy. The international rediscovery of Old Austrian culture contributed to a general awareness of the region's historical identity. In "Eastern" Europe (geographically Prague was never east of Vienna) the decline of Soviet power and ideology made *Mitteleuropa* even more attractive as an alternative to Soviet domination and Communism. In Austria, the conservative party, traditionally more interested in Danubian activism than the Social Democrats, reentered the government in 1986. Through a number of initiatives in formal and informal cultural diplomacy Austria contributed to the ideological destabilization and political reorientation behind the Iron Curtain. In a widely publicized gesture of June 1989, the Austrian and Hungarian foreign ministers cut one of the remaining pieces of the barbed wire on the Austro-Hungarian border. In November of the same year, just three days after the fall of the Berlin wall, Austria, along with Italy, Hungary, and Yugoslavia, launched the so-called Quadruple Initiative. After Poland and Czechoslovakia joined it as well, it was respectively renamed "Pentagonale" and "Hexagonale." Finally it turned into the "Central European Initiative" as cooperation intensified and members multiplied following the disintegration of Yugoslavia. The aim was to create a forum of comprehensive dialogue and cooperation, including environmental issues such as atomic energy—with Austria unsuccessfully demanding the closure of all atomic energy plants in the region—and to fill the vacuum left by the collapse of the Soviet Empire.[60] Yet, the peak of Austria's Central European policy was followed by rapid decline as both in the reforming countries and in Austria itself the European Community became much more attractive than *Mitteleuropa*.[61]

If *Central European regionalization* contributed to balance Austria's selective Western European regionalization during the cold war and its immediate aftermath, it did so not only on the suprastate level but also *on the substate level.* Substate regions proved to be more qualified partners where practical issues of transborder cooperation were at stake, or where small states were still too prominent actors to take delicate initiatives. The model was taken from *substate regionalization in Western Europe*, more specifically from the so-called *ARGE Alp (Arbeitsgemeinschaft Alpenländer)*, a scheme of environmental and economic cooperation in the alpine region initiated in 1972 by Bavaria (West Germany) and Tyrol (Austria). It further included the Austrian provinces of Vorarlberg and Salzburg, the canton Graubünden (Switzerland), as well as the autonomous province Bozen-South Tyrol and the Lombardy region (both in Italy). The problem of South Tyrol was one of Austria's main motives for joining this initiative, closely followed by the increasingly important issue of transit between Italy, France, and the Federal Republic of Germany, via Austria which created growing environmental problems. However, the hopes to resolve these problems on a regional level were quickly disappointed.[62] In 1978, a similar initiative, the *ARGE Alpen-Adria*, started in South-Eastern Europe including provinces and regions of Austria, Italy, and Yugos-lavia. In 1983, the *ARGE Mittlere Donau* comprised part of the regions crossed by the Danube and, among other things, contributed to the weakening of the Iron Curtain between Czechoslovakia and Austria.[63] Transborder regionalization on the substate level became so important that, in 1987, the new Austrian government spoke of "a new dimension in foreign relations" and initiated a change in constitution allowing Austrian provinces to sign treaties with foreign states and regions on their own.[64]

Selective regionalization was not only balanced by regional diversification within Europe but also by the *extension of regionalization on a continental scale.* Austria actively participated in preparing the Conference of Security and Cooperation in Europe (CSCE), i. e. *Euro-*

pean security regionalization.[65] This complemented Austria's *détente* policy in Central Europe and gave Austria the opportunity to strengthen its record as a mediator between East and West. Similar motives led the country to enhance *globalization of its foreign policy.* As early as the late 1950s, Austria engaged in an active U.N. policy which further developed during the 1960s and 1970s and included repeated participation in peace-keeping missions.[66] To play a useful, if limited, role on the global stage was in the interest of Austria's security and prestige.[67] Especially during the 1970s this role compensated for the country's inability to play the important part in Europe it had hoped for before the the cold war broke out.

Originally, Austria had also hoped to raise more effective international interest in the still unresolved, regional issue of South Tyrol, which was also an important matter of internal politics.[68] Due to the federal structure of the state, the Austrian government had to take into account the regional interests of its provinces including their external affairs. Paradoxically, substate regionalization thereby became an important reason for the globalization of Austrian foreign policy.[69]

Economic globalization gained importance as well. For one, Austria continued to participate in global trade negotiations within GATT. These were particulary important during Austria's discrimination on the Common Market as they put the European Communities under global (especially US) pressure to open their markets. Thus *trade globalization*—along with alternative regionalization (EFTA)—served as a last resort *against discriminating regionalization.* Austria also tried to play a role in the North-South-dialogue where one-sided trade globalization constituted one of the major problems of developing countries. The Austrian motives for this involvement lay partly in the traditional anticolonialism of the Socialist party which then held an absolute majority in parliament. Clientelism among non-aligned countries was a more prosaic motive. Yet Austria wanted also to extend its role as mediator between East and West to mediate between North and South and show particularly the domestic public that small Austria was a disproportionally big player in international politics. Foreign policy globalization therefore was also conceived to strengthen the country's identity.

Compensated by regional diversification and globalization, and rebalanced by the trade agreements with the European Communities in 1972, selective regionalization evolved from necessity to virtue during the era named after the Socialist chancellor Bruno Kreisky (in office from 1970 to 1983).[70] While opening itself to economic stimulation by

ECSC/EEC, Austria remained an EFTA member along with countries like Sweden which provided its model for social welfare. Austria adopted what has been described as a "third option" among typical small state strategies vis-à-vis internationalization. It neither closed nor opened its economy but chose a mix of both policies – the so-called *Austrian way*.[71] In fact, it still held levels of protectionism considered "an anomaly" among the small states of Western Europe.[72] Despite or because of this, prosperity increased dramatically during the 1970s with levels of employment, growth rates, and living standards surpassing those in the European Community. What had once been "the problem of Austria" became "the Austrian model," a success story which made Austrians proud of their country like never before and brought the nation building process to definitive completion.[73]

In the late 1970s even foreign observers attested that Austria seemed to have found the right "balance between [political] autonomy and [economic] dependence."[74] In fact, Austria was among the small European states which entered the era of growing economic and political *interdependence* in a position in which interdependence, as Peter Katzenstein put it, largely meant *dependence*.[75] This was true for interdependence by globalization as well as by regionalization and became most evident when Austria's most important trading partner, the Federal Republic of Germany, fell into recession following the oil crisis. By a generous policy of redistribution and indebtment ("Austro-Keynesianism") Austria managed to limit the negative effects on its economy considerably. Thus, Austria, more than ever, resembled that "island of the blessed" evoked by the Pope on his visit to the country in 1971. However, the financial burdens of these policies were enormous. Consequently regionalization and globalization become increasingly ambivalent as they continued to intensify. Not only did they threaten Austrian finances, but they also called the very future of the "Austrian way" into question. Nevertheless, in the early 1980s an Austrian political scientist expressed a then still commonly shared view when he concluded that more regionalization—i.e. further rapprochement with the European Community—"would rather decrease than increase [Austria's] political and economic room to maneuver."[76]

In the mid 1980s this consensus broke under the rising pressure of external changes and internal crisis. Whereas globalization accelerated, regionalization in Western Europe went into a new phase with the European Community finally deciding to complete the Common Market (declaration of Stuttgart, White Book, Single Act). After more than a decade of stabilized relations with the European Communities Austria once again faced discrimination. Furthermore, during the so-called Luxemburg process initiated to intensify EC-EFTA relations and the ensuing negotiations over the European Economic Area, Austria become dramatically aware of the impossibility of gaining the power of co-decision on relevant EC measures without full membership.[77]

Under these auspices both dependence and autonomy in "full sovereignty" were no longer what they had been.[78] The exporting industry called for alarm, while the foreign minister warned of Austria becoming "a second class state" and being forced into a "colonial status."[79] According to the new perception, selective regionalization had it been continued, would have further increased Austria's dependence in regional as well as in global terms and would have largely undermined Austria's autonomy. Obtaining co-decision powers in the European Community—including Community protection from globalization—was therefore worth sharing sovereignty in supranational institutions through *full regionalization.*[80] This seemed even more so when German unification pushed EC members to create a single currency and to found the European Union. Finally, the crisis and final collapse of the Soviet Union definitively shattered all conventional restrictions and made neutrality an internal rather than external issue. In Austria neutrality had become another word for independence and peace.[81]

While globalization and regionalization presented new challenges for Austria, its economy and part of its political system had plunged into crisis. Nationalized industry was in a structural crisis and could not be financed any longer. Economic modernization seemed urgent while unemployment, almost unknown for more than a decade, had reappeared and contributed to blocking reforms. Social partnership and the all-embracing paternalism of the two main political parties had run out of success provoking the rise of protest parties including Jörg Haider's FPÖ. Even worse, the internal image crisis of the formally praised Austrian political system was doubled by an external image crisis due to the Waldheim affair. This came as a shock to a country which during the previous three decades had acquired a considerable reputation and was proud of it. All these factors had destabilizing effects and, among other things, made the need for accession to the European Community more plausible. Conversely, Community membership became a stimulus for reform as it permitted the government to legitimate unpleasant measures by referring to Brussels.[82]

Austria's candidacy for membership in the European Communities was the first among European neutrals and came as early as July 1989. However, Austria had to wait three and a half years for the opening of negotiations which the EC held simultaneously with Finland, Sweden, and Norway. They were concluded after another fourteen months, on 1 March 1994. On 12 June of the same year a record two thirds of Austrian voters cast their ballots in favor of the accession treaty in a referendum the government had fought with the slogan "We are Europe *(Wir sind Europa).*"[83] It was noted that this slogan had formerly been used by the German SPD.[84] While this may explain why it resounded well with the governing Social Democrats in Austria, their conservative partners in coalition could have remembered former Chancellor Figl's "Austria is Europe" slogan dating back to 1945. The official appeals to identify Austria with Europe were essentially the same in 1945 and 1994. Yet, it had taken five decades of dramatic changes both in Austria and in Europe to get the equation right.

In the wake of EU accession the federal government had to strike a deal with the provinces to compensate them for giving up competences to Brussels. The federal government thus lost parts of its sovereignty both to supra- and substate institutions.[85] The weakening of the central, federal authorities (along with important subsidies for individual regions from the Union's structural fund) was indeed the major interest of the provincial authorities in Community membership. In the case of the Tyrol, for example, a "Europe of regions" would allow the creation of a "Tyrolian region in Europe" *(Europaregion Tirol)* which could reduce to insignificance the border separating the Austrian province from Italian South Tyrol.[86] Suprastate regionalization thus opened new perspectives for regional foreign policy which (as mentioned earlier in this paper) had already developed to a considerable extent before.[87] All provinces but one now have their bureaus in Brussels and are active in the Committee of Regions. In short, Austria's accession to the European Union meant at the same time *suprastate and substate regionalization in a globalizing world.*

Conclusion

Regionalization has been a dominating issue of modern Austrian foreign policy ever since the country's foundation in 1918. This is as true for suprastate as for substate regionalization and has mainly to do with Austria's longlasting difficulties to accept its identity as an independent small state. After the dissolution of the Habsburg monarchy and the prohibition of Austria's accession to Germany, various schemes of regionalization were developed to resolve the "Austrian question," which was as much a Danubian and European question as it was a German one. Yet, no proposition could surmount the conflicting interests among the powers and within Austria itself. For most of its early existence, Austria pursued revisionist aims by any form of regionalism it adopted: Great German regionalism (e.g. through a customs union) as a substitute for state union and substate regionalization within Germany (*Anschluss*); Great Austrian regionalism as an imperial multinational alternative to integral nationalism; Danubian or Central European regionalism (with *Mitteleuropa* including Germany) as economic and eventually political substitute for different variants of the Great Austrian or German imperial idea; and, finally, European regionalism, like *Paneuropepe*, which tried in vain to square the circle.

After the Nazis had taken power in Germany, however, Austria, at least officially, redefined its identity and turned, somewhat reluctantly, from offensive to defensive regionalism, hoping to secure its independence from Nazi Germany. Even more importantly, Europeanism became a constituent element of the Austrian identity discourse and was destined to counterbalance German nationalism. This new form of regionalism failed just like all previous forms. In the end, Austria's annexation by Germany brought no regionalization but centralization within another state and disintegration of the old one. German nationalism and imperialism prevailed.

After Austria's reestablishment at the end of World War II, re-regionalization on substate level was an essential part of rebuilding the state. Another important part was suprastate regionalism which was instrumental in redefining Austrian identity as a basically European, not German, one. It also provided a potential remedy for Allied occupation and Austria's involvement in the mounting tensions between the United States and the Soviet Union, which put at risk not only the recovery of full independence but also the unity and very existence of the country. Yet, the cold war frustrated European hopes and led Austria to engage only selectively in Western European regionalization. It participated in intergovernmental cooperation and trade liberalization within OEEC but kept out of (open) military cooperation (Western Union, NATO) and supranational economic cooperation (ESCE).

After gaining full sovereignty in 1955, Austria persisted in selective Western regionalization after some hesitation. It acceded to the Council of Europe with its loose form of intergovernmental cooperation in political and cultural affairs but finally refrained from candidacy for membership in the European Communities. While Austria intensified its Western European regionalization on the basis of trade liberalization by participating in the creation of EFTA and negotiating free trade agreements with the European Communities finally signed in 1972, it continued to exclude supranational cooperation, i.e. Community membership. The most prominent reasons for this decisions were external concerns of a small neutral state recently separated from Germany in a Europe divided by a global conflict. Yet, other important reasons included internal motives like economic, social, and political protec-tionism. Regionalization in Western Europe therefore remained partly an external affair, confronting Austria with the particularly exclusive character of supranational communities.

Austria counterbalanced its selective regionalization in Western Europe by developing a Central European regionalism which mainly involved the successor states of the Danubian monarchy. This was a small states regionalism, further "softened" by the moderate perspectives of an international climate in which mutual respect and *détente* amounted to bold steps forward, whereas close cooperation was no real option. Austria particularly concentrated on cultural foreign policy and, in the long term, contributed to the revival of a cultural regionalism which should play a not so small part in the decomposition of the Soviet empire. The same can be said of Austria's active engagement in security regionalization on a continental scale within the CSCE.

At least as important were substate regionalization and globalization of foreign policy which would become complementary movements in Austria's selective regionalization in Western Europe. For both developments regional issues, such as the question of South Tyrol or environmental problems, offered important motives. With varying success, Austria tried to further regional interests blocked on the bilateral state level by using either unconspicuous, "little," entries on the substate level or—as within GATT or the U.N.—the largest possible ones open to the entire international community. Furthermore, Austria could effectively foster its image as a useful, small neutral state able to build bridges between East and West, North and South. Together with selective regionalization in Western Europe, global image building was an important element of the successful nation building process which culminated during the 1970s in the Kreisky era. At the same time, the provinces sharpened the profile of their substate identity in a complementary and supportive movement including regional foreign policies on the provincial level.

Selective regionalization and complementary moves on the global scene had provided Austria with an internationally respected small state strategy which, until the early 1980s, succeeded in holding the difficult "balance between autonomy and dependence" in a globalizing world (Peter Katzenstein). Nevertheless, this "Austrian way"—some even talked of an "Austrian model"—failed to provide continued orientation when globalization and supranational regionalization accelerated. Full membership in the European Communities now seemed to be the only way out of threatening marginalization and totally unilateral dependences. In order to avoid renewed regional discrimination and to counterbalance unescapable globalization, Austria turned to full regionalization and finally entered the European Union in 1995. It accompanied this forward leap into suprastate regionalization by more, if limited, steps towards substate regionalization.

When celebrating the beginning of Austria's presidency of the European Union on 1 July 1998, the federal president, Thomas Klestil, declared to tens of thousands of people gathered before the Imperial Palace in Vienna that a longstanding hope had become reality: "Today, Austria is at the same time small and great. It is independent and forms part of a greater whole ... After multiple detours and sacrifices we Austrians have finally found back to our European vocation."[88] One purpose of this paper was to show how anachronistic it is to speak of "detours" when developments go in other directions than the most recent one. Repeated breaks, crises, and shiftings in Austrian identity make any determinism implausible. Nevertheless, the president struck the right cord and delivered an eloquent summary of the problems which, in conflicting and repeatedly changing ways, specifically motivated regionalization and globalization as complementary strategies in Austria's foreign policy since 1918: how to be small if one was great, and how to join others if one ought to or wanted to remain independent.

Notes

1. An earlier version of this paper was presented at the 19th International Congress of Historical Sciences, Oslo, 6-13 August 2000. It was delivered in the session of the Commission of History of International Relations, on "Globalization, Regionalization, and the History of International Relations" published as part of the commemorative CD-Rom of the Oslo Congress. For the current publication, the text has been reviewed and the footnotes have been expanded. I partly draw on a more comprehensive article: "De l'Autriche germanique à l'Autriche européenne? Identités nationales et internationales de

l'Autriche depuis 1918," in *La place et le rôle des petits pays en Europe au XXe siècle*, ed. Gilbert Trausch (Brussels: Bruylant, forthcoming). I wish to thank Dr. Michael Gehler (Innsbruck), Dr. Wolfram Kaiser (Düsseldorf) and Dr. Günter Bischof (New Orleans) for valuable comments.

2. See J. A. Scholte, "The Globalization of World Politics," and Fiona Butler, "Regionalism and Integration," in *The Globalization of World Politics: An Introduction to International Relations*, ed. John Baylis, Steve Smith (Oxford: Oxford UP, 1997), 13-30, 409-428.

3. Helmut Rumpler, "Österreich vom *Staat wider Willen* zur österreichischen Nation (1919 - 1955)," in *Die Deutsche Frage im 19. und 20. Jahrhundert: Referate und Diskussionsbeiträge eines Augsburger Symposions 23.-25. 9. 1981*, ed. Joseph Becker and Andreas Hillgruber (Munich: Vögel, 1983), 239-67; Gerald Stourzh, *Vom Reich zur Republik: Studien zum Österreichbewußtsein im 20. Jahrhundert* (Vienna: Atelier, 1990); idem, "Erschütterung und Konsolidierung des Österreichbewußtseins - vom Zusammenbruch der Monarchie zur Zweiten Republik," in *Was heißt Österreich? Inhalt und Umfang des Österreichbegriffs vom 10. Jahrhundert bis heute*, ed. Richard G. Plaschka, Gerald Stourzh, and Jan Paul Niederkorn, Archiv für österreichische Geschichte 136 (Vienna: Österreichische Akademie der Wissenschaften, 1995), 289-311; Ernst Bruckmüller, *Nation Österreich: Kulturelles Bewußtsein und gesellschaftlich-politische Prozesse*, Studien zu Politik und Verwaltung 4, 2nd ed. (Vienna: Böhlau, 1996); Ernst Hanisch, *Der lange Schatten des Staates: Österreichische Gesellschaftsgeschichte im 20. Jahrhundert*, Österreichische Geschichte 1890 – 1990 (Vienna: Ueberreuter, 1994), 154-64.

4. Scholte, "Globalization," 14. See, ibid., 15, "Globalization: A Collection of Definitions". See also Ulrich Teusch, "Zwischen Globalisierung und Fragmentierung: Theoriedebatten in den Internationalen Beziehungen," *Neue Politische Literatur* 44 (1999): 402-25, Jürgen Osterhammel, "Internationale Geschichte, Globalisierung und die Pluralität der Kulturen," in *Internationale Geschichte. Themen – Ergebnisse – Aussichten*, ed. Wilfried Loth and Jürgen Osterhammel, Studien zur internationalen Geschichte 10 (Munich: Oldenbourg, 2000), 387-408.

5. Scholte, "Globalization," 15.

6. Kurt Skalnik, "Auf der Suche nach der Identität," in *Österreich 1918 - 1938: Geschichte der Ersten Republik*, vol I, ed. Erika Weinzierl and Kurt Skalnik (Graz : Styria, 1983), 11-24; Hanns Haas, "Staats- und Landesbewußtsein in der Ersten Republik," in *Handbuch des politischen Systems Österreichs: Erste Republik 1918 - 1933*, ed. Emmerich Tálos, Herbert Dachs, Ernst Hanisch and Anton Staudinger (Vienna: Manz, 1995), 472-87.

7. Klemens von Klemperer, "Das nachimperiale Österreich, 1918 - 1938: Politik und Geist," in *Österreich und die deutsche Frage im 19. und 20. Jahrhundert: Probleme der politisch-staatlichen und soziokulturellen Differenzierung im deutschen Mitteleuropa*, ed. Heinrich Lutz and Helmut Rumpler, Wiener Beiträge zur Geschichte der Neuzeit 9 (Vienna: Geschichte und Politik, 1982) 300-17.

8. Moritz Csáky, "Zentraleuropa: Ein komplexes kulturelles System," *Études danubiennes* 13 (1997): 1-16.

9. William D. Bowman, "Regional History and the Austrian Nation," *Journal of Modern History* 67 (1995): 873-97; Gunda Barth-Scalmani, Hermann J. W. Kuprian, and Brigitte Mazohl-Wallnig, "National Identity or Regional Identity: Austria Versus Tyrol/Salzburg," in *Contemporary Austrian Studies*, vol. 5, *Austrian Historical Memory* (1997): 32-63; Bruckmüller, *Nation Österreich*, 67-69, 191-199.

48   Contemporary Austrian Studies

10. Günter Bischof, "The Historical Roots of a Special Relationship: Austro-German Relations Between Hegemony and Equality," in *Unequal Partners: A Comparative Analysis of Relations Between Austria and the FRG and Between Canada and the US*, ed. Harald von Riekhoff and Hanspeter Neuhold (Boulder: Westview, 1993), 57-92; Hanns Haas, "Die unvollendete Republik: Österreich 1918 - 1920," in *Die Achter-Jahre in der österreichischen Geschichte des 20. Jahrhunderts*, ed. Karl Gutkas, Schriften des Instituts für Österreichkunde 58 (Vienna: Österreichischer Bundesverlag, 1994), 54-68.

11. Alfred D. Low, *The Anschluss Movement 1918-1919 and the Paris Peace Conference*, Memoirs of the American Philosophical Society 103 (Philadelphia: American Philosophical Society, 1974); Gerald Stourzh, "Zur Genese des Anschlußverbots in den Verträgen von Versailles, Saint-Germain und Trianon," in *Saint-Germain 1919: Protokoll des Symposiums am 29. und 30. Mai 1979*, ed. Isabella Ackerl and Rudolf Neck, Veröffentlichungen der Wissenschaftlichen Kommission zur Erforschung der Geschichte der Republik Österreich 11 (Vienna: Geschichte und Politik, 1989), 41-53.

12. Alan K. Henrikson, "Mental Maps," in *Explaining the History of American Foreign Relations*, ed. Michael J. Hogan and Thomas G. Paterson (Cambridge: Cambridge UP, 1991), 177-92.

13. Gerhard Botz, "Das Anschlußproblem (1918 - 1945) aus österreichischer Sicht," in *Deutschland und Österreich: Ein bilaterales Geschichtsbuch*, ed. Robert A. Kann and Friedrich E. Prinz (Vienna: Jugend & Volk, 1980), 179-98; Alfred Ableitinger, "Der *Deutschlandkomplex* der Österreicher in der Ersten Republik," in *Österreich 1934 1984: Erfahrungen Erkenntnisse Besinnung*, ed. Joseph F. Desput (Graz: Styria, 1984), 173-98; Maria Ormos, "Le problème de la sécurité et l'Anschluss," *Études Historiques* [Budapest] 2 (1975): 5-44; Rolf Steininger, "12. November 1918 bis 13. März 1938: Stationen auf dem Weg zum *Anschluß*," in *Österreich im 20. Jahrhundert*, vol. I, ed. Rolf Steininger and Michael Gehler (Vienna: Böhlau, 1997), 99-150.

14. Hanns Haas, "Österreich im System der Pariser Vorortverträge," in *Handbuch des politischen Systems Österreichs: Erste Republik*, 665-81.

15. Martin F. Polaschek, "Eine *platonische Volksabstimmung:* Die Maßnahmen zu einer österreichweiten Anschlußbefragung im Jahr 1921 im Spannungsfeld von Bund und Ländern," *Zeitschrift für neuere Rechtsgeschichte* 20 (1998): 49-70.

16. Rolf Steininger, "*... Der Angelegenheit ein paneuropäisches Mäntelchen umhängen ...:* Das deutsch-österreichische Zollunionsprojekt von 1931," in *Ungleiche Partner? Österreich und Deutschland in ihrer gegenseitigen Wahrnehmung: Historische Analysen und Vergleiche aus dem 19. und 20. Jahrhundert*, ed. Michael Gehler, Rainer F. Schmidt, Harm-Hinrich Brandt, and Rolf Steininger, Historische Mitteilungen 15 (Stuttgart: Steiner, 1996), 441-78.

17. Helmut Rumpler, *Eine Chance für Mitteleuropa: Bürgerliche Emanzipation und Staatsverfall in der Habsburgermonarchie*, Österreichische Geschichte 1804 – 1914 (Vienna: Ueberreuter 1997).

18. Klaus Breuning, *Die Vision des Reiches: Deutscher Katholizismus zwischen Demokratie und Diktatur (1929 - 1934)* (Munich: Hueber 1969).

19. Peter M. R. Stirk, "Ideas of Economic Integration in Interwar Mitteleuropa," in *Mitteleuropa: History and Prospects*, ed. Peter M.R. Stirk, Studies in European Unity (Edinburgh: Edinburgh UP, 1994), 86-111; Arnold Suppan, "Mitteleuropa-Konzeptionen, zwischen Restauration und Anschluß", and Herbert Matis, "Wirtschaftliche Mitteleuropa-Konzeptionen in der Zwischenkriegszeit: Der Plan einer Donauföderation," in *Mitteleuropa-Konzeptionen in der ersten Hälfte des 20. Jahrhunderts*, ed.

Richard G. Plaschka, Horst Haselsteiner, Arnold Suppan, Anna M. Drabek, and Birgitta Zaar, Zentraleuropa-Studien 1 (Vienna: ÖAW, 1995), 171-97, 229-55; Drahomír Jancík and Herbert Matis, *"Eine neue Wirtschaftsordnung für Mitteleuropa...* Mitteleuropäische Wirtschaftskonzeptionen in der Zwischenkriegszeit,"* in *Österreich und die Tschechoslowakei 1918 - 1938: Die wirtschaftliche Neuordnung in Zentraleuropa in der Zwischenkriegszeit,* ed. Alice Teichova and Herbert Matis, Studien zur Wirtschaftsgeschichte und Wirtschaftspolitik 4 (Vienna : Böhlau, 1996), 329-87.

20. Éric Bussière, "L'Organisation économique de la SDN et la naissance du régionalisme économique en Europe," *Relations internationales* 75 (1993): 301-13.

21. Jacques Bariéty, "Le *plan Tardieu* d'aide aux pays danubiens et la France," *Revue d'Europe Centrale* 5 (1997): 1-14; Barbara Kronsteiner, "L'Autriche et le plan Tardieu," ibid., 63-72; idem, "La politique de la France envers l'Autriche dans les *années* 1930: l'invention de l'espace centre-europ'éen," in *L'Europe centrale et orientale en recherche d'intégration économique 1900 - 1950,* ed. Eric Bussière, Michel Dumoulin, and Alice Teichova (Louvain-la Neuve: Institut d'études européennes, 1998) 143-60.

22. Peter M. R. Stirk, "The Idea of Mitteleuropa," in *Mitteleuropa. History and Prospects,* 1-35; Werner Abelshauser, "Between Myth and Reality: The Concept of Mitteleuropa," in *A Missed Opportunity? 1922: The Reconstruction of Europe. Proceedings of the International Conference Florence 1 - 3 October, 1992,* ed. Marta Petricioli and Massimiliano Guderzo (Bern: Lang, 1995), 397-412.

23. Reinhart Frommelt, *Paneuropa oder Mitteleuropa: Einigungsbestrebungen im Kalkül deutscher Wirtschaft und Politik 1925 - 1933,* Schriftenreihe der Vierteljahrshefte für Zeitgeschichte 34 (Stuttgart: Oldenbourg, 1977); Harro Molt, *"...Wie ein Klotz inmitten Europas": "Anschluß" und "Mitteleuropa" während der Weimarer Republik 1925 - 1931,* Studien zum Kontinuitätsproblem der deutschen Geschichte 4 (Frankfurt am Main: Lang, 1986); Matthias Schulz, *Deutschland, der Völkerbund und die Frage der europäischen Wirtschaftsordnung 1925 - 1933,* Beiträge zur deutschen und europäischen Geschichte 19 (Hamburg: Krämer, 1997); Gerald Horst Brettner-Messler, "Richard Riedl. Ein liberaler Imperialist. Biographische Studie zu Handelspolitik und *Mitteleuropa*-Gedanken in Monarchie und Erster Republik," PhD. diss., University of Vienna, 1998; Jürgen Elvert, *Mitteleuropa! Deutsche Pläne zur europäischen Neuordnung (1918 - 1945),* Historische Mitteilungen Beiheft 35 (Stuttgart: Steiner, 1999).

24. Lubor Jilek, "Paneurope dans les années vings: la réception du projet en Europe centrale et occidentale," *Relations internationales* 72 (1992): 409-32; Michael Gehler, "Richard Coudenhove-Kalergi, Paneuropa und Österreich 1923 - 1972," *Demokratie und Geschichte. Jahrbuch des Karl von Vogelsang-Instituts zur Erforschung der Geschichte der christlichen Demokratie in Österreich* 2 (1998): 143-93; Jacques Bariéty, "Le projet d'union européenne d'Aristide Briand," in *L'ordre européen du XVIe au XXe siècle. Actes du colloque de l'Institut de Recherches sur les Civilisations de l'Occident Moderne, 15-16 mars 1996,* ed. Jean Bérenger and Georges-Henri Soutou (Paris: Presses de l'Université de Paris-Sorbonne, 1998), 137-49; *Le Plan Briand d'Union fédérale européenne. Perspectives nationales et transnationales, avec documents. Actes du colloque international tenu à Genève du 19 au 21 septembre 1991,* ed. Antoine Fleury and Lubor Jilek (Bern: Lang, 1998).

25. Gehler, "Richard Coudenhove-Kalergi, Paneuropa und Österreich," 145 and 183.

26. For more details see Angerer, "De l'Autriche germanique à l'Autriche européenne?"

27. Jan Tombinski, "Die österreichische Antwort auf den Plan Briands," in *Le Plan Briand,* 445-454; Anita Ziegerhofer, "Austria and Aristide Briand's 1930 Memorandum," *Austrian History Yearbook* 29 (1998) 139-160.

28. Peter Krüger, *Die Außenpolitik der Republik von Weimar* (Darmstadt: Wissenschaftliche Buchgesellschaft, 1985), 530; Andreas Rödder, *Stresemanns Erbe: Julius Curtius und die deutsche Außenpolitik 1929 - 1931* (Paderborn: Schöningh, 1996), 201-2.

29. Dieter A. Binder, "Alte Träume und neue Methoden. Das deutsch-österreichische Verhältnis als Produkt aggressiven Revisionismus von 1933 bis 1938," in *Ungleiche Partner?*, 497-512.

30. Gottfried-Karl Kindermann, *Hitlers Niederlage in Österreich: Bewaffneter NS-Putsch, Kanzlermord und Österreichs Abwehrsieg von 1934* (Hamburg: Hoffmann & Campe, 1984), 48. For a more detailed presentation of the argument and further references see Angerer, "De l'Autriche germanique à l'Autriche européenne?", and idem, "'Österreich ist Europa': Identifikationen Österreichs mit Europa seit dem 18. Jahrhundert," *Wiener Zeitschrift zur Geschichte der Neuzeit* 1 (2001): 55-72.

31. Wolfgang Häusler, "Wege zur österreichischen Nation: Der Beitrag der KPÖ und der Legitimisten zum Selbstverständnis Österreichs vor 1938," *Römische historische Mitteilungen* 30 (1988): 381-411.

32. Dieter A. Binder, "Der *Christliche Ständestaat*: Österreich 1934 - 1938," in *Österreich im 20. Jahrhundert*, vol. 1, 203-253; Laura Gellott, "Recent Writings on the Ständestaat, 1934 – 1938," Austrian History Yearbook 26 (1995): 207-38.

33. Dieter Stiefel, *Die große Krise in einem kleinen Land: Österreichische Finanz- und Wirtschaftspolitik 1929 - 1938*, Studien zu Politik und Verwaltung 26 (Vienna: Böhlau 1988).

34. Maria Ormos, "Sur les causes de l'échec du pacte danubien (1934-35)," *Acta Historica Academiae Scientiarum Hungaricae* 14 (1968): 21-83; Dieter A. Binder, *Dollfuß und Hitler: Über die Außenpolitik des autoritären Ständestaates in den Jahren 1933/34*, Dissertationen der Universität Graz 43 (Graz: Universität Graz, 1979); Marian Wrba, "Genfer Politik. Österreich und das System der Kollektiven Sicherheit, 1932 – 1935," Master thesis, University of Vienna, 1989; Marco Bertolaso, *Die erste Runde im Kampf gegen Hitler? Frankreich, Großbritannien und die österreichische Frage 1933/34: Eine Untersuchung der Außenpolitik der Westmächte in den ersten 18 Monaten des "Dritten Reiches" auf der Grundlage diplomatischer Akten* (Hamburg: Kovac, 1995).

35. Erwin A. Schmidl, *Der "Anschluß" Österreichs: Der deutsche Einmarsch im März 1938* 2nd ed. Bonn: Bernard & Graefe, 1994); Gerald Stourzh, "Der Weg zur Einverleibung Österreichs," in *1939. An der Schwelle zum Weltkrieg. Die Entfesselung des Zweiten Weltkrieges und das internationale System*, ed. Klaus Hildebrand, Jürgen Schmädeke, and Klaus Zernack (Berlin: De Gruyter, 1990), 141-9; Gerald Stourzh and Birgitta Zaar, ed., *Österreich, Deutschland und die Mächte. Internationale und österreichische Aspekte des "Anschlusses" vom März 1938*, Veröffentlichungen der Kommission für die Geschichte Österreichs 16 (Vienna: Österreichische Akademie der Wissenschaften, 1990).

36. Hermann Hagspiel, *Die Ostmark: Österreich im Großdeutschen Reich 1938 bis 1945* (Vienna: Braumüller, 1995); Evan Burr Bukey, *Hitler's Austria. Popular Sentiment in the Nazi Era, 1938 – 1945* (Chapel Hill: The University of North Carolina Press, 2000).

37. Wolfgang Neugebauer, "Ideas of the Austrian Resistance on Postwar Europe," in *Documents on the History of European Integration, I: Continental Plans for European Union 1939 - 1945*, ed. Walter Lipgens, European University Institute, series B 1/1 (Berlin: De Gruyter, 1985), 203-14; Helene Maimann, "Views of Austrian Exiles on the Future of Europe," in *Documents on the History of European Integration, II: Plans for*

European Union in Great Britain and in Exile 1939 - 1945, ed. Walter Lipgens, European University Institute, series B 1/2 (Berlin: De Gruyter, 1986), 629-50.

38. Erika Weinzierl, "The Origins of the Second Republic: A Retrospective View," in *Austria 1945-95. Fifty Years of the Second Republic*, ed. Richard Luther and Peter Pulzer (Aldersholt: Ashgate, 1998), 3-27.

39. Robert Kriechbaumer, "Liebe auf den zweiten Blick – Die Länder und der Bund 1945: Zu Vorgeschichte und Geschichte der Länderkonferenz 1945," in *Liebe auf den zweiten Blick: Landes- und Österreichbewußtsein nach 1945*, ed. Robert Kriechbaumer, Geschichte der österreichischen Bundesländer seit 1945, vol.6 (Vienna: Böhlau, 1998), 15-46.

40. For this and the following see more details and references in Angerer, "De l'Autriche germanique à l'Autriche européenne?", and idem, "'Österreich ist Europa'."

41. Gerald Stourzh, *Um Einheit und Freiheit. Staatsvertrag, Neutralität und das Ende der Ost-West-Besetzung Österreichs 1945 - 1955*, Studien zu Politik und Verwaltung 62, 4th ed. (Vienna: Böhlau, 1998); Günter Bischof, *Austria in the First Cold War, 1945-55. The Leverage of the Weak* (Basingstoke: Macmillan, 1999).

42. Günter Bischof, "Zum internationalen Stand der Marshallplan-Forschung: die Forschungsdesiderata für Österreich," in *3. Österreichische Zeitgeschichtetage 1997. 26. bis 28. Mai 1997*, ed. Gertraud Diendorfer, Gerhard Jagschitz and Oliver Rathkolb (Innsbruck: Studienverlag, 1998), 60-72; Günter Bischof and Dieter Stiefel, *"80 Dollar": 50 Jahre ERP-Fonds und Marshall-Plan in Österreich* (Vienna: Ueberreuter, 1999).

43. Wolfgang Burtscher, "Österreichs Annäherung an den Europarat von 1949 bis zur Vollmitgliedschaft 1956," in *Österreich im Europarat, 1956 - 1986. Bilanz einer dreißigjährigen Mitgliedschaft*, ed. Waldemar Hummer and Georg Wagner, Veröffentlichungen der Kommission für Europarecht, Internationales und Ausländisches Privatrecht 7 (Vienna: Österreichische Akademie der Wissenschaften, 1988), 37-52, (here 44-5); Florian Weiß, *"Gesamtverhalten: Nicht sich in den Vordergrund stellen: Die österreichische Bundesregierung und die westeuropäische Integration 1947 - 1957*," in *Österreich und die europäische Integration 1945 - 1992: Aspekte einer wechselvollen Entwicklung*, ed. Michael Gehler and Rolf Steininger, Arbeitskreis Europäische Integration, Historische Forschungen 1 (Vienna: Böhlau, 1993), 21-54; Oliver Rathkolb, "Austria and European Integration after World War II," *Contemporary Austrian Studies*, vol. 1, *Austria in the new Europe* (1993): 42-61; Robert Knight, "Austrian Neutrality and European Integration: The Historical Background," in *Austria's Contribution towards European Union Membership*, ed. Karl Koch (Guildford: University of Surrey, 1995), 28-47.

44. Stourzh, *Um Einheit und Freiheit*, 192-220; Bischof, *Austria in the First Cold War*, 111-23.

45. Thomas Angerer, "Integrität vor Integration: Österreich und *Europa* aus französischer Sicht, 1949 - 1960," in *Österreich und die europäische Integration*, 178-200.

46. Alan S. Milward and Vibeke Sørensen, "Interdependence or Integration? A National Choice," in Alan S. Milward et al., *The Frontier of National Sovereignty. History and Theory 1945 – 1992* (London: Routledge, 1993), 1-32, here 16-18; Thomas Angerer, "Exklusivität und Selbstausschließung: Frankreich, Österreich und die Erweiterungsfrage in der europäischen Integrationsgeschichte," *Revue d'Europe Centrale* 6 (1998): 25-54.

47. Michael Gehler, "Austria & European Integration 1947 – 1960: Western Orientation, Neutrality and Free Trade," *Diplomacy & Statecraft* 9 (1998): 154-210.

48. Stourzh, *Um Einheit und Freiheit*; idem, "The Origins of Austrian Neutrality," in *Neutrality: Changing Concepts and Practices*, ed. Alan T. Leonhard (Landham, MD UP of America, 1988), 35-57.

49. Rudolf Kirchschläger, "Integration und Neutralität," in *Die Ära Kreisky. Schwerpunkte der österreichischen Außenpolitik*, ed. Erich Bielka, Peter Jankowitsch, and Hans Thalberg (Vienna: Europaverlag, 1983), 61-95; Maximilian Oswald, "Wirtschaftliche Integration und österreichische Neutralität von 1960 bis 1972," in *Die Neutralen und die europäische Integration 1945 - 1995 / The Neutrals and the European Integration 1945 - 1955*, ed. Michael Gehler and Rolf Steininger, Arbeitskreis Europäische Integration, Historische Studien 3 (Vienna: Böhlau, 2000), 645-79.

50. Angerer, "Exklusivität und Selbstausschließung," 40-45.

51. Peter J. Katzenstein, "Trends and Oscillations in Austrian Integration Policy Since 1955: Alternative Explanations," *Journal of Common Market Studies* 14 (1975): 171-97; Michael Gehler and Wolfram Kaiser, "A Study in Ambivalence: Austria and European Integration 1945-95," *Contemporary European History* 6 (1997): 75-99.

52. Thomas Angerer, "L'Autriche précurseur ou ‚Geisterfahrer' de l'Europe intégrée? Réflexions dans la perspective des années 1950," *Revue d'Allemagne et des pays de langue allemande* 24 (1992): 553-61, here especially 556.

53. Jürgen Nautz, "Wirtschaft und Politik: Die Bundesrepublik Deutschland, Österreich und die Westintegration 1945 - 1961," in *Österreich und die europäische Integration 1945 - 1992*, 149-77; Waltraut Urban, *Österreichische-deutsche Wirtschaftsbeziehungen. Zwischen Westintegration und Ostöffnung*, Laxenburger Internationale Studien 8 (Vienna: Braumüller, 1995).

54. Oliver Rathkolb, "La politique européenne du parti socialiste. Théorie et pratique," *Austriaca* 32 (1991): 106-19.

55. Angerer, "Integrität vor Integration."

56. William T. Bluhm, *Building an Austrian Nation: The Political Integration of a Western State* (New Haven: Yale UP, 1973); Peter J. Katzenstein, "The Last Old Nation: Austrian National Consciousness Since 1945," *Comparative Politics* 9 (1977): 147-71; Bruckmüller, *Nation Österreich*.

57. Oliver Rathkolb, "The Austrian Case: From *Neutral Association* to a *Special Arrangement* with the EEC 1961 - 1963, in *Courting the Common Market. The First Attempt to Enlarge the European Community 1961 - 1963*, ed. Richard T. Griffiths and Stuart Ward (London: Lothian Foundation Press, 1996), 285-302; Michael Gehler, "In the EEC's Waiting Room: Austria and Europe, 1957 - 1963," in *Widening, Deepening and Acceleration: The European Economic Community*, ed. Ann Deighton and Alan S. Milward (Baden-Baden: Nomos, 1999), 317-30; Rolf Steininger, "Österreichs *Alleingang* nach Brüssel 1963 - 1969," in *Die Neutralen und die europäische Integration*, 577-644; Hans Mayrzedt, Hans Christoph Binswanger, eds., *Die Neutralen in der Europäischen Integration: Kontroversen - Konfrontationen - Alternativen*, Schriftenreihe der Österreichischen Gesellschaft für Außenpolitik und internationale Beziehungen 5 (Vienna-Stuttgart: Braumüller, 1970); Gehler, Steininger, *Die Neutralen und die europäische Integration*.

58. Hans-Georg Koppensteiner, ed., *Rechtsfragen der Freihandelsabkommen der Europäischen Wirtschaftsgemeinschaft mit den EFTA-Staaten*, Schriften zum gesamten Recht der Wirtschaft 14 (Vienna: Orac, 1987).

59. Vladislav Marjanović, *Die Mitteleuropa-Idee und die Mitteleuropa-Politik Österreichs 1945 - 1995*, Europäische Hochschulschriften XXXI/360 (Frankfurt am Main: Lang 1998) 77-93, here especially 83-87; Oliver Rathkolb, "Austria's *Ostpolitik* in the 1950s and 1960s: Honest Broker or Double Agent?," *Austrian History Yearbook* 26 (1995): 129-45.

60. Hanspeter Neuhold, "From the *Mitteleuropa* Debate to the Pentagonale," in *The Pentagonal / Hexagonal Experiment: New Forms of Cooperation in a Changing World*, ed. Hanspeter Neuhold (Vienna: Braumüller 1991), 113-25; Marjanović, *Die Mitteleuropa-Idee und die Mitteleuropa-Politik*, 118-26.

61. Marjanović, *Die Mitteleuropa-Idee und die Mitteleuropa-Politik*, 145-52.

62. Michael Gehler, "Selbstbestimmung - kulturelle Landeseinheit - Europaregion? Die Tiroler Südtirolpolitik 1945 - 1998," in *Tirol. "Land im Gebirge": Zwischen Tradition und Moderne*, ed. Michael Gehler, Geschichte der österreichischen Bundesländer 3 (Vienna: Böhlau, 1999), 569-728, here 672-77; Karin Schermann, "Niederösterreich und Europa: Von der Grenzregion zur EU-Musterregion," in *Niederösterreich: Land im Herzen – Land an der Grenze*, Geschichte der österreichischen Bundesländer seit 1945 (Vienna: Böhlau, 2000), 717-40, here 723-25.

63. Marjanović, *Die Mitteleuropa-Idee und die Mitteleuropa-Politik*, 94-96.

64. Ibid, 111-12; Friedrich Koja, "Die außenpolitischen Möglichkeiten der österreichischen Bundesländer: Eine Untersuchung aufgrund der Bundesverfassung," in *Die regionale Außenpolitik des Landes Salzburg*, ed. Roland Flomair, Salzburg Dokumentationen 108 (Salzburg: Landespressebüro Salzburg, 1993), 48-65.

65. Sigrid Pöllinger, *Der KSZE/OSZE-Prozess. Ein Abschnitt europäischer Friedensgeschichte. Mit einem Geleitwort von Wolfgang Schüssel*, Laxenburger Internationale Studien 12 (Vienna: Braumüller, 1998); Stefan Lehne, *Conference of Security and Cooperation in Europe: The Vienna Meeting of the Conference on Security and Cooperation in Europe, 1986 - 1989: A Turning Point in East-West Relations*, Austrian Institute for International Affairs series (Boulder: Westview, 1991).

66. Erwin Schmidl, "*In the Service of Peace:* 35 Jahre österreichische Teilnahme an UN-Friedensoperationen," *Österreichische Militärische Zeitschrift* 33 (1995): 125-34.

67. Helmut Kramer, "Strukturentwicklung der Außenpolitik (1945-1990)," in *Handbuch des politischen Systems Österreichs: Die Zweite Republik*, ed. Herbert Dachs et al., 3. ed. (Vienna: Manz, 1997), 715-39, here 723-8.

68. Gehler, "Selbstbestimmung - kulturelle Landeseinheit - Europaregion?," passim.

69. Erwin A. Schmidl, *Blaue Helme, Rotes Kreuz: Das österreichische UN-Sanitätskontingent im Kongo 1960 bis 1963*, Innsbrucker Forschungen zur Zeitgeschichte 13 (Innsbruck: Studienverlag, 1995).

70. See more in Angerer, "De l'Autriche germanique à l'Autriche européenne?"

71. Otmar Höll, "Abhängigkeit oder Autonomie: Österreich im Internationalisierungsprozeß," *Österreichisches Jahrbuch für Internationale Politik* 1 (1984): 26-63, here 45-46; idem and Helmut Kramer, "The Process of Internationalization and the Position of Austria. Problems and Current Development Trends of the *Austrian Model*," in *Small States in Europe and Dependence*, ed. Otmar Höll, Laxenburg Papers 6 (Boulder/Vienna: Westview/Braumüller, 1983), 184-219.

72. Peter J. Katzenstein, "Dependence and Autonomy: Austria in an Interdependent World," *Österreichische Zeitschrift für Außenpolitik* 19 (1979): 243-56, here 248.

73. Anton Pelinka, *Modellfall Österreich? Möglichkeiten und Grenzen der Sozial-partnerschaft*, Studien zur österreichischen und internationalen Politik 4 (Vienna: Braumüller, 1981); Günter Bischof, Anton Pelinka and Oliver Rathkolb, eds. *Contemporary Austrian Studies*, vol. 7, *The Kreisky Era* (New Brunswick: Transaction, 1999).

74. Katzenstein, "Dependence and Autonomy," 243. Manfred Rotter, "Austria's Permanent Neutrality and the Free Trade Agreement with the EEC: Strategies to Reduce Dependences?," in *Small States in Europe and Dependence*, 306-28.

75. Peter J. Katzenstein, *Small States in World Markets. Industrial Policy in Europe* (Ithaca: Cornell UP, 1985).

76. Höll, "Abhängigkeit oder Autonomie," 60.

77. Paul Luif, "The Evolution of EC-EFTA Relations and Austria's Integration Policy," in *The European Neutrals in the 1990s. New Challenges and Opportunities*, ed. Hanspeter Neuhold (Boulder: Westview, 1992), 55-88; Thomas Pedersen, *European Union and the EFTA Countries. Enlargement and Integration* (London: publisher, 1994).

78. Angerer, "L'Autriche, précurseur," 559-60.

79. Kramer, "Strukturentwicklung," 728-32; Idem, "Austrian Foreign Policy from the State Treaty to European Union Membership (1955-95)," in *Austria 1945 - 1995*, 161-80, here 164.

80. There is still controversy about whether elements of continuity or discontinuity prevailed in this shift of policy. See the exchange of views between Michael Gehler and the author in *Europäische Integration und Erweiterung: Eine Herausforderung für die Wissenschaften*, ed. Rosita Rindler-Schjerve, Biblioteca Europea (Neapel: Vivarium, 2000), 67-89 and 91-98. For a general and detailed presentation of Austria's Community policy see Michael Gehler, *Der lange Weg nach Europa: Österreich vom Paneuropa-Engagement zum EU-Beitritt 1923 - 1995: Darstellung und Dokumentation in zwei Bänden* (Innsbruck: Studienverlag 2001, forthcoming).

81. Ludmilla Lubova, "Österreich in der Außenpolitik der UdSSR und Rußlands: Die Rolle der Neutralität Ende der 80er und Anfang der 90er Jahre," in *Europäische Rundschau* 27 (1999/3) 67-86; Herbert Krejci, Erich Reiter and Heinrich Schneider, eds., *Neutralität. Mythos und Wirklichkeit*, (Vienna: Signum, 1992). Thomas Angerer, "Für eine Geschichte der österreichischen Neutralität: Ein Kommentar," in *Die Neutralen und die europäische Integration*, 702-8.

82. Heinrich Schneider, *Alleingang nach Brüssel: Österreichs EG-Politik* (Bonn: Europa Union, 1990); Kurt Richard Luther and Wolfgang C. Müller, eds., *Politics in Austria: Still a Case of Consociationalism?* (Portland: Cass, 1992); Gerhard Kunnert, *Österreichs Weg in die Europäische Union: Ein Kleinstaat ringt um eine aktive Rolle im europäischen Integrationsprozeß* (Vienna: Österreichische Staatsdruckerei, 1993); Günter Bischof and Anton Pelinka, eds., *Contemporary Austrian Studies* vol. 1, *Austria in the New Europe* (New Brunswick: Transaction, 1993); Anton Pelinka, Christian Schaller and Paul Luif, *Ausweg EG? Innenpolitische Motive einer außenpolitischen Umorientierung*, Studien zu Politik und Verwaltung 47 (Vienna: Böhlau, 1994); Paul Luif, *On the Road to Brussels. The Political Dimension of Austria's, Finland's and Sweden's Accession to the European Union*, Laxenburg Papers 11 (Vienna: Braumüller 1995); Michael Gehler, "17. Juli 1989: Der EG-Beitrittsantrag: Österreich und die europäische Integration 1945 - 1995," in *Österreich im 20. Jahrhundert*, vol. 2, 515-93; Wolfram Kaiser, "The Silent Revolution: Austria's Accesion to the European Union," *Contemporary Austrian Studies*, vol. 5, *Austrian Historical Memory* (1997): 136-62.

83. Anton Pelinka, ed., *EU-Referendum: Zur Praxis direkter Demokratie in Österreich*, Schriftenreihe des Zentrums für angewandte Politikforschung 6 (Vienna: Signum, 1994); Wolfram Kaiser, et al. "Die EU-Volksabstimmungen in Österreich, Finnland, Schweden und Norwegen: Folgen für die Europäische Union," *Integration* 18 (1995): 76-87.

84. Ruth Wodak et al. *Zur diskursiven Konstruktion nationaler Identität* (Frankfurt am Main: Suhrkamp, 1998), 264-66. Compare Angerer, "Österreich ist Europa."

85. Heinrich Neisser, "Souveränität - Mitbestimmung - Föderalismus: Perspektiven der Europäischen Union," *Juristische Blätter* 116 (1994): 713-20; idem, "Verfassungsreform im Lichte des EU-Beitritts," in *Grundfragen und aktuelle Probleme des öffentlichen Rechts: Festschrift für Heinz Peter Rill zum 60. Geburtstag*, ed. Stefan Griller, Karl Korinek and Michael Potacs (Vienna: Orac, 1995), 335-58.

86. Gehler, "Selbstbestimmung - kulturelle Landeseinheit - Europaregion?," 680-90; Günther Pallaver, "Kopfgeburt Europaregion Tirol: Genesis und Entwicklung eines politischen Projekts," *Geschichte und Region/Storia e regione* 9 (2000).

87. Koja, "Die außenpolitischen Möglichkeiten der österreichischen Bundesländer." For concrete examples see Peter Mittermayr, "Die Praxis der regionalen Außenpolitik des Landes Salzburg," in *Die regionale Außenpolitik des Landes Salzburg*, 103-16; and Andreas Kiefer, "Salzburgs Mitwirkung in europäischen Regionalinstitutionen," in ibid., 147-76.

88. Speech of the federal president of the Republic of Austria, Thomas Klestil, at the *Europafest* on the *Heldenplatz*, on 1 July 1998 (http://www.hofburg.at/de/vorg./d1tk/rd98/inla/Heldenplatz.htm, 9.11.2000). Translated by the author.

The Austrian Crisis as Seen by a French Scholar of Germanic Culture

Jacques Le Rider

In the history of the French perception of Austria since the beginning of the 20th century, it is possible to identify two constant factors: First, the French perception of Austria has always been selective. It is critical of certain aspects of Austria but looks with favor on what French scholars and scholars of Germanic languages have defined as the "real and good Austria." Second, it has never been possible to dissociate discussions of Austria from discussions of Germany and European equilibrium.

The 1980s were characterized by the infatuation of a growing French public with every aspect of the Viennese modernity (from the turn of the century till 1938), including its art, literature, philosophy, and politics. This veritable Viennese craze started with the special issue of *Critique*, "Vienna, the Beginning of a Century," published in 1975 (No. 339/340), and reached its climax in 1986 with the exhibition at the Centre Pompidou entitled "Vienna, 1880-1938. The Joyous Apocalypse." The popularity of similar Viennese subjects over the past fifteen years gives rise to questions about the reasons for their topicality. Recent discussions of the notion of post-modernity can provide some of the answers: What our epoch especially remembers about the artistic and intellectual production of turn of the century Vienna are its critical approach to modernity based on aesthetic, ethical, and psychological concerns and its scepticism of "modern ideas." This new interest in the Viennese legacy of the 20th century is spontaneously multidisciplinary: The rediscovery of the Viennese Sigmund Freud and "Austrian" thought from Mach to Wittgenstein, goes hand in hand with the revalua-tion of the Viennese school of art history, investigations of Austrian Jewish culture, and reflections on the political identity of Central Europe.

However, the "archaeological" interest in the *Wiener Moderne* does not necessarily mean that present-day Austria enjoys the same positive evaluation as its glorious past. It is obvious to everyone that Vienna has become a *Stadt (fast) ohne Juden*—a city with (practically) no Jews—and is no longer the capital of Central Europe, a multicultural melting pot characterized by creative plurality.

There has never been any doubt that French intellectuals instinctively showed a preference for Germany. Today it is fair to say that despite their apprehension about the reunification of 1989-1990, the French cultural, economic, and political elites have a more positive opinion of big Germany than of small Austria. It is worth emphasizing that while the huge wave of racist and anti-Semitic violence that surged through Germany in 2000 certainly provoked a great emotional response in France, it did not erode the trust in our German partner, whose high culture of democracy is universally accepted. However, the crisis sparked by the Austrian coalition between the traditional Right and the national-populist Right raised questions about the very foundations of the Austrian political system.

It is interesting to note that neo-Nazi incidents have been much more frequent in the "new *Länder*" of the former GDR than in the "old *Länder*" of the FRG. Contemporary historians can very easily compare the eastern German *Länder* with the "discursive neo-Nazism" supported by the leaders of the Austrian FPÖ. Austria and East Germany had one thing in common: They both based their legitimacy on a version of history that absolved them of guilt. In this interpretation, one was a country that had fallen victim to the Anschluss; the other a Socialist state that had inherited the positive and revolutionary traditions of the German people. In Austria, it took the Waldheim affair of 1986 to make people fully aware of their *versäumte Vergangheitsbewältigung,* their failure to come to terms with the past. As in the GDR, the ideological façade of official antifascism hindered a genuine confrontation of the Nazi past.

Until the end of the 1990s, it was apparently natural to speak of Austria *sine ira et studio.* Since the 1970s, Austria had generally been respected for its international role and its system of social democracy. At the time of the Reder case, the FPÖ minister implicated had made public apologies. The Waldheim affair had only involved an isolated president and his entourage. After 1986, the "symbolic Nazism" of the leaders of the FPÖ was reduced to the problem of a party excluded from the circle of the ruling parties. Some Austrians who supported the "black-blue" coalition formed in February 2000 failed to understand the vast differences between the improper behavior of an FPÖ excluded from the government and the improper behavior of an FPÖ that had become part of the government.

These considerations allow us to understand the enormous confusion in the French perception of Austria since the beginning of 2000. Having contributed to French discussions of the Austrian political crisis myself, I admit that my point of view is not entirely "scientific and objective," but I would like to add that nobody, at the present time, can claim to be "scientific and objective" in their opinions.

A secondary effect of the crisis of 2000 was that it revealed the discrepancy between the foreign view of Austria and the debates taking place within the country. One constantly recurring motif in domestic discussion—a defense against the "sweeping generalizations" from abroad—is that the Austrian is a terribly complex, subtle, and delicate being. Outsiders understand little or nothing about that. Is it true that in Austria appearances are deceiving? Are Austrian relationships so esoteric that they can only be interpreted by the natives entangled in them? I don't believe that, nor do I believe that foreign "Austriazists" (scholars of Germanic culture specialized in Austria) can do so any better. Still, it is foolish to insinuate that only Austrians can interpret Austrian woes.

Since 2000 there have been indications that the "real and good Austria" as interpreted by the French is being threatened by an imprudent government alliance between the traditional Right and the party that appears to succeed the parties which have always wanted to destroy Austria.

On the other hand, the year 2000 marked a serious crisis in the overall "Europe-building." Even if the condemnation of the "black-blue" government's policy was entirely justified with regard to the funda-mental values of Europe's political culture, the manner in which the sanctions were carried out was awkward and counterproductive. Instead of destabilizing the Austrian coalition government, the sanctions pro-voked a nationalist reaction in Austria; they exposed the absence of cultural and political unity in Europe and showed that European integration is limited to commercial and financial considerations. The obvious failure of the sanctions ultimately rushed the "normalization" of what had been considered abnormal six months earlier, and the strong criticism of the national-populist party contained in the report of the three wise men was considered negligible.

Those who disagree with me may say that without the sanctions Mr. J.H. might have become vice-chancellor or even chancellor instead of withdrawing to his Carinthian position. Perhaps. However, the "J.H. effect" has repeatedly led the Austrians to delude themselves with the idea that the national-populist issue is, in essence, all about one person. The surprising acceptance of Jörg Haider by his party and his electorate shows how much more complex things are. Since 1986, the FPÖ has owed everything to its "charismatic" leader and he, in turn, has thoroughly reshaped the identity of his own party, which has become less and less "liberal" and more and more national-populist.

Finally, the debate on European enlargement orchestrated the idea of a *Mitteleuropa* (Central Europe) versus a Europe consisting of the founding members of the European Community. Enlargement stood in opposition to deepening; the vision of *Mitteleuropa* stood in opposition to Europe as defined in the Treaties of Maastricht and Amsterdam. Many interpreted the failure of the French presidency at the Nice summit conference in November 2000 as the result of an act of revenge by Austria and the "small countries." They had disapproved of the sanctions and now seemed to respond to "a certain image of Europe" supported by France. At the same time, Franco-German solidarity on the sanctions (a solidarity that certainly would not have been maintained so strongly if Joseph Fischer had not been the German minister for foreign affairs) became a valuable point of agreement at a time when co-operation between France and Germany appeared to be in a serious crisis.

The French perception of the Austrian cultural identity has, for the most part, been influenced by the internal debate of the French on their own culture and by the debate of the Austrians on their own identity. Today, French observers of Austria tend to listen to Elfriede Jelinek much as they listened to Thomas Bernhard in the past, and they have been shaken by this Austrian novelist's solemn allusions to a *Zivilisationsbruch* (breakdown of civilization).

In the 1980s and 1990s, France suffered the rise of a racist and revisionist extreme right wing party; it experienced the havoc wreaked by local and regional alliances between the traditional Right and the extreme Right, made at the cost of violating the "coalition prohibition" declared by the leaders of the traditional Right. France observed how the left wing parties seriously discredited and harmed themselves by backing the extreme Right in order to weaken the traditional Right. Thanks to the usual routine in which the Left and the Right alternate,

France was able to avoid the historical catastrophe that the access of an extreme right wing party to the central government would have triggered.

This explains why the French were so astounded and worried when the Austrian Conservative Party entered a dangerous and compromising alliance. This high-risk game could only have been won if it had quickly led to the marginalization of the extreme Right. When such an alliance is long-term, it inexorably results in the degradation of an entire society's political culture, compromising the traditional Right, normalizing the extreme Right, and perverting all political life through the demagogy and violence of its discourse and actions.

The political solidarity between the ruling coalition partners makes the traditional conservatives susceptible to blackmail by their national-populist partners. The level of tolerance for specific forms of discourse and behavior increases. In the end, all the rhetoric of the democratically elected government, which can do anything in the name of democracy, including violating the basic values of our culture, is revealed as a pure cynicism. Suddenly any criticism is construed as a "declaration of war against a democratically elected government." But even when anti-Semitism, the revision of our collective memory, racism, xenophobia, and chauvinism are "democratically" elected, they are anti-democratic.

In both Austria and France, the relation of the extreme Right to collective memory is conflict ridden. In France, its judgements of the Vichy regime, Nazism, and the Shoah are incompatible with the fundamental values of democracy. This also applies to the wars of decolonization: Like a palimpsest, the "subtext" of anti-Semitic racism of the 1930s and 1940s has been overlaid with a xenophobia hostile to fellow citizens from Africa. Blacks and Maghrébins, even if they are French nationals, are simply reduced to the status of *immigrés*. The same observations can be made in Austria, in a different historical and geopolitical context. The racism and anti-Semitism of the 1930s and 1940s is really the "subtext" of a xenophobia directed against the refugees and immigrants of today.

I see no reason to retract the theory I formulated and voiced several times in 2000, that "symbolical fascism and Nazism" are propagated by the national-populist trend. The placating counter-arguments have one great weakness: They vastly underestimate the role that *Erinnerungskultur* (the culture of remembrance) and *Erinnerungspolitik* (the policy of remembrance) play in the strategies of gaining and maintaining power. The Third Reich, National Socialism, and European fascism are not things of the past. In the words of Henry Rousso, they belong to "*un passé qui ne passe pas*" (a past that does not pass away), especially since the 1980s. Dealing with the past is a permanent obligation, one that applies of course *not only* to Austria, but to the whole of Europe.

To understand the extent of the Austrian transgression from the French point of view, it is helpful to recall Henry Rousso's analyses. In *Le Syndrome de Vichy de 1944 à nos jours* (Paris: Seuil, 1987 ; reed. 1990) , *Vichy. Un passé qui ne passe pas* (Paris: Fayard, 1994), and *La Hantise du passé* (Paris: Textuel, 1998) this famous contemporary historian convincingly proves that the French culture has undergone different phases in attempting to come to terms with its past and its remembrance. The first was the *phase de deuil* (mourning period) between 1944 and 1955, to be understood more as an affliction than a proper mourning process, a *deuil inachevé* (unfinished mourning). It was a phase marked by the aftermath of the civil war, from the purge to the amnesty; a "choking back" phase favored by the myth of "resistancialism," promoted by the Communist and Gaullist parties. Then came the *phase du retour du refoulé* (the reappearance of the repressed): The mirror breaks and the myth is shattered (see the film *Le Chagrin et la pitié* or the Touvier affair). And we have now entered the phase of obsession, characterized in internal political debates by the awakening of the Jewish collective memory and the importance of memories of the occupation.

This is why I have felt a profound need to denounce a political strategy that I have interpreted as a betrayal of the historical heritage of the Austrian cultural and political identity rebuilt since 1945 and 1955, as well as an unbearable provocation to French sensitivities. I insist that my rejection was not prompted by partisan political preferences. I see clearly that in October, it was not the extreme Right that won, but the Socialist Left that lost; it was not the success of national-populism that radically changed the Austrian political landscape, but the deterioration of the grand coalition that had been feeding the desire for a change. The responsibility for the *Wende* (turning point) of February 2000 must be shared. In the same way, it can be said that by losing credibility in Austria, the left wing opposition has, for more than a year, allowed the black-blue coalition to consolidate.

In the meantime, the publication of my *Mr Haider's Austria. A Journal of the Year 2000* has called attention to the divergent sensitivities in our two countries. I note that, by and large, my book was well received in France despite all its weaknesses (which are inevitable when a book is written so quickly). It seems, though, that some Austrian readers perceived it as an affront to the Austrian identity.

I am sincerely sad about that, but I have the uneasy feeling that the recent evolution in Austrian political life and the political campaign for the March 25 municipal and regional elections of Vienna have confirmed my somber analysis of the situation. The prospect of a victory for the Left in Vienna would be within the continuity of 20th century "Red Vienna." However, history has shown that this tradition was not able to hinder the rise of Austro-fascism.

The crisis that broke out in February 2000 has done irreparable damage to France's image of Austria. The positive image of "Austria as a fellow country" was brutally supplanted by the resurgence of negative images of Austria. Those negative images may well have been present since the turn of the century; but if they were, they had been relegated to the background.

I draw two lessons from this serious Franco-Austrian crisis, which might also be a European one. First of all, one should certainly take a step back from analyses that reduce the crisis to an "Austrian problem" rooted in the particularities of the political culture of Austria and possibly even in some sort of "Austrian soul." Those particularities exist, yet what catches our attention is the "universal European" dimension of the Austrian issue. On Tuesday, March 22, *Le Monde* published an article entitled "The Report of the Human Rights Commission Reveals Alarm at the Increase of Racism in France." According to the research carried out by the consultative national human rights commission, "60% of the French believe that there are too many people of foreign extraction in France." Moreover, "80% of the racist crimes committed in France in 2000 were of an anti-Semitic nature" (the conflicts between the Israelis and Palestinians have, unfortunately, incited more acts of anti-Semitic racism).

I recall this to emphasize that the *morbus austriacus* is in fact one strain of a widespread European malady. In the face of this crisis in European human rights, the political parties have, now more than ever, an obvious *normative* responsibility. The founding consensus of Western Europe since 1945, repeated and reformulated after 1968, was the definitive rejection of fascism and racism. It also meant the rejection of colonialism for France and the other nations that had been involved in colonial wars. In 2000, the founding consensus of the European Union should have retained the strong and unconditional rejection of national-populists who are unscrupulous in their exploitation of the basest tendencies of the electorate and who use democratic procedures to undermine the principles of democracy. All attempts to deny the "true nature" of those national-populist parties can only result in their coalition partners' losing their own identity and losing sight of their founding values.

The second lesson I have learned from the current crisis is that the work of cultural reconciliation must be constantly restarted. The events of 2000 have caused exaggerated and polemic stereotypes of the Austrian to resurface in France, but they have also revealed the lasting antipathy towards France and the French which permeates all levels of Austrian society. It is as if we were back in the era of Andreas Hofer or still felt the rancor of Saint-Germain-en-Laye.

The work of cultural reconciliation and dialogues should be taken up again. This is why the Austrian government's recent decision to close the Austrian Cultural Institute of Paris is so dismaying. But the present circumstances also show that traditional cultural foreign policies are in crisis and that the only way to strengthen European culture is to stimulate all forms of non-governmental co-operation, from collaboration between associations to schools, universities, and local organizations.

To combat the process of alienation between Austria and France, it is not enough to protest the closing of the Austrian Cultural Institute in Paris. The evaluation of the true results of the traditional cultural institutes is still on the agenda. I regret the decision to close it, a resolution that, seen in the present context, can only be understood as retaliation for the sanctions. In my opinion, however, the issue is not maintaining the cultural institutes, but encouraging real cultural co-operation between the two countries.

Thomas Angerer and I have analyzed Austro-French cultural transfers since 1945 under the heading *Ein Frühling, dem kein Sommer folgte* (A Spring Not Followed by Summer). Cultural transfers have the particular ability to escape the will of centralized politics. Like the mechanisms of affective transfer (French also uses *transfert* for the Freudian term *Übertragung*), the mechanisms of the cultural transfer can only be influenced and energized if we proceed with tact and delicacy. The governmental policy of cultural co-operation led by the foreign office is not especially suitable in times of crisis.

In the interest of ensuring that the Franco-Austrian cultural transfers do not become *Ein Herbst, dem ein Winter folgte* (An Autumn Followed by a Winter), let us hope that our two societies will find a way to renew the dialogue suspended by the serious crisis of confidence in 2000 and to rekindle the flame of the cosmopolitan ideal of Europe. Although we have a single European currency and a European central bank, we still do not have a common political culture. During the recent political crisis, we behaved much the same as Europeans at the beginning of the last century, the era of nationalism, might have behaved. It is this *Gleichzeitigkeit des Ungleichzeitigen* (simultaneity of non-simultaneity) that creates *Zerrissenheit,* tearing apart European civilization today.

After the Viennese elections of March 25, French friends of Austria were extremely relieved and hopeful again. Those elections were a huge challenge: The national-populist party of Jörg Haider had posted amazingly successful results in the local elections of 1996, with 27.94% of the votes in the Austrian capital. More recently, there has been speculation as to whether the trend observed in the regional elections since the middle of 2000, which showed the extreme Right wave receding, would continue. Would the test of governmental responsibilities demystify this protest party? The March election results turned out to be more than a backward movement: They indicated a real defeat, with the FPÖ getting only 20.15% of the votes.

The Socialist Party (SPÖ) benefited from the return of voters who had been seduced by the populist topics of Haider's party, which had received an exceptionally high proportion of votes in the wealthy neighborhoods of Vienna. The middle classes, shocked by Jörg Haider's violent rhetoric, voted for the Left rather than for the conservative party of Chancellor Schüssel, who had formed an alliance with the Freedom Party in the government coalition of February 2000.

In Vienna, Chancellor Schüssel lost his majority, while the opposition (Socialists and Greens) enjoyed an overwhelming majority, thus presenting a real "republican front" to the provocations of extreme Right leader Jörg Haider. Following a period of doubts and depression, the opposition has now recovered its self-confidence, and for the next parliamentary elections it can expect to regain the ground it lost in autumn 1999.

Nonetheless, the damage done by the coalition between the Right and the extreme Right has been considerable. It had been a long time since Austria had last witnessed such an outburst of xenophobia and anti-Semitism from a party which counted among its members several ministers and the vice-chancellor of the national government. Jörg Haider's verbal attacks on Ariel Muzicant, the representative of the Jewish community of Austria, were intended to galvanize national-populist voters, and it must be pointed out that these provocations kept the FPÖ from falling under the 20% mark. Unfortunately, anti-Semitism and xenophobia are still a profitable business. 20.15% is admittedly much lower than the 1996 results, but it is nevertheless significant.

There is no choice but to note that the conservative leaders, starting with Chancellor Schüssel, maintained a prudent silence on the subject of Haider's speeches and articles. Evidently, the Conservative Party is bent on remaining in power and dealing tactfully with its coalition partner. For that reason, they are ready to make concessions that I for one consider excessive and dishonorable. This evolution has proven to be unsuccessful in Vienna, a fact all Europeans will be delighted to hear.

What does the future hold for the FPÖ? I would first like to draw attention to the evolution of the extreme Right in France: The recent municipal elections of 11 and 18 March 2001 revealed that the global retreat of this movement, divided into two rival parties, had not impeded the development of local bastions on a municipal level. Will Carinthia and some Austrian regions function as fallback positions for the national-populist extreme Right in Austria? Will Red Vienna be an island surrounded by a black-blue Austria, as was the case in the 1920s and 1930s? Will the traditional Right, in order to remain in power as long as possible, have to help the extreme Right maintain a sufficient level?

The future of the FPÖ will be the future that the major democratic parties of Austria are willing to give it. In October 1999, it was not the FPÖ that won, but rather the SPÖ-ÖVP grand coalition that lost. The grand coalition system had gone on for too long: It had squelched democratic debate, paralyzed the practice of alternating power, discredited institutions by means of dubious compromises and corruption, and energized the FPÖ by giving it the prestige of being an *ausgegrenzte* (excluded) party. Since February 2000, the SPÖ has not recovered the energy or momentum a major opposition party should have. There is some reason to believe that votes cast for the Socialists on March 25 were more anti-FPÖ than pro-SPÖ.

The future of the SPÖ will also depend on the economy and European policy. The return of a period of slowdown in both economic growth and the European integration process could create favorable conditions for the FPÖ and urge them to go back into opposition to play the role of a protest party opposed to "the system."

Bibliography

Angerer, Thomas and Jacques Le Rider, eds. 1999. *Ein Frühling, dem kein Sommer folgte? Französisch-österreichische Kulturtransfers seit 1945.* Vienna, Böhlau (see also the review of this book by Kurt Tweraser, pp. 333ff.).

Ferry, Jean-Marc. 2000. *La Question de l'Etat européen.* Paris, Gallimard.

Le Rider, Jacques. 2001. *L'Autriche de M. Haider. Un journal de l'année 2000.* Paris, Presses Universitaires de France.

Martens, Stephan, ed. 2001. *L'Allemagne, l'Autriche et l'espace centre-européen.* Paris, La documentation française (Problèmes politiques et sociaux, vol. 850).

Ricoeur, Paul. 2000. *La Mémoire, l'histoire, l'oubli.* Paris, Le Seuil.

Small States—Big States:
Who Has the Political Clout in the European Union?

Johannes Pollak and Sonja Puntscher Riekmann

I. Introduction

In a famous remark about the decision-making process in the EU Council of Ministers the former vice president of the Commission Leon Brittan (1994: 232) has singled out two basic principles: "stopping the big fish from eating the small fry, and preventing the small fry from ganging up on the big fish." Whereas it might be quite clear for insiders who are the sharks and who are the herring, from an outside perspective, a veil of secrecy lies on the decision-making processes in the European Union. It largely prevents scholars from charting a clear picture of the role and the weight that states and their representatives have in single negotiations. Moreover, the picture might change from one policy field to another, if not in principle certainly in important details. And, the fact remains that no single state—be it big or small—can prevail without forming alliances with others. Alliances are of uttermost importance, but they may be constructed along varying lines. Last but not least, the Council is only one, if the most important, of the legislative actors on the European level. Hence, alliances might also be formed with the Commission and to an increasing degree with the factions of the European Parliament.

This article is focused on the role and capabilities of small member states to influence European politics, with special emphasis on Austria. However, the distinction between *big* and *small* is all but easy in that it rests on quantitative as well as qualitative elements. Small states belonging to the group of founders of the Union may have another impact than those who joined only recently. Economic strength, military importance and political culture may figure as distinguishing factors relevant to all members. Moreover, roles may change due to economic and/or political developments of the member state itself and due to more global transformation processes. Thus, the role of Spain derives not only from its size but also from its continuously expanding economic strength after EU membership, while today's dominant position of Germany, beyond its economic performance, is owed to the demise of the Soviet empire entailing German reunification and considerable growth in population. But then the latter phenomenon has visibly altered the position of France and the working of the Franco-German tandem as a driving force of European integration. Another important factor is a member's commitment to the construction of the new European polity, the lack of which can reduce the impact also of big states, the United Kingdom being an important case in point.

To offer a possible way out of this maze of variables is rather difficult. This article will only be one of few attempts, as the literature largely ignores the subject. The interest scholars have taken in problems resulting from the size of states with regard to international relations in general has so far had little reverberations in the studies on European integration. However, the issue has gained in relevance particularly in the course of the recent intergovernmental conference (IGC) leading to the Treaty of Nice. Interestingly, but perhaps not all that surprisingly, the row about small and big broke out rather vehemently, with the main bone of contention being indeed the voting weights of the members in the Council in view of the next enlargement. Enlarging the Union towards Central and Southern Europe does entail the accession of a considerable number of medium and small states, Poland being the only exception. However, here again problems arise not only from a dichotomy of big versus small, but also from one of rich versus poor and of old versus new. Size is a variable rather than a constant!

In order to shed some light on the general topic this article will try to depict the debate as it unfolded throughout the IGC negotiations 2000. This is of course a special situation in several respects. IGCs generally lead to new institutional arrangements and thus are of *constitutional* importance. In IGCs the heads of states and governments decide about the principles of the distribution of power in the Union and between the Union and the member states. Hence, scholarly judgments about them cannot easily be transposed onto the everyday policy-making process. However, the peculiarity of this context notwithstanding, it offers good empirical material for the issue we are dealing with in this article. Furthermore, this IGC differs from the negotiations which led to the Single European Act (1987) or the Treaty of Maastricht (1992) as its challenges are determined by a policy of enlargement differing in quantity and in quality from everything the Union has realized in its history. It failed already in Amsterdam in 1996/97 when trying for the first time to create new structures suiting to this task. At that time institutional reforms which were declared as the *conditio sine qua non* of any new enlargement have been postponed to the next IGC. Hence, the pressure on the negotiators in Nice to produce at least some results worth the name of institutional reform. Finally and undeniably, since Amsterdam, discourses on European integration have latently or overtly changed towards a greater emphasis on the nation state as the unalterable pillar of co-operation in the Union. However, evoking the nation state as the main actor in the Union almost inevitably brings about the discussion about their single status. The debate about *big* and *small* has its roots also in this changed environment.

As has been said before, the focus of this article is on Austria. But again, Austria in the year 2000 is a special case. Due to its government coalition of FPÖ and ÖVP—i.e of the Freedom Party qualified as a part of the "New Radical Right in Europe" (Kitschelt 1997) and the conservative People's Party—the other fourteen members of the Union decided to impose diplomatic measures against Austria. They were lifted eight months later after a trio of "wise men" had investigated Austria's democratic record and counseled the French presidency to revoke this decision as it had become counterproductive. One argument surfacing in the debate inside and outside of Austria concerned the question about the measures being imposed on a small member state. It was argued that, had a similar government been formed in Germany or France, no other state would have dreamed of putting it under observation. And indeed, there were evidences for this when the German chancellor Gerhard Schröder announced a similar procedure if in Italy a right-wing coalition were formed taking on board the post-fascist *Alleanza Nazionale* and the radical *Lega Nord*: Schröder had to beat a retreat after heavy protests of the incumbent Italian left-wing government.

This special event will play a role in this article, partly because it obviously influenced the Austrian position in the IGC with particular regard to the reform of Article 7 of the Treaty on the European Union (TEU) concerning the question of how to deal with members—actually or potentially—violating the democratic values of the Union. But beyond this case, the general attitudes of the Austrian representatives in the IGC will be analyzed in comparison with other member states. Collecting reliable information on the positions of the member states still is a daunting task since the nature of the IGC negotiations reminds more of secret privy councils than of a democratic process.

This article proceeds as follows: We will first make a short excursion into international relations theory because one is to expect that this branch of political science has to come up with a sound catalogue of criteria enabling us to define what *big* and *small* means. Secondly, we will describe the positions of the member states in the IGC 2000 concerning the extension of qualified majority voting, the weighting of votes in the Council, the size of the Commission, enhanced cooperation, and the Charter of Fundamental Rights trying to find a pattern which allows to see a confrontation between large and small member states.[1] In chapter four we will briefly deal with the future of the European Union—more precisely with the prominent voices heard calling for a *constitutionalization* of the EU. In the aftermath of the negotiations on the Treaty of Nice the cleavage between large and small member states became the object of the debate on a new European constitution which might be considered as a potential remedy to avoid open power struggles and to render bullying impossible or at least mitigated.

II. Big or Small in Relation to What?

In the literature on International Relations several attempts have been made for a quantitative approach aiming at the definition of small states. Perhaps the most extensive analysis is the UNITARY-study "Small States and Territories: States and Problems" (Rapaport et al. 1971) which measures size by three variables: area, population and Gross National Product (GNP). But the definition of the size of states can be undertaken by measuring their potential influence, which also uses to some extent quantitative variables. Robert O. Keohane (1969) distinguishes small and big by focusing on whether their leaders think their states have a decisive impact on the international system. Others have defined a small state as being unable to exercise its political will, or protect its interests, by power politics (Jaquet 1971) or as a state that does not have the capabilities to guarantee its own security (Rothstein 1968). It was also argued that it is not possible to arrive at more specific definitions. Quite logically some of the literature contends that "the idea of small power is meaningless unless used relative to other states" (Bjol 1971).

Whereas the economic literature focuses on the expected characteristics of the states' economies, "the political literature takes as a starting point that a small state has a larger security problem and proceeds to examine the various available solutions" (Griffith/Pharo 1995: 29). The question of whether smaller states are able to influence larger states by forming alliances is a widely discussed issue. When theories have dealt with smaller states by "studying foreign policy the highest priority has been given to the study of the adaptive policy of small states in regard to the power politics of superpowers or 'big' powers and not to the participation of small states in integration processes. ... Thus, there is a special need for attention to the relationship between small states and integration." (Kelstrup 1993: 137).

A more recent study (Thorhallsson 2000) applies Peter J. Katzenstein's approach based on the economic characteristics small states have in common with regard to European integration. Katzenstein's basic assumption is that "size affects, in particular, both economic openness and the characteristics of the political regime" (1985: 80). He discerns three distinctive characteristics of the smaller states in Europe. Firstly, smaller states can be distinguished from larger ones in their economic openness which reinforces their corporatist arrangements. Secondly, the corporatist difference is evident in the three defining characteristics of corporatism: "an ideology of social partnership, a centralized and contested system of economic interest groups, an uninterrupted process of bargaining among all of the major political actors across different sectors of policy" (Katzenstein 1985: 80). And thirdly, corporatism also results from the distinctive party systems of the small states in Europe, where "political opponents tend to share power and jointly influence policy" (Katzenstein 1985: 80).

According to Katzenstein the domestic policy-making of smaller states differs from larger states: "[C]orporatist arrangements set the small European states apart from the large industrial states . ... One can distinguish the strong corporatism of the small European states from the weak corporatism of the large industrial states." (Katzenstein 1985: 30). This corresponds to the findings of Arend Lijphart (1999: 177) on interest group pluralism. Lijphart uses aggregate data located on a five-point scale: Austria (0.62), Belgium (1.25), and Finland (1.31) show a high degree of corporatism whereas France (2.84) and the United Kingdom (3.38) count as highly pluralistic countries. Germany (1.38) also shows a corporatist political structure which may be due to its strong federalism. Thus, small states have, besides mere quantitative restrictions, different styles of policy-making compared to large states.

However this does not automatically mean that they have the same range of interests.

By applying and refining Katzenstein's approach Baldur Thorhallsson (2000: 12 ff) reaches the following conclusions for the policy fields "Common Agricultural Policy" (CAP) and "Regional Policy of the EU": Smaller states prioritize within these policy fields—they concentrate only on issues from which they gain considerable benefits. The administrative working of the smaller states in the decision-making in CAP and Regional Policy is characterized by greater informality and flexibility. In questions of low relevance they have more room to maneuver. Size obviously also affects the relationship between the member states and the European Commission: The larger states are able to exert a stronger influence upon the Commission. The smaller states compensate for this by using the characteristics of their small administrations to develop a special relationship with officials of the Commission. Secondly, due to the limited capacity of the administrations of the smaller states, they rely more upon the Commission to get their proposals through the Council. Concerning the negotiation style Thorhallsson's study has shown that the distinctive corporatism of Peter Katzenstein's theory does not provide a satisfactory explanation for the behavior of small states in the decision-making process of the CAP and the Regional Policy. This is because in negotiations larger states are as restricted by their domestic interests as the smaller states.

Concerning "low politics" the main decision-making body in the European Union is the Council of Ministers. Besides the formal allocation of votes all member states try to increase their power in the Council. It is tricky, though, to establish what endows particular participants with effective power. Much attention has been given to the relative voting power (Hosli 1994; Widgrén 1994). The Banzhaf power index and the Shapley-Shubik power index both show similar results: the relative decline in voting power of larger member states and the relative increase in voting power of smaller member states. But small member states do not actually outvote large member states in any systematic way. When votes are taken, it is almost unheard of for two large member states to be outvoted. On unanimity decisions it is exceptional for a single small member to sustain opposition and highly exceptional for a small member state to attempt a veto on decisions otherwise subject to majority voting (comp. Hayes-Renshaw/Wallace: 268). Various coalitions are very common while long-term stable alignments are almost never seen.[2] Moreover, the fact that the EU deals simultaneously in so many policy areas makes it possible in principle for negotiations to embrace a wide variety of topics and thus be subject to cross-trading (Hayes-Renshaw/Wallace 1997: 18).

But whatever the voting weights, it is a fact that Germany has the most economic power as a country, which strengthens the force of some German government arguments. For instance, there was simply no question about whether to establish the European Monetary Union (EMU) without German consent. On specific issues individual member states have specific endowments and stakes that bear in the policy-making process. The size of the Spanish fishing fleet has to be acknowledged in order to understand the outcome of the EFTA accession package on fish. Austria's crucial position between two big member states explains the rather exceptional "transit agreement" regulating heavy traffic through the north-south passage. Voting weights had nothing to do with it. Additionally the personal reputation of a minister depending on his or her competence irrespective of representing a large or a small member state can add political weight. Thus, the reflex in the Council has mostly been to operate by consensus. Unfortunately "we lack detailed and authoritative accounts of meetings, voting records and how business is transacted, leaving too much to be read into the resulting texts and anecdotes" (Hayes-Renshaw/Wallace 1997: 3).

Thus, the ability of a state to influence its environment within the framework of the EU will largely depend on a favorable constellation of circumstances. Recognizing the right moment for launching an initiative or knowing when to put the brakes on depends on competent pundits informing their respective capitals on important trends. Sometimes this can amount to a situation of mutual siege—but he who is the first to grab the initiative is also the one to gain the most. Winning and blocking coalitions in the Council are typically constructed of a range, not primarily to attain a specific voting threshold, but based on affinities and/or interests. Everything depends on making a proposition "yesable" to as many participants as possible (Fisher/Ury 1982).

III. The Bazaar of Nice

On 3 and 4 June 1999, in view of the coming enlargements, the European Council in Cologne decided to convene an IGC as early as the beginning of 2000, under the Portuguese presidency, to resolve the institutional issues left open in Amsterdam that needed to be settled be-

Table 1a
Small and Big Fish in the European Union: Some Quantitative Indicators

EU Members	Council of Ministers Voting allocation		Seats in EP		Population in m	GDP**
	Current	New*	Current	New*		
Germany	10	29	99	99	87.0	2,134.205
Britain	10	29	87	72	59.2	1,357.197
France	10	29	87	72	59.0	1,426.967
Italy	10	29	87	72	57.6	1,171.865
Spain	8	13	64	50	39.4	553.230
The Netherlands	5	13	31	25	15.8	381.819
Greece	5	12	25	22	10.5	120.724
Belgium	5	12	25	22	10.2	248.184
Portugal	5	12	25	22	10.0	106.697
Sweden	4	10	22	18	8.9	226.492
Austria	4	10	21	17	8.1	211.858
Denmark	3	7	16	13	5.3	174.870
Finland	3	7	16	13	5.2	123.502
Ireland	3	7	15	12	3.7	81.949
Luxembourg	2	4	6	6	0.4	17.500
Total	87	237	626	535	375.3	

Table 1b

Candidates	Council of Ministers Voting allocation		Seats in EP	Population in m	GDP**
	Current	New*	New*		
Poland	8	27	50	38.7	158,574
Romania	6	14	33	22.5	34,158
Czech Republic	5	12	20	10.3	56,379
Hungary	5	12	20	10.1	47,807
Bulgaria	4	10	17	8.2	12,258
Slovakia	3	7	13	5.4	20,362
Lithuania	3	7	12	3.7	10,736
Latvia	3	4	8	2.4	6,396
Slovenia	3	4	7	2.0	19,524
Estonia	3	4	6	1.4	5,202
Cyprus	3	4	6	0.8	4,125
Malta	2	3	5	0.4	2,455
Total	134	345	732	481.2	

* Provisional
** Gross Domestic Product in Millions of USD, 1998
+ Allocation if country were an EU member
Sources: Council of the European Union, *The Economist, Agence Europe,* no. 7870, *Fischer World Almanach 2001*

fore enlargement. The aim was to keep this IGC as short as possible completing its work already by the end of the year 2000 under the French presidency. At the meeting in Helsinki on 10 and 11 December 1999 the European Council defined the following issues to be reviewed by the IGC: the possible extension of qualified majority voting in the Council, the weighting of votes in the Council, and the size and composition of the European Commission. The "IGC on Institutional Matters" was officially inaugurated on 14 February 2000 in Brussels. At the meeting of the Council in Feira on 19 and 20 June 2000 it was agreed to add the question of enhanced co-operation as a further item to the conference's agenda.

On the occasion of the informal meeting in Biarritz on 13 and 14 October 2000 it was decided to ask the IGC to examine the proposals aimed at reforming Article 7 TEU. A reform of this article became relevant in the wake of the measures set by the fourteen against Austria, as indeed the wording of the existing article had not provided an appropriate legal basis for those measures.[3] The matter was discussed at a meeting on international law held in the Austrian ministry of foreign affairs while at the same time the Belgian negotiators at the IGC offered a similar proposal. The main task was to find a formula enabling the member states to evaluate possible dangers of infringements of democratic values and to act preventively on the basis of sound procedures.

In the following we will briefly describe the member states' positions on the so-called Amsterdam leftovers.[4] These positions varied in the course of the negotiations. Furthermore, it seems that national positions made public via the media sometimes contradicted the positions taken in the IGC. For instance France's Minister for European Affairs Pierre Moscovici had to oppose the impression that France was professing a restrictive attitude on the subject of qualified majority voting. It was largely believed that the so-called uncoupling of Germany (more votes in the Council for Germany than France due to its population size) will be on the agenda of the negotiations, but Moscovici repeatedly countered by saying that the only public declaration of Germany he knows is that "this is not a problem" (*Agence Europe,* 26 October 2000).

Extension of qualified majority voting in the Council

The extension of the qualified majority voting (QMV) in the Council is of considerable importance for guaranteeing the ability to function and the efficiency of the decision-making process in an enlarged Union. The Portuguese and French presidencies have identified around fifty articles where unanimity should be replaced by QMV. Among these articles five sensitive areas were singled out where the transition to QMV is particularly important for an enlarged Union, but hard for certain delegations to accept: coordination of social security and minimum requirements in social policy; visas, asylum, and immigration; taxation, common commercial policy; economic and social cohesion policy. Italy, France, Germany, the Netherlands, Austria, and Belgium were largely in favor of extending QMV. From their point of view unanimity should be restricted to very important issues only, such as treaty revisions. The United Kingdom, Denmark, and Sweden have voiced their concerns about an excessive extension. Equally, Portugal and Greece had strong reservations in environmental policy, Spain and Portugal in the area concerning the structural and cohesion funds, the United Kingdom, Ireland, and Luxembourg with regard to taxation. But even within the group advocating for an extension of QMV requests for exceptions have been heard: France pointed to its difficulties in the field of justice and home affairs, and Austria announced reservations concerning water resources, land use, choice of energy resources, and regional planning. The Austrian Chancellor Wolfgang Schüssel, in an interview with an Austrian newspaper (*Die Presse,* 1 December 2000) confirmed his opposition to the introduction of QMV for immigration and asylum policy, saying that these issues must foremost be decided by "Austrian, German and Italian societies."

In the last summary paper of the French presidency Foreign Minister Hubert Védrine stated that "12 countries out of 15 have serious problems with applying QMV to such or such a subject" (*Agence Europe,* 4 December 2000), only Belgium, Italy, and the Netherlands have no reservations.

After three days of intensive and rather difficult negotiations at the concluding conference in Nice, a Finnish proposal was accepted which more clearly indicates the cases where the rule of unanimity is upheld. No progress was possible over the dossier of taxation and social security, notably because of the total refusal by the United Kingdom. A rather modest progress was made with regard to the Structural and Cohesion Funds[5]: application of QMV as of 1 January 2007 with, in addition, the guarantee requested by Spain that, if there is no agreement on the new financial perspectives at this date,[6] the application of QMV would be postponed. In the future QMV will be applied, among others, to Article 7.1 TEU Establishment of a breach of fundamental rights in a member state (by four-fifths of the members of the Council) and common commercial policy (Article 133).[7] In only six areas was the extension of QMV matched immediately by the commensurate extension of co-decision with the European Parliament (EP).[8] Indeed, as Jacques Chirac has said in the concluding press conference, "things are evolving at a wise and necessarily slow pace" (*Agence Europe,* 11 December 2000). Commission President Romano Prodi probably came nearer to the truth when he deplored the existence of "insurmountable vetoes that have not even allowed to have a discussion" on qualified majority voting in key sectors like taxation and social provisions (ibid).

Weighting of votes in the Council

As with every previous enlargement, the accession of Austria, Sweden, and Finland prompted only an arithmetical adjustment to the weighting of votes in the Council. In allotting votes the population of the new member states and the balance between larger and smaller states was taken into account. The threshold required for a qualified majority remained unchanged at just over 71% of all the votes. Since, apart from Poland and Romania, all the prospective new members fall into the category of smaller states, a further adjustment in the weighting to their advantage is to be expected. The proposal of a "simple dual majority" (votes and population),[9] favored by the Commission, the European Parliament, Germany, Greece, Ireland, and Austria, did not meet with great enthusiasm from the other EU members.

The style of the negotiations in the short hours of 11 December can only be compared to horse-trading. Rough transcripts of the discussion, which were leaked to the British weekly *The Economist,* show a stunning obsession with national power interests (*The Economist,* 16 December 2000: 24). During these final negotiations the French presidency provoked protests from Portugal, Finland, and Greece when it tabled its first plan, which envisaged tripling the votes of the four biggest countries to thirty while increasing those of the small states (in terms of population) by a factor of two or less. This prompted Portuguese Prime Minister Antonio Guterres to speak of an "institutional coup d'etat" (*European Voice* 6/46: 2). According to this proposal,

Poland would have had two votes less than Spain, despite having only 700,000 fewer people. The French suggested increasing the Netherlands' share of the vote from twelve to thirteen, thus giving them more than Belgium, and at the same time reducing the votes allocated to the four biggest members to twenty-nine. But it also proposed increasing the qualified majority needed to pass decisions from 71% to around 74%. This, together with a new criterion requiring all decisions to be approved by votes representing at least 62% of EU citizens,[10] was seen as a way to make it easier for big countries to block decisions. Contrary to public expectations a clash over the parity of votes between Germany and France was avoided, giving Germany greater political weight by introducing this 62% threshold. It was the Belgian Prime Minister Guy Verhofstadt who averted failure in this very dense atmosphere: The qualified majority threshold was set at 71% until the Union expands to twenty-seven members, then it will rise to 74.8%. The votes supporting this decision (258 of the total 345) must represent a simple majority; or, in case the Council has made the initiative, two thirds of the member states will be required to vote. The blocking minority will be ninety-one votes. The deal was made final when Portugal, Greece, and Belgium were allocated twenty-two members of parliament after enlargement.[11] This did not meet with great enthusiasm in the Czech Republic and Hungary (twenty seats each in the EP) because the Czech Republic's population is bigger than that of Belgium and Portugal, and Hungary's population is larger than that of Portugal.

As it turned out later the various thresholds agreed on in Nice were contradictory and remained to be resolved by the Permanent Representatives Committee (COREPER).[12] The interpretation runs now as follows (*Agence Europe*, 23 December 2000): In a Union of fifteen, decisions are secured if they gather at least 169 votes (170 in the text agreed on in Nice). Out of a total of 237 votes, the minority block would, in such a case, be 69 votes whereas, in the Nice text, 68 votes would have sufficed.[13] The "declaration on the threshold for a qualified majority and the number of votes for a minority block in an enlarged Union" would be modified and would stipulate that, in case the candidates for membership had not yet joined the EU on 1 January 2005, the threshold for a qualified majority "will evolve, depending on the rhythm of accessions, from a percentage lower than the current percentage" (71.26%) to a maximum of 73.4%. Both the declaration and the Nice text state that, once all candidates have joined, the minority block will be taken to 91. However, in order to eliminate the contradiction in the figures, the declaration adds that, in a Union of twenty-seven the threshold for a qualified majority "will automatically be consequentially adapted." In a Union of twenty-seven, decisions will be secured if they receive at least 258 votes out of the 345. Thus, the IGC, which was supposed to streamline the decision-making, has produced an arrangement that raises the threshold for QMV at the same time as it increases the weight of the votes. The disappointment of the Commission can easily be perceived through Prodi's comment about the system that will function, but, he regrets, "is not understandable" (*Agence Europe,* 11 December 2000). Furthermore, the unhappy comments by Chirac, who during the negotiations in Nice said that it was natural for new member states to have a "handicap" that existing members do not share, are apt to lead to a new cleavage between *old* and *new* member states.

Size of the Commission

In an enlarged Union a Commission with twenty-seven members hardly seems to be a manageable body. Besides, the mere restriction due to the number of reasonable available portfolios upholding the strict principle of collegiality in such a large body seems quite difficult. Consequently France, Germany, and Italy have opted for a ceiling on the number of commissioners. But there was no agreement about what to do after the accession of more than five countries. Germany proposed a hierarchization of the Commission differentiating between vice-commissioners and junior commissioners. Italy put forward a suggestion which emphasized the equal status of the member states and the collegiate nature of the Commission and pleaded for a rotation model in which groups of member states could then nominate one commissioner.

The Austrian Foreign Minister Benita Ferrero-Waldner said in an interview published in an Austrian newspaper (*Der Standard,* 1 December 2000) that, in Nice, "there will be no room for negotiations" over an immediate ceiling for the Commission. Concerning the suggestion of a rotation of commissioners she stated that "there must be no decision [in Nice] on the rotation," but that "we can imagine a review process for the issue, once we have seen how a future Commision works." Her comment that "we neither want rotation nor hierarchization" (*Agence Europe,* 4 December 2000) was supported by Sweden, Portugal, and Ireland. The principle of "one state, one commissioner" favored by Denmark, Luxembourg, and Greece has been a "commandment" for the Austrian position ever since. The symbolic value of "having" one national in the Commission must not be underestimated. Especially in the case of Austria it was always argued that this is an important means to bring Europe closer to its citizens. Moreover, the Danish prime minister has cynically questioned whether one could imagine a Commission without a German commissioner.

In the concluding negotiations France proposed a ceiling and a 2010 deadline for introducing the new system, with posts to be shared on the basis of equal rotation. But the smaller states won the deal by demanding that this should not happen until the EU comprises twenty-seven members. The setting of a limit on the number of commissioners was put on hold at this time by simply stating that it should be "less than twenty-seven." The next Commission, which will start its term in January 2005, will consist of one commissioner for each member state. Once twelve new countries join the EU, the number will be decided by unanimous vote. Additionally the future Commission president, to be chosen by QMV, has been given further powers to reorganize the Commission and the distribution of portfolios. But it is not clear how far a future president will be able to go in creating a core Commission cabinet whose members have direct responsibility for the key portfolios, while others would be left with minor or more symbolic tasks.

Enhanced Cooperation

The Treaty of Amsterdam provided the possibility for closer cooperation within the existing institutional framework based on strict conditions. Member states may establish closer cooperation between themselves on matters covered by the EC Treaty and matters concerning Police and Judicial Cooperation in Criminal Matters. There was no possibility for closer cooperation in the area of Common Foreign and Security Policy (CFSP). The existing provisions required a majority of members to start enhanced cooperation.

France, Italy, and Germany advocated an overhauling of the existing rules on flexibility (Article 40 and 43-45 TEU), whereas the United Kingdom, Sweden, and Denmark have been more restrained. But also Finland, Greece, Ireland, Austria, and to some extent Portugal have shown no great passion. The argument for facilitating enhanced cooperation derives from the increasing economic and geographic differentiation of the Union: Closer cooperation may be more necessary if the Union is to develop.[14] Those who were reticent to change argued that the Amsterdam provisions have only just entered into force and any change should be on the basis of a clear identification of future areas for closer cooperation. According to the last summary paper of the French presidency, a majority of member states were pleading in favor of a small number of member states being able to trigger closer cooperation (three to four in the area of Common Foreign and Security Policy against eight states in other fields) but several states were categorically against this proposition (*Agence Europe,* 4 December 2000).

Finally, the conditions for the operation of enhanced cooperation under the first pillar (European Community) were improved: Eight member states may decide to cooperate more closely, if approved within the Council by a qualified majority. In the first and the third pillars (Police and Judicial Cooperation in Criminal Matters) there is the added stipulation that closer cooperation must reinforce the integration process. The national veto at the level of the European Council was abolished in the first pillar. As to the second pillar new possibilities for enhanced cooperation were confined to the CFSP (which must not be related to matters having military or defense implications[15]). But enhanced cooperation may still be envisaged as a last resort only and after a reasonable period of trying to reach agreement between all member states. These rather strong provisions against an easy use of enhanced cooperation can be seen as a means to secure cohesion of potentially twenty-seven members.

Charter of Fundamental Rights

In November the French presidency took advantage of the IGC ministerial conclave to invite member states ministers to express their view on the advisability of introducing, as requested by the European Parliament, a reference to the Charter of Fundamental Rights in Article 6 of the Treaty. Six delegations, the United Kingdom, Ireland, Denmark, the Netherlands, Finland, and Sweden voiced opposition although not all of them rejected a subsequent legally binding nature of the Charter to be proclaimed at the Nice Summit. While Spain expressed some comprehension for the Parliament's proposal, it also seemed reluctant. All other countries, including Austria, supported, if without conviction, the EP's proposal which was interpreted as reflecting the simple concern of giving a sign of good will to the EP (*Agence Europe,* 22 November 2000).

With regard to the Charter the role of Austria has been highly constructive. In particular at the level of the European Parliament it was the Austrian Green member and vice president of the Constitutional Committee Johannes Voggenhuber who, together with the British Liberal member Andrew Duff, was the rapporteur of the Parliament on this matter and was subsequently delegated to the Convention in charge of drafting the Charter. But also the other two Austrian members of the Convention, the former vice president of the Austrian Parliament Heinrich Neisser, representing the Austrian government, and the former minister of science and transportation Caspar Einem, representing the national parliament, played an important role. Moreover, all three engaged in promoting a public debate on the Charter in Austria.

In a very general evaluation of the Nice process we can observe that national interests buttressed by vetoes continued to dominate and superimpose the rhetoric of creating more efficient and transparent procedures and institutions. The media have reported about a deep cleavage between small and big member states with rather drastic words. For example *The Financial Times* (12 December 2000) titled a report about Nice "Europe's Meeting of Unequals" and went on to say that "it has been a battle between the big and the small." A Greek newspaper complained that the big countries "did everything they could to create a directorate, which will control all decisions, leaving the little countries at the margins" (*The Economist*, 16 December 2000: 23). Criticism of the outcome and style of the negotiations was widespread. Hans-Gert Pöttering, leader of the center-right European People's Party said: "This IGC did not produce any kind of result. This should never be allowed to happen again. Let's try another model." The president of the Socialist group of the EP Enrique Baron, and the president of the Liberal group, Patrick Cox, also showed their dissatisfaction stating that the "emphasis was more on blocking things rather than on promoting them" (*European Voice*, 6/46: 1; *Agence Europe*, 13 December 2000; ibid, 10 January 2001). British Prime Minister Tony Blair admitted that the EU could not "continue to take decisions as important as this in this way" and continued: "Reform is essential so a more rational way of decision-making is achieved" (*European Voice* 6/46: 1). Even French President Chirac, whose handling of the negotiations came under fierce attack from virtually all sides, told the members of the EP that IGCs might no longer be a suitable method. It seems that even the negotiators themselves were taken by surprise about the confrontational style of the negotiations, which might have been a "foretaste of the power struggles to come" (*The Economist,* 16 December 2000: 23). When it comes to day-to-day politics a rather conciliatory climate prevails in the Council of Ministers.[16] But it would be naive to expect politicians who are socialized in the political framework of the nation-state to put their national interests last. The future hot topics like tax harmonization, constitutionalization, or common defense touch on most sensitive areas of hitherto national sovereignty. Thus a more confrontational style will emerge—aggravated by the fact that the supranational and national executive elites are confronted with a reluctant public who increasingly shows signs of disaffection if not utter disapproval of European politics (Wolton 1993; Andersen/Eliassen 1996; Scharpf 1996, 1999; Puntscher Riekmann 1998; Bach 1999; Gusy 2000). Besides the fact that this new style can also lead to a broader public discussion, the so-called post-Nice process[17] will be less along the lines of "big vs. small," but more along the divergencies of "old vs. new" or "north vs. south." Moreover, it will be a matter of shared interests and skillful plotting of alliances which by definition means the transgression of trodden paths.

IV. A Constitution for Europe?

The debate about a Constitution for Europe is not a new one. The predecessor of the EP, the European Coal and Steel Community's Common Assembly began to draw up a European Constitution on just the second day of its existence in 1952. This was closely connected to the initiative about creating a European Defence Community (EDC). Article 38 of the draft text about the EDC provided for the drafting of a constitution which in the end comprised 117 articles mainly dealing with the institutional structure of the EC. But the constitutional model never had to prove its value since the EDC failed in 1954. It took until 1984 when the EP started a new initiative to create a "Union" (the so-called Spinelli Report, see the Official Journal, part C, 1984/77) based on a constitution which foresaw a federal structure with jurisdiction over economic and social policy, and international relations. In 1994 the EP launched a second proposal (the Herman Report, see the Official Journal, part C, 1994/61) also calling for a federal structure which was never put to vote in the plenary but was considered the basis for further discussions.

Today, a number of prominent politicians have started yet another debate about a European constitution, whose central terms and concepts are sometimes rather ambiguous and often highly controversial. On the occasion of the 50-year-celebrations of the Schuman declaration Jacques Delors (2000) has argued for a "treaty within the Treaty" which would unite the forces of the six founding states and thus build a European avant-garde aiming at deeper integration. This concept of a "core Europe" was introduced in a position paper by CDU/CSU floor leader Wolfgang Schäuble and the parliamentarian Karl Lamers (CDU) in September 1994,[18] earning mainly negative comments. A few days later, the British prime minister at the time, John Major, proposed his own version of flexibility, under which governments could choose integration *à la carte*. The idea of a core group was also advocated by Valéry Giscard d´Estaing and Helmut Schmidt in an article for the French newspaper *Le Figaro*.[19]

Besides the idea of a core group, the simplification of the treaties figured prominently in the debate. In a resolution of 19 November 1997 on the Treaty of Amsterdam, the EP requested the Commission to submit before the European Council of December 1998 a report with proposals for a comprehensive consolidation of the treaties. In order to prepare the EP for the Commission's report, the Parliament asked the The European University Institute (Robert Schuman Centre) in Florence to explore possible ways of bringing the European treaties closer to the form of a classical constitution.[20] The study aims at simplifying the existing European Communities treaties by merging them into just one treaty, divided into a fundamental part (aims, fundamental rights, institutions, competences) and a policy part. This was already proposed by a group of "wise men" set up by the Commission in October 1999.[21] The rapporteurs of the EP Committee of Constitutional Affairs, Giorgos Dimitrakopolous and Jo Leinen, also argued for such a simplification.[22]

In his speech at Berlin's Humboldt University on 12 May 2000, German Foreign Minister Joschka Fischer outlined a *finalité* of the integration process: a European federation that will create a government from either the Council or the Commission and will resolve the democratic deficit through a bicameral European parliament with real legislative power.[23] This federation is to be brought to life by a "consti- tuent treaty."[24] The international reactions ranged from cautious acceptance to disapproval (comp. Hrbek 2001; Börzel/Risse 2000; Müller-Graff 2000). The foreign ministers of Portugal and Italy, Jaime Gama and Lamberto Dini (see *Agence Europe*, 18 May 2000, 20 May 2000, 22/23 May 2000) were in favor of Fischer's proposals, and Belgium and Luxembourg supported them as well. The EP and the Commission voiced some concerns especially with regard to the role of the Commission as motor of the integration (see *Agence Europe,* 24 May 2000, 26 May 2000). The United Kingdom, Sweden, Finland, Ireland, and Greece were more reticent either because the term *federation* is still equated with centralism, red tape, and insufficient democracy, or because the idea of an avant-garde triggers fears of being left out (see *Agence Europe,* 15/16 May 2000, 5 June 2000). France's reaction was also rather cautious since France prepared for taking over the presidency of the Council. Besides the harsh comments by then Minister of the Interior Jean Pierre Chevènement, who later entered into dialogue with Fischer (*Le Monde,* 21 June 2000), Foreign Minister Védrine (*Le Monde,* 13 June 2000) answered positively to some of Fischer's ideas. Nevertheless, all commentators agreed about the importance of Fischer's speech in initializing a public debate about the future European political order.

The debate was enriched by Blair's speech in Warsaw, entitled "Europe: Building a Superpower Not a Superstate."[25] Blair called for Europe to become a global superpower to rival the economic and political strength of the United States. A charter of competences should be drawn up that would clearly set the limits of the EU's powers but would fall short of being a fully-fledged European constitution. As a move towards more democratic accountability, the Commission should be required to publish an annual agenda of its plans as well as a master plan set by the European Council. Blair rejected all ideas about the creation of a "hard core" of EU members and called on EU's elected parliaments and governments to impose their authority onto Brussels. A "council of nations," consisting of national parliamentarians functioning as a second chamber of the EP, should become the watchdog over the "masters of the treaties."[26] Quite interestingly, Austrian officials did not take part in this debate.

V. Conclusion

Now that the Treaty of Nice has formally introduced a link between voting weights in the European Council and population size we can justifiably differentiate between large and small member states, independent, though, from political power. So far the various contributions about the future shape and role of the EU have not reflected upon the relation between the two. A constitutionalization of the EU might contribute to the democratic principle of equality of all members by setting a clearer distribution of competences between the European and national levels, thus reducing the possibilities of "bullying." Nevertheless, the re-emerging ideas about a variable geometry now phrased in the more fashionable term *avant-garde* raise concerns among all member states. The fear of being left out can easily lead to the construction of an *arrière-garde,* composed of member states whose populations are reluctant to trust the rather clandestine European policy-making processes any further. This reluctancy may be instigated by openly anti-European parties and candidates, emerging in all member states, which re-evokes Charles De Gaulle's vision of "l'Europe des patries."

It proves fairly difficult to describe the Austrian position in the ongoing debate because the official statements are rather modest both in terms of quantity and quality. Besides paying lip service to an enhanced role of national parliaments in the post-Nice process, a clear position is still missing. This is all the more unfortunate since the principle "first-come-first-served" perfectly fits this debate. However, even the Austrian self-definition of being an "honest broker" in the policy process, invented during its first presidency of the Council in the second half of 1998, has been significantly reduced by the so-called sanctions. While in 1998 the Austrian government had put the accent mainly on enlargement and tax harmonization (see Puntscher Riekmann/Pollak 1999: 148), the follow-up created a kind of disillusionment within and outside Austria. In particular the neighboring accession countries, which put their hopes on Austria as a committed advocate of their membership, were utterly disappointed.

By way of conclusion it may be maintained that there is no systematic cleavage between small and large member states of the European Union. The delicate balances of influence of the past have been constructed to protect small members against over-weaning large partners and to diffuse brute questions of power, political muscle, and economic leverage (comp. Hayes-Renshaw/Wallace 1997: 295). Though the negotiations in the short hours of Nice and the still infant debate about the future of the EU give the impression that the EU is dominated by a directory of Great Britain, France and Germany, the overall facts allow for a more differentiated picture. *Small* and *big* are idle categories in the context of European integration in that they do not live up to the complexity of multi-level governance and the differences between constitutional issues and the package-dealing in everyday policy-making. While in the former the sovereign status of the single member state is at stake, this is less so in the conundrums of day-to-day politics.

Moreover, the status is more visible in the constitutional issues and more opaque in the daily maze.

References

Andersen, Svein S. and Kjell A. Eliassen. 1996. *The European Union: How Democratic Is It?*. London: Sage Publications.

Arter, David. 2000. "Small State Influence Within the EU." In *Journal of Common Market Studies*, vol. 38 (5): 677-98.

Bach, Maurizio. 1999. *Die Bürokratisierung Europas. Verwaltungseliten, Experten und politische Legitimation in Europa.* Frankfurt a.m.: Campus.

Börzel, Tanja and Thomas Risse. 2000. "Who is Afraid of a European Federation? How to Constitutionalize a Multi-Level Governance System," to be published in: Christian Joerges, Yves Meny, and Joseph H. H. Weiler, *Responses to Joschka Fischer*, 17 July 2000. Draft available at: http://www.iue.it/Personal/Risse/Rissedoc/Welcome.html

Bjol, Erling. 1971. "Small states in international politics." In *Small States in International Relations*. Ed. August Schou and Arne O. Brundtland. Stockholm: Almqvist & Wiksell.

Britton, Leon. 1994. *Europe. The Europe We Need*, London: Hamish Hamilton.

Delors, Jacques. 2000. "Le pardon et la promesse. L'héritage vivant de Robert Schuman, Commémoration du cinquantenaire de la Déclaration Schuman." Luxembourg. Edited by the Groupement d'études et de recherches Notre Europe, Paris.

Fisher, Roger, Ury, William. 1982. *Getting to Yes: How to Succeed in Negotiation Without Giving In.* London: Hutchinson.

Griffiths, Richard T. and Helge Ø Pharo. 1995. *Small States and European Integration. Literature Survey and Evaluation.* ARENA Working Paper no. 19.

Gusy, Christoph. 2000. "Demokratiedefizite postnationaler Gemeinschaften unter Berücksichtigung der Europäischen Union." In *Globalisierung und Demokratie.* Ed. Hauke Brunkhorst and Matthias Kettner. Frankfurt a. M.: Suhrkamp. 131-150.

Hayes-Renshaw, Fiona and Helen Wallace. 1997. *The Council of Ministers.* London: Macmillan.

Holsti, Madeline. 1994. "Coalitions and Power: Effects of Qualified Majority Voting in the European Union's Council of Ministers." Maastricht: European Institute of Public Administration (mimeo).

Hrbek, Rudolf. 2001. "Europäische Föderation durch Verfassungsvertrag." Joschka Fischers Leitbild und der Beginn einer neuen europapolitischen Orientierungs-debatte. In *Europäische Leitbilder. Festschrift für Heinrich Schneider.* Ed. Roland Hierzinger and Johannes Pollak. Baden-Baden: Nomos.

Jaquet, Louis M.G. 1971. "The Role of Small States within Alliance Systems." In *Small States in International Relations.*

Katzenstein, Peter J. 1985. *Small States in World Markets; Industrial Policy in Europe.* Ithaca/London: Cornell University Press.

Kelstrup, Morten. 1993. "Small States and European Political Integration; Reflections of Theory and Strategy." In *The Nordic Countries and the EC.* Ed. Teija Tiili-kainen and Damgaard Petersen. Copenhagen: Copenhagen Political Studies Press.

Keohane, Robert. 1969. "Lilliputians Dilemmas: Small States in International Politics." *International Organization* 23 (2): 291-310.

Kitschelt, Herbert. 1997. *The Radical Right in Western Europe. A Comparative Analysis.* Ann Arbor: University of Michigan Press.

Lijphart, Arend. 1999. *Patterns of Democracy. Government Forms and Performance in Thirty-Six Countries.* New Haven: Yale University Press.

Müller-Graff, Peter-Christian. 2000. "Europäische Föderation als Revolutionskonzept im europäischen Verfassungsraum?." *Integration* 23/3: 157-70.

Pernthaler, Peter and Peter Hilpold. 2000. "Sanktionen als Instrument der Politikkontrolle – der Fall Österreich." *Integration* 23/2: 105-19.

Puntscher Riekmann, Sonja. 1998. *Die kommissarische Neuordnung Europas.* Vienna: Springer.

Puntscher Riekmann, Sonja and Johannes Pollak. 1999. "Austria and the European Union: From Nation State to Member State." *Journal of International Relations and Development* 2/2: 136-53.

Rapaport, Jacques, Ernest Muteba, and Joseph J. Theratill. 1971. *Small States and Territories: States and Problems.* New York: Arno Press.

Rothstein, Robert. 1968. *Alliances and Small Powers.* New York: Columbia University Press.

Scharpf, Fritz W. 1996. "Democratic Policy in Europe." *European Law Journal* 2, no.2: 136-55.

Scharpf, Fritz W. 1999. *Regieren in Europa. Effektiv und demokratisch?.* Frankfurt: Campus.

Schäuble, Wolfgang and Karl Lamers. 1994. "Reflections on Europe." Retrieved 25 January 2001 from the World Wide Web: http://www.keele.ac.uk/socs/ks40/reflect.html or http://www.evpp.org.

Thorhallsson, Baldur. 2000. *The Role of Small States in the European Union.* Aldershot: Ashgate.

Widgrén, Mika. 1994. *The Relation between Voting Power and Policy Impact in the European Union.* CEPR Discussion Paper no. 1033. London: CEPR.

Wolton, Dominique. 1993. *La Dernière Utopie. Naissance de l´Europe démocratique.* Paris: Flammarion.

Notes

1. In this part the article largely relies on press sources since it was written shortly after the negotiations in Nice were completed.

2. With the exception of the alliance between the Benelux countries which is explicitly referred to in Article 233 TEU. The most visible alliance in former times has been the Franco-German axis. In both cases the cooperation has been more concerned with the overall development of the EU rather than with specific policies, and both alliances have come under considerable strain in recent time. A new initiative calling for greater cooperation between the Nordic states is the Northern Dimension Initiative launched in 1997 by Finland (see Arter 2000).

3. For the relevant legal analysis see Pernthaler, Hilpold 2000.

4. See the *Protocol on the institutions with the prospect of enlargement of the European Union* attached to the Treaty of Amsterdam as well as the *Declarations* to that protocol by Belgium, France, and Italy urging for a braver attempt to institutional reform.

5. As well as with regard to Article 137 on social provisions.

6. It is to be expected that a Spanish "yes" to the new perspectives and thus the shift to QMV will be a costly one.

7. With the exception of cultural and audiovisual service—as France has demanded.

8. Articles 13.2, 18.2, 65, 157, 159, 191 TEC.

9. Besides dual majority the Amsterdam protocol also cited re-weighting as a possible way of determining the qualified majority.

10. But only when formally challenged for a verification by any member state.

11. The ceiling of 700 seats in the EP has now been breached. British Liberal MEP Andrew Duff commented that the distribution of seats in the EP in an enlarged EU was contrary to Article 190 TEC—which states that the allocation of seats should ensure an adequate representation of the people of the States making up the Community—and that it should therefore be the subject of a complaint to the Court of Justice (see *Agence Europe,* 11 January 2001).

12. The percentage of votes in the Council of Ministers required to pass new laws did not match the exact number of votes needed.

13. Which leads Spain to observe, for example, that Italy, France, and Portugal, with 70 votes, may block a decision, whereas Italy, Portugal, and Spain would not manage it, having only a total of 68 votes.

14. The idea of an avant-garde was also brought forward by Wolfgang Schäuble, Karl Lamers, Jacques Delors, Valéry Giscard d'Estaing, and Helmut Schmidt.

15. This phrase was inserted on insistence of the UK.

16. This impression may also be due to the lack of information, about how a decision is reached there.

17. Not satisfied with having "opened the way for enlargement," however, the heads of government call for a "deeper and wider debate about the future development of the European Union" in the *Declaration on the Future of the Union* which was added to the final act of the IGC in Nice. The declaration calls on the Swedish and Belgian presidencies of the Council in 2001 "in cooperation with the Commission, involving the EP" to encourage wide-ranging discussions. The Laeken European Council in December 2001 will adopt a declaration on how to pursue this process.

18. In 1974 German Chancellor Willy Brandt suggested that the varying economic strengths of the then nine EC members would require different levels of integration.

19. Partly reprinted in *Agence Europe,* 17/18 April 2000.

20. See http://www.iue.it/RSC/Treaties.html.

21. See the Richard Weizsäcker/Jean-Luc Dehaene/David Simon report for the European Commission: "The institutional consequences of enlargement," Brussels, 18 October 1999, clause 3.

22. Report on the EP's proposals for the IGC, Committee on Constitutional Affairs, http://www.europarl.eu.int/igc2000/offdoc/pdf/repa50086_1en_en.pdf.

23. For the full text of the speech see http://www.auswaertiges-amt.de/6_archiv/index.htm.

24. The English translation of Fischer's speech is sometimes misleading, e.g. *Verfassungsvertrag* is translated 2constituent treaty rather than "constitutional treaty."

25. See http://www.pm.gov.uk/news.asp?NewsId=1341&SectionId=32.

26. Shortly after Blair's speech *The Economist* published its own version of a constitution for Europe which strongly argued for an intergovernmental approach. See *The Economist* 357, no. 8194, 28 October – 3 November 2000.

President of the European Commission Jacques Santer (Luxembourg) in a press conference with Austrian Chancellor Viktor Klima during the Austrian EU-Presidency in the second half of 1998 (photo Harald Hofmeister, *Die Presse*)

The European Council and EU Summitry:
A Comparative Analysis of the Austrian and German Presidencies

Michael G. Huelshoff

Since the founding of the European Council in 1974, the role of member governments in EU decision-making has been significantly transformed. The reassertion of national sovereignty often associated with the Luxembourg Compromise and the establishment of the Council has not so much eroded as evolved. While the relationships among national, subnational, and supranational actors are hotly debated in the academic literature, there is a growing consensus that relations among political actors in the European Union (EU) are different from what is common outside the Union. James Caporaso, for example, speaks of three models of EU statehood, the Westphalian, the regulatory, and the post-modern, and argues that the latter is apparently the direction in which Europe is going.[1] This post-modern form of politics is characterized by rather chaotic, episodic, and unstructured relations across multiple levels of authority, so that the policy-making process is highly flexible and unstable. Yet strong national governments remain important actors, albeit not the only ones in EU decision-making in Caporaso's post-modern EU analysis.

In this article, I examine the role of national governments in EU decision-making. In a comparative study of the Austrian and German presidencies of the European Council and the Council of Ministers, I explore the ability of national governments to affect the pace, scope, and content of the EU's policy agenda, and to use the Council and its summits to pursue both EU and national goals. I find a complicated mix of national prerogative and supranational guidance largely consistent with the pattern noted by Caporaso. Yet I also find that national initiative is not eroding, as some assert. Rather, national governments still enjoy considerable opportunities to shape the agenda in the EU.

Unlike the findings of much of the literature on policy-making, however, I also assert that agenda-setting powers result in considerably weaker influence over outcomes in the EU than is common in national policy-making systems.

The paper is divided into three parts. First, I review the literature on EU policy-making, with special emphasis on studies of the European Council. In the second section, I compare the Austrian and German Council presidencies. Finally, I link the patterns found in the two cases to the broader literature on EU policy making.

The European Council in EU Policy-Making

As Neill Nugent notes, the primary reason that the member governments formalized the irregular summits into the European Council at the Paris Summit in 1974 was to jump-start the EU.[2] In the view of the heads of government, especially French President Giscard d'Estaing and German Chancellor Schmidt, neither the Commission nor the Council of Ministers were able to offer leadership to the EU. The Luxembourg Compromise had politically weakened the Commission, at a time when the completion of tariff reductions in the EU (negative integration) required a shift in focus to more difficult areas of cooperation (positive integration).[3] Sectoralism and unanimity voting rules constrained the Council of Ministers from playing its policy-coordination role, as it found itself bogged down in technical issues. The European Council, then, would provide much-needed leadership. The European Council and regular summits would also help tie the EU to the citizenry of Europe, and assist heads of government in restraining sectoralism and conflict within national governments. Finally, summits would enhance the public visibility of national leaders, generating much hoped-for political support at home.[4]

In its original form, then, the European Council was an informal body designed to increase understanding and exchange ideas among the members, direct the development of policy, resolve disputes among the members, and garner public attention. As it evolved over the next two and a half decades, the European Council has become increasingly formalized, even making explicit mention in major treaty reforms, all without becoming a formal and legal part of the EU. Today, the European Council meets at least twice a year (on average about three to four meetings per year), at the end of each government's tenure as president of the Council of Ministers. The European Council informally incorporates heads of government into the EU's policy-making process. Summits are seen as the cap to a government's turn as president, when expectations to reach a significant number of agreements are high. Indeed, the summits are seen as yardsticks of a member government's leadership in the EU. Further, the recent string of Inter-Governmental Conferences (IGCs) and other initiatives that have re-written the Treaties of Rome (Maastricht, Amsterdam, and Nice, as well as the program to complete the internal market), have all been concluded in the course of European Council summits. Simon Bulmer notes nine specific roles the Council plays:

• Facilitation of informal exchanges about the overall direction of the EU;
• Facilitation of strategic planning about the overall direction of the EU;
• Specification of detailed guidelines in policy areas;
• Negotiation of enlargements of the scope of EU policy making;
• General policy coordination;
• Facilitation of collective declarations about foreign policy issues;
• Decision-making, in the form of a quasi special session of the Council of Ministers;
• Problem-solving for issues deadlocked at lower levels; and
• Coordination of policy control and implementation.[5]

Despite the importance of the European Council, it has received comparatively little attention in the academic literature. There are a large number of studies about specific Council meetings that have resulted in major treaty revisions, such as the 1992 Project,[6] the Maastricht meeting,[7] and the Amsterdam meeting.[8] Many of these studies refer to earlier summits and presidencies, but usually only selectively. Very few studies look at Council summits comparatively, and even fewer offer an overview of all summits, including those that did not result in major treaty revisions.

In a brief study published just as the Council was being formalized, Juliet Lodge explores the "malintegrative" and integrative functions of summits.[9] She finds that summitry before 1974 largely furthered integration in Europe. Writing a decade after the formalization of summits, Bulmer argues that summits were designed to balance internal and external affairs in the EU.[10] He examines four important areas of summitry: distributive bargaining, integrative bargaining, attitudinal structuring, and intra-organizational behavior (an early version of what is now called multi-level governance). Bulmer argues that while the presidencies were able to balance external and internal foci during their first five years, presidencies thereafter became too focused upon internal developments.

Neither study offers much in the way of systematic or detailed empirical analysis of summits, relying instead on ad-hoc empirical observations to support theoretical generalizations. Colm O Nuallain's collection examines individual presidencies in greater detail, but the focus in the different contributions is on the technical aspects of Council presidencies.[11] Little attention is paid to the content of summits or their impact on the development of the EU, and comparisons of summits are drawn only on narrow, public administrative lines.

Mary Troy Johnston is also interested in institutions, but shifts the focus more explicitly to institutionalization and policy-making.[12] She poses the same question as Lodge about pre-1974 summits: Does the European Council facilitate, or hinder integration? Like Bulmer, she avoids a systematic examination of the European Council summits, in favor of a broader empirical analysis of the development of the Council, of its relationships with other institutions (especially the Commission,) and of Council activities in several broad policy areas. She finds that the European Council has become increasingly institutionalized, has improved its technical capability, and has developed a tight and mutually supportive relationship with the Commission. As a result the prospects for further integration in Europe have been enhanced, although Johnston notes that this result is dependent in part on the quality and experience of leadership in the Council,[13] and on general developments in the international system.

Despite the utility of the findings of these studies, none of them systematically analyze summitry in the EU. In contrast, Andrew Moravcsik examines five of the major summits that resulted in significant treaty revisions, and finds that national governments driven by economic interdependence were key in shaping the outcomes.[14] Yet such a sample is biased toward the importance of member governments, as they can be expected to pay especially close attention to, and to try to dominate, both the scope and details of negotiations and renegotiations of treaties that so clearly define their inter-relationships and raise issues of national sovereignty. Thus, it is difficult to know if the patterns of national predominance found in this sample is representative of general European Council presidencies and summitry.

Emil Joseph Kirchner also examines Council presidencies and summitry.[15] Unlike Moravcsik, Kirchner studies eight presidencies and their summits between 1986 and 1989, irrespective of the treaty implications of each summit. Thus, he avoids potential case selection bias that would result from picking a non-contiguous subset of presidencies and summits. Like Bulmer and Johnston, Kirchner finds that the European Council's role in European politics grew during the period he studied. Both the management of technical areas and scope expansion was noted during this period. Further, as Johnston argues, Kirchner finds that the European Council has come to work more closely with the Commission, defying the projections of some commentators that the Council would come to usurp the Commission. Rather, Kirchner argues, "[t]he emphasis is now on legislative and political planning, involving the Commission, a seamless flow of Presidencies and, increasingly, the European Parliament as well."[16] Further, he notes that the Council president functions on two related planes. The first emphasizes the "management and mediating" role that presidencies must perform. This role is encouraged by the six-month duration of each presidency, the impact of the *Troika* in maintaining both continuity and limiting policy initiative,[17] the continued importance of the Commission as policy initiator, cultural expectations emphasizing *European-ness*, and domestic economic and political conditions among the members. The second plane emphasizes the leadership role of Council presidents. Both the general logic and pace of integration in Europe, and events outside the Union, encourage presidents to become champions of scope expansion. In other words, Kirchner finds that Council presidents must be responsible for maintaining and furthering the existing agenda of cooperation in the EU, and they must be on the lookout for new challenges that may require collective policy-making.

The Kirchner study is the only project that examines Council presidencies and summitry in the EU in a systematic fashion. It identifies a historically contiguous sample of cases, and rigorously explores the behavior of members through eight presidencies. Yet it does suffer from one potential flaw. By choosing presidencies and summits dominated by the completion of the internal market, the continuity/management plane of Council presidencies may be over-emphasized. By its very nature, the Single European Act (SEA) posed a particular set of management problems for the Union and the Council. The Act spelled out a finite (if rather large) set of policies that were to be adopted by a fixed date. It did not specify how these agreements would be negotiated, even if least-common denominator solutions were discouraged. Thus, much of the agenda of the Councils was fixed, and a selection of cases drawn from this period alone might well bias the results toward the continuity/management set of observations. Regardless, Kirchner's study remains one of the few detailed, systematic, and rigorous studies of the European Council to date. Its results directly inform this research.

In sum, despite its seeming importance, the European Council has received strikingly little rigorous empirical examination. Drawing on this limited theoretic and empirical base, the next section of this paper will examine the following research questions:

- To what extent are Council presidents able to alter the EU agenda during their tenures?
- To what extent does the Council share policy initiative responsibilities with the Commission?
- What is the impact of domestic preferences on the outcomes of Council presidencies?
- To what extent are Council presidencies immune to, or held subject to, events outside the Union, and/or outside the Union's immediate agenda?

These research questions will be explored in a preliminary analysis of two presidencies, that of Austria during the second half of 1998 and that of Germany during the first half of 1999. There are several advantages to the choice of these two presidencies. First, both countries are wealthy advanced industrial societies with substantial manufacturing sectors. Thus, issues of resource allocation between the Union's rich and poor are unlikely to bias the results. Further, both countries enjoy similarly structured social systems, and both have federal systems of government characterized by coalition governments. Thus, both Austria and Germany face similar domestic political environments. Center-left political parties led both governments at the time of their presidencies. Additionally, both states shared similar broad perspectives on essential policy issues at the time, including expansion of the Union into Central and Eastern Europe. Finally, there were no overwhelmingly dominant and highly structured sets of issues on the EU agenda during these two presidencies. Two of the most important issues, expansion and unemployment, did not have clearly defined and treaty-based sets of solutions as did the SEA.

However, several important differences also mark these two cases. First, the Austrian presidency was its first opportunity to lead the Council since Austria entered the Union. Thus, as will be seen, there was some concern (unfounded, as it turned out) that the Austrians would not have sufficient experience to perform well as Council president. Germany, in contrast, had served many turns as Council president. This was somewhat offset by the change in government in Germany after the September 1998 elections (in the middle of the Austrian presidency), which returned the Social Democratic Party (SPD) to power after sixteen years in opposition. As will be seen, the SPD-Green coalition suffered a bumpy start to its presidency, in part due to its inexperience. Second, the size differences should not be underestimated. The German economy is the largest in the EU, and its model of finance policy has more or less dominated the drive to monetary union in Europe. Thus, it might be expected that the Germans, especially after the election of a more independent-minded government, might be in a position to wield more influence in the EU than might Austria. Finally, it must be emphasized that an "n" of two is quite small. While a study of these two countries avoids the temporal choppyness and context-determining influences that plague earlier studies, generalizations from these two cases must remain tentative due to potential biases resulting from outlier events.

The Austrian and German Presidencies

In this section, I compare the Austrian and German presidencies along several dimensions. First is an analysis of how both governments prepared for their turn as president. Second, I explore the agendas both states brought to the presidencies. Finally, I examine the fit between agendas and outcomes. While reference will be made to the questions of agenda-setting, the role of the Commission, domestic politics and outcomes, and the impact of outside events, these specific questions will be examined in the conclusions.

Preparing for the Presidency

At the time Austria joined the EU in 1995, its turn as president was fixed for the latter half of 1998. Thus, the government knew several years in advance when it would assume responsibility for the European Council. As Alexander Schallenberg and Christoph Thun-Hohenstein make clear, preparations for the Austrian presidency began shortly after 1 January 1995.[18] This involved not only administrative adjustments in the Austrian federal government, but also the assimilation of considerable information and analyses so as to guarantee that Austrian policy-makers would be fully informed about EU policy issues. Finally, this also required that the Austrian government begin to develop and to plug itself into the dense network of contacts and consultations that is so common in the EU. Initially expectations for the Austrian presidency were not high. Many feared that Austria, a small country, would have a difficult time as president.

Germany was set to assume the European Council presidency immediately after the Austrian presidency. Thus, both governments were involved in the Troika during the Austrian presidency. Further, the Kohl government had considerable experience in EU politics. The government's close policy coordination with other EU member governments, especially with France, guaranteed that it would have the sort of policy network that the Austrians had to spend so much time to develop. Additionally, Helmut Kohl had taken a personal interest in the development of the EU, and was a major political force in EU decision-making. Thus, it would seem that the Germans were in a particularly strong position to have a major impact on the EU during its turn as president.

Yet the German voters turned out the Kohl government in September 1998. The election results had significant impacts upon German preparation for the presidency. The transition from the CDU/CSU-FDP coalition to the new SPD-Green coalition was not particularly smooth. Since both sides blamed the other for the lack of communication, there was little continuity in German preparations for the presidency during the six months before 1 January 1999. Several reasons accounted for this situation.

First, one should not underestimate the animosity between the two political camps. Sixteen years in opposition did not endear the SPD to the CDU/CSU. Further, generational gaps divided the leadership of the two parties. Helmut Kohl often spoke of his experiences in World War II as motivations for his almost visceral commitment to European union. While Gerhard Schröder of the SPD and Joschka Fischer of the Greens also spoke the rhetoric of European integration, many believed that their commitment was not as personal and strong as that of Kohl. Further, Schröder and the SPD also inherited Helmut Schmidt's ambivalence toward the EU. Finally, the long-standing animosity between the CDU/CSU and the Greens—lessened only slightly by infrequent periods of coalition partnership at the *Land* level—further soured the transition. This situation got even worse when it became clear that the Greens would receive the foreign ministry in the new government.

Second, there was conflict within the SPD camp as well. The uneasy alliance between Schröder and his main rival in the party, Oskar Lafontaine, broke down almost immediately after the new government came to power. One source of conflict between the two was the EU policy, especially the policy about the European monetary union (EMU). Soon after assuming leadership of an expanded finance ministry in the new Red-Green government, Lafontaine tried to reverse long-standing German policies regarding several key EMU issues. First, he argued for a relaxation of the convergence criteria, suggesting that the criteria should not take precedence over the fight against unemployment. The Maastricht Treaty had specified rather strict convergence criteria that were to be tightened over time after the EMU began to operate; these criteria were relaxed significantly when the original eleven members joined EMU in the spring of 1998. Lafontaine wanted even more national flexibility, directly in opposition to the prior government's position and somewhat at odds with the rather vague positions of the new chancellor.

Further, Lafontaine began calling for interest rate cuts to stimulate growth. The controversy here was not so much over the desirability of cuts, but over the appropriateness of national governments trying to apply political pressure on the soon-to-be European Central Bank (ECB). The issue of political direction over the ECB had been hotly debated in the IGC leading to the Maastricht Treaty. The French, among others, had lobbied hard for political control over ECB policy-making, which ran directly counter to German central bank independence. The result was fudged. The so-called Euro-X (later to be named the Euro-11 and currently Euro-12) of EMU-member finance ministers was created, but its powers were vague. After Maastricht, the French pushed, and the Kohl government resisted, defining Euro-X's role in ways that would give it power to direct ECB policy. The new German government, in the person of Finance Minister Lafontaine, seemed to be moving toward the French position. Again, however, Chancellor Schröder's position remained unclear. While speaking in the fall of 1998 about the need to stimulate growth and employment, he failed to explicitly support his finance minister's position. Lafontaine's eventual resignation, and the appointment of a more conservative finance minister, Hans Eichel, seemed to signal that Schröder was closer to Kohl's rather than Lafontaine's position on ECB independence.[19]

The controversy over the ECB was indicative of a broader conflict in the SPD, between Lafontaine's more traditional interventionist views of government and Schröder's largely undefined "Third Way" between free market and intervention. There was also great personal animosity between the two, as Lafontaine's caustic memoirs make clear. As a result, German economic policy in general, and EU policy in particular, remained the subject of an internal tug-of-war until Lafontaine's resignation in March 1999.

In sum, the Austrian government enjoyed some forty-two months to prepare for its presidency, the new German government only three months (actually less due to coalition negotiations). While the Germans had a much greater pool of experience to draw upon in preparing for their presidency, much of this was squandered in inter-party and intra-party conflict. What, then, were the two able to accomplish?

Agendas

As stated above, there are two general pressures on member governments when they assume the Council presidency. First, they inherit an agenda, which via the Troika they both are familiar with and helped to shape. Further, the Commission works to try to focus each presidency upon this agenda. Second, as Kirchner points out, presidents are also keen to respond to events outside the agenda, either broader issues facing the Union or events taking place outside the Union. In each case, members are motivated by a variety of incentives when beginning their presidencies, including the opportunity to shape EU policy-making in directions beneficial to domestic groups, to win the respect of other member governments by concluding many agreements, and to demonstrate international prominence and leadership to the domestic public.

The agenda that the Austrian government inherited in the summer of 1998 was quite busy. In its program for the presidency, the Austrian government noted ten broad goals:

* fighting unemployment, in light of the inclusion of unemployment into the Amsterdam Treaty, and the strengthening of this responsibility at the Luxembourg Employment Summit;
* completion of preparations for the monetary union;
* Agenda 2000, especially as regards reform of agricultural policy, structural policy, and budget reform;
* expansion, especially continuation of negotiations with potential members in Central and Eastern Europe;
* environmental protection;

- internal security, especially as regards police and judicial cooperation in the fight against international crime, drug smuggling, and
  terrorism;
- reform of common foreign and security policy, especially in light
  of the changes specified in the Amsterdam Treaty (which was due
  to become Union law at the end of 1999);
- final completion of the internal market, especially tax harmonization;
- strengthening of the EU's international profile, especially as regards
  universal human rights standards; and
- strengthening of the democratic legitimacy of the Union by impro-
  ving contacts between the Union and its citizens.

All these policy areas clearly represent existing foci of the Union,
but several stand out. First, the priority placed on fighting unemployment was certainly less an immediate concern for the Austrians than it
was for many other EU members. Austria had one of the lowest unemployment rates in Europe in the summer of 1998. That employment
received such prominence on the Austrian agenda is an indication of the
influence of other actors, the Troika and the Commission, in setting the
agenda. Second, the completion of EMU was probably high on the
agenda both because of its political prominence, and because EMU was
largely finished by July 1998. Members of EMU had been chosen, and
exchange rates among them fixed. The only remaining issues of significance involved relations with third parties, especially the IMF and the
G-8. Thus, by putting monetary union at the top of the agenda, the
Austrian government was virtually assuring visible successes during its
presidency.

The next set of issues, Agenda 2000 and expansion, were both related and of significant importance to Austria. Agenda 2000 reforms were
closely linked to expansion, as many of these reforms were seen as
necessary to prepare the Union for as many as twelve new members in
the next decade. An essential reform was the budget, and agriculture
remained the largest item in it. That an Austrian, Franz Fischler, was the
commissioner responsible for agricultural policy in the EU also elevated
the issue. Progress on Fischler's proposed Common Agricultural Policy
(CAP) reforms would strengthen the visibility of Austria in EU affairs,
and might offer opportunities to protect and enhance the interests of
Austrian farmers. Finally, Austria's common borders with states in
Central and Eastern Europe, and the fears of immigration should some

or all of Central and Eastern European countries enter the Union, raised the visibility of these issues in Austrian politics.

Finally, the prominence of criminality, the environment, and democratic legitimacy reflected domestic Austrian concerns. Criminality was related to expansion and the greater openness in Austrian society as a result of EU membership. The environment was important due to the effects of cross-border road traffic through Austria. Democratic legitimacy was also important in light of the continued public ambivalence toward EU membership in Austria. Additional issues on the agenda, such as tax harmonization and common foreign and security policy were both driven by the Commission and were necessary due to treaty obligations.

In sum, the Austrian agenda for its tenure as Council president represented a mixture of continuity and initiative, clearly weighted toward continuity. The primary policy areas on the agenda were inherited from the prior presidencies, and heavily influenced by the Commission. The Austrian freedom of movement could be found primarily in the issues relating to criminality, environment, and democratic legitimacy. Each of these issues, of course, was also on the EU's policy-making agenda. The Austrians, however, were able to raise their visibility by emphasizing these issues in their agenda.

The contrasts with the German agenda are striking. The German program for its presidency had three main parts: *Standort Europa*, the EU and the world, and justice and home affairs. Each had several sub-categories. *Standort Europa*, for example, specified three major areas: one, employment, focusing on two strategies, a European Employment Pact and National Employment Plans (as specified in the Amsterdam and Luxembourg Summits); two, Agenda 2000, with special emphasis on budget reform; and, three, the completion of the internal market, as well as research and development, with emphasis on company law, intellectual property rights, tax harmonization, social policy, industrial policy, telecommunications, information and communication, consumer protection, energy, agriculture, and environment. The second part of the German program, the EU and the world, focused on a variety of policy areas, the fifth of which was expansion. Finally, justice and home affairs specified mutual assistance in criminal matters, the EU-wide fight against fraud and corruption, the fight against organized crime, civil law reform and transparency, asylum policy, illegal immigrants, and a charter of fundamental human rights.

What was striking about the German policy agenda for its turn as Council president was its detail, and the changes from the Austrian agenda. The term *Standort Europa* came directly out of domestic German policy debates about the implications of globalization for the German social model. Of prime interest on the German agenda, as was the case with the Austrian agenda, was employment. The European Employment Pact, which had been discussed in general terms at the Vienna Summit, became a key focus of the German presidency. Such a pact had been under discussion for some time in Europe, especially among trade unionists and socialist and social democratic parties. The German government clearly hoped that this would be a major achievement of their presidency.

The German stand on the internal market is another example of national preferences shaping presidency agendas. While tax harmonization remained on the agenda, the new German government clearly wanted to reverse the position of the prior government on a range of social issues. The Kohl government had blocked some of these directives, including the company statute. Other, so-called *new economy* issues, such as intellectual property rights, support for small and medium-sized enterprises, and vertical obstructions to competition (selective and exclusive distribution arrangements, franchising rules, etc.) would have fit easily into a Kohl presidency. This suggests a welding of traditional social democratic interests and the post-industrial/ globalization agenda that Chancellor Schröder brought to Berlin.

The Agenda 2000 issues were particularly important to the new German government. The Vienna Summit mandated emphasis on the budget in the German presidency. The Austrians made important progress on the budget that could not be finished by December 1998. Hence, it was agreed at the Vienna Summit that a special summit would be held in March 1999 to resolve the remaining differences. Chancellor Kohl had signaled a more stringent German attitude toward its regular surplus contribution for several years. This position was echoed by the SPD and chancellor candidate Schröder during the election campaign, and after the electoral victory in September. Yet, as will be seen, rhetoric did not match reality on the budget issue.

Perhaps the most glaring change in agenda from the Austrian to the German presidency is in the treatment of expansion. First, by placing expansion into the category *EU and the World*, the German government seemed to signal a distancing from the desirability of expansion. Expansion was seen as an external issue, not an internal issue. Indeed, there were groups in both coalition parties that opposed expansion for a range of reasons, from fear of further unemployment to hostility towards the EU in general. Second, the issue was virtually buried in the agenda. A number of other international issues were regarded as more important. Finally, very little was said about expansion in the German agenda. Only a few lines were devoted to the topic, and they were of the most general character. Again, the signal seemed to be that the new German government would do little to further the membership applications of states in Central and Eastern Europe.

This position seemed to be in contrast to that of the prior German government. Expansion had raised some eyebrows in the conservative parties, especially by those who feared a loss of German identity due to economic immigrants out of the east, and those who still harbored revanchist beliefs (especially in some parts of the CSU). Yet these were minor views in the old coalition, which were more than counter-balanced by Helmut Kohl's passion for all things European. As will be seen, the SPD changed its public stance on expansion very quickly, even before formally assuming the presidency in January 1999.

In the final policy area, justice and home affairs, the German presidency closely followed the lead of the Austrian presidency. The issue of a charter of fundamental human rights was strongly emphasized, as were police and legal cooperation, organized crime and drugs, and civil law reform. The new German government, however, put perhaps more emphasis on cooperation in such issues as illegal emigrants and asylum policy than what might have been expected from the former German government.

In sum while the German agenda followed the Austrian agenda closely in some ways, it also reflected a healthy dose of national preferences. It further showed significant deviance from prior German positions. Most notable was the virtual disappearance of expansion from the agenda (a position that the new government would have to change quickly, not without embarrassment), and a significant strengthening of the employment agenda. The emphasis on high tech issues was largely consistent with the former German government's preferences, but the rise of social policy in the German order of preference did not please the conservative parties.

In comparing agenda setting, it seems that the German government exercised significantly more independence than did the Austrian government. The Austrian agenda was much more derivative of the existing agenda than was the German agenda. However, both exhibited significant elements of continuity and path dependence, both put distinctly national spins on agenda items, and both added items important to themselves. In the next section, I explore the results of the presidencies.

Outcomes

Since the Austrian agenda was so heavily influenced by the agenda it inherited, it is not surprising that the results of its presidency are best characterized as *incremental*. Several important, if not very flashy, accomplishments marked the Austrian presidency. First, the final details regarding the launching of the ECB were worked out during the Austrian presidency. These included observer status for the ECB on the IMF Executive Board; the ECB, Ecofin and Euro-X's status vis-à-vis the G-8 meetings; and general representation of the EU in third-party financial negotiations. Second, the Austrian government made progress toward preparations for negotiations with potential new members. At that time, the Commission was in the midst of a review of compliance with the *acquis communitaire* on thirty-one specific issues. Seven of these issues had been resolved by the beginning of the Austrian presidency. While the Austrian government had hoped to finalize the remaining twenty-four, it completed only twelve (better than the seven completed by the UK, the prior president). This left four areas unresolved and eight more to work on.

Areas where the progress of the Austrian presidency was more halting included the Agenda 2000, especially CAP, the budget, and the structural funds reform. In these areas, Austrian success was heavily constrained by events outside the government's control. First, the period between the German election and the Vienna Summit was very short. It was hoped that the Kohl government would be in a position to be more flexible on its budget contribution after the election. When Kohl lost the election, the period to negotiate got even shorter. The new German government was involved in difficult coalition negotiations. Additionally, there was apparent conflict within the SPD, represented by the cool relations between Lafontaine and Schröder. As finance minister, Lafontaine played a significant role in formulating the new government's position on these reforms. Lafontaine represented the more critical wing of SPD opinion on the German budget contribution. Schröder also supported cutting German contributions. Finally, the lack of a smooth transition between the outgoing and incoming governments hampered the development of a clear German position on CAP, budget, and structural funds reform. Since Germany was the largest net contributor to the EU budget, and since both major German parties had campaigned on promises to lower Germany's contribution, it was difficult for the Austrians to negotiate compromises. Despite these constraints, the Austrians were able to negotiate a deadline for budget reform: March 1999. Thus, specific reforms were passed to the Germans to negotiate.

Despite high expectations, the Austrian government faced difficulties in furthering the employment dimension of the agenda. The task of reviewing National Action Plans to fight unemployment was delayed. However, by emphasizing equal opportunity issues, training and retraining as an essential component of the EU employment program, the Austrian government was able to put a distinctly Austrian stamp on the employment issue. If the Employment Pact remained largely undefined, at least the Austrians were able to shape future debates.

Finally, during the Austrian presidency progress on a number of other issues was mixed. The Austrians pushed a strong environmental agenda, but were unable to negotiate a deal on sustainability across policy areas, or to develop a comprehensive EU strategy on climate change. The issue of cross-border traffic pollution, highly sensitive in Austria, was successfully negotiated with the agreement on road user charges (*Eurovignette*). The Austrians also succeeded in raising the visibility of a number of issues of specific national concern, including prevention of violence, AIDS, drug use, and social models to accommodate both family and professional life. Again, while these issues had been on EU agendas in the past, the Austrian presidency was able to bring greater attention to them. Other successes included the adoption of the Fifth Programme of Research and Development, budgets for the Leonardo, Socrates, Kaleidoscope, and Ariane programs, and an agreement to clarify the legal bases of budgets for non-governmental organizations involved in human rights and social exclusion issues.

The reasons Austria was unable to make greater progress on the agenda are found primarily outside of Austria. First, as noted, the German election, and the resulting change in government in Germany, greatly hampered progress. Germany remains such a central player in European politics that indecision in Berlin can slow any presidency. That the incoming German government was so divided and unsure of its priorities only complicated Austria's job. Second, the growing crisis in the Balkans in the fall of 1998 further complicated the Austrian presidency. Austria has traditional ties in the region, and as president of the European Council Austria was expected to take the lead in developing a common foreign policy toward the Serb government and its policies in Kosovo. An important Austrian success here, however, was to change the nature of the debate about European security cooperation. The combination of events in Kosovo and changing national political leadership opened an important door to closer European military cooperation. At the Vienna Summit, both the United Kingdom and France agreed to develop a European defense capability. The German government would be ready to march the EU through this door once the conflict in Kosovo escalated in March 1999. Thus, while the government was able to make significant progress on a number of issues it inherited, outside events prevented the Austrians from making as much progress as they might have hoped. Yet outside events also created future possibilities for closer cooperation.

Inexperience and confused priorities hampered the German presidency from the beginning. Ill-conceived public comments from members of the new government, as well as the seeming attempt to bury EU enlargement down the German agenda, resulted in controversy even before Germany officially began its presidency on 1 January 1999. Both the Austrian government and several of the potential first round members sharply criticized the new German government for trying to push enlargement in the EU agenda. New Foreign Minister Joschka Fischer had to make a quick tour of Central and Western European capitals in December 1998 to reassure these governments that the Germans remained committed to enlargement. Yet the publication of the official German agenda in January 1999, with its lack of attention to enlargement, guaranteed that the controversy would not die quickly. More reassurances about German commitment to enlargement in January and February 1999 were needed. This whole process suggested that the new government simply failed to make its priorities clear, rather than sought to delay enlargement. Regardless, it was a poor start to the German Council presidency.

The emphasis on Agenda 2000 in the German presidency suggested that the government thought enlargement could only take place once the EU had its own house in order. The list of issues to be addressed in Agenda 2000 was long, and there was no hope that all could be completed by June 1999.[20] As agreed at the Vienna Summit, EU members met in Berlin in March 1999 to negotiate a budget package that would meet several goals. First was the need to prepare the EU for the financial burden of adding new and poorer members. The Commission argued that this could be accomplished with little financial pain, but the final costs of enlargement are largely unknown. Second, the Germans insisted that their net contribution to the budget had to come down sharply.

The Berlin Summit was very contentious. Three issues were at the top of the agenda: the CAP reform, the British rebate, and the reform of structural and cohesion funds. On the CAP reform, the French government essentially blocked any major changes. While a freeze was placed on payments to farmers, two of the most costly areas, milk products and cereals, were not fully addressed. Prices of milk products were to be set later, in 2005/6, by the technical council for agriculture. These technical councils are notorious for supporting the interests of farmers. In the second area of concern, cereals, phased-in price cuts totaling fifteen percent were offset by increases in area payments from fifty-four to sixty-three Euro. This still resulted in a net loss for farmers, but one much smaller than it would seem. The unwillingness of the French government to consider deeper cuts, or to negotiate German proposals for co-financing of farm subsidies, put severe strains on the Franco-German relationship.[21]

On the issues of contributions and rebates, the British position was unbending. The rebate that Thatcher negotiated in the 1980s could not be reduced, at least not directly. Rather than directly cutting contributions, it was agreed that contributions would no longer be calculated by reference to value-added taxes, but to the GDP. This helped to reduce the size of the British rebate, and increased the contributions of Italy and Belgium (where the existence of shadow economies reduced overall VAT contributions). This also resulted in a slight decrease in the German contribution, knocking about DM 1.4 billion off the then DM 22 billion German net contribution. Finally, slight cuts were negotiated in the structural and cohesion funds, lopping 8.9 percent off the 2000 figures, 9.4 percent off the structural fund, and 4.0 percent off the cohesion fund. This was accomplished by reducing the number of objective areas, but with special transition regimes totaling 4.7 billion Euro (or about sixteen percent of the structural funds budget) for the affected areas.

As Foreign Minister Fischer put it, "*wir haben die Europäische Union zusammengehalten*" (we kept the European Union together), but the price was high. Franco-German relations were strained by the French unwillingness to negotiate a reform of the CAP. Additionally, the small cut in the German net contribution did little to alter domestic perceptions that Germany was paying too much. Most importantly, the Berlin budget compromise probably did not do enough to financially prepare the EU for expansion. Consequently, one might expect that there will be even greater pressure on the EU to negotiate lengthy transition periods for potential new members, especially in the areas of agriculture and structural funds. By the completion of the German presidency in June, further progress was made toward completing the thirty-one chapters of the *acquis* review, and a timetable to complete the Agenda 2000 preparations for enlargement was negotiated.

Clearly, the issue of employment was at the forefront of the German Council presidency. At the time, German unemployment was above ten percent, and the new government had promised to reduce unemployment in the election campaign. During the course of the German presidency, a number of proposals were floated to lower unemployment. First were Finance Minister Lafontaine's calls, supported by the French, for a more pro-labor policy of the ECB, coupled with greater political control over the bank. Lafontaine's resignation left these proposals in doubt, but the new Finance Minister Eichel's positions at the *Ecofin* Summit in Dresden, shortly before the budget summit in Berlin, emphasized structural reform among the members over Keynesian-style demand stimulation. Thus, the revised Schröder government moved back to a position closer to that of the prior government. The only interventionist-style policy proposals were calls for exchange-rate coordination in the G-8, and restrictions on disruptive capital flows.

Other Lafontaine positions that collapsed after his resignation were policies regarding minimum wages and explicit growth targets. Strongly supported by the French, a European-wide minimum wage could stimulate employment, as could the setting of growth targets. Yet at the time Germany was wracked by debate about the taxing of so-called 630-Mark jobs, i.e. part-time employment. European-wide minimum wages were strongly opposed by German business, which was increasingly critical of Schröder's apparent failure to keep his campaign promises to industry. Additionally, growth targets were viewed as potentially inflationary. Eichel dropped all reference to minimum wages and growth at the Dresden *Ecofin* Summit.

The Cologne Summit, at the end of the German presidency, introduced a new initiative on unemployment, the European Employment Pact. It had three central goals. First, the members pledged themselves to stable, inflation-free economic and finance policies, and to fight unemployment. Second, they committed themselves to reform their economies and to make them more competitive by liberalizing labor markets, within national constraints. Finally, the members committed themselves to active labor market policies, as laid out in the Luxembourg Summit. All these goals were to be facilitated by regular but loosely defined and non-binding meetings among the representatives of labor, capital, the Commission, and the ECB. The Pact may be a useful restatement of commitments expressed elsewhere, but it does not constitute much that is new. No specific action was proposed on either of the first two goals, and the "active labor market policy" was not defined. Talk of minimum wages and growth targets was dropped. Thus, while the verbal commitments expressed at the Cologne Summit helped to galvanize public attention on unemployment, little of a concrete character was accomplished. Further, the company statute regulation that the Germans had pushed very strongly was vetoed by Spain.

However, the Cologne Summit proved hugely successful in other ways. Most significant was the negotiation of the end to Serbian presence in Kosovo, and the end to the NATO bombing campaign. Negotiated by the Germans under EU and NATO auspices, the success of the initiative clearly signaled, for virtually the first time in the troubled Balkan region, that the EU could be an effective agent. It also strengthened EU security and military policy coordination, although the Germans were unsuccessful in pushing a plan to merge the EU's nascent foreign and security policy apparatus with the Western European Union. Yet progress was made toward institutionalizing the Common Foreign and Security Policy (CFSP), and the appointment of former NATO Secretary General Javier Solana as "Mr. CFSP" gave prominence to the EU's foreign and security policy cooperation.

In sum, the German presidency began with a seemingly strong departure from the Austrian presidency, but veered back into established patterns. The failure of the Germans to negotiate a larger cut in their net contribution suggests that they felt pressure to go along once in the presidency. The rather weak agreement on employment was indicative of both early internal splits in the government, and the impracticability of addressing unemployment at the EU level. The major German successes were setting agendas for future summits (an important, but rather anemic success) and in negotiating an end to the conflict between NATO and Serbia.

There were a number of reasons why the German presidency was less successful than originally hoped. Internally, the split between Lafontaine and Schröder complicated the formation and pursuit of consistent policy preferences. Lafontaine's resignation in March helped to resolve this dispute, but also left little time to negotiate agreements that were more significant. Additionally, *Land* elections in Germany returned control of the German *Bundesrat* to the opposition parties, requiring more complicated internal negotiations. Environment Minister Jürgen Trittin's policies on ending the foreign recycling of nuclear wastes also complicated relations with France and the UK. Finally, the government's inexperience in European affairs led to several misunderstandings, including the initial confusion about German positions on EU expansion.

The German presidency was also troubled by significant external crises, all of which had important internal ramifications. The Kosovo campaign was important not only as it consumed much time in negotiating its end, but also because it caused a crisis in the Green Party. The Greens were split over the use of force to resolve disputes, and only a courageous position taken by its most prominent leader, Foreign Minister Fischer, led to the government's support for the air campaign. A breakdown of the governing coalition over the Kosovo issue was a real possibility in the spring of 1999. Additionally, the resignation of the Commission in March of 1999 added significantly to Germany's woes. Not only did the resignation mean that Germany would not receive the usual support from the Commission for running its presidency, but also that German appointments to a new Commission would touch off a domestic controversy. Traditionally, the two German commissioners come from the parties in power. The Greens, however, were split over the desirability of assuming one of the two positions (there remains a strong anti-EU wing in the party), and a Green appointment was opposed by the opposition parties. In the end, the Greens supported the SPD's candidate for Bundespräsident, Johannes Rau, in exchange for a commissioner from the Green party.

Finally, significant timing problems plagued the German presidency. The June European Parliament elections in June, which are seen as measures of popular support for sitting governments and which are often won by opposition parties, prevented bold German policy proposals. Additionally, it was widely expected that a new Commission would not be appointed until after the new Parliament was in place and at work, i.e. in late summer or early fall. Within these constraints, it was hard for the German presidency to make any further accomplishments.

In sum, the Austrian and German presidencies exhibit elements of both path dependence and national initiative. They also demonstrate the key role that external events can play in Council politics, sometimes in unexpected ways and with unexpected consequences. In the final section, I explore these implications.

Conclusions

What can we learn from comparing the Austrian and German Council presidencies? First, it is important to restate the caveats to generalization that result from the design of this research. Two cases are insufficient for generalization, in part because they may over-emphasize the importance of rare events. Both the resignation of the Commission in the midst of the German presidency, and the Kosovo crisis that extended through both presidencies represent situations that are unlikely to be common. Further, the differences in influence between the two suggest that Germany might be expected to be in a better position to shape EU agendas and affect outcomes than is Austria. Regardless, several observations relevant to the academic literature can be drawn from this study.

First, Council presidencies, as Kirchner, Johnston, and Bulmer point out, are path dependent to a considerable degree. The institutionalization of the Council, via the Troika and via the Council's relationship with the Commission, creates powerful incentives for presidents to stick to existing agendas. This path dependence exists for all members, but it seems to be greater for smaller, and hence less influential, member governments than it is for larger and more powerful member governments. Regardless, both Germany and Austria found themselves drawn to the existing agenda. The German failure to push for a larger cut in its budget contribution can be seen as an indication of the pressure on presidents to sacrifice national preferences if they block regional agreement.[22] As Foreign Minister Fischer put it, the Germans held the Union together at the Berlin Summit, and they did so at their own expense.

Path dependence, however, needs to be offset by recognition that national governments do, indeed, have room to shape their presidencies. Both Austria and Germany drew upon the broad range of issues that fall within the ambit of the EU to shape the agenda. In Austria's case, this meant an emphasis on criminality, the environment, and democratic legitimacy. For Germany, this meant re-shaping a broad range of economic issues into *Standort Europa*, a uniquely German way of looking at Europe's competitive challenges. Further, in both cases these initiatives have roots in domestic politics. Thus, both the past and national priorities shape Council agendas. In this way, the European Council, while not wresting policy initiation from the Commission, competes with the Commission for policy initiation rights.

These two cases highlight the importance of outside events, but do so in ways that are more complex than has been noted in the literature. European Councils have often been hijacked by outside events, as was the case in both the Austrian and German presidencies. Yet these events can both hinder, and propel, cooperation in Europe. In the Austrian case, both the indecision caused by the German election and the growing crisis in Kosovo greatly hampered the Austrians from making more progress on the policy agenda. A similar election result in Greece or Luxembourg would in all probability not have had the same effects. Yet, Kosovo also helped to propel the EU forward in important ways. The informal agreements on foreign policy cooperation reached at the Vienna Summit were crucial in setting the stage for the Cologne Summit.

In the German case, outside events also hampered and helped cooperation in Europe. The Commission resignation complicated both summit preparations and German domestic politics, at a time when the inexperienced government was trying to develop a more consistent set of priorities for its Council presidency. Yet with the help of informal agreements reached in Vienna, the German government was able to significantly move forward the debate about CFSP and the future of European security arrangements by negotiating an end to the NATO bombing campaign in Serbia and Kosovo. Thereafter, negotiations among EU members about common defense policy, the development of non-NATO intervention capabilities, closer military procurement programs, and the development of common logistical capabilities seemed to take on new life. In the future, the German-led solution to the crisis in the Balkans will probably be seen as a turning point in the development of European security arrangements independent of NATO. In other words, an outside event in these two cases helped to expand the EU's agenda.

The balance, therefore, between inherited agenda and national initiative is complex. Power seems to play an important role in agenda independence, within a context of path dependence. Unlike the findings of much of the policy literature, however, evidence from these two cases suggests that agenda-setting powers are not as important in the EU as they are in national politics. Governments that try to alter agenda priorities (either by intention or by mistake) or that try to introduce new priorities will find it difficult to achieve much in the short period that they lead the European Council. This reflects both the pressure of time and the continued difficulty of negotiating with otherwise sovereign nation-states, which are not constrained in the ways that bureaucratic actors are. Finally, agendas mean little when outside events divert attention, and sometimes create opportunities for presidents. The path of European integration is indeed "post-modern" in Caporaso's meaning when such events alter priorities.

In sum, it is surprising to note the lack of systematic attention to the European Council in the academic literature. While this study makes only limited progress toward filling this gap in our knowledge, it suggests that the fruits of such an effort might prove quite satisfying. While implications for theorizing about European integration are beyond this paper, a focus on the Council may also help to reshape our understanding of the European Union.

Notes

1. See James A. Caporaso, "The European Union and Forms of the State: Westphalian, Regulatory, or Post-Modern?," *Journal of Common Market Studies* 34 (March 1996): 1-34.

2. Neill Nugent, *The Government and Politics of the European Union*, 4th ed. (Durham, NC: Duke University Press, 1999).

3. See Simon Bulmer, "The European Council's First Decade: Between Interdependence and Domestic Politics," *Journal of Common Market Studies* 24 (December 1985): 89-104.

4. Ibid.

5. Ibid., 99.

6. This literature is truly voluminous. For a sample see Wayne Sandholtz and John Zysman, "1992: Recasting the European Bargain," *World Politics* 42 (1989): 95-128; Paul Taylor, "The New Dynamics of EC Integration in the 1980s," in *The European Community and the Challenge of the Future*, ed. Juliet Lodge (New York: St. Martin's, 1989), 3-25; Jeppe Tranholm-Mikkelsen, "Neo-Functionalism: Obstinate or Obsolete? A Reappraisal in the Light of the New Dynamism of the EC," *Millennium* 20 (1991): 1-22; Robert O. Keohane and Stanley Hoffmann, "Institutional Change in Europe in the 1980s," in *The New European Community: Decisionmaking and Institutional Change*, ed. Robert O. Keohane and Stanley Hoffmann (Boulder: Westview, 1991), 1-40; Andrew Moravcsik, "Negotiating the Single European Act," in *The New European Community*, 41-84; David R. Cameron, "The 1992 Initiative: Causes and Consequences," in *Euro-Politics: Institutions and Policymaking in the "New" European Community*, ed. Alberta. M. Sbragia (Washington, DC: Brookings, 1992), 23-74; and Geoffrey Garrett, "International Cooperation and Institutional Choice: The European Community's Internal Market," *International Organization* 46 (1992): 533-60.

7. While Maastricht did not receive as much attention as did the Single European Act (SEA,) it still generated another flood of academic analysis. A sample includes Richard Corbett, *The Treaty of Maastricht: From Conception to Ratification* (White Plains, NY: Longman, 1993); Peter Ludlow, "Reshaping Europe: The Origins of the Intergovernmental Conferences and the Emergence of a New European Political Architecture," in *The Annual Review of European Community Affairs*, ed. Peter Ludlow, Jorgen Mortensen, and Jacques Pelkmans (London: Brassey's, for the Centre for European Policy Studies, 1992), 400-406; Neill Nugent, "The Deepening and Widening of the European Community: Recent Evolution, Maastrict, and Beyond," *Journal of Common Market Studies* 30(September 1992): 311-28; Richard Corbett, "The Intergovernmental Conference on Political Union," *Journal of Common Market Studies* 30 (September 1992): 271-89; and Michael J. Baun, "The Maastricht Treaty as High Politics: Germany, France, and European Integration," *Political Science Quarterly* 110 (Winter 1995-96): 605-24.

8. Andrew Duff, ed., *The Treaty of Amsterdam: Text and Commentary* (London: Sweet and Maxwell, 1997).

9. Juliet Lodge, "The Role of EEC Summit Conferences," *Journal of Common Market Studies* 12 (December 1974): 337-45.

10. Bulmer, "The European Council's First Decade."

11. See Colm O Nuallain, ed., *The Presidency of the European Council of Ministers* (Beckenham: Croom Helm for the European Institute of Public Administration, 1985).

12. Mary Troy Johnston, *The European Council: Gatekeeper of the European Community* (Boulder: Westview Press, 1994).

13. All three of the leaders she singles out for praise, Thatcher, Mitterrand, and Kohl, have since left the stage of European politics.

14. Andrew Moravcsik, *The Choice for Europe: Social Purpose and State Power from Messina to Maastricht* (Ithaca, NY: Cornell University Press, 1998).

15. Emil Joseph Kirchner, *Decision-making in the European Community: The Council Presidency and European Integration* (Manchester: Manchester University Press, 1992).

16. Ibid., 115.

17. The *Troika* refers to the consultation that takes place among the current presidency, the one prior to it, and the one immediately following it. Thus, when a member government assumes the presidency of the Council of Ministers and the European Council, it will already have worked for six months with the last president, and will continue to consult for six more months with the next president once its term concludes. The intention of this arrangement is to encourage continuity and consistency in the Councils, but also functions to limit the independence of presidents.

18. Much of the following is drawn from Alexander Schallenberg and Christoph Thun-Hohenstein, *Die EU-Präsidentschaft Österreichs* (Wien: MANZ Verlag, 1999).

19. The issue, however, remains unresolved. Belgian Finance Minister Didier Reynders recently reopened debate about Euro-12, calling for a tight political control over the ECB. See Peter Norman and Brian Groom, "Political Role Forecast for Informal Euro Finance Group," *Financial Times*, 14 February 2001.

20. Indeed, most of the controversial issues, like voting rules and Commission composition, were only negotiated, and negotiated incompletely, at the Nice Summit in December 2000.

21. Some analysts suggest that French intransigence at the Berlin Summit led Schröder to be equally difficult on other Agenda 2000 issues negotiated at Nice in December 2000. See Robert Graham, "Chirac Rules Out CAP Changes," *The Financial Times*, 18 February 2001.

22. This point is further demonstrated in the public criticism of France before the Nice summit, which many suspected to have become a venue for negotiating French preferences at the expense of common positions.

III. DOMESTIC POLITICS PERSPECTIVES

Haider's Revolution or The Future Has Just Begun

Hans-Georg Betz

On the last day of January 2000, Portugal, as chair of the European Union (EU), announced that the EU was about to impose a catalogue of sanctions against one of its members, the Austrian republic. Among the most significant measures adopted by the 14 member governments were the indefinite suspension of bilateral relations with Austria, a drastic reduction of all contacts with Austria's ambassadors, and the withholding of support for Austrian candidates to international posts. The measures were intended to express the EU members' extreme displeasure with the inclusion of several ministers from the Freedom Party (FPÖ) in the newly formed coalition government in Vienna, a party that many observers at home and abroad considered right-wing extremist and therefore outside of the politically acceptable. The boycott represented a clear attempt to influence, if not reverse, the outcome of a democratic election and thus constituted a blatant interference, a "quantum leap in the union's intrusion in the affairs of a member state."[1] As Theo Sommer, the editor of the highly regarded German weekly *Die Zeit*, put it, this was an unprecedented event, "a sort of Breshnev Doctrine in reverse," where "a cabal of EU chiefs-of-government decides whether the people's democratic decisions are valid or not."[2] In a similar vein, Lord William Rees-Mogg in his weekly commentary for *The Times* characterized the measures against Austria as "an unlawful attempt to coerce the democratic choice of a small European nation," adding somewhat hyperbolically that this was something that had not happened "since 1938."[3]

What caused the EU to adopt measures, which were meant to isolate Austria and turn it into an international pariah, was much more than the nature of the Freedom Party. After all, the EU had shown no reaction to the inclusion of postfascists (*Alleanza nazionale*) and xenophobic regionalists and soon-to-be separatists (*Lega Nord*) in Silvio Berlusconi's short-lived government in 1994 in Italy. The deeper cause of the EU's reaction—or at least that of some of its key members—was alarm over the success of a new type of politics, which was increasingly seen as a potential, serious challenge to Western Europe's political establishment; and this at a time where in a number of countries the conservative right was in disarray, giving the far right an opportunity to fill the void.[4] At the same time the EU's reaction reflected an acute fear of a man who, more than any other politician in Europe, has been identified with this new politics during the past fifteen years: Jörg Haider. "Allow Jörg Haider's Freedom Party into government, their argument ran, and the extreme right will have won political respectability; defining the bounds of what is politically acceptable in the European Union may help to stop the new century from taking the continent the way of the old one."[5]

Haider has not only been one of the most important postwar Austrian politicians, he has arguably also been "Europe's most successful politician of the past decade", whose impact extends far beyond the small stage of Austrian politics.[6] More than anything else, it was fear that the "Haider effect" might prove contagious that led to the sanctions against Austria in an attempt to contain the virus before it could spread and cause further and more serious political damage. This was an implicit admission that Haider was more than a provincial politician from a country better known for its cultural heritage and natural beauty than political radicalism. To be sure, as Haider has not tired to explain, the FPÖ's success is to a significant degree a distinctly Austrian phenomenon, which can only be fully understood in the context of the idiosyncrasies of Austrian postwar history and the Austrian socioeconomic and sociopolitical model.[7]

However, this is only part of the story. The main reason Haider's appeal has extended beyond Austria's borders is that he, more than any other prominent contemporary Western European politician, speaks to the emotional state of contemporary Europe caught in a maelstrom of rapid and often bewildering transformation. As Roger Cohen puts it, Haider "emerged in a Europe uncertain what place, if any, nations and national identity should command as the attempt to build a federal United States of Europe is pursued. A continent worried by immigration and the idea that calls to Islamic prayer will drown out church bells. An uneasy polity that is growing increasingly Americanized and has swapped the Communist threat for fears of globalization."[8] To this list one might add a growing sense that, in the face of rapid global change, national governments are less and less capable of controlling economic conditions; that they are less and less willing to protect the ordinary citizen against the vicissitudes and turmoil inherent in the New Econo- my; and that political elites care more about themselves than the interests of those who elected them into public office. The series of political scandals that rocked a number of Western European democra- cies in recent years only confirmed the growing perception that the political establishment could not be trusted. The result was widespread voter disenchantment, cynicism and a general political malaise.[9]

This is the larger context, which has provided Haider with ample opportunities to create and continuously expand political space for himself and his party. To be sure, Haider was neither the first nor has he been the only contemporary politician to pursue a new politics on the right.[10] But he has been significantly more successful than the leaders of other comparable political movements in Western Europe and else- where, not only in advancing his party's position at the polls but also in maintaining its organizational integrity and political maneuverability in the face of intense external pressure and despite the occasional defection of key personnel.

What explains this extraordinary success? Is it merely the result of a strategy that consciously "picked up the thread of the Nazi-tradition of the FPÖ" in an attempt to "return to the past," as some of Haider's Austrian detractors have maintained?[11] In what follows I will argue that an interpretative framework that takes the Nazi past as its point of departure for understanding Haider's rise and success is far too reductionist to explain the extent of his appeal in and outside of Austria. The Haider phenomenon represents neither a "resurgence of Nazism" nor is it a "new type of fascism." Making these charges can only contri- bute to the trivialization of the genuinely revolutionary nature of fascist ideology and the genocidal nature of Nazism. I would even question those who have labeled Haider and his party right-wing extremist. For extremism to remain a meaningful and useful concept, it should be reserved for those groups, movements, and parties, which accept and promote violence as a legitimate means for attaining political goals and negate the fundamental principle of human equality—which are both anti-democratic and racist in the original sense of the word.[12] The FPÖ has been neither.

Haider is perhaps best described as a charismatic populist, whose politics is as much, if not more, about style than it is about content. His is a new type of politics, which seems to defy the traditional notions of left and right. This is a postmodern style of politics, which treats the history of political traditions and struggles like a quarry from which it extracts whatever appears to be useful for the moment, and then reassembling the pieces into new patterns of political discourse. A central characteristic of this style is its reliance on spectacle and provocation, on the deconstruction of the dominant elite and their ideas, and, perhaps most important of all, on the mobilization of diffuse *ressentiments*. This is a new type of populism, which is both radically and often uncompromisingly customer-oriented and, at the same time, well-adapted to the realities and logic of a media-dominated, personality-centered political market, where politics can successfully compete for air time only if it has entertainment value.[13]

Programmatically, the new politics of the right has generally come in two guises, either as what the British political scientist Roger Griffin calls "ethnocratic liberalism" or as what the anthropologist Douglas Holmes from New Zealand characterizes as "exclusionary welfarism." Roger Griffin defines ethnocratic liberalism as a type of party politics, which "enthusiastically embraces the liberal system" while at the same time considering "only one ethnic group full members of civil society."[14] In Griffin's view, what distinguishes the contemporary radical right from the traditional extreme right is its ready adoption of a language of liberalism. The contemporary radical right speaks in terms of 'rights'—rights of ethnic peoples, rights to a culture—which addresses deep-seated and understandable fears about the erosion of identity and tradition by the globalizing (but only partially homogenizing) forces of high modernity." The radical right's response to these fears has been the promotion of a particular form of "exclusionary welfarism," defined as a reaffirmed claim to social welfare "regulated by a radicalized delimitation of citizenship."[15] As Douglas Holmes has shown, exclusionary welfarism has had particular appeal in traditional working-class areas faced with deindustrialization and the resulting loss of community, such as the East End of London.

Under Haider, the FPÖ has either oscillated between these two seemingly incompatible positions or even tried to fuse them into a programmatic synthesis, without, however, committing itself too much to the new type of welfarism. Exclusionary welfarism was perhaps most pronounced with respect to the party's pronounced stance against immigration, which it combined with an equally determined and vociferous defense of Austrian interests. The latter found its most succinct expression in the party's election slogan of "Austria (and Austrians) First." With this relatively simple program, the party managed to appeal to a broad constituency including a growing number of workers that transformed it into a new type of catch-all party of protest, albeit with a strong working-class base.[16]

Undoubtedly, much of the party's (and with it, Haider's) success can be attributed to its determined pursuit of a populist politics of resentment, which to a large degree has derived from Haider's own deep-seated animosities and *ressentiments*.[17] At the same time, the party (and Haider) has sought to present and establish itself as a genuine alternative to the established political parties intent on bringing about far-reaching reforms that would result in a radical transformation of the Austrian political and particularly institutional system. As a result, the party has presented a bewildering array of different, often conflicting and contradictory images, reflecting the various roles Haider himself assumed—and abandoned—depending on the occasion: an Austrian Robin Hood acting as an advocate for ordinary people; an outlaw and rebel revolting against established conventions; a "teller of unpalatable truths" (Mazower); an entertainer and "media gladiator" (Sully) who provokes for the sake of provocation; a tireless fighter for greater transparency and greater democracy; an Austrian patriot defending the interests of the Austrian nation; a statesman who demands to be taken seriously as a potential candidate for chancellor.[18]

In the process, Haider became one of the best-known and most heavily scrutinized contemporary politicians in Western Europe and beyond. Yet, as Melanie Sully has observed, despite his visibility, Haider has largely remained an "enigma" and "the true Haider, despite journalistic inquiries, [has] remained elusive." Particularly his ability to constantly reinvent himself, quickly adopting new trends, while discarding positions that are no longer deemed promising or are seen as too compromising, has earned him the reputation of being a postmodern politician, a manipulative opportunist without true beliefs and convictions. Much of this reputation is well-deserved. Yet it is only half of the truth. As I will try to demonstrate in the following analysis, behind all of Haider's rhetorical twists and turns is a core of goals and convictions that has informed his politics from the time he attained national prominence in the late 1980s to today. It forms the basis of a political project that has little to do with historical revisionism or his urge to rehabilitate the war generation, the two main focal points of those who have critically followed Haider's political career. As I will suggest in what follows, the core of Haider's project is the radical transformation of Austrian society, and via Austria, of European society into something fundamentally new, which has a striking resemblance to the United States. What Haider envisions is not a return to an idealized European past but the advent of a thoroughly Americanized future. This, I believe, is the real challenge of Haider's version of populism, which too often, however, has been obscured by the obsessive concentration on his provocative remarks on the past.

Haider's Populism

In recent years, Haider has readily adopted the notion that he is a "populist politician who simply wants to ask the people before decisions are made."[19] This was not always the case. In his account of Haider's rise to prominence, Andreas Mölzer, FPÖ chief ideologue and one of Haider's closest confidants, recognized that the charge that Haider was a right-wing populist contributed to the defamation campaign, which his boss had had to endure since assuming the party chair.[20] It was not until his Vienna Declaration from 1992 that Haider acknowledged that his was a populist movement. What made it populist was that "we think with the head of the citizens," that "we fight for the consent of the citizens," and that "we, unlike the traditional parties, don't depend on power and the pressure to conform, which are supposed to make the citizen docile (*gefügig*)."[21] By the time of the publication of his first book, in 1993, Haider had fully accepted the populist label as a badge of distinction that stood for the fact that his party fought for the ordinary people by encouraging them to freely articulate whatever was troubling them.[22]

Haider's initial reluctance to accept the populist label probably had a lot to do with the fact that, by the early 1990s, the notion of populism had taken on a negative connotation. In both journalistic and academic debates, populism was increasingly made out to be nothing more than a pseudo-democratic, manipulative, opportunistic, even demagogic way to market politics to an increasingly cynical electorate.[23] The problem with this characterization is that it seriously underestimates both the nature of the populist challenge as well as its appeal in contemporary politics. This raises the question of definition. Margaret Canovan has recently proposed to define contemporary populism as "an appeal to 'the people' against both the established structure of power and the dominant ideas and values of the society." To this one might add a second characteristic, namely the aim "to redress the balance of power" in society "in such a way that genuinely popular government might persevere."[24] This means that a movement or party is only genuinely populist if it goes beyond merely mobilizing "the people" against the political and intellectual establishment; i.e., if it advances a strong claim for greater popular participation and representation in the political process brought about via a radical reform of the way politics is conducted. Given this definition, how seriously should we take Haider's claim to be a populist? And what exactly is behind it?

When Haider assumed the chair of the FPÖ in 1986, his first priority was to shape the party into an instrument capable of effecting a fundamental transformation of the Austrian political and institutional system. This meant above all to create a new image for the party that would identify it as "the driving force behind the political renewal of Austria," as the party described itself in the mid-1990s.[25] Haider himself made it quite clear that the FPÖ wanted considerably more than a mere correction of the established political course: "What we want is an Austrian cultural revolution with democratic means, what we want is to overthrow the ruling political class and the intellectual caste."[26] One year later, the FPÖ officially stated that it not only aimed at transforming Austrian society, but that it was "pursuing a strategy of system change" whose goal it was to liberate the citizens from the political parties.[27] It was again Haider, who in an interview with a French international relations journal, laid out what in his view distinguished the FPÖ from all the other parties in Austria:

> Our objective is to promote the emergence of a new politics, more democratic and more humane, based particularly on the self-limitation of the power of the state and on greater freedom of opinion. Until now, the large parties have exercised an excessive influence on the private life of the citizens. This situation has to stop, especially with regard to the media. . . . It is without doubt because we attack the privileges of the traditional parties that they try to discredit us by brandishing us as extremists.[28]

In order to advance this goal, Haider and the FPÖ pursued several different routes. One was a frontal attack against certain of Austria's critical left-wing and liberal intellectuals (particularly those of the 68-generation) who, in Haider's view, through their dominant position in the public media had managed to set both agenda and tone of the public discourse in Austria. Haider made it quite clear that he intended to challenge the left's intellectual predominance with respect to all things cultural ("cultural hegemony") as a first step toward reversing the damaging influence it had exerted—and continued to exert—on Austrian society. Although Haider took most of his examples from Germany, it took little imagination to realize that he saw similar tendencies unfold in Austria, such as the attempt to denigrate and discredit the concept of the nation; "criminalize" the nation's history; and promote multiculturalism while fostering national self-hatred.[29] For those who know the history of the German nationalist right of the past fifty years, these are familiar charges.

A second route was the promotion of an extensive neo-liberal economic program that called for decentralization and privatization, deregulation, tax reform, the creation of new incentive structures, and a restructuring of the welfare state while at the same time extolling the virtues of individual initiative, responsibility, and entrepreneurship. The party could reasonably argue that all of its demands and proposals were solely intended to improve Austria's competitive position in a rapidly changing world. The measures it proposed were rather radical in the Austrian context. But they were hardly different from the actual policies that were introduced by a growing number of governments in Western Europe designed to shift the focal point of "governmental policy away from the general maximization of welfare within a nation (full employment, redistributive transfer payments and social service provision) to the promotion of enterprise, innovation and profitability in both private and public sectors."[30]

In most cases, this neo-liberal offensive was informed by concern that the state had taken on too many tasks and, as a result, had been weakened. Following the Thatcherite lead, the objective was both to free the economy and to strengthen the state by making it more efficient and thus more effective.[31] This, however, was not the FPÖ's goal. On the contrary. As the party emphasized itself, it was not primarily interested in strengthening the state but in "redimensioning" its power and reach through a substantial reduction of the areas over which it had control. In other words, its goal was not so much to create an effective state, but to bring about a minimal one (only as much as absolutely necessary).[32] The reason for that was that the party clearly believed that this was the most effective way to deprive its declared enemies, namely the established political parties and their allies in the country's economic and cultural elite, of their material power base. This, in turn, would break the "power cartel's" hold on Austrian society and thus bring about the envisioned "liberation of the citizens from the political parties," which would automatically lead to the transformation of the Austrian system from a "party state to a citizens' democracy."[33] Haider spelled out his party's goals in a speech from 1998 when he said: "What we want is to bring about a redistribution from the top to the bottom, from the functionaries to the workers, from the protected [i.e., public] sector to the unprotected sector, from the lazy to the industrious in this country. That must be possible."[34]

The party's strategy, as well as the way it crafted its image and defined its role established the FPÖ as a quintessentially populist party. To a large degree the party marketed itself as a radical force for reform and renewal against Austria's political and cultural establishment and an entrenched socio-political system, which, in the party's view, prevented any progress toward greater democracy. In his second book Haider referred to the FPÖ as "a kind of liberation movement from Proporz, privileges, and bureaucratic intellectual narrowmindedness [*geistiger Funktionärsenge*]," and in an interview with the *Süddeutsche Zeitung* in 1996 he even called it "Austria's PLO."[35] Much of the concrete program was not all that different from the projects adopted by a growing number of center-right and particularly center-left parties in Europe and elsewhere. What made the FPÖ distinctive was the degree of radicalism of its tone as well as the fact that its program represented above all a frontal attack against Austria's (and, by extension, Western Europe's) entrenched centers of political power.

Particularly the party's vision of a minimal state, grounded in a view that sees the state as fundamentally inimical to the interests of the citizens and the common good, was a radical departure from the European view of the state. Rather, it was an import from the United States by a Haider, who increasingly drew his lessons from Anglo-Saxon countries like New Zealand, which had managed to reshape the state into what Philip Cerny has called a "quasi-'enterprise association'"[36]—something Haider also envisioned for the Austrian state. As he wrote: "We have to learn to understand the state as an enterprise and to lead it accordingly."[37] This found a reflection in the new program of 1998, where the party called for a "fundamental and profound administrative reform," which would bring the state in line with the private sector by creating a "lean state."[38] For those who have followed the policies adopted by a series of small countries in Europe, Australia, and New Zealand the FPÖ's ideas have a familiar tone.[39] Of course, in most of those cases, the adaptation of private sector models to the public sector was pushed by formally left-wing parties.

Haider's populist bent was also reflected in his ideas on Austria's institutional system. What he envisioned was a substantial weakening of parliamentary democracy, which he considered a thing of the past.[40] In his view, representative democracy ("*Stellvertreterdemokratie*") meant above all that the people were prevented from exerting influence on decisions that directly affected them.[41] The result was a "profound identity crisis between people and their representatives" which stemmed from the "irresponsibility and anonymity of the decisions made by polit-buroes and semi-state institutions."[42] In order to alleviate this situation, the FPÖ proposed a number of institutional reforms designed to complement parliamentarism with elements of direct democracy, i.e., referenda and popular initiatives, and to strengthen the legislative organs at the expense of the executive. Among other things, the FPÖ called for the direct election of a range of representative and executive offices as a guarantee for more responsibility on the part of the elected and more transparency with respect to decision-making processes. As Andrew Bacevich has noted, initiative, referendum, and the direct election of representatives (in this case of United States senators) were key demands of the American populist movement in the nineteenth century.[43]

It is probably not too far-fetched to suspect that Haider got many of his ideas about institutional reform from his visits to California, which seem to have made a deep impression on him.[44] Curiously enough, Haider's alleged fascination with the United States was one of the main things held against him by the European far right, who, by the late 1990s, increasingly saw in him a dangerous Trojan horse.[45] They were probably not completely wrong. There can be no doubt that Haider harbored a not so secret fascination with the United States and was increasingly looking for inspiration and new ideas across the Atlantic. This might explain why, in 1995, the party advanced its "contract with Austria" and even floated the idea of a flat tax, "around 20 percent."[46] It might also explain why, for some time, Haider had three flags in his office, one Austrian, one American, and one Californian, and why Haider, the leader of a self-proclaimed Austrian patriotic movement, when asked at his fiftieth birthday where he would like to live, did not respond with Klagenfurt, Linz, or Bregenz but – New York City.[47]

It is doubtful that even a minority of those who voted for the FPÖ in the 1990s knew, or cared much about, Haider's goal to bring about a substantial "Americanization" of Austrian society. There are good reasons to believe that the vast majority of FPÖ voters considered their vote an expression of their political disaffection and discontent. As Fritz Plasser and Peter Ulram put it, for many of them election time was pay-back time.[48] And a vote for the FPÖ was seen as the most effective way to voice their disaffection. This was a tribute to the party's (and especially Haider's) imaging ability: Within a few years of Haider's assumption of power in the party, the FPÖ had not only managed to identify itself closely with fighting corruption and privileges and preventing the waste of public funds but also to be seen by the public as the party most competent in dealing with these issues.

Surveys suggest that the party's rise in the 1990s was primarily a result of the appeal of its populist stance. In 1995, 79 percent of its voters said they had voted for the FPÖ because of its efforts to disclose scandals; only 51 percent because of the party's position on immigration. Given this appeal, it should come as no surprise that Haider adopted the image of a populist fighter for justice, truth ("He has not lied to you"), and more democracy, and promoted himself as a rebel leading a revolt against entrenched interests and the party state. Comparative work shows that contemporary radical right-wing parties in general seem to have a particular appeal to voters who are outside traditional channels of social integration, such as religious communities or unions. In contemporary sociological terms, the radical right appeals particularly to those voters most affected by processes of individualization, who are most likely to stress "individual freedom, non-conformism with respect to traditional norms, the rejection of moral authorities, the refusal of compromises in politics and a vague desire for social change."[49] Haider's populist style was clearly tailored to appeal to these new constituencies. At the same time, he proved very skillful in couching his attacks against the established system in terms that were designed to appeal to more broadly-based latent *ressentiments*: the notion of the "criminalization" of history, which was bound to resonate in Austria, even if Haider talked about it in the German context; or his attacks against those who he charged with exploiting the welfare system.

By presenting himself as "Austria's answer to Robin Hood," it was easy for Haider to attribute the animosity toward him and his party in and outside of Austria not to his controversial statements on the past or his and his party's attitude towards foreigners and immigrants, but to the fact that his party stood outside the political establishment.[50] There might be something to this charge (but then, again, it was Haider himself who had built his whole image campaign on portraying himself as the outsider).[51] However, the fact remains that Haider would have never evoked the extent of revulsion and hostility he did if he had not made those statements. They stamped him as a crypto-Nazi, neo-fascist, or worse; undermined his respectability; and prevented him from being considered a serious contender for the office of chancellor to which he aspired. It was not until recently that some observers have offered a more tempered, and in a way more sympathetic, interpretation of Haider's way of dealing with the past, which seems to have been driven more by *ressentiments* than genuine conviction. Yet it was Haider's statements on the past that shaped Haider's image far more profoundly than any of his—in the long run potentially far more significant—ideas about the future shape of Austrian society and the Austrian state. At the same time, these statements were bound to undermine any real chance for him to get into a position that would have allowed him to bring about the revolution, which he envisioned.

Master of the Past

It is tempting to put the rise of Jörg Haider in the context of Austria's "unmastered past." In this interpretation, Haider has been possible because Austria and the Austrians, unlike (West) Germany and the (West) Germans, had not been forced to deal with their past, i.e., the extent to which Austrians were implicated in the genocidal program of the Third Reich; or because in Austria, Nazi terminology and Nazi ideology was not as discredited after the war as was the case in Germany. Yet, as Tony Barber has suggested, "the rise of the Austrian far right under Mr Haider is not simply a matter of history being swept into the national unconscious after 1945 and now bursting out in a putrid flood," even if Haider's controversial statements as well as his provocative use of language might have suggested the opposite.[52] There is no reason to suggest that the majority of FPÖ voters voted for the party because of Haider's ambiguous stance on the past. In fact, as an Integral Survey from spring 2000 showed, FPÖ voters and supporters hardly distinguished themselves from the average Austrian with regard to their attitudes toward the past. Thus 80 percent of FPÖ voters agreed with the statement that during the Nazi period, millions of Jews were killed (compared to 83 percent of the whole population); and 68 percent agreed that the Austrians shared responsibility for the mass murder of the Jews (compared to 70 percent of the whole population). Only with regard to the question of whether or not the past should be put to rest ("*Gras über die Vergangenheit wachsen lassen*"), FPÖ voters were significantly more likely to agree with the statement (51 percent) than the general public (33 percent).[53] Thus, what distinguished FPÖ voters was not a lack of historical sensitivity (i.e., the refusal to acknowledge historical realities) but a strong yearning not to be reminded of the past any longer. This, however, did not prevent them from voting FPÖ, despite the fact that Haider's statements on the past and the reactions they provoked were a major reason for the return of the unmastered past into Austria's collective consciousness at century's end.

Much has been written about Haider's "record of defending the policies of Nazi Germany and of justifying individual actions during those years."[54] Among the most notorious examples were his comment on the Third Reich's "sound employment policy," which cost him his job as governor of Carinthia in 1991; his 1995 reference to *Waffen-SS* veterans as "decent people" who "remained true to their convictions until today"; and, the same year, his characterization of the concentration camps as "penal camps" during a speech he gave in the Austrian parliament in the same year.[55] For many observers, these statements represented clear evidence that Haider was a right-wing extremist, intent on minimizing the crimes of the Nazi period while absolving the perpetrators of all responsibility and guilt. Or even worse, they represented "signals to hardcore fascist supporters that Haider is really with them, constrained only by legislation that outlaws holocaust denial and efforts to reestablish the Nazi Party."[56] This was "all the more disturbing for occurring in a country that has shown very little remorse for its own past. Preferring to think of themselves as Hitler's first victim, too many Austrians have forgotten that one million of their forebears fought in Hitler's armies."[57]

These concerns do have a certain legitimacy; but, as Andrew Nagorski has suggested, they also tend to distort reality and lead to that "reckless oversimplification," which "is a common feature of today's politics of guilt," i.e., the tendency to "distinguish only between 'good guys' who use reassuringly familiar terms about the need to atonement and 'bad guys' who raise troubling questions."[58] In Haider's case, what most critics failed to appreciate was the fact that he had been one of the first major post-war Austrian politicians to publicly question the myth of Austria as Hitler's first victim.[59] On the contrary, some of his detractors asserted that "he and his party have consistently opposed efforts aimed at encouraging Austrians to come to terms with their considerable role in the Holocaust."[60] This, however, is simply not true. An example to the opposite is Haider's Vienna Declaration from 1992, where he, somewhat cryptically, referred to the Austrian "dogma" of neutrality as the "ideological superstructure for the victim theory, which is designed to make Austria's role between 1938 and 1945 appear in a milder light and which neglects the question of the perpetrator." A year later, in his first book, he chastised the Austrian political leadership for having taken fifty years to finally admit that "Austrians too had taken part in the crimes" committed by the Nazis.[61] Since then, Haider has repeatedly stated in public that "Austria was not only a victim of the Nazis, it also collaborated with them," or that Austrians "are not only victims but were also perpetrators (*Täter*)."[62] At the same time he abandoned the party's traditional German-nationalist position and refurbished himself as an "Austrian patriot" who, had he lived during the Third Reich, "wouldn't have accepted that a foreign army came to occupy this country" and therefore would have probably "been in prison during the Nazi period."[63] Haider's new position was not lost on the European radical right, which denounced him for, among other things, having stated that Austria had a "collective responsibility" with respect to the past.[64]

There are a number of explanations for Haider's highly idiosyncratic way of coming to terms with the past. One has a lot to do with his own background and biography. As is well-known, both of his parents were convinced Nazis. But neither attained high-ranking positions in the Third Reich. In Haider's own words, they were "small Nazis." And yet, after the war, they were ostracized and prevented from getting anything but menial jobs while, at the same time, "prominent Nazis recycled themselves as prominent Austrian politicians."[65] Although Haider has publicly denied it, there can be little doubt that the differential treatment of the war-generation in Austria left a strong impression on him. It quite likely gave rise to deep-seated *ressentiments* toward a system that allowed once high-ranking Nazis who made careers in the two major parties, to dictate the terms of how to deal with the past.[66] From this perspective, Haider's pointed remark on the Nazi economic policy could also be interpreted as a deliberate attempt to provoke a self-righteous response from those Haider considered to have no right to be self-righteous.[67] As Rudolf Burger has put it, "Haider is the personified antithesis of political correctness, and therefore for many a symbolic liberation. He formulates the uneasiness with hypocrisy."[68]

At the same time, as Melanie Sully has persuasively argued, Haider has always felt a fierce loyalty to his parents, which led him to forcefully rally to the defense of the whole war generation.[69] In his view, what distinguished this generation was not that they had been involved in monstrous crimes, but that they had fought and risked their lives on the Eastern front in order to safeguard democracy in Europe through their sacrifice.[70] This, of course, is a rather idiosyncratic interpretation of the Wehrmacht's role in the East, to say the least. It reflected as much traditional right-wing anti-Communism as it represented a conscious act of provocation against the attempts on the Austrian left to deconstruct the Wehrmacht's image in the Austrian public by showing the public to what extent the Wehrmacht had been implicated in the Nazi crimes.[71] For Haider, this was nothing more than an attempt to turn "the biography of the parents and grandparents" into a "single rogues' gallery."[72]

This was a careful choice of words designed to revive *ressentiments* among those circles in Austrian society that were most susceptible to, and offended by, what Andrew Nagorski has aptly referred to as the "politics of guilt." It was meant to appeal to those voters who had always felt that Austrians (and Germans) had been singled out; that the attribution of innocence and guilt had been more or less arbitrary; and, perhaps most importantly, that crimes and suffering had been measured unevenly. As Rainer Bauböck has put it, Haider "stands for a different attitude of resentful remembrance."[73] It is hard to tell how widespread these sentiments still are in the Austrian public (or, for that matter, in the German public). The public protests against the Wehrmacht exhibition as well as the most recent debate about the Benesch decrees in Austria seem to suggest that some of these sentiments are still rather strong and can mobilize political action. In this respect, many of Haider's remarks quite likely resonated among some segments of the Austrian public and further established Haider as the one politician "who says what you think:" as, for example, that the former Italian prime minister, a former Communist, "did not have to don sackcloth and ashes and explain that he had been reformed"; or Haider's implicit equation of Churchill's decision "to destroy cities such as Dresden, where there were no soldiers of the German army" with Hitler's policy to "drop bombs on cities where only civilians and children live;" or his most recent demand that Germans expelled from the Sudeten region be provided with some kind of restitution because they "also suffered from crimes against humanity, and they deserve some kind of moral recognition," which seemed to link "the expulsion of the Sudeten Germans to the destruction of the European Jewry" and thus trivialize the latter.[74] This was Haider, the rebel and "ice breaker"(Mölzer), who dares to challenge taboos and to question the notion that given the experience of Nazism, there have to be "restrictions on political debate on sensitive subjects."[75] At the same time, this was part of a larger strategy of political mobilization that relied on the appeal to diffuse *ressentiments*.

Haider's controversial statements on the Nazi past were thus inspired by several rather apparent motives: Loyalty to an "older generation which has lost lots of blood during the war" and "which is no longer in a position to defend itself effectively;" personal *ressentiments* toward "red [SPÖ - Socialist Party of Austria] and black [ÖVP – Austrian People's Party] politicians, who want to hold a speech at every meeting of veterans' organizations, but at the same time make sure that thousands of students are driven into the despicable *Wehrmacht* exhibitions intended to incite them against their parents and grand parents"; and, last but not least, the conscious intention to mobilize latent *ressentiments* in the Austrian public.[76] Had he stopped here, it would be easy to dismiss him as an apologist and revisionist, who had marginalized himself.

However, this is only half of the story. The other, and by far more interesting half of the story, regards the most recent twist in Haider's dealing with the past, which has at least three major components. The first component is Haider's public acknowledgment of the true nature of the Nazi regime and of the centrality of the Holocaust. Already in his first book he wrote that the "worst thing about National Socialism was undoubtedly its anti-Semitism and racism, which led to mass extermination. Such crimes can never be put right." And: "There is nothing that can justify National Socialism."[77] Two years later, he claimed in an interview with Michael Wolffsohn that he constantly told his older voters and members, "how criminal the Nazis were."[78] At the same time, he publicly referred to "the barbarities of the Nazi period."[79] But the most important statement was his lengthy November 1999 declaration, in which he apologized for his past comments on the Third Reich. Among other things Haider stated that he understood the anxiety and fears of Austria's Jewish citizens: "The very uniqueness and incomparability of the crime of the Holocaust demands from an Austrian politician that he takes those fears seriously."[80] The same language was incorporated into the declaration on "The Responsibility for Austria – A Future in the Heart of Europe," which was a precondition for the acceptance of the FPÖ/ÖVP coalition government by the Austrian president. It stated that "Austria accepts her responsibility arising out of the tragic history of the 20th century and the horrendous crimes of the

National Socialist Regime. . . . The singularity of the crimes of the Holocaust which are without precedent in history are an exhortation to permanent alertness against all forms of dictatorship and totalitarianism." When asked why he had signed this statement Haider responded: "Yes, because an industrial mass extermination of human beings has only happened once in this form."[81] At the same time, Haider insisted that there was no collective guilt, only individual responsibility. That, however, did not absolve his generation from "observing" what he called a "*Gedächtnislast*," a "specific responsibility for that time," which had to inform "our political activities."[82] Haider stated the new course perhaps most succinctly in his interview with the German TV station ARD on the day of the inauguration of the new government when he said: "It is our problem as young people to observe loyalty toward our older generation, which has rebuilt this democracy in Austria, but on the other hand also to make clear that there is no room for ways [sic], sympathies with totalitarian regimes or the time of National Socialism. For the Holocaust was [sic] in its uniqueness as a crime simply such a dimension that it reaches far beyond the twentieth century."[83] With these words Haider managed to accept the central elements of the consensus position on the Nazi regime and on the Holocaust without abandoning the core of his position with respect to his parents' generation.

The second component of Haider's dealing with the past was his acceptance of the idea that Austria had an obligation to compensate Word War II forced and slave laborers.[84] Ironically, it was under a government that included the FPÖ that the question of compensation was finally tackled, while earlier governments had always refused to deal with this issue. Although Haider's insistence to link compensation to slave laborers with restitution for the German victims of expulsion from Czechoslovakia after the war tainted the government's gesture, it represented an important step forward in Austria's attempt to come to terms with the past.[85] As Stuart Eizenstat, the American official in charge of the negotiations, pointed out, "with respect to the slave and forced labor issues [the Austrians] have acted with great alacrity, great courage, and shown leadership not just in Austria but leadership to the rest of Europe and to the world about how one can reconcile with one's past, and how one can heal wounds even many decades later."[86] Undoubtedly, this was possible because Haider had not only embraced the idea (against internal resistance by the far right, represented by Andreas Mölzer), but was actively promoting it, particularly among those most likely to object to it: In October, when Haider once again joined the veterans of Hitler's army at the annual Ulrichsberg meeting he "called for the compensation for slave laborers" during his speech to the crowd.[87]

The third component of Haider's dealing with the past was his active promotion of a settlement with the Slovenian minority in Carinthia, another legacy of the past. As in the case of slave laborers, this was a rather astounding turnaround: As even those unsympathetic to Haider readily admitted, while the SPÖ had been in the majority in Carinthia, "the demands of the minority were not even discussed." Once Haider was in charge, he quickly initiated a campaign to woo the Slovenian minority by showing a new flexibility with respect to some of the thorniest issues that had soured majority-minority relations in Carinthia for decades: the question of putting up bilingual place name signs, setting up bilingual kindergartens, and the creation of a mandate reserved for a representative of the Slovenian minority in the Carinthian *Landtag*.[88] For Haider, this was an important issue, if for no other reason than that its generous settlement would improve Carinthia's image and make it a model for the rest of Europe of a successful minority politics, "which does not ignore the problems of the majority."[89]

What accounts for these dramatic shifts in Haider's strategy? Some observers have suggested they constituted above all an attempt to improve his personal image as a politician who still aspired to become chancellor. Although there is good reason to believe that this played a part, I would suggest that other considerations were more important. This is derived from a remark Haider made during an interview with the German weekly, *Die Zeit*, in early 2000. In response to the question whether Austria should have a genuine debate about the past, Haider responded: "I think we should concentrate more on the future, in order to prevent these things from happening again. . . . But at one point one also has to be able to break out of the past. . . . [F]or the Austrian there is a point where he says the issue has been sufficiently discussed. It would be good if the country would finally occupy itself with the future." And he quoted Gerhard Schröder who had once said: "now it is enough, now we turn towards the future."[90] In an interview with the *Washington Post* a few days later, Haider expressed once again his exasperation with the "obsessive quest to flagellate his country for its wartime role and denigrate him as representing a new brand of fascism," adding that as governor of Carinthia, he was trying "to focus on the future."[91]

What these words betrayed was a growing general impatience and frustration, but also a growing awareness that his own past remarks represented the most important reason why he was not allowed "to focus on the future" as much as he wanted. This came at the time when Haider tried to convince the world that he was not a backward-oriented provincial right-wing extremist but Austria's version of Tony Blair. He laid out the similarities in an article for the *Daily Telegraph* a few days after the inauguration of the new government. Among the similarities between the FPÖ and New Labour he saw that both "want to escape from the rigidity of the welfare state without creating social injustice. They want a fair deal for more self-sufficient citizens to develop their real potential instead of state hand-outs, which can only perpetuate the poverty trap."[92] Given his record on economic issues, there is little reason to doubt his sincerity. But he also realized that his past statements on the Nazi period had increasingly become a liability and distraction which threatened to hamper and impede the new government's ability to bring about the far-reaching transformation of Austrian politics and society that he had envisioned when he took over the party. This, more than anything else, explains why he embarked on a path that to his critics on the far right looked like nothing short of a complete capitulation to the forces of political correctness. This path, of course, made perfect sense, even from a perspective of purely electoral politics, given the fact that a majority of FPÖ sympathizers and voters, as we have seen, wanted to see the past laid at rest as quickly as possible and get on with their lives. This, however, meant that the past had to be "overcome" first; and what better person to do that than Jörg Haider.

Back to the Future

What, then, is the nature of Haider and the FPÖ? It has been suggested that Haider is nothing more than a postmodern political opportunist who "is this, [who] is that, and in the end he is nothing, so what is left is the image onto which people project."[93] There is some truth to this, but it is only part of the story. A closer reading of the available evidence suggests that Haider does have convictions as well as a project, and that he has remained quite faithful to both. Haider's claim that he is Austria's Tony Blair should be taken seriously. If he points out that both the new Labour and the FPÖ are "conservative and revolutionary" because both "want to deregulate and leave everything to market forces," both "work for reform in the state and a society without taboos," and both "seek flexible possibilities for independent people in a changing society," then he only reaffirms what he has been saying and writing since he took over as party chair.[94] This suggests that Haider is indeed part of the post-Thatcherite neo-liberal wave, which, largely inspired by Tony Blair, has been transforming Western Europe during the past few years. Douglas Holmes has pointed out that one of the core aspects of the Thatcherite revolution was its assault on traditional authority. It derived from the insight that the left's "agenda of social reformism and progressivism, intended to protect the interests of the working class, ratified its subaltern position." By equating "welfarism with dependency and subordination," and by advocating "individual enterprise and contempt for the entitlements of socialism," Thatcherism "subverted precisely those social values of deference to authority that have kept people in their place."[95] This has been even more so the case in Austria, as even Haider's most ardent critics would admit. From this perspective, Haider's claim that his is a movement of liberation ("Austria's PLO") represents more than merely a marketing gimmick.

The public shock of the measures introduced by the FPÖ's finance minister, Karl-Heinz Grasser, in the fall of 2000 and designed to balance the budget suggests that Austria was less than prepared for a Thatcherite revolution.[96] Ironically, by focusing most of their attention on Haider's verbal acrobatics regarding the past, critical observers and commentators failed to initiate a debate about the question whether Austria really wanted to see their country undergo the fundamental socioeconomic transformation which Haider and his new breed of yuppy technocrats seemed to have prepared for the country. However, this is hardly the end of the story. As Haider wrote himself, his party stands not only for the unleashing of market forces and initial initiatives, but also for supporting "the weak and underprivileged: Without freedom there can be no social security, and without social security there can be no freedom."[97] Austria's Robin Hood might have to get back on his horse, this time to save Austria from his own revolution.[98]

Notes

1. Roger Cohen, "A Haider in Their Future," *The New York Times Magazine*, 30 April 2000, 59.

2. Theo Sommer, "Contra – Bann über Österreich? Europa leistet sich aus moralischen Gründen eine große Heuchelei," *Die Zeit*, 10 February 2000.

3. William Rees-Mogg, "We Are Acting Like Nazis Over Austria," *The Times*, 13 June 2000.

4. Anson Rabinbach, "EU Says the Right Stops Here," *Los Angeles Times*, 6 February 2000.

5. Mark Mazower, "Haider Is Not Alone," *Civilization* 4 (2000), retrieved 3 October 2000 from the World Wide Web: http://www.civmag.com/articles/C0004wor.html.

6. Cohen, "A Haider," 54.

7. Jörg Haider, *Befreite Zukunft jenseits von links und rechts* (Vienna: Ibera & Molden, 1997), ch. 6.

8. Cohen, "A Haider," 54.

9. See Russell J. Dalton, "Political Support in Advanced Industrial Democracies," in *Critical Citizens: Global Support for Democratic Governance*, ed. Pippa Norris (Oxford: Oxford University Press, 1999), 62-65.

10. For an overview of this trend see the contributions in Hans-Georg Betz and Stefan Immerfall, eds., *The New Politics of the Right* (New York: St. Martin's Press, 1998).

11. Sonja Puntscher Rieckmann, "The Politics of *Ausgrenzung*, the Nazi-Past and the European Dimension of the New Radical Right in Austria," *Contemporary Austrian Studies*, vol. 7, *The Vranitzky Era in Austria*, ed. Günter Bischof, Anton Pelinka, and Ferdinand Karlhofer (New Brunswick: Transaction Publishers, 1999), 79.

12. It is interesting to note that Haider has found it necessary to emphasize that his party not only "excludes violence as a means of politics" but also clearly distances itself from "every form of totalitarian, chauvinist, and national-socialist thinking." *Wiener Erklärung zur Situation von Staat und Gesellschaft am Vorabend der Beitrittsentscheidung über ein gemeinsames Europa* (Vienna: Freiheitliches Bildungswerk, 1992), 13.

13. For a discussion of the importance of the media in the new "audience" democracy see Wolfgang C. Müller, "Elections and the Dynamics of the Austrian Party System since 1986," English version of a contribution to *Das österreichische Wahlverhalten*, ed. Fritz Plasser, Peter A. Ulram, and Franz Sommer (Vienna: Signum, 2000), PDF file, retrieved 8 January 2001 from the World Wide Web.

14. Roger Griffin, "Interregnum or Endgame? Radical Right Thought in the 'Post-fascist' Era," *Journal of Political Ideologies* 5, no. 2 (2000): 173.

15. Douglas Holmes, *Integral Europe: Fast-Capitalism, Multiculturalism, Neofascism* (Princeton: Princeton University Press, 2000), 122.

16. On this development see Fritz Plasser and Peter Ulram, "Wandel der politischen Konfliktdynamik: Radikaler Rechtspopulismus in Österreich," in *Wählerverhalten und Parteienwettbewerb*, ed. Wolfgang C. Müller, Fritz Plasser, and Peter A. Ulram (Vienna: Signum, 1995), 471-503.

17. See Rudolf Burger, "Romantisches Österreich," *Leviathan* 28, no. 1 (2000): 3-13.

18. See Klaus Ottomeyer, *Die Haider-Show. Zur Psychopolitik der FPÖ* (Klagenfurt: Drava, 2000).

19. "Haider: EU-Sanktionen als 'Hornberger Schießen'," *Kurier*, 13 September 2000.

20. Andreas Mölzer, *Jörg! Der Eisbrecher* (Klagenfurt: Suxxes, 1990), ch. 6.

21. *Wiener Erklärung zur Situation von Staat und Gesellschaft*, 6.

22. Jörg Haider, *Die Freiheit, die ich meine* (Frankfurt: Ullstein, 1993), 54.

23. Michael Frank, "Jörg Haiders Populismus auf Höhenflug," *Süddeutsche Zeitung*, 14 March 1989, 4.

24. Margaret Canovan, "Trust the People! Populism and the Two Faces of Democracy," *Political Studies* 47 (1999): 3; A. J. Bacevich, "The Impact of the New Populism," *Orbis* 40, no. 1 (1996): 34.

25. *The Nationalrat Election in Austria: Information on October 9, 1994* (Vienna: The Federal Press Service, 1994), 19.

26. Haider, *Die Freiheit, die ich meine*, 201.

27. *Freiheitliche Thesen zur politischen Erneuerung Österreichs* (Vienna: Freiheitliches Bildungswerk, 1994), 4.

28. "Entretien avec Jörg Haider: Une autre voix pour l'Autriche?" *Politique Internationale* 66 (Winter 1994/95): 134.

29. Haider, *Die Freiheit, die ich meine*, ch. 2.

30. Philip G. Cerny, "Paradoxes of the Competition State: The Dynamics of Political Globalization," *Government and Opposition* 32, no. 2 (1997): 260.

31. Andrew Gamble, *The Free Economy and the Strong State* (Durham: Duke University Press, 1988).

32. In the FPÖ's new party program, the emphasis is clearly on a drastic reduction of the scope of the state and its limitation to the "*ureigensten*" (most fundamental) tasks, such as internal and external security, legislation, education, and monetary politics. *Das Programm der Freiheitlichen Partei Österreichs*, 1998, 22.

33. *Vom Parteienstaat zur Bürgerdemokratie: Der Weg zur Dritten Republik* (Vienna: Freiheitliche Akademie, no date); *Freiheitliche Thesen zur politischen Erneuerung Österreichs*, 4.

34. "Rede des Bundesparteiobmannes Dr. Jörg Haider."

35. Jörg Haider, *Befreite Zunkunft jenseits von links und rechts* (Vienna: Ibera &Molden, 1997), 100. "'Wir sind die PLO Österreichs'," *Süddeutsche Zeitung*, 18 October 1996, 8.

36. Philip Cerny, "Paradoxes of the Competition State: The Dynamics of Political Globalization," *Government and Opposition* 32, no. 2 (1997): 251.

37. Haider, *Befreite Zukunft*, 160.

38. *Das Programm der Freiheitlichen Partei Österreichs*, 33.

39. See Herman Schwartz, "Small States in Big Trouble," *World Politics* 46, no. 4 (1994): 527-55.

40. Melanie A. Sully, *The Haider Phenomenon* (New York: Columbia University Press, 1997), 41-42.

41. See Christa Zöchling, *Haider: Licht und Schatten einer Karriere* (Vienna: Molden, 1999), 87.

42. *Vom Parteienstaat zur Bürgerdemokratie*, 11.

43. Bacevich, "The Impact," 34.

44. Sully, *The Haider Phenomenon*, 40.

45. Gerhoch Reisegger, "Jörg Haider – Aufbruch zu neuen Ufern oder Fußnote der Geschichte?," in *Jörg Haider: Patriot im Zwielicht?*, ed. Rolf-Josef Eibicht (Stuttgart: DS-Verlag, 1997) 149; Brigitte Sob, "Welche Freiheit meint Jörg Haider," in ibid., 122-

23.

46. Haider, *Befreite Zukunft*, 192.

47. On the flags see his interview with Melanie Sully in Sully, *The Haider Phenomenon*, 216; on New York City see "Über Frauen, Männer und das Altern," *Kleine Zeitung*, 23 January 2000.

48. Fritz Plasser and Peter A. Ulram, "Wahltag ist Zahltag," *Österreichische Zeitschrift für Politikwissenschaft* 18, no. 2 (1989): 151-64.

49. Jaak Billiet, "Church Involvement, Ethnocentrism, and Voting for a Radical Right-Wing Party: Diverging Behavioral Outcomes of Equal Attitudinal Dispositions," *Sociology of Religion* 56, no. 3 (1995): 322; Marcel Lubbers and Peer Scheepers, "Individual and Contextual Characteristics of the German Extreme Right-Wing Vote in the 1990s. A Test of Complementary Theories," *European Journal of Political Research* 38, no. 1 (2000): 82

50. So, for example, in an interview with CBC News, 7 February 2000, retrieved 5 September 2000 from the World Wide Web: http://cbc.ca/national/magazine/austria/index/html.

51. It might be tempting to compare Haider with Gianfranco Fini, who became one of Italy's most respected politicians after he had formally disavowed the Fascist past. The crucial difference was, of course, that Fini never sought a confrontation with the political establishment. On the contrary, he did everything to become part of the new political establishment in Italy.

52. Tony Barber, "Do They Remember?," *The Independent*, 15 October 1996, 18.

53. Integral Marktforschung, "Umfrage Holocaust," April 2000. I would like to thank Manfred Tautscher for sharing the results of this study with me.

54. Anti-Defamation League (ADL), "Joerg Haider: The Rise of an Austrian Extreme Rightist," February 2000, 6.

55. English translations of the latter two speeches can be found in Sully, *The Haider Phenomenon*, 73-76 and 138-40.

56. Rick Kuhn, "The Threat of Fascism in Austria," *Monthly Review* 52, no. 2 (2000): 23.

57. Ivo H. Daalder, "Squeeze Austria to Cleanse its Government," *Newsweek*, 14 February 2000, A25.

58. Andrew Nagorski, "The Politics of Guilt – Austria's Bigot, Europe's Burden," *Foreign Affairs* 79, no. 3 (2000): 19.

59. One of the few exceptions was Mark Tran, "Austria's Freedom Party," *The Guardian*, 28 January 2000.

60. Robert S. Wistrich, "Haider and His Critics," *Commentary*, April 2000, 31.

61. *Wiener Erklärung*, 24-25; Haider, *Die Freiheit, die ich meine*, 116. In the well-known interview with the *Falter* magazine, Haider even claimed that he had been the first Austrian politician to publicly declare that Austria was both victim and perpetrator (at the occasion of the fiftieth anniversary of the *Anschluss* in 1988). See "Jörg Haider – Das Interview," retrieved 24 February 2000 from World Wide Web: http://store.falter.at/interview.html.

62. "Wir sind eine österreichische Sonderanfertigung," *Die neue Gesellschaft/Frankfurter Hefte* 42, no. 7 (1995): 628; "Une autre voix pour l'Autriche?," 141; Eran Tiefenbrunn, "Haider: 'Sono più vicino a Blair che a Le Pen'," *Il Messaggero*, 4 February,

2000.

63. *Newsweek*, 13 January 1997, cited in Rolf-Josef Eibicht, "Konstruktive Kritik im Dienst an der Nation: Dr. Jörg Haider im Zwielicht," in *Jörg Haider – Patriot im Zwielicht*, 50; Dominic Lawson, "I Lead. I Lead. I Lead the People," *Sunday Telegraph*, 13 February 2000.

64. Eibicht, "Konstruktive Kritik, " 50-51.

65. Cohen, "A Haider in Their Future," 57; Zöchling, *Haider*, 54; interview with Haider in Sully, *The Haider Phenomenon*, 212.

66. The denial can be found in the interview with Dominic Lawson in the *Sunday Telegraph*, in which he answered the question of whether there were feelings of anger or bitterness about the way his parents had been treated and about the fact that his was "more or less a poor family": "No. It was a beautiful childhood."

67. Zöchling, *Haider*, 53.

68. Burger, "Romantisches Österreich," 8.

69. See the interview with Wulf Schmiese, where Haider said: "It was always my interest to spare the older generation, which has gone through terrible things during the war, a generalized disparagement (*pauschale Verunglimpfung*). And I stand by that." "Der nette Herr Haider...," *Die Welt*, 7 February 2000.

70. *Profil* interview, 21 August 1995, cited in Brigitte Bailer-Galanda, *Haider wörtlich* (Vienna: Löcker Verlag, 1995), 103.

71. With regard to the *Wehrmachtsausstellung* (exhibition), Haider said in 1998 in Graz: "This is not a forum for a dialogue, when an industrial family and cigarette producer from Hamburg [i.e., the Reemtsma family], which has its own brown shadows, believes that it can cure its own family history by rendering a collective verdict of guilt over a whole generation of soldiers. That is not what we want." See "Rede des Bundesparteiobmannes Dr. Jörg Haider, Neujahrstreffen 11. Jänner 1998 – Graz," mimeo, 27-28.

72. "'Ich bin auserkoren' – Ein Gespräch über das Teuflische im Menschen (Teil I)," *Der Tagesspiegel*, 14 June 2000.

73. Rainer Bauböck, "Austria: Jörg Haider's Grasp for Power," *Dissent* (Spring 2000): 3.

74. See "Ich lasse mir nicht alles gefallen," *Die Zeit*, 3 February 2000; Lawson, "I Lead. I Lead. I Lead the People;" and William Drozdiak, "Haider Baffled by Western Protests," *Washington Post*, 10 February 2000.

75. William Pfaff, "Right Turn in Austria," *Commonweal*, 25 February 2000. Pfaff leaves the question open whether or not such restrictions are, in fact, justified.

76. "Rede des Bundesparteiobmannes Dr. Jörg Haider Neujahrestreffen 11. Jänner 1998 – Graz," January 1998, mimeo, 28.

77. Haider, *Die Freiheit, die ich meine*, 116, 117.

78. Interview in *Bunte* 51 (1995), cited in Eibicht, "Konstruktive Kritik," 49.

79. Cited in Tony Barber, "Do They Remember?," *The Independent*, 15 October 1996.

80. "Erklärung Dr. Haiders vom 12. November 1999 Zur Lage der Republik und zur Situation der FPÖ," retrieved 24 February 2000 from the World Wide Web: http://www.fpoe.at/aktuell/november-rede.htm.

81. *A Future in the Heart of Europe. A New Governance for Austria: The Programme of the Federal Government*, February 2000, 4; "'Ich bin auserkoren' (Teil I)"; see also Haider's interview with *Il Messaggero*, where he said that "the Holocaust has been the most terrible crime against humanity in the history of humanity. The systematic extermination, Auschwitz, the industry of death (*l'industria della morte*) are things that the world had never seen before," in Tiefenbrunn, *"Haider: 'Sono più vicino'."*

82. "There is no collective Guilt," *Newsweek International*, 21 February 2000; Richard Gizbert, "Haider Speaks," ABC News, 7 February 2000; "Erklärung Dr. Haiders."

83. "Farbe bekennen, " TV interview, ARD, 4 February 2000.

84. Haider in *Die Zeit* interview: "I see it as our task more to advance in the humanitarian area, for example in the question of compensation for forced laborers or in student exchange," in "'Ich lasse mir nicht alles gefallen'."

85. Haider was hardly the only one to link compensation for the victims of Nazism with that of the victims of expulsion. Thus Chancellor Schüssel said in an interview with the *Neue Züricher Zeitung* that "there is great support in all parties for dealing with all aspects of our past history. . . . We have made it clear that we want to resolve the question of forced labor and the issues of the Holocaust. But that must not prevent us from making progress on other open, bilateral questions in a spirit of good neighborly relations." "Vienna's New Coalition: An Interview with Chancellor Schüssel," *NZZ Online*, 19/20February 2000.

86. "Unofficial Transcript: Schaumayer, Eizenstat on Nazi Slave Labor Fund," retrieved 17 August 2000 from the World Wide Web: http://www.usis.it/wireless/wfa00517/A0051718.htm.

87. Melissa Eddy, "Haider Defends WW2 Soldier Meeting," *The Associated Press*, 2 October 2000; surveys show that a large majority supported compensating the victims of the Nazi regime, from Jews, Sinti, and Roma to slave laborers (between 59 to 74 percent). At the same time, a two-thirds majority also agreed with the notion that the question of compensation (*Wiedergutmachung*) should finally come to an end. See "Umfrage: Österreicher betreffend Entschädigungszahlungen positiv eingestellt," *Der Standard*, 11 July 2000.

88. Ernst Sittinger, "Kärntner Slowenen: Politik zwischen Taktik und juristischem Zwang," *Die Presse*, 17 August 2000; for more information on the situation of the Slovenian minority in Carinthia see http://www.volksgruppen.orf.at/kaernten/de/aktuell/aktuell/mi_aktuell.htm.

89. "Haider und die Slowenen," ORF Report, 8 August 2000, retrieved 3 October 2000 from the World Wide Web: http://tv.orf.at/report/000808/000808_3.htm; see also the interview with Haider "'Keine Chance für Wirrköpfe' – Interview mit LH Jörg Haider," *Kleine Zeitung*, 5 October 2000.

90. "'Ich lasse mir nicht alles gefallen'."

91. William Drozdiak, "Haider's Rise Rooted in Conservative Home Soil," *The Washington Post*, 13 February 2000.

92. Jörg Haider, "Blair and Me Versus the Forces of Conservatism," *Daily Telegraph*, 22 February 2000.

93. André Glucksmann, quoted by Cohen, "A Haider in Their Future," 58.

94. Haider, "Blair and Me."

95. Holmes, *Integral Europe*, 189.

96. See Klaus Dutzler and Petra Stuiber, "Operation Staatshaushalt," *Format* 29 (2000); K. Grubelnik and P. Stuiber, "Eine Nation im Steuerschock," *Format* 39 (2000).

97. Haider, "Blair and me."

98. See Klaus Dutzler, "Haider gegen alle," *Format* 41 (2000).

The Freedom Party of Austria (FPÖ)—an Austrian and a European Phenomenon?

Walter Manoschek

1. Introduction

When in February 2000 the Austrian government formed a coalition between the Freedom Party (FPÖ) and the People's Party (ÖVP), the controversy surrounding the FPÖ, its *political nature*, and the potential threat to democratic political life became the talk of Europe. The bilateral diplomatic measures put in place by EU members against the Austrian government between February and September 2000—incorrectly termed "EU sanctions"—have clearly shown that the FPÖ is perceived as more than just an Austrian domestic problem. Indeed, it has triggered varying degrees of anxiety in all the nations of the EU. They fear that the success of the FPÖ—or, more precisely, the "Haider-FPÖ"[1]—could develop into a European-wide phenomenon. Consequently, in December 2000, the EU heads of government enacted an "alarm system" as part of the Treaty of Nice (Article 7) to place controls on governments that violate fundamental European values.[2]

Article 7 was not conceived specially for the FPÖ though, but was designed to be applied to all EU member states in which governments are formed with the participation of extreme right parties. This became clear when just before the Italian parliamentary elections on 12 May 2001 Belgian Foreign Minister Louis Michel issued a warning in the Italian media of a possible governmental coalition involving Silvio Berlusconi's *Forza Italia* (FI) and Umberto Bossi's extreme right party, Northern League.[3]

It remains to be seen whether the complicated body of rules in Article 7 can actually be implemented. A precondition for this is the creation of a catalog of criteria providing a concrete list of "serious breaches of basic European values." Furthermore, the EU member states will have to determine whether any parties now exist in Europe whose "political nature" is such that their participation in a governing coalition would per se constitute a "clear risk of a serious breach of basic European values." In the contemporary European political landscape, several parties might "qualify," especially the nationalistic extreme right parties which have emerged over the last fifteen years in Austria, France, Italy, Belgium (Flanders), and Scandinavia, and have developed into significant players in the political life of their countries.[4]

Indeed, it is not easy to reduce these various European extreme right parties to a common political denominator. They have developed in dissimilar fashion and exhibit distinctive, locally specific characteristics. Thus, they confront both the political scientist and the politician with problems of definition and conceptualization.

This paper will therefore begin with a discussion of the heuristic value of various terms such as "neo-populist" and "extreme right," followed by a comparison of the FPÖ and other extreme right parties with special attention to their central political elements and fields of political activity. I will then investigate the roots and history of the FPÖ, the extreme right party with the most votes, which is to date the only one to join a governing coalition in an EU member state. Thereafter, I will look into the causes—both internal and external—of the Haider-FPÖ's success and its rise from a party garnering a mere 5% at the polls to Austria's second strongest party with almost 27% of the vote. The following section will examine the repercussions and feedback effects that the FPÖ's participation in the governing coalition has had for the party. Finally I will attempt to advance hypotheses dealing with the possible consequences of the success of the Haider-FPÖ for other EU member states.

2. European Far-Right Parties: Neo-Populist or Extreme Right Parties?

A significant growth of extreme right parties became evident in several EU states at the same as, or even prior to, the following historic events: the collapse of *Realsozialismus* and the end of the bipolar balance of power, German reunification, the establishment of a New World Order, the expansion of the EU to include new members as well as the integration processes within the framework of the EU, and, last but not least, the dynamic growth of turbocapitalism in the sense of nearly unlimited concentration of financial capital and the globalization of markets. These parties verbally distance themselves from the extreme rightist, Fascist, or National Socialist parties and movements of the interwar period and thereby achieve their aim of being played down as "neo-populist parties." Nevertheless, uneasiness towards these parties pertains, since, despite all their professions of commitment to a pluralistic, parliamentary-democratic form of government, they continue to espouse basic political attitudes with specific views that contradict or oppose fundamental liberal values of democratic societies. For social scientists, it is a difficult task to establish definitions and typologies of this complex phenomenon of extreme right parties in their highly divergent national manifestations. As Martin Blinkhorn so aptly formulated it, this has to do with the fact that "the definitions, typologies and taxonomies beloved of social scientists tend to fit uncomfortably the intractable realities which are the raw material of the historian. ... Lines stubbornly refuse to be drawn, ... exceptions disprove more rules than they prove."[5]

From the plethora of definitions that have been advanced, I will cite here just a few that are relevant to the effort of typologizing the FPÖ.[6] Most authors agree that, despite instances of overlapping and shared values—particularly in the areas of law and order, immigration, and moral traditionalism—the extreme right parties belong to a different political family that is distinguishable from the traditional right wing.[7] In spite of certain substantive commonalities with the traditional right, these parties distinguish themselves in the political discourse by dealing with issues in a completely different way, i.e. through radicalization, xenophobia, and racism.[8] This difference in political style and in the political discourse is characterized by some authors as "populist," "neo-populist," "national-populist," or "right-populist,"[9] because these parties "have been rather careful to stress their commitment to representative democracy and the constitutional order."[10]

Indeed, Michael Minkenberg, who uses Giovanni Sartori's discussion of anti-system parties as a starting point, defines a new right radical or extreme right party as one that "abides by a belief system that does not share the values of the political order within which it operates."[11] In this dichotomy between democratic pretensions and anti-democratic values, and in the effort "not to be associated with outright fascism or with violent methods, these parties display several similarities with the extreme right-wing parties of the inter-war years."[12]

Indeed, as we have seen, the label "extreme right" is not acceptable to all observers. As far as the Haider-FPÖ is concerned, it should be kept in mind that the party's policies "must be seen alongside his controversial and well-publicized eulogy to unreconstructed Nazis. Thus, nominal commitment to democracy and constitutionalism should not simply be taken as evidence of its actual realization. As Ignazi ... again explains, the anti-party, anti-establishment, anti-pluralistic values of the extreme right serve overall to undermine, not to strengthen, the liberal democratic representative system."[13]

One of Jörg Haider's political goals is the transformation of the Second Republic into a Third Republic[14] (analogous to Le Pen, who wants to abandon the constitution of the French Fifth Republic and replace it with a new Sixth Republic). The objective of this is to weaken representative democracy and thus, at the very least, to call the constitutional order into question.[15] To typologize the Haider-FPÖ as an extreme right party can therefore be justified from a scholarly point of view. An analysis of the political content and the preferred political issues of the Haider-FPÖ supports this categorical ascription.[16]

In many aspects, the extreme right parties can be seen as antiparty-parties. They benefit from popular disillusionment with mainstream parties: "Crisis of representation, anti-elitism, corruption, the electorate's disaffection with established political parties and their policies"[17] are the vehicles of extreme right parties.[18] The most important aspects of the extreme right's agendas in Western Europe are immigration, anti-Semitism, rejection of multiculturalism, a racist representation of the nation ("Germany for the Germans—Foreigners Go Home" and "Austria First"), and welfare chauvinism (in practice, this means propagating the idea of reserving or prioritizing state-provided goods and benefits such as jobs, housing, and social payments only for people with national citizenship). These political agendas shared by extreme right parties admittedly do not yield a concise, clearly formulated *Weltanschauung* (they take various different forms in the respective countries and display specific national traits). What these parties do have in common, though, is a world view characterized by more or less concealed nationalism-chauvinism, anti-Semitic leanings or unabashed anti-Semitism, anti-Enlightenment thinking, national Darwinism, xenophobia, a party structure centered on a powerful leader, the demand for a strong state, and a political platform hostile to other races and ethnic groups.

All of these elements are present with some degree of prominence in the Haider-FPÖ. For example, a study conduced by Fritz Plasser and Peter Ulram revealed that the competence of the FPÖ for the issue "solving problems with foreigners" rose from 11% to 36% between 1990 and 1994, and that since 1992, the FPÖ has been ranked first among all political parties in respect to "solving problems with foreigners."[19] Welfare chauvinism is one of the main agenda points of the Haider-FPÖ's anti-foreigner policy: "One characteristic of this policy was to point out that foreigners would exploit the Austrian system of social welfare."[20] However, the FPÖ never produced any concrete proof for these assertions. Plasser and Ulram call this technique "political dichotomization by constructing concepts of an enemy"[21] ("scapegoat strategy") which can be successfully used to create xenophobia. Anti-Semitic remarks by FPÖ politicians are legendary.[22] A typically racist representation of the nation was the "Austria First" referendum initiated by the FPÖ in 1993, the primary goal of which was to mobilize anti-foreign attitudes.[23] Cautiously formulated, it would seem indicative of an overly constricted perspective when empirical social research comes to the conclusion that most of those who vote for the Haider-FPÖ do so as a form of protest and not for ideological reasons. In Austria, xenophobic political campaigns can call upon a considerable reservoir of prejudices against "foreigners," which "has been a necessary, though not sufficient, condition for Haider's electoral success."[24]

Besides incorporating the traditional elements of extreme right parties, the FPÖ has added a central agenda point that is unique among the new parties of the extreme right: the "defense of the war generation."[25] This substantive issue is connected with both the roots and the history of the FPÖ, as well as with the postwar history of Austria.

3. The History of the FPÖ in the Context of the Second Republic

If we review the history of the FPÖ, we see that references made by politicians of that party to ideological elements of National Socialism are in fact structural characteristics of the FPÖ worldview and not "verbal slip-ups," as those who wish to play down outrageous statements would have us believe. The FPÖ grew out of the *Verband der Unabhängigen* (Association of Independents, VdU),[26] which was founded in 1949 with the active assistance of the SPÖ. The Socialists hoped that the new movement—688,000 disenfranchised ex-NSDAP members were allowed to vote for the first time in the 1949 parliamentary elections —would split the bourgeois vote, cutting into the support for the ÖVP. The VdU also hoped to profit from this new block of voters, as its own functionaries were old Nazis, neo-Nazis, Pan-Germans, and a few liberals. The VdU received a respectable 12% of the 1949 vote and began to agitate for its main goal, the abolition of all laws governing de-Nazification procedures. The arguments the VdU employed to this end were a typical reversal of the perpetrator-victim dichotomy: the real victims were not those persecuted by the Nazi regime but those who had profited from acquiring Jewish property ("Aryanizers") and ex-members of the NSDAP, who had been prosecuted and punished on the basis of emergency legislation after 1945.

The fascism concept of the VdU was a crude version of the totalitarianism theory. Fascism was defined in a very general way as a dictatorship and the suppression of all dissent. As far as the VdU was concerned, Stalinism, Red Vienna of the interwar period, and even the post-1945 Second Republic were fascist since, now as before, Nazis (dissenters) were persecuted on the basis of emergency laws. Accordingly, the "real fascism" problem for the VdU was the de-Nazification policies pursued since 1945. Other kinds of fascism belonged to the past; the governments of the Second Republic represented the present fascist danger. By portraying anti-fascist laws or anti-fascist politicians as fascist, the VdU turned meaningful political concepts upside-down. The new party used this grotesque fascism concept to attack the de-Nazification policies of the government. In equating Nazism with other political systems, VdU spokesmen really played down the crimes of the Hitler regime. When the VdU spoke about fascism, it mentioned neither National Socialism nor the Holocaust, referring instead to the "positive sides" of German fascism, such as full employment and economic growth. When seen against this political background, notorious remarks made in recent times by Haider and his cohorts cannot be treated as "verbal slip-ups" but rather as being fully in the tradition of the FPÖ and its predecessor VdU. Haider's statement in the Carinthian provincial parliament about "the correct employment policies of the Third Reich," for example, were specified the following day by the FPÖ leader: "Just to make sure that there is no misunderstanding: What I said was just establishing the facts; namely, that in the Third Reich, an intensive employment policy led to the creation of many new jobs and so abolished the unemployment problem."[27]

Haider follows the same tradition when he answers the question as to the difference between Nazism and other dictatorships: "It is not my task to examine whether one form of dictatorship is more humane than another." When asked in an interview "Was the Nazi dictatorship the most inhumane?," Haider answered "You have passed that value judgment. I don't rate them."[28]

Nazi leitmotifs belong to the vocabulary of the FPÖ. In the spring of 2000, Ernest Windholz, the new chairman of the FPÖ in Lower Austria, thanked those officials who had elected him with the oath of allegiance of the Waffen-SS, "Our honor is loyalty" (*"Unsere Ehre heißt Treue"*). His sentence was greeted by enthusiastic applause. He later stated that he did not know the real meaning of the quotation. Haider's commentary: "It can't be wrong, if somebody confesses in decency, loyalty, honesty and performance."[29] Relativizing or playing down key elements of Nazism in different ways is part of the political ideology of the FPÖ.

Many of the FPÖ's leading functionaries over the years were previously members of the VdU. The FPÖ was formed as the successor organization of the VdU in 1955 after the proclamation of the Austrian State Treaty. The FPÖ had never been a normal *third party* like the German Liberals (FDP) or other small liberal parties in Western European countries. The FPÖ was also at least indirectly the successor of the Austrian NSDAP. The first chairman of the party was Anton Reinthaller, an illegal member of the NSDAP in the pre-1938 era and minister of agriculture, member of the Reichstag and SS-*Standartenführer* following the incorporation of Austria into Germany in March 1938. After his demise, the candidates for the election of FPÖ chairman were Hermann Neubacher, ex-mayor of Vienna in the Nazi era, Lothar Rendulic, ex-general of the Wehrmacht, and Friedrich Peter, SS-*Obersturmbannführer*. All candidates thus had a strong Nazi past. An undefined attitude to the Nazi past and an uninterrupted continuity to German nationalism also characterized the opinions of top FPÖ functionaries and the content of the party program (declaration of adherence to "the German cultural nation").

When SPÖ Chancellor Kreisky formed a minority government in 1970 with the support of the FPÖ, he appointed four ex-NSDAP members to ministerial posts. That was a signal to the FPÖ that the SPÖ, in order to gain power, would do business with former Nazis in a pragmatic way. Five years later Simon Wiesenthal disclosed that FPÖ leader Friedrich Peter had been a member of the First SS Brigade, a unit responsible for the murder of tens of thousands of civilians—mostly Jews—in the Soviet Union. Kreisky and with him the most prominent Socialists then unleashed a campaign of defamation against Wiesenthal, culminating in the charge that he had collaborated with the Gestapo.[30]

The case aroused international comment and severe criticism of Kreisky's behavior. While the controversy did not produce any international consequences in the 1970s, it played an essential part in demonstrating that Austria had a scandalous attitude to its Nazi past. It further contributed to the belief held in informed circles abroad that the country was not yet prepared to face up to that portion of its history in an honest way.

With the election of Haider as party leader in 1986, the FPÖ was led by a man who maneuvered skillfully between allusions and plain speaking in respect to the Nazi past. With regard to Wehrmacht soldiers during the Second World War, Haider said "they made the Europe as we know it today possible. If they had not resisted [Stalin], they would not have been in the East, if they had not fought, then we would have. ... "[31] ("*Hätten sie nicht Widerstand geleistet, wären sie nicht im Osten gewesen, hätten sie nicht die Auseinandersetzung geführt, dann hätten wir ...* ")

In answer to the question whether the German invasion of the Soviet Union was a war of conquest, Haider replied that one had to ask oneself nowadays "what is was really like back then."[32] He answered that very question the same year in a public speech before veterans of the Waffen-SS in Krumpendorf in Carinthia. Although the Waffen-SS had been condemned as a criminal organization at the Nuremberg Trials, Haider described its members as "decent individuals with character who stick to their beliefs despite strong opposition and remain true to them today as well. That is a good basis, my dear friends, for us younger people to inherit."[33]

Regarding the German invasion of the USSR as "a preventive war," admiring the strength of character and ideological loyalty of Waffen-SS members, describing concentration camps as labor camps, playing down the crimes of Nazism by equating it with other totalitarian regimes, all this belongs to Haider's standard repertoire. His views are shared and supported by the FPÖ as a whole. John Gudenus, now an FPÖ member of the Austrian second chamber (*Bundesrat*), said about the existence of gas chambers: "Gas chambers? I am not going to get involved in that! I believe everything which is dogmatically prescribed." ("*Gaskammern? Ich halte mich da raus! Ich glaube alles, was dogmatisch vorgeschrieben ist.* ")[34] In 1993, the FPÖ Member of Parliament Reinhard Gaugg defined the letters NAZI as "new, attractive, single-minded, and ingenious" ("*neu, attraktiv, zielstrebig, ideenreich* ").[35] Dieter Böhmdorfer, Haider's attorney and minister of justice in the present government, has expressed the opinion that one could not view Nazism "exclusively in the sense of all-out rejection."[36] The list of similar quotations from other FPÖ politicians is endless. Edmund Stoiber, the head of the Bavarian CSU and prime minister in that German province, while being one of the most ardent supporters of the present FPÖ-ÖVP government in Vienna, remarked recently that the kind of views expressed by FPÖ politicians on the Nazi past would force any German politician to resign on the same day.

Haider is a typical product of the FPÖ. As the son of parents who had been active Nazis,[37] he has stated to climb the FPÖ party hierarchy in his early youth, and he was by far Austria's longest serving political party chief. Haider is thus no more a *new* politician than the FPÖ is a *new* kind of party. Since 1949, the FPÖ and its predecessor, the VdU, have been an anti-system party in one key respect: They stood squarely in the political tradition of German nationalism, and—in stark contrast to the three founding parties of the Second Republic (ÖVP, SPÖ, and KPÖ)—vehemently rejected the "Magna Carta" of Austrian identity, the national foundational myth of Austria as the first victim of Nazi Germany. Accordingly, the FPÖ almost exclusively recruited its functionaries, its rank and file, and its grass-roots supporters from the German nationalist "community of believers" consisting of former National Socialists and Nazi sympathizers. When, in the 1970s, the SPÖ was forced to seek support for its government from the FPÖ, it signaled the effort that it was prepared to take a pragmatic approach (*pragmatische Haltung*) to the FPÖ's clientele of former Nazis; and at the same time, though, the SPÖ attempted to inflate the significance of the FPÖ's insubstantial liberal elements. The fact that this occurred while Friedrich Peter, a former member of the Waffen-SS, was FPÖ chairman is not without a certain amount of irony.

As a true dyed-in-the-wool politician possessing intimate knowledge of the FPÖ's inner circle, Haider recognized that neither the party's traditional German nationalist orientation nor the strained efforts by his predecessor as chairman, Norbert Steger, to make a liberal party out of the FPÖ would ever succeed in elevating it beyond the status of a fringe group attracting a mere 5% at the polls. The FPÖ seemed condemned to the role of insignificant coalition partner of one of the major parties —either the SPÖ or the ÖVP. Haider's putsch-like takeover of the FPÖ in 1986 was indeed highly undemocratic but nevertheless decisive for its political future and the transformation of the FPÖ into a "catch-all party." This brilliantly unscrupulous move by Haider laid the foundation of his image as "Jörg, the one who dares to do it," a slogan used by the FPÖ.

This tactics seemed to appeal to the FPÖ, a party organized according to the masculine social Darwinist principle of survival of the fittest, and one whose functionaries display corresponding mental structures.

Thereafter, Haider systematically eliminated all of his enemies and critics within the party. And in 1993, a group surrounding Heide Schmidt, his former party vice chair, broke away to found the Liberal Forum (LIF) together with a few other ex-FPÖ politicians. Since then, the FPÖ has been a classic *Führerpartei*. All of the FPÖ provincial organizations and party functionaries are directly dependent on Haider. One example *pars pro toto*: When, in 1998, Haider became dissatisfied with the FPÖ organization in the province of Salzburg, he directed his then-assistant Susanne Riess-Passer to simply dismiss all three hundred functionaries, and it was not until they humbled themselves and joined together in hymns of praise to Haider that he reversed his decision and just as promptly reinstated them.

Haider also recognized that the FPÖ's traditional German nationalist ideology constituted an impediment, preventing the party from attracting more voters. In the early 1990s, he simply abandoned this ideology in favor of an Austrian super-patriotism, and, in a move patterned after Newt Gingrich, drew up a "Contract with Austria."[38] At the same time, in order to enhance his vote-maximizing strategy, he put an end to the FPÖ's historical tradition of anti-clericalism and began currying favor with the fundamentalist wing of the Catholic Church. The protests within the party never went beyond the level of ineffectual grumbling.

Even Haider's tactical withdrawal in February 2000 to the position of governor of the province of Carinthia had no effect upon his omnipotence within the party. Susanne Riess-Passer, now by the grace of Haider vice chancellor in the coalition government, put it in a nutshell at the FPÖ Party Convention in May 2000: "The FPÖ is the party of Jörg Haider."[39]

4. Reasons for the Rise of the Haider-FPÖ

Haider's talent as an unscrupulous politician has not been the only reason for the party's success. The person of Jörg Haider was a necessary condition for the FPÖ's rapid rise over the last fifteen years, but is inadequate to completely explain it, since the realization of his charismatic drive to power within the arena of *Realpolitik* has required corresponding structural framework conditions. Since the mid-1980s these conditions were ideal for an opposition politician with an uninhibited, audaciously populist political style who was determined to really stir things up in the Austrian political system. At the end of the Kreisky Era in 1983, the SPÖ lapsed into a crisis; under the leadership of Fred Sinowatz, the party became a mere shadow of its former self. When in the fall of 1986 Haider took over the chairmanship of the FPÖ, the so-called small coalition between the SPÖ and the FPÖ came to an end. [40] The ensuing SPÖ – ÖVP coalition, however, soon acquired the image of a "coalition of losers." The *Neue Kronen Zeitung*, Austria's highest circulation daily paper, whose overwhelming influence upon national political life is unparalleled elsewhere in the world, cultivated this image and promoted Haider as the only politician capable of radically reforming the stultified Austrian political system. At the same time, the plot was thickening in the Waldheim Affair, and with it one of the central pillars of the Austrian postwar identity that had been promulgated by the Grand Coalition—the victim myth—was beginning to totter.[41] Social Partnership, the core element of Austro-corporatism that had stabilized the entire system up to that point, was jeopardized by the economic crisis of the mid-1980s.[42] The three political camps— Christian Social, Social Democratic, and German National—that had been solidly established in the interwar period, were beginning to break down.

To sum this all up: The victim myth, concordance democracy, the patronage system, the party state, corporatism, and social partnership— that is to say, the entire political system[43]—was undergoing destabilization. Additional momentum was imparted by the collapse of the bipolar world order—which, in turn, called Austrian neutrality into question—and by Austrian EU membership since the mid-1990s. University of Klagenfurt social psychologist Klaus Ottomeyer produced a short but remarkable paper in which he analyzed the political psychology with which Haider reacted to these systemic developments.[44] He proceeds under the assumption that it is not so much facts that engender this fascination with the Haider phenomenon, since they can be rationally perceived (such as unemployment or poverty statistics, according to which Austria continues to number among the world's ten richest nations). To a much greater extent, it is certain (social) psychological factors, products of the postmodern society, that become politically decisive under particular national conditions when someone like Haider

with a highly developed feel for the human subconscious instrumenta-
lizes them politically. Ottomeyer identifies three personae that Haider
stages with great virtuosity: "The first persona is a Robin Hood who
promises to take from the rich and powerful—for example, to scare the
beneficiaries of the Austrian *Proporz* system—and give to the poor. The
second persona is a male athlete who bears a certain resemblance to
Sylvester Stallone and who triggers a kind of infatuated, blinding
enthusiasm among men and women. The third persona is the 'beer tent
Socialist.' ... This figure, a regular guy you can pat on the back and
refer to familiarly as 'Jörgl,' gives people the illusory feeling that
society's class hierarchy has just been, or is about to be, transcended.
For many of those who sympathize with, vote for, or tolerate the FPÖ,
the three personae cited above mask the party's extreme rightist
component, which ... constitutes a dangerous reality ever-present in the
background. ... The overall picture of this *mise-en-scène* also includes
the 'smoke and mirrors' of inconsequential denials ... or even lies,
which are dished out to the public when the meanness and persecution
that emanates above all from this extreme rightist background become
all too visible."[45]

5. An Anti-System Party as a Governing Party in a Strategic Dilemma

For years, Haider never tired of making loud-mouthed predictions
of the year in which he would become Austrian chancellor. But despite
his prognoses, Haider did not become chancellor in 2000; rather, the
FPÖ became junior partner in a coalition government, and was immediately faced with a political dilemma. It is simply a difficult undertak-
ing for an extreme right party with a populist approach to politics to
successfully market itself as a governing party. Haider was clearly the
first to recognize this problem and to draw the obvious conclusions,
demoting himself to "simple party member" only three weeks into the
coalition. Formally, he withdrew to his function as governor of the
province of Carinthia, though of course without giving up his exclusive
grip on the reins of power in his party. Through this tactical move
Haider could avoid being identified with the government's neo-liberal
measures which were clearly directed against the weaker and more
vulnerable classes of society. In his role as "Robin Hood of Carinthia,"
riding forth from the Bärenthal, Haider attempted to continue
"oppositional activities" against the FPÖ-ÖVP federal government and

to keep up his personal image as the "advocate of the respectable and industrious." As far as his party is concerned, this has produced scant success, as the FPÖ's success at the polls declined—sometimes considerably—in all regional elections held since February 2000. The extent to which this has damaged Haider's own image indeed remains to be seen. It is breathtaking to witness how the FPÖ has appointed such absolute political dilettantes to ministerial posts (within ten months, the party saw itself forced to replace three ministers due to political incompetence), how it bombarded party critics with lawsuits, and with what unscrupulousness it has undertaken an exchange of elites in the most important social sectors in order to get to the feeding trough of power. And yet, opinion polls conducted after the FPÖ's first year in government have shown a considerable support decline in FPÖ support from 27% to about 20%.

The tactical and strategic options left open to the FPÖ are dwindling down to zero: If Haider breaks up the coalition, then the FPÖ's chances in new elections look bleak; if the party remains in the coalition, it can sit back and watch its grassroots support dry up from one election to the next. FPÖ politicians are left with the rather naïve, but, for them, characteristic hope: "Jörg will make everything turn out all right in the end."

6. Summary

After the first year of the FPÖ-ÖVP coalition, it is to be feared that the long-overdue "Westernization"[46] of Austria is turning into a "Westernization the Austrian way."[47] At least in the intermediate run, this development is heading in the direction of an amalgamation of neo-liberal economics with reactionary-provincial social policy measures. For the other EU member states, this represents neither a model to be followed nor a political threat to be feared. If the political developments in Austria have international significance, then as a cautionary tale illustrating what can happen when a bourgeois-conservative party obsessed with power decides to enter into a governmental coalition with an extreme right party. However, there have been historical precedents that were much more dangerous than the Alpine duo of Haider & Schüssel.

The Austrian democratic political culture, and especially the way it deals with National Socialism, is a world-class scandal and a shame. In the wake of the Waldheim Affair, the FPÖ's participation in the governing coalition is additional proof that Austria still has a long way to go before coming to terms with the past. This unwillingness of dealing with National Socialism is responsible for the fact that the Haider-FPÖ, despite having to permanently apologize for its inappropriate remarks about National Socialism, has not been stigmatized and excluded from the democratic political arena, but has rather increased its support for almost fifteen years. In Austria, however, coming to terms with the Nazi past in a meaningful fashion has hardly commenced, and a politician's career is not in jeopardy when he or she makes scandalous remarks on that subject. The political culture of Austria is such that as long as a politician does not actually break the law when commenting on National Socialism, his or her views thereon are of no consequence and have no consequences. Thus, there are no grounds for excluding from power a party whose leaders play down the criminal nature of National Socialism.

The Haider-FPÖ is a typical European extreme right party, although its comparatively spectacular political success is primarily an Austrian phenomenon. Austria's delayed nation-building process,[48] the country's underdeveloped democratic culture, the tendencies toward erosion that have marked the Austrian political system since the mid-1980s, the de facto print monopoly of a single daily newspaper, the SPÖ's lack of political and ideological orientation, the "institutionalized racism" that is also a component of the ÖVP and SPÖ policies,[49] and the ÖVP's unrestrained craving for power comprise the biotope that enables a political creature like Haider to thrive.

"Haiderism" is by no means an Austrian political export product. The successes of the Haider-FPÖ pose no danger to Europe, though they certainly do to Austria itself. The ÖVP has proven that it is prepared to drop any and all restraints when it comes to holding on to power. But the SPÖ, too, negotiated with the FPÖ in early 2000 and explored the FPÖ's readiness to tolerate an SPÖ minority government. Thus, in the near future it is not to be expected that either the ÖVP or the SPÖ will pursue a policy of fundamental exclusion toward the FPÖ similar to the way all French parties have closed ranks in refusing to enter into a coalition on any political level with the *Front National*. The French parties have shown how tightly the boundaries setting off extreme right parties can be drawn in a developed democratic culture, and how simple and effective it is to combat extreme right parties on this basis. After all, the strength of extreme right parties is directly related to the state of a country's democratic political culture.

In light of this, it is to be feared that Haider's FPÖ will remain for some time to come a key player in Austrian politics.

Notes

1. I use the term "Haider-FPÖ" for the following reasons: the Haider-FPÖ is a classic *Führerpartei*; the other FPÖ functionaries are, with few exceptions, mediocre, small-time politicians at best. If Haider would ever leave the party, the "FPÖ phenomenon" would vanish into thin air.

2. Article 7 of the Treaty of Nice provides that the EU Council, responding to a proposal by either one third of its member states, by the European Parliament, or by the EU Commission, and acting with a majority of four-fifths of its members, may determine that there is a "clear risk" of a serious breach of European principles by an EU member state. It would subsequently address "appropriate recommendations" to that state. However, the Treaty of Nice will take effect only after all national parliaments have ratified it; until then, the complicated body of rules in Article 7 remains a mere theoretical construction.

3. See *Süddeutsche Zeitung*, "Warnung vor Italiens Haider," 1 March 2001.

4. For a very good overview of the European extreme right parties (including those in the post-Communist countries) see Paul Hainsworth, ed., *The Politics of the Extreme Right. From the Margins to the Mainstream* (London: Pinter, 2000). However, with the exception of Hainsworth's general introduction, this work lacks a comparative perspective. It does include, though, an outstanding article on the FPÖ by Duncan Morrow, "Jörg Haider and the New FPÖ: Beyond the Democratic Pale?," 33-63. I hereby express my thanks to Reinhold Gärtner (Innsbruck) for having made this book available to me while I was writing this paper (it was not to be found in any scholarly library in Vienna). Due to the limited scope of this work, I am unable to address here the extreme right parties in the post-Communist countries, or the success at the polls of Christoph Blocher's extreme right party in Switzerland (*Schweizerische Volkspartei*, SVP). This party succeeded in raising its proportion of the vote from 15% to 22.5% in the October 1999 Swiss parliamentary elections.

5. Martin Blinkhorn, ed., "Introduction: Allies, Rivals or Antagonists? Fascists and Conservatives in Modern Europe," in *Fascists and Conservatives* (London: Unwin Hyman: 1990), 1-2.

6. For further discussion, especially of the relationship between fascism and the extreme right, see Roger Eatwell, *Fascism: A History* (London: Chatto and Windus, 1995); Piero Ignazi, "The Extreme Right in Europe: A Survey," in *The Revival of Right Wing Extremism in the 90s*, ed. Peter H. Merkl and Leonard Weinberg (London: Frank Cass, 1997) 47-64; Paul Wilkinson, *The New Fascists* (London: Grant McIntyre, 1981).

7. See Paul Hainsworth, ed., *The Extreme Right in Post-War Europe and the USA* (London: Pinter, 1992).

8. Piero Ignazi, "New Challenges: Post-materialism and the Extreme Right," in *Developments in West European Politics*, ed. Martin Rhodes (Basingstoke: Macmillan, 1997), 300-19.

9. Sebastian Reinfeldt, *Nicht-wir und Die-da. Studien zum rechten Populismus* (Vienna: Braumüller, 2000).

10. Hans-Georg Betz, "Introduction," in *The New Politics of the Right: Neo-Populist Parties and Movements in Established Democracies*, ed. Hans-Georg Betz and Stefan Immerfall (Basingstoke: Macmillan, 1998), 3.

11. Michael Minkenberg, "The New Right in France and Germany: *Nouvelle Droite, Neue Rechte*, and the New Right Radical Parties," in *The Revival of Right Wing Extremism*, 65-90.

12. L. Karvonen, "The New Extreme Right-Wingers in Western Europe: Attitudes, World Views and Social Characteristics," in *The Revival of Right Wing Extremism*, 91-110.

13. Paul Hainsworth, "Introduction: the Extreme Right," in *The Politics of the Extreme Right*, 8.

14. See Sonja Puntscher-Riekmann, "The Politics of *Ausgrenzung*, the Nazi-Past and the European Dimension of the New Radical Right in Austria," in *Contemporary Austrian Studies*, vol. 7, *The Vranitzky Era in Austria*, ed. Günter Bischof, Anton Pelinka, and Ferdinand Karlhofer (New Brunswick: Transaction, 1999), 91.

15. In 1995, Andreas Khol, current chairman of the ÖVP, responded to these objectives by characterizing the Haider-FPÖ as standing beyond the constitutional fringe.

16. Significantly, hardly any studies dealing with the FPÖ and other extreme right parties on a comparative basis have been produced to date. One exception is the collection published by Ruth Wodak et al., *Racism at the Top. Parliamentary Discourses on Ethnic Issues in Six European States*, vol. 2, *The Investigation, Explanation and Countering of Xenophobia and Racism* (Klagenfurt: Drava, 2000); and the essay by Jessika Ter Wal, "Anti-Foreigner Campaign in the Austrian Freedom Party and Italian Northern League: The Discursive Construction of Identity," in *The Haider Phenomenon*, ed. Anton Pelinka and Ruth Wodak (New Brunswick: Transaction Publishers, forthcoming).

17. Hainsworth, "Introduction", 9.

18. For the Haider-FPÖ see Fritz Plasser and Peter A. Ulram, "Trends and Ruptures: Stability and Change in Austrian Voting Behavior 1986-1996," *Contemporary Austrian Studies*, vol. 7, 41-43.

19. Fritz Plasser and Peter A. Ulram, "Wandel der politischen Konfliktdynamik: Radikaler Rechtspopulismus in Österreich," in *Wählerverhalten und Parteienwettbewerb. Analysen zur Nationalratswahl 1995*, ed. Wolfgang C. Müller et al. (Vienna: Signum, 1995), 477.

20. Reinhold Gärtner, "The FPOe, Foreigners and Racism in the Haider Era," in *The Haider Phenomenon*.

21. Plasser and Ulram, "Wandel der politischen Konfliktdynamik," 480.

22. See Brigitte Bailer-Galanda and Wolfgang Neugebauer, *Haider und die "Freiheitlichen" in Österreich* (Berlin: Elefanten Press, 1997), 96-98. In the spring of 2001, during the election campaign for Vienna, Haider made anti-Semitic jokes about the president of the Jewish Community of Vienna and provoked international reactions about his anti-Semitic statements.

23. See Ruth Wodak and Martin Reisigl, "The Petition Austria First 1992-93. A Discourse-Historical Analysis," in *The Semiotics of Racism*, ed. Ruth Wodak and Martin Reisigl (Vienna: Passagen Verlag, forthcoming).

24. Richard Mitten, "Austria all Black and Blue: Jörg Haider, the European Sanctions, and the Political Crisis in Austria," in *The Haider Phenomenon*.

25. Fritz Plasser and Peter A. Ulram, "Rechtspopulistische Resonanzen: Die Wählerschaft der FPÖ," in *Das österreichische Wahlverhalten*, ed Fritz Plasser et al. (Vienna: Signum, 2000), 225-41.

26. For a history of the VdU and the FPÖ see Brigitte Bailer and Wolfgang Neugebauer, "Die FPÖ: Vom Liberalismus zum Rechtsextremismus," in *Handbuch des österreichischen Rechtsextremismus*, ed. Stiftung Dokumentationsarchiv des Österreichischen Widerstandes (Vienna: Deuticke, 1994), 357-94.

27. *Morgen-Journal,* Ö1 (Austrian State Radio), 14 June 1991.

28. *Profil*, 18 February 1985.

29. *Falter* 27 (2000): 8.

30. See Ingrid Böhler, "Wenn die Juden ein Volk sind, so ist es ein mieses Volk. Die Kreisky-Peter-Wiesenthal-Affäre 1975," in *Politische Affären und Skandale in Österreich. Von Mayerling bis Waldheim*, ed. Michael Gehler and Hubert Sickinger (Vienna: Thauer, 1996), 502-31.

31. *Profil*, 21 August 1995.

32. Ibid.

33. *Profil*, 8 January 1996.

34. *Kurier*, 19 October 1995.

35. *Kurier*, 12 November 1993.

36. *Der Standard*, 11 April 2000.

37. See Christa Zöchling, *Haider. Licht und Schatten einer Karriere* (Vienna: Molden, 1999).

38. Anton Pelinka, "The FPÖ in the European Context. The Haider Phenomenon in Austria," in *The Haider Phenomenon*.

39. Cited from Klaus Ottomeyer, *Die Haider-Show. Zur Psychopolitik der FPÖ* (Klagenfurt: Drava, 2000), dust jacket blurb.

40. Anton Pelinka, *Kleine Koalition. SPÖ - ÖVP. 1983 - 1986* (Vienna: Böhlau, 1993).

41. Richard Mitten, *The Politics of Anti-Semitic Prejudice* (Boulder: Westview, 1992).

42. Emmerich Tálos, "Entwicklung, Kontinuität und Wandel der Sozialpartnerschaft," in *Sozialpartnerschaft: Kontinuität und Wandel eines Modells*, ed. Emmerich Tálos (Vienna: Manz, 1993), 11-34.

43. Anton Pelinka, *Austria. Out of the Shadow of the Past* (Boulder: Westview Press, 1998).

44. Ottomeyer, *Die Haider-Show*.

45. Ibid., 7-8.

46. Pelinka, *Austria*, 205-32.

47. Walter Manoschek, "FPÖ, ÖVP and Austria´s Nazi Past," in *The Haider Phenomenon*.

48. See Rainer Bauböck, "Constructing the Boundaries of the Volk. Nation-building and national populism in Austrian politics," in *The Haider Phenomenon*.

49. Peter Gstettner, concurring with Hans-Martin Lohmann, argues that an "extremism of the middle" has already taken root in Austria. See Peter Gstettner, "Die gefährliche Mischung des Jörg Haider: Rechtspopulismus plus Rassismus," in *Kurswechsel* 1 (2000): 97-107.

Austria's Welfare State:
Withering Away in the Union?

Gerda Falkner

1. Introduction

While the effects of EU membership on Austrian social policy basically confirm what has been expected (see below), it came as a surprise to most observers that EU social policy itself underwent a quite significant change, whose final effects are only to be seen in the future.

Since EU social policy evolved to such a large degree after the Austrian membership application and decision, it seems necessary to give the reader an overview on its overall development (section 2). Subsequently, the expectations and realizations of social aspects of EU adhesion concerning direct effects (3) and indirect effects (4) will be summarized. Then the implications of this shall be analyzed along different redistributive dimensions (5). The final section presents conclusions and an outlook.

2. The Development of EU Social Policy Before and After the Austrian Membership Decision

The 1957 EEC-Treaty did not directly provide for a Europeanization of social policies since too many delegations had opposed this.[1] It only contained a small number of concessions for the more *interventionist* delegations, notably the provisions on equal pay for both sexes (Art. 119, EEC-Treaty) and the establishment of a "European Social Fund" (Art. 123-128, EEC-Treaty). The other provisions of the EEC-Treaty's title III, *social policy*, were rather solemn statements that did not empower the EEC to act. "Underwriting this arrangement was the relative feasibility of nation-state strategies for economic development in the first decades after World War II. The common market, as it was constructed, was designed to aid and abet such national strategies, not transcend them."[2]

Where necessary or functional for market integration, intervention in the social policy field was nevertheless implicitly allowed, via the so-called subsidiary competence provisions (Art. 100 and 235, EEC-Treaty). They provided, from the 1970s onwards, a *backdoor* for social policy harmonization at the EU-level. The necessary unanimous council votes, however, constituted high thresholds for joint action. Accordingly, social regulation slowly became a corollary of the EC's market-making activities. During the 1970s a persistent pro-social-regulation advocacy coalition together with functional pressures brought about a number of spillovers[3] from market integration to social policy (which can only be crudely summarized here).[4]

In the field of *gender equality*, the European Court of Justice became a major actor with its extensive interpretation of Article 119 of the EEC-Treaty. Matters such as equal pay and equal treatment of men and women at the workplace were finally even regulated at the EU level in directives.[5] In the field of *labor law*, a number of directives were adopted during the late 1970s (on collective redundancies, on the transfer of undertakings, and on securing of workers' rights in cases of employer insolvency), and many more followed during the 1990s (worker information on conditions of work contract, working conditions of posted workers[6] and atypical workers,[7] parental leave, etc.).

By then, the Single European Act had already come into force as the first major EEC-Treaty revision (in 1987). Like in the 1950s, an economic enterprise had been at the heart of a fresh impetus for European integration. But while the Internal Market Program had been solemnly put on track by the European Commission and the governments, social policy had again constituted a controversial issue: How much social state building should go along with even more far-reaching market integration? In various, so-called *flanking* policy areas, notably environmental and research policy, EEC competence had been formally extended. Not so for social policy: the delegations had not been willing to give the EEC a greater role in this field. Only two exceptions had been made to this general rule. Art. 118b of the EEC-Treaty had provided that "[t]he Commission shall endeavor to develop the dialogue between management and labor at European level which could, if the two sides consider it desirable, lead to relations based on agreement." The second and crucial concession had been Article 118a of the EEC-Treaty on minimum harmonization related to health and safety of workers. This one had provided an escape route out of the unanimity requirement that had blocked EC social policy in many instances.[8] It had allowed, for the first time in European social policy, for directives based on only a qualified majority of the council members. This had been agreeable to all delegations because occupational health and safety was closely connected to the Internal Market.[9] Quite wrongly, the Thatcher government had not expected this perceivably *technical* issue to significantly facilitate social policy integration in the decade to come. In fact, the EEC increasingly intervened under the heading of *worker health and safety*. Directives included not only protection of workers exposed to emissions and loads, or protection against risks of chemical, physical, and biological agents at work (e.g. lead or asbestos).[10] Beyond these indeed more technical aspects, working conditions in a broader sense were also taken into consideration (e.g. working time).

Although this list of EC social activities may—against the background of an absent social policy agenda in the original treaties (as opposed to the later Maastricht and Amsterdam Treaties)—appear impressive at the first glance, the eclectic character of EC social policy is obvious if compared to national provisions. In the absence of a commonly accepted theory on which parts of the enterprises' *social costs* actually constitute a distortion of competition, the Community has pragmatically followed a step-by-step approach of suggesting selective harmonization of the disparate conditions which both enterprises and citizens find in the various member states of the Common Market. The Council, by contrast, often blocked directives suggested by the European Commission, at least before the Maastricht Treaty reforms.

As mentioned above, there has been a significant change in the character of E(E)C[11] social policy since Austria joined the EU, based on the Maastricht Treaty reforms. It is true that the crucial innovations of this 1991 treaty were already known when Austria negotiated its membership. However, they only came into legal force by November 1993 and did not have their full effect until they were integrated in the Amsterdam Treaty in late 1997. By the early 1990s, by contrast, EC social policy seemed in a complete stalemate.

This is why social policy was one of the crucial areas in the 1991 Intergovernmental Conference (IGC), set up to reform the EEC-Treaty. The originally envisaged extension of the provisions in the EEC social chapter could not be realized because of strong opposition from Great Britain. In order not to endanger the rest of the IGC's compromises, the UK was finally granted an exception (opt-out) from the social policy measures agreed on by the rest of the member states. In the *Protocol on Social Policy,* appended to the renewed EEC-Treaty, the other (then eleven) member states were authorized to have recourse to the institutions, procedures, and mechanisms of the treaty for the purposes of implementing their *Agreement on Social Policy.*[12]

This so-called *Social Agreement* represented a significant change in governance if compared to the earlier treaty provisions. There is now an explicit *Community competence* for a wide range of social policy issues, including working conditions, information and consultation of workers, equality between men and women with regard to labor market opportunities and treatment at work; and the integration of persons excluded from the labor market. Consequently, both the EU member states and the Community now share the power to act in the social realm. Action under the Social Agreement can in most areas even be taken under the supranational mode of *qualified majority voting*, e.g. in the area of information and consultation of workers as well as on working conditions. Unanimous decisions are restricted to social security and social protection of workers; protection of workers where their employment contract is terminated; representation and collective defense of the interests of workers and employers, including co-determination; conditions of employment for third-country nationals legally residing in Community territory; and financial contributions for the promotion of employment and job creation.

The Agreement in practice shows that the member states which had signed up for the Social Agreement were careful not to endanger the integration process as such, and had particular regard for the unity of EU law. Indeed, the Social Agreement was more frequently used as a legal basis only when it seemed highly probable that the UK would be bound by its effects as the new social directives came into force. The changes to the institutions and the financial consequences of the Agreement were kept as limited as possible.[13]

Nevertheless, to re-establish a single legal basis for EC social policy was a central social policy stake in the IGC in 1996-97 for all governments except the UK. The British government joined these ambitions after the defeat of the Conservatives by Labor in the elections of May 1997, and the inclusion of the Social Agreement into the EC-Treaty (TEC) was agreed on at the Amsterdam Council in June 1996. That this would change the character of EC social policy to a large extent was, however, not yet known when Austria reflected on whether or not to become a member.

3. Social Aspects of Austrian EU Adhesion:
Direct Effects in Theory and Practice

The specific character of EU social policy, as described above for the early 1990s, suggested that becoming an EU member would not legally require any major changes in the structure of the Austrian welfare state. The first reason was that by the early 1990s, the EU impinged only marginally in the most costly aspect of national welfare systems, i.e. social security. It is true that various principles restricted the individual member states' sovereignty over some welfare issues (above all, the freedom of movement of workers and equal treatment of EU-nationals at the workplace, as well as the co-ordination of national social security systems to assure the welfare of migrant workers). As long as these principles were respected, however, all basic characteristics of social security were left to be decided at the national level (most importantly, the number and type of insurance or benefit schemes, beneficiaries, as well as the type and level of allowances).[14]

The second reason an EU membership would not require major changes was that, while the EU's Council of Ministers had been more active in the field of labor law (see above), these measures were so eclectic that many issues of national labor law were not even touched. Furthermore, they typically followed the principle of minimum harmonization, so member states were allowed to keep or introduce higher standards at any point. Since Austria considered itself a particularly advanced welfare state, little attention was paid to these minimum standards and some were surprised when it became clear that various Austrian laws needed a lifting of standards in order to comply with EU social standards (see below).

Finally, a third reason why social policy played only a small role in the pre-accession debates was that most adaptations were needed and many indeed were already effectuated well before Austrian EU membership. It should be mentioned that the Agreement on the European Economic Area (in effect after 1 January 1994) had already covered most of the EU's social policy measures.

As a consequence of this state of affairs, it was uncontroversial among politicians as well as social scientists that the existing EU social laws would not directly impinge on the quality of the Austrian welfare state after EU accession. In actual fact, the only contested aspect in that regard concerned the prohibition of night work for women. While the Austrian Constitutional Court had only in early 1993 deemed the prohibition of female night work as constitutional and well-founded due to the presumed particular need for protection of women with double obligations (job and family), it is crucial to mention that most women's organizations actually did not consider abandoning this ban as a lowering of social standards. In any case, long before Austrian EU membership, the European Court of Justice had interpreted the Equal Treatment Directive's basic principle of equal working conditions to mean that a unilateral restriction of nightwork for women was discriminatory.[15] In principle, this had to be accepted as part of the EU law, but in the Austrian membership negotiations, an exception clause was agreed on with the EU. Therefore, the ban on nightwork for women would have to be abolished only by 2001.[16]

All other discrepancies between EU gender law and relevant Austrian provisions were not contested with a view to their progressive social character but, if at all, for their costs to employers. It should be mentioned that following a ruling of 6 December 1990 by the Austrian Constitutional Court on the discriminatory quality of unequal pension ages for women and men, a number of compensatory measures for women (whose pension age was subsequently lifted) were agreed on under the leadership of then Minister for Women Affairs Johanna Dohnal. In the framework of a so-called women's package, the equal treatment law was also reformed in December 1992. Since, in view of the European Economic Area and of possible later membership, EU rapprochement was already considered crucial, important parts of the EC's laws were incorporated into Austrian law already then.[17] This included the prohibition of indirect discrimination (unequal treatment on the basis of a presumably objective criterion that, in fact, disadvantages women more than men) and of unequal pay for work of equal value (as opposed to *equal work* only). While these were important improvements to the Austrian equal treatment legislation, it should be noted that other Austrian provisions (e.g. on gender neutral job offers and on a balanced quota in public service) were already more favorable for women than EU gender legislation. However, the legal adaptation to some details of EU legislation (most notably the amount of penalties for breach of the equal treatment principle) was not effectuated as and when it should have been.[18]

Other important aspects where labor law had to be adapted to EU standards include most notably health and safety at the workplace. The relevant EU directives went in part far beyond what was known in worker protection before Austrian membership, e.g. concerning digital display units. How to implement these rules raised manifold conflicts between parties and social partners. A relevant law would long have been required for the European Economic Area but did not come into force until EU membership.[19]

4. Social Aspects of Austrian EU Adhesion:
Indirect Effects in Theory and Practice

As outlined above, the expectation that existing EC social laws would not harm Austrian social standards (but rather improve some) was not controversial at all. By contrast, two other issues were extremely contested in the Austrian pre-membership debate: the role of decision gaps in EU social policy (1), and the social relevance of EU policies outside the proper social policy realm and their impact on national social policy-making (2). The contested issues hence concerned social *political* aspects in the wider sense, in contrast to the narrower perspective of looking exclusively at the standards of EU social *law*.

1) Some argued that it was necessary to look not only at what the EC did in social policy, but also at what it didn't do (or: had not done, by then).[20] This referred above all to the fact that the Internal Market Program effectuated economic liberalization without always securing that corresponding social provisions were also in place. The most frequently cited example was the question of which labor law to apply in cases of posted workers. Should Portuguese construction workers on German sites be paid according to Portuguese rules? If so, the German economy (just like the Austrian and others) would suffer from significant competitive disadvantages, and workers at the same construction site would be treated unequally because of their nationality. This problem had not been regulated in a satisfactory way under the various EU and international rules. Nevertheless, the relevant 1991 European Commission proposal was blocked in the Council until well after Austrian membership.

Another example for a side effect of the Internal Market on social policy, which was not counterbalanced by EU social policy for a long time, was the issue of European works councils (institutions for enterprise-level information and consultation of workers). With increased Europeanization, the national laws on worker information and consultation had de facto become void of substance. Transnational enterprises escaped from their scope because their important decisions were taken outside the national realm. Therefore, only *European* works councils could guarantee that the status quo ante of worker participation was being upheld in the unified European market. Nevertheless, a Commission draft directive from 1980(!) was waiting to be adopted until late 1994.[21]

Although the issue of decision gaps in EU social policy[22] was much debated within the EU,[23] it was not always welcome to bring it up within Austria, where the government had adopted a strategy based on overt advertising for EU membership and not on discussing those aspects where the EU's performance may possibly not (yet) have been optimal. In this context, the publication of an intense 550 page study on various potential social policy effects of EU membership, elaborated for the Austrian Ministry of Labor and Social Affairs, was not allowed.[24]

After a two-thirds majority of the Austrian population opted for EU membership in the referendum of 12 June 1994, both the directives on posted workers and on European works councils were adopted. The new possibility for majority voting in many social affairs and the new decision rules involving the EU-level social partners (adopted in Maastricht without the UK and extended in the Amsterdam Treaty to all member states) had the effect of finally unblocking almost all Commission draft directives that had not been adopted during the 1980s and early 1990s.[25] Despite the *Euro-sceptic* initial assessments of most academic commentators,[26] the social dimension of the Internal Market as developed by the European Commission was finally implemented[27]-- although with great delay compared to the economic liberalization program.

2) Another very contested aspect in the discussion of the social consequences of an Austrian EU membership was the potential relevance of EU policies outside the proper social policy realm for national social policy-making. In particular, this concerned the liberalization and competition-oriented character of most European integration measures which might draw attention to possible competitive disadvantages stemming from higher social costs. It might also reinforce the public discourse on social spending cuts, which continued to be enforced despite an ever growing economic prosperity and which, in the end, only served the well-to-do.[28] The discussion also raised the issue of the Maastricht convergence criteria for Economic and Monetary Union which pointed to the harmonization of monetary and fiscal indicators without paying attention to other classic macro-economic policy goals, notably employment rates.[29]

Although the need for budgetary consolidation had already been widely acknowledged in Austria during the early 1990s, the additional external justification of the EU membership was necessary to push through the specific short-term consolidation measures adopted during the second half of the 1990s. As an EU member, Austria was suddenly under the critical supervision of the European Commission and the other member states' governments. That the Austrian government wanted to be among the first countries to join the Economic and Monetary Union also created an immediate need for cutting the budget deficit from 6.2% of Gross Domestic Product (GDP) (1995) to the mere 3% allowed by the Maastricht criteria. The public debt had to be brought down from 69.2% (1995) to 60%. However, while the EU was clearly useful as an external justifier for budgetary consolidation, one should also keep in mind that "an appreciable part of the high budget deficit recorded in 1995 was attributable to the costs of accession; according to Commission estimates, around 2 percentage points of the total 5.2 percent deficit."[30]

Already in 1995 and 1996, two *austerity packages* were adopted by the then grand coalition government of Social Democrats and Christian Democrats. These packages consisted of some hundred measures touching key aspects of social policy (without, however, changing the structure of Austria's welfare state itself). In some cases, these measures hit low income earners, the unemployed, and single mothers particularly hard, while transfer payments which also benefited those with higher incomes (like subsidies for owned housing, some family transfers) were hardly touched at all.[31] Quite obviously, though, it is not possible to measure the influence of EU policies in this process or to know which strategies for budgetary consolidation Austrian actors would possibly have chosen outside the Union.

5. Developments Along Different
Redistributive Dimensions

According to the classic definition by T.H. Marshall, social policy is the use of political power to supersede, supplement, or modify operations of the economic system in order to achieve results which the economic system would not achieve on its own.[32] More specifically, in a welfare state such operations include the redistribution of money, rights, or influence. By differentiating explicitly between various lines of redistribution in the Austrian welfare state, it may be easier to summarize the effects of Europeanization on Austria five years after her entry into the EU.

The most crucial dimensions along which one can conceptualize the impact of the EU on the Austrian welfare state seem to be the following: redistribution between high income and low income earners (1), between employers and employees (2), between the employed and the unemployed (3), between the sexes (4), and between generations (5).[33]

(1) Redistribution between *high income and low income earners* can primarily be captured in terms of the level of financial transfers in cases of unemployment or lack of income for other reasons (e.g. invalidity). It is very difficult (and impossible in this chapter) to quantify the changes effectuated during recent years, aggregating across different insurance systems and individual benefits. As mentioned above, however, it is clear that Austrian austerity packages have included some measures that particularly effected the poorer part of the population (e.g. reduced levels of and restricted access to unemployment compensation, increased co-payment levels in health care, non-valorization of benefits in the general care allowance system). Furthermore, the proportion of Austrian wealth spent for social welfare has been decreasing since the mid-1990s (1995: 29.8%; 1998: 28.5%).[34] While this was in practice a choice taken at the national level, commentators argued that this choice might not have been politically feasible without the external justifier provided by the Maastricht convergence criteria.[35] The EU itself has no binding rules on how to fight poverty and social exclusion, only a number of recommendations (from the early 1990s) and some discussion documents (rapidly increasing in recent years).

(2) Concerning the relationship between *employers and employees*, EU intervention touches on the dimension of employee rights and protection. As outlined above, a number of specific standards of worker protection had to be lifted during the implementation of relevant EC directives (notably in the field of health and safety at the workplace, and concerning parental leave, working time, and other working conditions). In all these fields, dense national rules had already existed in Austria. Although they often went beyond what was demanded by the relevant EU counterparts, amendments were needed to comply with higher EU standards in some particular details. Furthermore, some specific new rights were created at the EU level, most notably, the right to be informed about and consulted on important enterprise-related decisions if one is employed in a multinational enterprise (as defined in the relevant EU directive on the European works councils). While all these aspects improved rights or created new ones for employees, they also accounted for higher corresponding costs for employers.

Beyond this, there are also the indirect effects of EU membership which are hard to measure. In any case, multiple examples show that Austrian employer representatives cite lower standards and lower costs in other countries within the EU's Internal Market in order to gain savings at home—as the highest government official in the field had feared before membership.[36] While outright cutbacks seem not to have occurred so far,[37] it is impossible to know for sure how much this pressure affected the level of Austrian labor law via potential advances that were not realized. When this essay was written (2000), the new center-right government had just moved the competencies for worker protection from the social to the economic ministry, and cutbacks were on the agenda.

(3) Another important dimension of de facto redistribution in modern welfare states is that between the *employed and the unemployed.* This refers to efforts to create jobs and to improve placement services to speed up transfer into employment. As expected, EU membership brought about beneficial effects in terms of overall budgetary means. Since the European Social Fund (ESF) co-finances the active labor market policies of all member states, accession to the EU led to an increase in the resources available for such projects.[38] At the same time, the leeway for unilateral national action withered away since the major part of domestic funds had to be used for co-funding projects accepted under the ESF schemes.[39]

Since Austria almost directly adopted the EU's priorities, the Union's innovative employment policy, which in recent years went hand in hand with ESF activity, became very important. The 1997 Amsterdam Treaty added a chapter on employment policy to the EC-Treaty. Articles 125 to 130 now specify how the "Member states and the Community shall … work towards developing a coordinated strategy for employment and particularly for promoting a skilled, trained and adaptable workforce and labor markets responsive to economic change." The member states "shall regard promoting employment as a matter of common concern and shall coordinate their action in this respect within the Council."[40] Without transferring any specific powers to the Council of Ministers, this provision aims to redirect the member states' hitherto largely independent actions towards mutual adaptation. This is encouraged in a coordination procedure (set out in Article 128 EC-Treaty) that was already informally practiced before the Amsterdam Treaty (in the so-called Essen process[41]).

The European Council now monitors the employment situation in the Community, and draws its conclusions from a joint annual report by the Council and the Commission. On the basis of these conclusions, the EC Council of Ministers draws up guidelines to be followed by the member states. Subsequently, each member state must report "the principal measures taken to implement its employment policy in the light of" the Council's guidelines for employment.[42] The Council examines whether the member states implement policies according to the guidelines for employment; the Council then may make recommendations to member states "if it considers it appropriate in the light of that examination."[43] The joint annual report by the Council and the Commission to the European Council, concerning the employment situation in the Community and the implementation of the guidelines for employment, closes the cycle by serving as the relevant input for the next annual employment policy conclusions of the European Council.

According to a decision taken at the so-called Luxembourg Jobs Summit in November 1997, the European employment strategy is built on four main pillars: employability, entrepreneurship, adaptability, and equal opportunities. Every year, a set of guidelines are adopted for each of the pillars, which set out a number of specific targets for member states to achieve in their employment policies. These employment policy guidelines are transposed into concrete and administrative measures by each member state through a National Action Plan for Employment (NAP). [44]

On the one hand, Austria welcomed all these activities as a fresh impetus for her labor market and employment policy. On the other hand, money for activities outside the EU priorities became ever scarcer. At the same time, the quality of some retraining and reintegration measures seemed to suffer, at least in some instances. The new framing of employment policy in terms of employability, the goal of including at least 20% of all unemployed in retraining measures (in principle a good strategy), and the obligation to report periodically on achievements and current unemployment figures may have prompted a system in which ever more long-term unemployed are included in ever more short-term training programs with ever less practical effect (except for erasing those covered by such programs from the statistic of long-term unemployment).

(4) Concerning redistribution between the *sexes*, both rights and money (notably via the social security systems) are crucial. Equal treatment rights are granted in various EC labor law directives. They

have brought important innovations to the Austrian *status quo* (see above). Redistribution of wealth is more difficult to analyze along the gender dimension. However, commentators point to the fact that various aspects (e.g. in the pension reforms) of the austerity packages were exercised with a view to budget consolidation work to the detriment of women, in particular.[45]

(5) Redistribution between *generations* happens notably via the pension system. The EU has, at least to date, no binding rules in this field (exceptions concern the aspects of non-discrimination, in particular of other EU nationals, and women). As outlined above, the various austerity packages, which aimed at (and succeeded in) propelling Austria to become an early member of the Economic and Monetary Union, included some important reforms in this area. However, it should be mentioned that spending on the elderly has extremely increased both before EU adhesion and after, due mainly to demographic factors. Considering that the Austrian government's net spending on the elderly is roughly twice its overall deficit and approximately one fifth of the central government's budget (some 38 percent of all social expenditure),[46] and that Austria is thus well above the average EU spending in this field,[47] steps to close this gap are considered indispensable. The misbalance between the generations can hardly be denied even by those who try to block reforms. This makes the role of the EU in legitimating these changes seem smaller than, for example, with the redistribution between rich and poor.

6. Conclusions and Outlook

All in all, the effects of EU membership on the Austrian welfare state did not bring any major surprises within the first five years. Rather, *de facto* developments confirmed scholarly expectations. One surprise was that the EC was, after all, capable of closing the labor law gaps created by the initial lack of *social dimension* in the Internal Market Program of the mid-1980s.[48] In any case, the basic setup of national social policy was not touched upon, as expected and discussed before 1995. Some labor law standards had to be lifted in order to comply with EU norms, but most aspects of Austrian social law stayed as they were. The more indirect effects on the national welfare state cannot be analyzed as easily as the direct ones. In instances such as those outlined above, EU policies outside the narrow realm of the *social* have a certain impact on national welfare issues. However, it is impossible to discern the exact degree of this influence (as opposed to the changes in national ideology or government, internationalization in general, or the changes in national demand due to different circumstances, e.g. demographics). One cannot really know what kind of budgetary reform the Austrian grand coalition government, in office during the first five years of EU membership, would have adopted if the EU had not provided an external *justifier*. One can only try to analyze the discourses observable before and after 1995, but no *hard* scientific method is available. Just because these indirect effects cannot be analyzed scientifically, though, it would be a mistake to simply ignore their existence at all.

It is important to stress that even at the turn of the millennium national influences are still much more decisive in welfare state reform than supranational ones. In other words, a national government with preferences other than welfare and social justice can induce many more relevant changes than the EU membership could bring about. As I pointed out almost a decade ago, this policy would even be easier within the EU. The EU's rather neo-liberal bias can help to justify such measures, and its non-transparent character can serve to blur real responsibility. (The EU can easily be used for such blame avoidance since the distribution of competencies, especially but not exclusively in social policy, is not transparent for the uninitiated.) Finally, such a government can block many social policy initiatives at the EU level, either alone (where unanimity is still the rule) or with ready coalition partners, such as the UK. While EU membership *per se* never constituted a profound danger to the national welfare state (for most problematic issues appropriate measures for countersteering seemed, at least potentially, available), the twin conditions of EU membership and a welfare-adverse national government in Austria could easily alter the traditional social policy balance in a profound manner.[49]

For this reason, the forthcoming five years of EU membership may possibly be more interesting to watch than the last ones. This is further underlined by the latest developments in the so-called *social dimension of European integration*. Currently, the preferred method of EU intervention in social affairs (in the wider sense) is changing rather fundamentally. As previously outlined through the example of employment policy, other means than regulative action are now being employed, and similar patterns shall be used for fighting poverty and for social security reform. This new method of *open coordination* is based on benchmarking, advertising best practice, establishing hegemonic discourses, and peer pressure at the EU level, but leaves regulative action to the national and sub-national levels. What actually results from such "neo-voluntaristic"[50] social policy-making in terms of concrete actions crucially depends, once again, on the individual national governments. For better or for worse (and this will differ from country to country), the EU will help the specific governments in office to more easily effectuate reforms, even against the protest of some national interests.

Notes

1. For a background on these negotiations and the opposing camps of neo-liberal marketers (notably in the German delegation) versus social-interventionists (predominantly in the French delegation) see for example Bengt Beutler et al., *Die Europäische Union. Rechtsordnung und Politik,* 4ᵗʰ ed. (Baden-Baden: Nomos, 1993).

2. George Ross, "Assessing the Delors Era and Social Policy," in *European Social Policy: Between Fragmentation and Integration,* ed. Stephan Leibfried and Paul Pierson (Washington, DC: The Brookings Institution, 1995), 360.

3. In a simple formulation by Ernst Haas, the *founding father* of neo-functionalism, "spillover" refers to a situation where "policies made in carrying out an initial task and grant of power can be made real only if the task itself is expanded." See Ernst B. Haas, *Beyond the Nation-State. Functionalism and International Organization* (California: Stanford University Press, 1964), 111.

4. For more details see for example Gerda Falkner, "European Integration and Social Policy: Between Stalemate and Spillover," in *The European Yearbook of Comparative Government and Public Administration,* ed. Joachim Jens Hesse and Theo A.J. Toonen (Baden-Baden: Nomos, 1997).

5. Catherine Hoskyns, *Integrating Gender* (London: Verso, 1996); Gerda Falkner, *Supranationalität trotz Einstimmigkeit? Entscheidungsmuster der EU am Beispiel Sozialpolitik* (Bonn: Europa Union Verlag, 1994).

6. E.g. Portuguese construction workers building houses in Belgium.

7. Part-time, fixed-term and temporary workers who, according to the new directives, may not be discriminated.

8. An extensive use of this provision was possible mainly because the wording and the definition of key terms of Article 118a were all but unequivocal.

9. If all goods should circulate freely, there has to be some common policy with a view to the security of those goods which are later on used in factories (e.g. machines) and constitute an important factor of human security. The elimination of "technical barriers to trade" made Community action attractive in the perception of relevant policy-makers; see Otto Schulz, *Maastricht und die Grundlagen einer Europäischen Sozialpolitik* (Cologne: Heymans, 1996), 18f.

10. Gerhard Schnorr and Johann Egger, "European Communities," in *International Encyclopaedia for Labour Law and Industrial Relations Supplement,* ed. Roger Blanpain (Deventer/Boston: Kluwer Law and Taxation, 1990), 82.

11. Note that the European Economic Community (EEC) was renamed European Community (EC) in the Maastricht Treaty, which also introduced the encompassing name European Union (EU) for all three European communities.

12. For details see Gerda Falkner, *EU Social Policy in the 1990s: Towards a Corporatist Policy Community* (London: Routledge, 1998).

13. In fact, the British members of all institutions except the council kept their full rights even under the Social Agreement. Despite a "technical solution" to the problem of potentially administering a part of the EC budget without UK contributions, no financial consequences of the Social Agreement occurred; see Gerda Falkner, "Das Maastrichter Sozialprotokoll: Differenzierte Integration wider Willen," in *Zur Zukunft flexibler Integration in Europa: Einheit oder "Europe à la Carte"?*, ed. Fritz Breuss and Stefan Griller, *Schriftenreihe der ECSA-Austria* (Vienna: Springer, 1998)

14. On indirect pressures in these fields see Stephan Leibfried and Paul Pierson, "Social Policy. Left to Court and Markets?," in *Policy-Making in the European Union*, ed. Helen Wallace and William Wallace, *The New European Union Series* (Oxford: Oxford University Press, 2000).

15. Judgement C-345/89; see for example Birgitt Haller, "Zwischen Paternalismus und 'Gleichmacherei' - Frauennachtarbeit im europäischen Vergleich," *Österreichische Zeitschrift für Politikwissenschaft* 22, no. 3 (1993): 277-90.

16. See for example Ingrid Mairhuber, "Gleichbehandlungs- und Frauenförderpolitik: Zu große Erwartungen oder frauenpolitischer Backlash?," in *EU-Mitglied Österreich. Gegenwart und Perspektiven: Eine Zwischenbilanz*, ed. Emmerich Tálos and Gerda Falkner (Vienna: Manz, 1996).

17. See for example Gerda Falkner, "Österreichische Gleichbehandlungspolitik und das EU-Recht," in *Frauenbericht 1995* (Vienna: Bundesministerium für Frauenangelegenheiten, 1995): 416022; Mairhuber, "Gleichbehandlungs- und Frauenförderpolitik."

18. Falkner, "Österreichische Gleichbehandlungspolitik und das EU-Recht."

19. See for example European Industrial Relations Review (EIRR), ed. Andrew Brode (London), 259/25.

20. Gerda Falkner, *Die Sozial- und Arbeitsmarktpolitik der Europäischen Gemeinschaft und ihre Auswirkungen auf Österreich im Fall eines Beitritts* (Vienna: Bundesministeriums für Arbeit und Soziales, 1992), 377-480; see also various authors in Klaus Firlei, ed., *Soziales Risiko EG?* (Salzburg: Kammer für Arbeiter und Angestellte für Salzburg, 1991).

21. For the genesis and contents of the European Works Councils Directive see for example Gerda Falkner, "European Works Councils and the Maastricht Social Agreement: Towards a New Policy Style?," *Journal of European Public Policy* 3, no. 2 (1996): 192-208.

22. For the concept of a "joint decision trap" see Fritz W. Scharpf, "The Joint-Decision Trap: Lessons from German Federalism and European Integration," *Public Administration* 66, no. 3 (1988): 239-278; for the "corporatist decision gap" see Wolfgang Streeck, "Politikverflechtung und Entscheidungslücke. Zum Verhältnis von zwischenstaatlichen Beziehungen und sozialen Interessen im europäischen Binnenmarkt," in *Die Reformfähigkeit von Industriegesellschaften. Fritz W. Scharpf - Festschrift zu seinem 60. Geburtstag*, ed. Karlheinz Bentele, Bernd Reissert, and Ronald Schettkat (Frankfurt: Campus, 1995), 101-30; for a discussion of both concepts with a view to EC social policy see: Falkner, EU *Social Policy in the 1990s.*

23. See for example Wolfgang Däubler, ed., *Sozialstaat EG? Die andere Dimension des Binnenmarktes* (Gütersloh: Verlag Bertelsmann Stiftung, 1989); Franz Steinkühler, ed., *Europa '92 - Industriestandort oder sozialer Lebensraum* (Hamburg: VSA-Verlag, 1989); Eliane Vogel-Polsky, "Maastricht ou la voie étroite du social," in *Quelle union sociale européenne?*, ed. Mario Telò (Bruxelles: Editions de l'Université de Bruxelles, 1994).

24. Falkner, "Die Sozial- und Arbeitsmarktpolitik."

25. For a detailed overview see Falkner, *EU Social Policy in the 1990s.*

26. See in particular Berndt Keller, "European Integration, Worker's Participation, and Collective Bargaining: A Euro-Pessimistic View," in *Convergence or Diversity? Internationalization and Economic Policy Response*, ed. Brigitte Unger and Frans van Waarden (Hants/Avebury: Aldershot, 1995), 252-77.

27. Gerda Falkner, "EG-Sozialpolitik nach Verflechtungsfalle und Entscheidungslücke: Bewertungsmaßstäbe und Entwicklungstrends," *Politische Vierteljahresschrift* 41, no. 2 (2000): 279-301.

28. Klaus Busch, *Umbruch in Europa. Die ökonomischen, ökologischen und sozialen Perspektiven des einheitlichen Binnenmarktes*, 2nd ed. (Cologne: Bund-Verlag, 1992).

29. See for example Alexander Van der Bellen, "Budget: Entgleisung im Schatten von Maastricht," in *EU-Mitglied Österreich. Gegenwart und Perspektiven: Eine Zwischenbilanz*, ed. Emmerich Tálos and Gerda Falkner (Vienna: Manz, 1996); Klaus Busch, "Europäische Integration und Tarifpolitik. Lohnpolitische Konsequenzen der Wirtschafts- und Währungsunion," (Cologne: Bund Verlag, 1994), Gerda Falkner, "Perspektiven der und Alternativen zur Sozialpolitik in der Europäischen Wirtschafts- und Währungsunion," in *Europäische Integration nach ökologischen und sozialen Kriterien (Sonderheft der Zeitschrift Kurswechsel)* (Vienna: Beirat für wirtschafts,- gesellschafts- und umweltpolitische Alternativen, 1994).

30. Emmerich Tálos and Christoph Badelt, "The Welfare State between New Stimuli and New Pressures: Austrian Social Policy and the EU," *Journal of European Social Policy* 9, no. 4 (1999): 354; Van der Bellen, "Budget: Entgleisung im Schatten von Maastricht," 128.

31. Tálos and Badelt, "The Welfare State between New Stimuli and New Pressures," 355.

32. See for example Paul Pierson and Stephan Leibfried, "Multitiered Institutions and the Making of Social Policy," in *European Social Policy: Between Fragmentation and Integration*, ed. Stephan Leibfried and Paul Pierson (Washington, DC: The Brookings Institution, 1995), 3.

33. A quite different category, which could nevertheless be framed in terms of *redistribution* (i.e. redistribution in terms of the political power balance), runs between labor and capital as organized groups. For the effects of EU membership on Austrian corporatism see Gerda Falkner, "How Pervasive Are Euro-Politics? Effects of EU Membership on a New Member State," *Journal of Common Market Studies* 38, no. 2 (2000): 223-50; Gerda Falkner, "Korporatismus auf österreichischer und europäischer Ebene: Verflechtung ohne Osmose?," in *Sozialpartnerschaft: Wandel und Reformfähigkeit*, ed. Ferdinand Karlhofer and Emmerich Tálos (Vienna: Signum, 1999): 215-40; Tálos and Badelt, "The Welfare State between New Stimuli and New Pressures"; Bernhard Kittel and Emmerich Tálos, "Interessenvermittlung und politischer Entscheidungsprozeß: Sozialpartnerschaft in den 1990er Jahren," in *Zukunft der Sozialpartnerschaft: Veränderungsdynamik und Reformbedarf*, ed. Ferdinand Karlhofer and Emmerich Tálos (Vienna: Signum, 1999), 95-136. In addition to the dimensions outlined above, Marshall's wide definition of *social policy* would also include redistribution between regions within the EU, but in most academic settings this falls within the realm of regional policy (not social policy) and cannot be included here. For more information on this topic see Gabriele Tondl, "Regionalpolitik: Neue Impulse durch die EU-Strukturfonds," in *EU-Mitglied Österreich. Gegenwart und Perspektiven: Eine Zwischenbilanz*, ed. Emmerich Tálos and Gerda Falkner (Vienna: Manz, 1996), 165-83.

34. *Der Standard,* 20 October 2000.

35. Tálos and Badelt, "The Welfare State between New Stimuli and New Pressures," 354.

36. Eva-Elisabeth Szymanski, "Arbeitnehmerschutz und EG-Recht," in *Österreichisches Arbeitsrecht und das Recht der EG*, ed. Ulrich Runggaldier (Vienna: Orac, 1990), 317.

37. That is, such cutbacks have not occurred on the legal level, and it is impossible to evaluate here the practice of controlling the application of norms.

38. Tálos and Badelt, "The Welfare State between New Stimuli and New Pressures," 356; Ehrenfried Natter, "Arbeitsmarktpolitik: Erweiterung und Veränderung durch den Europäischen Sozialfonds," in *EU-Mitglied Österreich. Gegenwart und Perspektiven: Eine Zwischenbilanz*, ed. Emmerich Tálos and Gerda Falkner (Vienna: Manz, 1996), 184-200.

39. Natter, "Arbeitsmarktpolitik," 195.

40. Article 126 paragraph 2 TEC.

41. See for example Stefan Griller et al., *The Treaty of Amsterdam. Facts, Analysis, Prospects*, vol. 15, *Series of the Research Institute for European Affairs* (Vienna: Springer, 2000), 527-48.

42. Article 128 paragraph 3 TEC.

43. Ibid.

44. The Joint Annual Reports, the Employment Guidelines, the National Action Plans for Employment, and the European Employment Pact launched at the 1999 Cologne Summit are published on the Commission Directorate General V homepage (http://europa.eu.int/comm/dg05/empl&esf/ees_en.htm).

45. Tálos and Badelt, "The Welfare State between New Stimuli and New Pressures," 355; Mairhuber, "Gleichbehandlungs- und Frauenförderpolitik," 233.

46. For further references see Tálos and Badelt, "The Welfare State between New Stimuli and New Pressures," 354. See also *Der Standard*, 20 October 2000.

47. *Der Standard*, 20 October 2000.

48. Falkner, "EG-Sozialpolitik," 290-2.

49. Falkner, "Die Sozial- und Arbeitsmarktpolitik," 505.

50. Wolfgang Streeck, "Neo-Voluntarism: A New European Social Policy Regime?," *European Law Journal* 1, no. 1 (1995): 31-59.

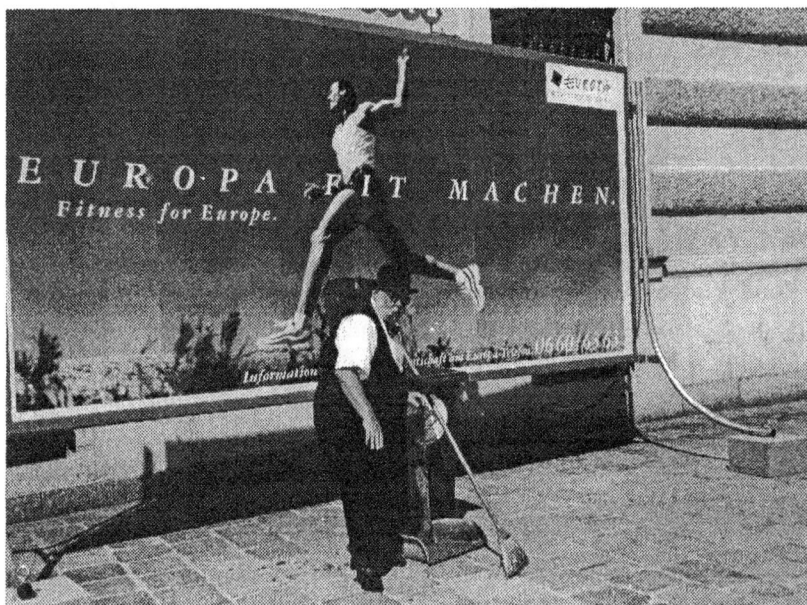

Good times in Europe - Austria's advertisement campaign for Europe during the Austrian EU-Presidency (photo Harald Hofmeister, *Die Presse*)

"Preventive Hammer Blow" or Boomerang?
The EU "Sanction" Measures against Austria 2000[1]

Michael Gehler

I. Introduction and Historical Background

The focus of this article is not the question of whether Jörg Haider is a right-wing populist, which is clearly the case, nor how he can effectively be confronted, which is the task of politics. It will deal with the motivations, attitudes, reactions, and consequences of the political and state representatives of the fourteen EU member states (hereafter referred to as "the EU 14") toward the emerging and completed formation of an ÖVP (Austrian People's Party)-FPÖ (Freedom Party of Austria) government in February 2000. In addition, it will discuss the behavior of the EU acting as a structure with multiple institutions.

The basic thesis which I would like to advocate is that Austria itself was also a pretext for the policy of "sanction" measures, and that the reasons for the measures of the fourteen Union states are not to be found primarily in the actions of the Socialist International as was rashly believed in Austria. Rather, the deep crisis of the German Christian Democrats (CDU) at the end of 1999 and the beginning of 2000 was decisive for the absence of mediation in the path of transnational party cooperation and for the lack of corresponding political support for the ÖVP-FPÖ government.

The threat of three "sanction" measures contained in the "Statement from the Portuguese Presidency of the European Union on Behalf of XIV Member States," was issued on 31 January 2000, before the ÖVP-FPÖ government was even formed. It reads as follows:

> Today, Monday, 31 January, the Portuguese Prime Minister informed both the President and the Chancellor of Austria, and the Portuguese Minister of Foreign Affairs notified his Austrian counterpart of the following joint reaction agreed by the Heads of State and Government of XIV Member States of the European

Union in case it is formed [sic] in Austria a Government integrating the FPÖ:

- Governments of XIV Member States will not promote or accept any bilateral official at political level with an Austrian Government integrating the FPÖ;
- There will be no support in favor of Austrian candidates seeking positions in international organisations;
- Austrian Ambassadors in EU capitals will only be received at a technical level.

The Portuguese Prime Minister and the Minister of Foreign Affairs had already informed the Austrians [sic] authorities that there would be no business as usual in the bilateral relations with a Government integrating the FPÖ.[2]

In this short proclamation about a government that was not even formed yet, the EU 14 issued a sort of act of rule without argumentative reasoning. This could not work in a communications-oriented and democratically formulated society. In the long run, this questionable policy could not be carried out against public opinion, particularly as there were no compelling reasons for maintaining the measures, in spite of the occasional statements of some FPÖ politicians. On top of that, the threat and implementation of the "sanctions" proved a great mistrust in the strength and resistance of the political opposition within Austria.

The EU 14 announcement triggered paralyzing dismay and complete bewilderment in large sections of the Austrian population.[3] Overnight, the EU's "model student" had turned into the EU's "boogieman."[4] Austria had committed itself very early to the pan-European idea under extremely difficult fundamental conditions (the statutes of the League of Nations, the period of occupation, the Cold War, neutrality, etc.) and in the face of resistance[5]. The country had made a contribution to peaceful and stable development in Europe and had distinguished itself as a pioneer and forerunner for rapprochement between the European Community and other European nations.[6]

On 12 June 1994 Austria voted for Maastricht Europe with the highest percentage of any *continental* European country (66.6 %). On 1 January 1995 the country joined the EU and shortly thereafter the European Monetary System (EMS), the precursor to the Economic and Monetary Union (EMU), as a net payer. Thanks to its continuous policy of European integration before 1989, Austria joined the EU in an economically advanced stage.[7]

The Grand Coalition, consisting of Social Democrats and Christian Democrats, tried to adhere to the criteria for convergence in the form of austerity programs and tax increases. These criteria were supported by the two social democrats and chancellors Franz Vranitzky (1986-1997) and Viktor Klima (1997-2000) and by the Christian Democratic vice chancellors Erhard Busek (1991-1995) and Wolfgang Schüssel (1995-2000). However, the criteria provoked criticism among the Austrian population. The influence of the FPÖ opposition leader and right-wing populist, Jörg Haider, grew steadily—from 8 % in 1986 to 27 % in 1999.[8] But in 1997, the FPÖ initiative for a petition to hold a referendum against the euro (for which the present-day vice chancellor, Susanne Riess-Passer, was responsible) was rejected by the people in relatively clear terms.[9]

Austria's assumption of the EU presidency in the second half of 1998 demonstrated its capability of taking on this new role and, with it, the responsibility for community policy.[10] Austria needed "Europe." Within a short time, two identity-forming core elements of the Second Republic were removed: The "victim thesis" was made questionable in the wake of the Waldheim debate;[11] and "permanent" neutrality became obsolete through the security policy in Europe (the Common Foreign and Security Policy and NATO).[12] The "return to the European stage" seemed to offer a sensible replacement for them. But this hope was deceptive.

Overnight the country was to become a pariah.[13] The "model student" of the EU was hit unexpectedly, unpreparedly, and undeservedly by the decision of the fourteen other EU countries to threaten (and later carry out) "sanction" measures in the event of the formation of an ÖVP-FPÖ government. In the history of the community there had never been a precedent for such an action. This made the Austrians very much aware of the political dimension of the Union, the loss of relevance of national sovereignty, and the worries of the other EU members regarding the change in government in the Alpine republic. Austrians had simply gotten too accustomed to Haider. The sensitivity in other countries affected by right-wing populist tendencies (Belgium, France, and others) was underestimated. The Austrian foreign ministry had indeed expected negative reactions, but not to this degree. Even the politicians appeared to be surprised. Critical comments had been counted on, but not such massive punitive measures against a member state. They were unique in the history of the community and thus unforeseeable.[14]

Soon there were doubts as to the permissibility and legality of these measures. They appeared to be disproportionate and without legal basis.[15] However, Social Democrats and members of the Green Party were at first in favor of the hard stance of the EU 14. They attempted to justify the "sanctions," and saw in them a reason for the resignation of Wolfgang Schüssel, who was still foreign minister at the time and presumedly the new chancellor.[16]

II. EU 14-Dealings with Austria –
"Bevormundete Nation" or an Example of
Smaller States Being Incapacitated?

Can an event which is so young be historicized? In any case such a great power tutelage as the EU 14 "sanction" measures is nothing new for Austria—it has often happened before. Austria seems to be fated in its geopolitical position to suffer great power tutelage. Even if the EU "sanctions" against Austria appear to be unique, acting under "foreign orders" is nothing new in Austria's foreign policy history. Vienna has learnt to deal with them. "Supervision" has repeatedly occurred since 1918 and has thus been "tested."[17]

In 1988 a study edited by Günter Bischof and Josef Leidenfrost was published, entitled *Die bevormundete Nation. Österreich und die Alliierten 1945-1949* ("A Nation under Tutelage. Austria and the Allies 1945-1949").[18] Plausible objections to the term *Bevormundung* (tutelage) were raised by the Viennese modern historian Thomas Angerer. According to him, the catchword was merely a good piece of political rhetoric and favored those who were under occupation at the time.[19]

The current coalition made up of the ÖVP and the FPÖ was accused by the opposition (the SPÖ and the Green Party) of exploiting the "sanctions" to distract from the unpopular austerity measures and to surreptitiously and decisively push through restructuring measures. Did the attempt at historicizing the *Bevormundung* thesis come too soon? How sovereign had Austria really been in its history and after 1955? Was it trustworthy? To what degree could it still be influenced, how independent was it, and to what degree were decisions made for it by other nations? Much that occurs in and around Austria during this time is not new. It is necessary to look further back.

The desire for Anschluss with Germany in 1918-19 was widespread and could hardly be tamed,[20] but the First Republic was obliged to maintain its existence by the *dictum* of the Treaty of St. Germain. The loans arranged in Geneva in 1922 and Lausanne in 1932 kept Austria under the thumb of the League of Nations. A general commissioner, the Dutchman Alfred Zimmermann, was responsible for overseeing Austria's redevelopment, that is, its budget policy.[21] A certain economic stabilization was indeed achieved, but not a political one.

The failed political experiment of the *Ständestaat* was viewed by the world in a critical manner. The Dollfuß-Schuschnigg regime had basically liquidated social democracy and suppressed the labor movement. With the agreement of July 1936, Austria already came close to being a Nazi satellite. The Anschluss was only a question of time;[22] also, it was often regarded as an expression of the Western Powers' inability to find an acceptable and lasting solution to the "Austria problem." The anti-Hitler coalition considered the *Ostmark* and the *Alpen- und Donaugaue* an important part of the war-waging Nazi Germany which had to be broken away from the *Reichsverband*. The thesis of Austria as the "first victim of Nazi aggression" was a means to this end.[23]

After the end of the war, Austria was thus supposed to be "liberated" and "independent," as the Allies had proclaimed in Moscow in 1943. Their trust, however, was not especially deep. Memories of budget crises, the civil war, and the Anschluss movement in the period between the wars were still too fresh. Unity and liberty were thus still to be awaited after 1945. Austria only received its State Treaty in 1955 with limits to its sovereignty.[24] On the international level, Austrian neutrality was only accepted with reluctance.[25]

There was a far-reaching fear among Western heads of government and foreign ministries that the Soviet Union wanted to bring Austria into play as a "model" for Germany.[26] France watched suspiciously over the relations with Austria's northern neighbor and found itself in good company with the USSR, which wanted to see a "prohibition against Anschluss" clause firmly written into the State Treaty. This "unholy alliance" between Paris and Moscow was to continue. Austria remained economically, politically, and militarily dependent on the goodwill of the European Great Powers and the superpowers.

The Austrian attempt at rapprochement with the EEC in the 1960s brought no relief, but rather more uneasiness.[27] The Belgian Paul-Henri Spaak, one of the fathers of the Treaties of Rome (EEC and EURATOM), studied the decision of the International Court of Justice concerning the customs union project with Germany of 1931, which had fallen through—by a narrow eight to seven vote—because of an indiscretion.[28] The specter of Anschluss continued in Europe.

Italy finally used its veto in Brussels in 1967 against further EC negotiations with Austria over a "special arrangement." Terrorism in South Tyrol and the "danger of a Greater Germany" served as excuses. Association with the EC was blocked.[29] There was relief not only in Moscow but also in Paris. It was not until five years later that Austria was granted simple customs and trade treaties along with the other EFTA nations.

Vienna still remained dependent on the goodwill of the East and the West. Kreisky's globalized foreign policy skillfully covered the monetary and security policy dependencies and practical constraints. How much the 1980s resembled the 1960s! Neither François Mitterrand nor Jacques Delors was glad about Austria's EC membership application of 17 July 1989. What was actually on the agenda was to expand the depth of the community. A few months later, German unification would follow. In addition, in the 1980s the true involvement of many Austrians in the Nazi system fully entered into international consciousness. This was the Austria that had voted for Kurt Waldheim with an absolute majority and had produced Jörg Haider, the German-nationalist opposition leader. An international commission of historians found that President Waldheim was not a war criminal but had been an accessory. The positive image of the Alpine country was in a process of considerable decline and slowly mutated into the "Scandal Republic."[30] Would Austria be one more unreliable member in the community? A disruptive factor in a community that strives toward greater depth? In any case, there would be eight million more German speakers.

Austrian EC membership could not be taken for granted and could only be realized with difficulty. The main advocates in the community were the West Germans. Helmut Kohl had striking arguments at hand for members of the Minister's Council of Europe which were also used in the final communiqué. However, there was strong resistance against the "expansion toward EFTA"[31] from the Benelux states, above all from the Netherlands, especially with regard to the debate about the wartime past of Kurt Waldheim.[32]

In this very difficult situation Helmut Kohl maintained political solidarity with Austria regarding its EC membership application. He was angry about the behavior of the German president, Richard von Weizsäcker, who had refused to shake hands with Waldheim at the Salzburg Festival. After the U.S. decision to put the Austrian president on the watch list, Italy's foreign minister, Giulio Andreotti, criticized this treatment of Austria in an EC Minister's Council meeting. Caution was necessary to avoid that the USA treated all European states in that way.[33]

The ÖVP followed a skillful double strategy in its policy toward Europe, which was not lacking in explosiveness because of the Waldheim debate: the "friends" on the outside were the prime ministers Poul Schlüter (Denmark), Rudolphus F.M. Lubbers (Netherlands), Jacques Chirac (France), and Wilfried Martens (Belgium), as well as the Belgian foreign minister Leo Tindemans; on the inside the necessary support for the EC membership application granting the advice note, for example was assured, above all, by German Chancellor, Helmut Kohl. There were regular preliminary discussions between Kohl and Mitterrand before the meetings of the EC Council of Ministers. Mitterrand coordinated these matters of concern with the Socialist representatives of the EC nations, and Kohl did likewise with the Christian Democrats. In these discussions Kohl could usually bring his European party friends to agree with him and Mitterrand.[34]

Reducing the Haider problem to mere (right-wing) populism explains little.[35] This simplification would cover up too much. Such populism has a historical dimension and is also a question of rank and prestige in the power structure between Paris and Berlin.[36] Fears of setting a precedent were also a particular motive for the measures by the EU 14.

The founding members of the EEC (Germany, France, the Benelux nations, and, to some extent Italy) took a very hard stance in the Austria "sanctions" affair. These states apparently have a mental reservation against the "latecomers to the Community." The Community has shifted from a union that spoke primarily Romance languages (predominantly French) to a German and English-speaking one. This had manifold consequences in view of how positions were filled and how personnel policy was handled.

Is *Bevormundung* (tutelage) a tool used out of fear and weakness, or is it a single harbinger of the incapacitation of the smaller states in Europe? The question of "sanctions" feeds old doubts throughout Europe about how reliable and responsible Austria really is. A consolidated state in the middle of Europe was brought into question, and thus the political destiny of the Union was put at stake.

In 2000 Europe obviously suffered from a lack of statesmanship. The old Kohl-Mitterrand axis would never have allowed such a rash action that threatened both the nature of cooperative Community solutions as well as the process of EU eastern expansion. The completely ossified situation in the spring of 2000 was also caused by stubborn, conceited, and vain politicians who were, at best, only of average quality.[37]

But there was also a change in Community politics.[38] The Treaty of Amsterdam of 1 May 1999 contained constitutional principles which were installed due to Article 6 of the European Union Treaty. They include the "principles of freedom, democracy, the respect of human rights, basic freedoms, and the rule of law." These principles are shared by all of the member states. Every member state is also obliged to adhere to these principles and to respect them. It is from this requirement of homogeneity that the thesis of a "community of values" resulted, to which all EU states should be obliged. From this perspective, measures of intervention seemed to be necessary in the case of Austria.[39]

Austria was used as an example to demonstrate that in the Europe of the year 2000 there is a limit to national sovereignty. The argument of "meddling in internal affairs" originated during the age of nation-states. Even though there is a prohibition against intervention under international law (Article 2, Paragraph 7 of the United Nations statutes), a precept for intervention under EU law appears to be emerging; in the case of a "grave and lasting violation" of the principles of the European Union Treaty, Article 7 of the treaty provides for a separate sanctions procedure based upon Article 6, paragraph 1.[40]

Such a policy undoubtedly requires some type of overseeing body, a controlling institution, or a supervising authority. The "sanctions" threat of January 31 and the following "sanction" measures that were instituted can be interpreted as deterrent actions. These are tolerable in the run-up to sanctioning as long as their effect is limited and proportional. They should also be suited to the attainment of a goal. The EU 14, however, did not explicitly refer to Article 7, paragraph 1 of the European Union Treaty. They imposed "sanction" measures that can be defined as disproportional since the preconditions in the case had not yet been present. The EU 14 also had not provided for an exit strategy for a lifting of the "sanctions," which might be a sign of their exaggeration.[41]

The EU 14 can be accused of deliberate coquetry and shadow boxing, and of intentionally giving the impression that the EU 14 was the entire Union. In Austria the EU 14 members also made believe that they represented all institutions of the European Union. There was much pretense. The Portuguese spoke "in the name of the 14," which caused irritation in British diplomatic circles. They could only speak in the name of all members or in their own name. The EU 14 was not the EU, which is a fact and has been correctly argued. On the one hand, the attempt was made to feign that the measures had come from "the Union"; on the other hand, in case of legal objections, only the bilateral level of the procedures was emphasized without making reference to the full EU.[42]

With these measures of the individual EU member states, a further Americanization of European politics was indicated. "Integration by (self-)containment" was already part of America's policy toward Europe and Germany in the 1950s. Waldemar Hummer speaks of the EU as a "self-contained regime."[43] "Humanitarian interventions" have become conceivable not only in operations outside of the "civilized" community of nations against the so-called "rogue states" of Saddam Hussein or Slobodan Milosevic, but also within the community of nations against "wrong politicians" such as Jörg Haider. The fact remains that in this case it is first and foremost a small state which is being dealt with, one whose supposed independence and freedom of action within the European Union could be affected.

III. International Reactions:
The Background of the Measures by the EU 14

From the very outset, there was not a unified line among the EU 14 because numerous states were not very happy about the idea of "sanctions." There was never a common front in this case, even though the German Christian Democrats quickly dropped out. It was therefore foreseeable that these "sanctions" would not hold up in the long run and that in the end they could only become grotesque and anachronistic.

The massive degree of the agreed-upon reactions was noteworthy, as was the fact that it was the Belgians and the French who led the polemic and the charge to isolate Austria. But their policy was not merely polemics: they tried to contain potential coalitions of the moderate center with nationalist far right elements in their own nations.

The actions against the Austrian government formation and the procedures by those who carried out the "sanction" measures did not fail to pressure the middle-sized and smaller partner states (Ireland, Denmark, Finland, and Luxembourg).[44] In some cases, their positions were even ignored. Therefore, not all of the EU 14 were in favor of these procedures. At the Holocaust Conference in Stockholm from 26 – 28 January 2000, where many European heads of state and heads of governments were present, the head of the Italian government, Massimo D'Alema, said that he was worried about the prospect of an ÖVP-FPÖ coalition, but, he continued, "I in no way want to meddle in the internal affairs of Austria."[45]

Luxembourg's premier, Jean-Claude Juncker, called the measures of the EU 14 "exaggerated."[46] The Greek foreign ministry made known that the developments in Austria were a cause for worry, but thought that such hasty "sanctions" represented a "meddling in internal affairs" and "a dangerous precedent."[47] Athens formally and publicly distanced itself. The decision was thus made under false pretenses—the assent of the Greeks was still lacking. However, those in favor of the measures against Austria feared appearing as a "defender of Haider" if a united front was not put up. Since the decision was made at the highest level of governments, the foreign ministries normally entrusted with this task were passed over and the parliaments were not consulted, which led to domestic criticism in Finland and Denmark.[48]

The Socialist International (SI) expressed solidarity (it would have been difficult to avoid such a stance), although its role should not be overestimated and its pragmatic approach to the issue should be noted. In Austria conspiracy theories soon sprouted up.[49] In any case, this issue involved prominent figures, since the Portuguese president of the Council of the European Union, Antonio Guterres, also served as president of the SI. In addition, socialists were in power in Europe: nearly all EU states had heads of government who were Social Democrats (Great Britain, France, Germany, Italy, Greece, Portugal, the Netherlands, Finland, Sweden, and Denmark). Belgium had a liberal premier. There were conservative prime ministers only in Spain with José Maria Aznar, Ireland with Bertie Ahern, and Luxembourg with the Christian Democrat Jean-Claude Juncker.

From February to April, the matter of concern for the SI was to help a threatened fellow party in Europe and for the individual Socialist parties to distinguish themselves in their respective countries with their own electorate. When the measures did not prove to be helpful or useful for the SPÖ, the Socialist party and government representatives signaled their readiness in May and June to consider the matter closed. Because of other motives, however, the French-Walloon alliance saw no reason to drop the "sanction" measures (from the very beginning, saving the

SPÖ was not their real concern). The SI alone, not taking into account the deviations from some of the Socialist parties in Europe, would not have been able to carry through this action against Austria. It needed additional help, in particular the personal reinforcing effect from some European personalities (Jacques Chirac, Gerhard Schröder, Louis Michel, and José Maria Aznar). Aznar needed to nail his colors to the mast considering the upcoming elections in Spain on March 12. He could distance himself from the repeated accusations of Francoist wishful thinking (*"Velleitäten"*) and thus demonstrate an "antifascist" image. After the elections, Aznar yielded with a more understanding attitude toward Austria.[50]

In the cases of France and Belgium, political motives that were primarily domestic were obviously at play as well. The fear of setting a precedent played a decisive role. Both countries feared that if they recognized the government participation of the right-wing populist FPÖ, negative repercussions with regard to the racist French *Front National* and the secessionist Belgian *Vlaams Blok* might unfold.[51] In contrast to his predecessor François Mitterrand, President Jacques Chirac had clearly distanced himself from the policy of the Vichy Regime and had pursued a strong course of exclusion against Jean-Marie Le Pen. Against this background, consistent reaction against Haider's FPÖ was on the agenda.

In Germany, the recommendation for an ÖVP-FPÖ coalition by Bavarian premier Edmund Stoiber of the Christian Social Union in the autumn of 1999 and the deep crisis in the CDU at the end of 1999 beginning of 2000 fed the worry that the spark could leap over to Germany and a populist party could be established there alongside the Christian Democrats.[52]

It is necessary here to look back in history. The question of French agreement to the EU's policy concerning Austrian EU membership had been first and foremost a result of decisions at the political level. The neo-Gaullist prime minister (1986-88), Jacques Chirac (UDR/RPR), was one of the first French politicians to be in favor of it, while the diplomatic representatives remained reserved and hesitant. Chirac's reaction ran counter to the line held by the Quai d'Orsay. Here, the European balance of power was considered, and it was not possible to be free of the fear that Austria would be "the second German voice" in the EU, strengthening the position of Germany. The Socialist president Mitterrand, however, had arrived at a positive attitude through the efforts of Helmut Kohl.[53]

The Schröder-Fischer government in Germany came out decisively against the ÖVP-FPÖ government. It attempted to avoid the impression of behaving in a historically insensitive and "politically incorrect" manner. Chancellor Gerhard Schröder and Foreign Minister Joschka Fischer stood fully behind Jacques Chirac, even though that went against German public opinion, which opposed "sanctions." How the problem was dealt with also touched on the question of rank and prestige in the relations between Paris and Berlin. The German government thus put itself in a position of being a sort of political hostage of France's policy vis-à-vis Austria. The SPD could not escape the constellations of domestic and coalition politics. Schröder and Stoiber had a sharp verbal exchange in Parliament because of Haider. Chancellor Schröder, who emphasized that Haider must not become "a German problem," feared that the Bavarian premier could, like Haider, exploit the Europe theme for the election.[54] There were recognizable attempts by the Social Democrats to push the CDU and CSU, parties that had traditionally supported the European idea, into the right corner.

For Foreign Minister Joschka Fischer the situation with Austria presented an opportunity to make a positive mark. After arguing for the war in Kosovo, which caused extreme tension within the party, he could now show himself in a favorable light to the party grassroots. With respect to foreign policy, he recognized Germany's historical responsibility towards the Nazi-period. "Anything else would arouse the suspicions of the EU partners,"[55] he made clear, with a view toward the ties to history. Fischer seemed to be a typical antifascist veteran of the demonstrations of 1968. Was that why he supported the "sanctions"?

The Swiss government distanced itself from the EU countries that boycotted Austria. The Austrian government should be judged according to its actions and "not because of any preconceived notions,"[56] declared Foreign Minister Joseph Deiss. In 2000 Switzerland was the first nation to which the head of the Austrian government made a foreign visit.

An especially problematic role was played by the Belgian foreign minister, Louis Michel. He acted as a hard-liner in the policy of "sanction" measures against Austria when he called upon his countrymen not to take any more ski vacations in Austria, which, as he called it, would be "immoral."[57] Until June Brussels was strictly in favor of maintaining the "sanctions" and proposed a regulated procedure for similar cases in the future.[58]

The Luxembourgers, however, acted with cautious hesitance, appearing to be amenable to an exit strategy. Also, the Dutch held back noticeably. And in spite of the clear line taken by their foreign minister,[59] the British side remained mostly in the background. Although Great Britain officially stood for the "sanction" measures, it deliberately hesitated and represented a position in the middle, while Ireland advocated the development of an exit strategy and an end to the "sanctions."[60] The British policy toward Europe under Foreign Minister Robin Cook had been strongly involved in the judgment against the FPÖ participation in the government. After several weeks, however, London realized the counterproductive effects: the conservative and Euro-skeptic press began to use Haider in his role as a Europhobe. It treated him as "a useful stick" with which "the EU donkey could be beaten."[61]

The United States reacted critically and admonishingly, but far less harshly than the EU 14. Haider had been developing contacts in the United States since 1994. A few weeks before the formation of the government, he was in Washington, and had meetings in the State Department.[62] Certain arrangements must have been reached there. The spokesman for the State Department made clear that the situation in Austria would be followed attentively.[63]

What was implicit was that the claims for compensation (for Jewish property confiscated during the Nazi period and for forced labor) had been linked to the American good will vis-à-vis the Austrian government. The head representative of the American Jewish interest groups, the attorney Ed Fagan, had already come to Vienna in February in order to carry on negotiations with the government and, in particular, with Maria Schaumayer, the former president of the Austrian National Bank.[64] Because of the international isolation and the increased media pressure, Austria was now without a doubt more ready to negotiate and more willing to pay.[65]

France was strictly against any abolition of the "sanction" measures as long as "the nature" of the FPÖ did not change. It was decided that during the course of the French EU presidency that began July 1, no member of the government would be sent to Vienna and Chancellor Schüssel would only be met in Brussels. Italy, however, spoke up for an end to "sanctions" through its spokesman, Foreign Minister Lamberto Dini. One reason behind this was the increasing pressure from the Italian right onto the Roman center-left government. Spain, which in the beginning favored the sharp course against Vienna, fell in with the group of countries that was looking for a way out.[66]

German Chancellor Schröder officially remained in favor of the "sanctions," but word soon came from government circles that the measures would not hold up any longer. Joschka Fischer publicly pleaded for "reflection." But Germany could not be expected to take a trailblazing role in the matter of an abatement of the "sanctions," since the historical responsibility still weighed too heavily.[67]

Finland called repeatedly for an abolition of the "sanctions," but an initiative by Prime Minister Paavo Lipponen was treated as though it had never been presented.[68] Sweden officially stood behind the "sanction" measures although they were regarded as controversial even in the Social Democratic government.[69]

Different reactions came from the Central and Eastern European candidates for membership in the EU. Poland supported the "sanctions," primarily for historical reasons.[70] The Czech Republic favored the measures, but only after the FPÖ declared in February that its agreement to Czech membership in the EU would depend on the abolition of the Beneš decrees.[71] Václav Klaus, president of the Czech Parliament, had originally referred to the "sanctions" as "a greater evil than Haider."[72] Slovakia showed understanding for the "sanctions" but was hesitant.[73] Hungary, though, was critical of the EU 14 policy from the very beginning and emphasized "the good neighbor policy" toward Austria. And while Slovenia hesitated, it expressed skepticism toward the "sanctions."[74]

Considerations of integration policy also surfaced during the debate. The classic dialectic, according to which the EU could not take on greater importance without expansion,[75] seemed endangered. This is another reason why France, the traditional advocate of a far-reaching EU,[76] reacted so strongly to Austria's anti-EU party.[77]

Possible measures of retaliation and selective vetoes by Austria could also no longer be excluded. However, claims such as that opponents of expansion were accused of being Haider supporters, that Austria was instrumentalized as a negative example for membership applicants,[78] or that the FPÖ was exploited as a scapegoat for a possibly unsuccessful eastern expansion of the EU sound more like conspiracy theories than realistic scenarios.

While the influence of the Socialist International on the Austrian affair was overestimated, the contributions of European Christian Democrats and Conservatives to the lifting of the "sanction" measures was widely ignored and often overseen. The European People's Party (EPP), founded in 1976,[79] was faced with a dilemma. On the one hand, fundamentalists and representatives of the Benelux nations and Italy only wanted to accept Christian Democratic representatives from current

EC member nations into the EPP. On the other hand, realists, supported especially by the CDU/CSU and smaller Christian Democratic parties, also wanted to accept British Conservatives, Gaullists and neo-Gaullists, and representatives of the EFTA member nations and the neutral states. The British were finally refused as members by the EPP, and the ÖVP was not even granted observer status. Talks regarding this failed in the 1970s.[80]

The founding of the European Democratic Union (EDU) in 1978 with the inclusion of the Conservatives and Gaullists was a reaction to this development. "No one would let us play anywhere, so we built our own sandbox," Andreas Khol explained.[81] With the help of this international party cooperation (former Foreign Minister Alois Mock advanced to the post of EDU president),[82] the way to Austrian EU membership was paved.

Those Christian Democratic parties of a smaller or centrist nature behaved in a historically continuous manner with respect to the 2000 conflict with Austria. Luxembourgian and Belgian Christian Democrats, French neo-Gaullists, and Italian politicians of the *Partito Popolare Italiano (PPI)* wanted to make gestures against the ÖVP, while the large center-right parties in Europe with few opponents further to the right, such as the CDU/CSU, *Forza Italia*, or the Tories, acted against such an ostracism of the ÖVP. The only exception was the Spaniards. Aznar even intended to throw the ÖVP out of the European People's Party faction, but he did not go through with it.[83]

The immobility of the CDU in the wake of the Kohl fundraising scandal greatly upset the political equilibrium in Europe at the end of 1999 and annulled a vital player. This was a decisive factor for the lack of balancing and moderate voices in the case of the ÖVP's government formation with the Austrian Freedom Party. It was largely responsible for the misfiring of the EU 14 policy. Kohl, as the leader of the Christian-Conservative *Lager*, could have played a crucial role in mode-rating the European response to the ÖVP/FPÖ government. His presence would have been a mediating one in the later diplomatic process and could probably have prevented the "sanction" measures. But by the spring of 2000, the former chancellor and the CDU were unable to play a part in foreign policy. Then, solidarity with the ÖVP reemerged, with a certain delay, within the framework of both the EPP and the EDU.[84]

Gestures of solidarity with the Freedom Party were made by the European far right. Jean-Marie Le Pen congratulated Haider in spite of his attempts at distancing. Messages of solidarity also came from

Umberto Bossi and the *Lega Nord*. In the Anglo-American world, the Right (Conservatives and Republicans, respectively) remained open, since they had had fewer problems with contact and in fact were far less amenable to a Europe that was too Socialist.[85]

The international press reacted in a far more sophisticated manner than did the European media world. The majority of public opinions in European countries did not support the measures taken by the EU 14, with the exception of France, the Benelux states, and Sweden.[86] The overall decrease in approval of the FPÖ was only hesitantly noted abroad, possibly because of the fear of making the "sanction" measures appear unjustified or of encouraging a playing down of the "Haider danger."

In the wake of the EU 14 declaration, various organs and institutions of the Union became active and made statements. On 1 February, the European Commission accepted unanimously—i.e. including the vote of the Commissioner for Agriculture, the Austrian Franz Fischler—a communication, noting the agreement of the EU 14 and referring to it as a common statement. The Commission shared the worry expressed therein without addressing the procedure of the EU 14. It was interpreted as a political declaration of intent and as a preliminary measure to Article 7 of the Union Treaty, as indicated by the Commission's reference to Articles 6 and 7 of the Union Treaty.[87]

In a resolution on the results of the parliamentary elections in Austria and on the February 3 proposal for the formation of a coalition government between the ÖVP and the FPÖ—which passed by a vote of 406 to 53 with 60 abstentions—the European Parliament welcomed the intent of the statement by the EU 14. It further agreed that the inclusion of the FPÖ in a coalition government would legitimize the extreme Right in Europe. This action was also a preliminary measure to Article 7.[88]

In an emergency session on February 16, the "Committee of the Regions," in a resolution on the coalition government in Austria, supported the statement of the EU 14 with an overwhelming majority. It stated that a party was participating in the Austrian government which had declared itself in favor of "intolerance," "hostility toward foreigners," "nationalism," and "inequality."[89]

Until the very end, there was controversy over whether the measures of the EU 14 had been encouraged or requested by the Austrian side.[90] While still in office as chancellor, Viktor Klima was accused of having warned about the threat of Haider's participation in the government at the Holocaust Conference in Stockholm on January 26-28. This had allegedly left a lasting impression with the conference participants because of the depressing atmosphere with respect to the persecution of the Jews and their mass annihilation. However, Chirac, Michel, and Aznar were not even present in Stockholm. Klima had certainly signaled consternation and worry in Stockholm,[91] but his role should not be overestimated. The not-so-distinguished socialist was really not in any position to give orders within the SI or among European socialists.

A different level of importance may be attributed to the attitude of President Thomas Klestil. He clearly still had worries on his mind about his country's loss of public image due to, among other reasons, his activity as ambassador to the United States during the Waldheim affair.[92] He created an alarmist atmosphere and turned to hectic telephone diplomacy for assistance and understanding from abroad. It would, however, also be an overestimation of Klestil's power if it were asserted that the measures of the EU 14 had been "ordered" by him.[93] But his behavior had some influence on the advance publication of the threat of "sanctions."[94]

Until the actual formation of the government, Klestil made intensive efforts toward the prevention of a "Black and Blue" coalition and finally spoke out in favor of an SPÖ minority government. With the agreement of three provincial governors (most likely Josef Pühringer of Upper Austria, Franz Schausberger of Salzburg, and Wendelin Weingartner of Tyrol), he hoped to prevent the formation of an ÖVP-FPÖ coalition.[95] However, Klestil had not rejected the declaration by the EU 14, but rather had agreed with it and demonstrated understanding for their action, thus compromising himself in a certain way before the Austrian public.

The hope of preventing the formation of the government by giving advance notice of the attitude of the EU 14 was a further fatal miscalculation. Because of the threat of "sanctions," Schüssel was basically compelled to take the bull by the horns. His withdrawal would have meant his political end, and the ÖVP would have had to face either going back to the old coalition with the SPÖ or else being in opposition.

IV. Short-term and Medium-term Effects
of the "Sanctions" Policy

The threats of the 14 EU states were not successful. The government was formed in spite of them. The objective of the poorly thought-through ad hoc decision was not achieved because the participation of the FPÖ in the government could not be prevented. In the sense of a "preventive hammer blow," however, a powerful shock effect was achieved and shook the political establishment of Austria. The leadership circles of the ÖVP and FPÖ had not counted on such rigorous gestures of threats and measures of isolation.

In the course of the threat of "sanction" measures, the new government declared itself ready to sign, in addition to the declaration of government, a preamble stating a clear commitment to the EU, to its mandate of being made more far reaching, and to its eastward expansion.[96]

Ironically, the "sanction" measures were counterproductive by strengthening Wolfgang Schüssel's domestic stature. It also seemed that Schüssel was somewhat strengthened by the massive foreign exertion of influence on Haider, enabling Schüssel to free himself from the latter. Nevertheless, Schüssel himself was the target of sharp attacks, such as the beseeching and admonishing appeals from the German foreign minister and Green Party politician Joschka Fischer. These open attacks represented an unprecedented interference in internal Austrian affairs by a prominent German foreign government official.

To keep faith with his electorate, Jörg Haider, as the FPÖ's chief negotiator, was forced not to give in to international pressure and to make his party's participation in the government a reality, in spite of strong resistance in the media. In so doing, however, he accepted disadvantages with regard to the assignment of ministers. Schüssel was the secret winner of the negotiations about the formation of the government—the controversial coalition partner received the ministries that are less popular with the public (finance, social services, and defense), while, in the face of sensitive international public opinion, the more popular ministries with public appeal (interior and foreign affairs) went to the ÖVP. The Freedom Party left the foreign policy damage control up to the "Europe party," the ÖVP. This lent respect to Foreign Minister Benita Ferrero-Waldner and, most importantly, brought about an improvement of the domestic image, thus representing a political bonus. Ferrero-Waldner has since become one of the most popular politicians in the government.

The short-term effects of the EU 14 national representatives—who appeared to act in a unified manner—consisted of appeasements and clarifications from representatives of the Austrian government, large-scale demonstrations against the "Black and Blue" coalition,[97] and Jörg

Haider's resignation from the FPÖ party chairmanship (announced at the end of February 2000). Haider withdrew to his agenda as provincial governor.[98]

The EU 14 implemented the "sanction" measures once the government was formed on 4 February 2000. In other words, they carried out their threats. Anything else would have represented a political loss of face. The boycott was more or less joined by the governments of Norway, the United States (which only informally demonstrated concern when recalling its ambassador), Israel (which also withdrew its ambassador from Vienna), Canada, Costa Rica, and Argentina.[99]

In the meantime, a debate had begun as to whether the "sanctions" were really *sanctions* at all. Those Austrian critics who later denied that the measures had indeed been sanctions were the same who, back in February, claimed that these measures against the "Black and Blue coalition" were not sufficiently sharp nor enough of an ultimatum. Compared to the original intentions of the hard-liners among the Union states, the measures implemented against Austria were actually moderate.

The measures should not be overly dramatized, which the representatives of the Austrian government tended to do, nor should they be minimized and played down, which the Austrian opposition parties did in the wake of the ineffectiveness of the "sanctions." There were calls for a boycott of Austrian goods and services. Other consequences, which were implemented, included: the suspension of student exchange programs, the refusal to consider the participation of the Austrian Archaeological Institute in the Area II Pilot Project, the exclusion of Austria from the opening ceremonies of "Brussels, European City of Culture" and of the "Anti-Racism Office" in Vienna, the revocation, by order of the Walloon government, of an already agreed-upon loan from a Belgian Museum for an exhibition about Charles V in Vienna, refusals to attend the Viennese Opera Ball, conference cancellations, the refusal to award honors to Austrians, cancellations of projects, obstruction of cooperation, condemning resolutions, and more. It was deemed to have been an "unfriendly act" when the "European partners" arrived at meetings in Brussels too late to have to greet the Austrian representatives, or else when they left the hall whenever an Austrian minister took the podium.[100] This attitude was of no use to the purpose of the Union; rather, it went against its values, which were supposed to include fairness, solidarity, and a willingness for dialogue.

The measures against Austria soon turned out to be unsuitable, disproportionate, surreal, and comical. The arguments by supporters and opponents of the "sanctions" were interchangeable, which was a sign of the rapid change in the development. The argument that the "sanctions" did not accomplish anything and should thus be neglected came in May and June from the opposition. If the same argument had been made in February by an FPÖ sympathizer, it would have been judged to be whistling in the wind. The medium-term effects were multiple, but from the point of view of those who instituted the measures, they were mostly counterproductive.[101]

There were considerable protest actions and demonstrations within the country, especially in Vienna. But aside from these, the general populace rather expressed solidarity for the national government that was under such intense pressure.[102]

The ÖVP party chairman and new chancellor, Wolfgang Schüssel, experienced an unexpected strengthening of his position. He had secured parity with the FPÖ after a perfect strategy of mobilization of the ÖVP voters on 3 October 1999. The new government team was virtually welded together because of the unrelenting pressure from abroad and the continuing mass demonstrations, especially in Vienna, in February and part of March. The "sanctions" and protests were what bonded this government together, leaving shortcomings, unprofessional conduct, and weak points in the cabinet in the background.[103]

The "sanction" measures, which hardly affected the average citizen, further served as an exploitable maneuver of distraction from the unpopular laws and measures by the new government (austerity measures, reduction of pensions, and cuts in social services). In addition, Haider received a massive amount of publicity on the international level that no public relations agency could have provided him. For him, bad news was still news. He thus inherited from Kurt Waldheim the title of best-known Austrian politician throughout Europe and the world.

The common argument that the measures were morally justified but politically questionable proved to be ambivalent, if not inappropriate. Taking the debate over the EU's values as a basis, a questionable double standard that was applied in different ways was recognizable. With regard to European policy this had never been so clear as with the Haider situation and the Austrian affair.

Regarding the Austrian domestic policy, the measures also backfired, since the Haider party could present itself as the safeguard of Austrian national interests. At the same time, the opposition lost face in the general public and was confronted with the accusation of having "betrayed Austrian interests" because it had initially justified and defended the "sanction" measures.

When the measures of the EU 14 increasingly proved to be problematic and ineffective, the opposition argued, on the one hand, that the "sanctions" were really not sanctions and, on the other hand, that it also wanted to contribute to their being lifted. The contradiction was obvious. With the exception of the Green Party, which for a brief period received higher opinion poll ratings, the opposition parties fell into a deep internal crisis. The Liberal Forum collapsed in the face of a leadership vacuum and was about to dissolve; the dreadful state of the SPÖ's debts came to light in its full extent, and the colorless successor to Klima, Alfred Gusenbauer, cut an unhappy figure on his image tour through various European capitals, particularly since he was compelled to explain, if not defend, the points of view of the advocates of the very "sanctions" whose lifting was now his declared matter of concern.

The scenario of the "sanction" measures was a signal that went beyond Austria and pointed toward a debate on renationalization in Western Europe. Growing discontent among the smaller countries toward the medium and larger powers was articulated with respect to the procedures of the EU 14. In no way did the EU 14 behave as if they were united, but they had been driven on primarily by France, Belgium, and Portugal. Skepticism toward the weak Euro was expressed in those countries which did not yet belong to the European Monetary System (EMS) (especially Denmark).[104]

The upcoming reform of EU institutions was increasingly criticized because it was expected to favor the large EU countries of Germany and France to the disadvantage of the smaller countries.[105] The matter of the eastern expansion of the EU appeared more and more questionable —opponents of a more far-reaching and enlarged EU found themselves on the upswing.[106] The EU 14's rough treatment of a small member state like Austria really shocked prospective applicants in the East. What will Slovenia or Hungary do if the "EU" doesn't like some of their leaders?

The EU 14 considered Haider's repeated debonair statements about the Nazi past as highly problematical. The "sanction" measures clearly tried to stigmatize such uncritical views of the Nazi past, especially since they came from an Austrian. Like in the Waldheim debate, ostracizing a prominent Austrian should send a message to the Austrian population that such views no longer were acceptable. To many Austrians and critics of the "sanctions" such EU moralism smacked of too much political correctness. While it was fairly easy to isolate Waldheim after his election, it was much harder to boycott an entire nation, as the EU would soon find out. Austria was represented in the EU institutions and not everyone agreed to ignore the presence of the Austrian representatives.

There were also noteworthy political and moral consequences to the "sanction" measures: Because of the transparency and superficiality of the spokesmen, the stigmatization of the problematic dealing with the Nazi past in order to create political advantages came more clearly to light than on previous occasions. The political and moral ostracism and isolation of problematic interpreters of the Nazi period no longer succeeded in such a consistent, believable, and convincing way as it did, for example, in the Waldheim debate. This affair was also already interspersed with attempts at instrumentalization—by the Austrian Social Democrats, the World Jewish Congress, and the Office of Special Investigation of the U.S. Department of Justice—but these were not so easily recognizable at the time. Besides, an individual could easily be isolated, ostracized, and prevented from traveling, but it was hard to boycott a member state which was in the heart of the home market and whose mountain passes lay at crucial crossroads of intra-European traffic and trade.[107]

As pedagogically grounded and justified as the "preventive hammer blow" might have appeared, the "sanction" measures, which were instituted on a national basis because they were bilateral, appeared anachronistic, if not ridiculous. With their integration policy the EU 14 fell into one of Haider's traps.[108] Their procedures were questionable with regard to democracy policy—the Austrian government had indisputably come into existence through a democratic process.

The argument by "sanctions" advocates that the measures ought to affect the government and not the populace did not catch on, since even individual citizens could be affected by politics. Thus the ÖVP-FPÖ government was able to reap political rewards from the "sanctions." The demonstrations against the government, which later on waned markedly, did not, as had been interpreted by proponents of the "sanction" measures, represent the opinion of average Austrians. The majority of the latter rejected both the "sanctions" and the demonstrations against the government.[109]

The goals of the protests (against xenophobia, racism, and animosity toward foreigners) conveyed a justifiable, all too obvious concern. But they distracted from the causes of and reasons behind the rise in popularity and continuing success of Haider. In order to be credible the protests should have been directed against the Austrian political system as a whole[110] and its media culture, which produced, allowed, supported, and raised the status of Haider, rather than only against its product, the FPÖ.[111] The chief goal of the demonstrations—to make the government resign—failed. Possible ways of affronting the Haider phenomenon were not indicated. The mass protests did not weaken the government; quite the contrary—the cabinet held together even more tightly.

V. The "Three Wise Men" and their Report
as a Way Out of the Dilemma

The "Council of Wise Men," which had been appointed in June and began its work in July, had a difficult task to accomplish. Its appointment was the expression of a failed policy and of the increasing helplessness of the EU 14, which was now at a complete loss. They indirectly admitted their failure by relying on "wise men" and elder statesmen to help them find a way out of the hopelessly muddled situation.

The civil rights and human rights situation has played and continues to play an important role with respect to the decisions of the EU Commission. Respecting these rights has more than ever become a condition of membership for new EU applicants. An example of this was the appointment of three so-called wise men to examine the rights of minorities, refugees, and immigrants in Austria and to report in detail on the development and the political nature of the FPÖ. The Portuguese presidency of the Council of the European Union conferred the task of selecting the wise men upon Luzius Wildhaber of Switzerland, president of the European Court for Human Rights in Strasbourg.

In its reports on Central and Eastern European candidates for EU membership, the Commission regularly notes the situation of minorities in these countries, such as the Russian minorities in the Baltic states or the Sinti and Romany peoples in Slovakia, Hungary, and Romania. In the 1998-99 annual report of the European Parliament, the existence of an extremist party in Austria had already been mentioned with apprehension. This existence could result in "a danger to the mainte-nance of human rights, and to the fight against racism and hostility toward foreigners." Other EU members were also criticized, though. Belgium and France were requested to better protect their minorities.[112]

Wildhaber's choices for the "three wise men" were the former Finnish prime minister, Martti Ahtisaari, the German professor of International Law, Jochen Frowein, and the former Spanish foreign minister and EU commissioner, Marcelino Oreja. The council began its work in July.[113] The choices proved to be good ones.

As much as the motives and intentions were justified and understandable, the procedure followed by the EU 14 against Austria was not acceptable. The ostracism of the center-right government in Vienna was fragile from the beginning.[114]

Under the leadership of the conservative French president, Jacques Chirac, and the liberal Belgian prime minister, Guy Verhofstadt, European governments referred for the first time to European basic values in order to place a partner into a state of quarantine. This falsely assumed that the quarantine could prevent the formation of a government. Well-meaning observers saw in this a chance for the crystallization of a common canon of values. But they were later disappointed because, as always, national interests still took precedence in the Union and different standards were applied to states outside of the community. While the Russian war of extermination in Chechnya was tolerated and Putin was merely viewed as a far-sighted politician, Austria remained ostracized. This went hand in hand with a loss of credibility regarding the policy of the members of the Union.

To rational observers, it was clear from the very beginning that the three-pronged isolation—no bilateral contact, no support for Austrian candidates for international organizations, and a diminution of the level of ambassadorial contact—could not be maintained in the long run. Boycott measures at the level of international trade would have violated Common Market regulations. What was meant as a preventive hammer blow for the yet-to-be-sworn-in Schüssel/Riess-Passer government became a lasting punishment after the government formation. The longer the EU 14 held on to their "sanction" measures—primarily for purposes of domestic politics—the more clearly the doubts and disagreements were evident among the isolationists. By summer there was not a single diplomat in Brussels who did not consider the situation to be muddled. Among those who had second thoughts from the very beginning was EU Commission President Romano Prodi who was noticeably reserved. The questionable intervention did not have a favorable effect on the internal climate of the Union.[115] With their "relapse into the gunboat diplomacy of a bygone era," the heads of state and government had badly damaged the idea of "Europe."[116]

Considering the unique pressure in February and March, the Austrian government reacted very moderately and in a manner which was both loyal to the Community and very determined in the rejection of the "sanction" measures. A "policy of the empty chair," like that of the French head of state Charles De Gaulle in 1965-66, was out of the question for Vienna.[117]

The government, which was seen as politically incorrect, behaved highly correctly in Brussels. Even the strongest critics of Haider could not prove any violation of the EU Treaty (Article 7 provides for sanctions only in the event of a "serious and lasting violation" of basic rights by a member nation), even though the governor of the province of Carinthia attempted to vent his anti-European resentment.[118] Thus, in June, the Viennese government was able to break the diplomatic isolation in the EU after less than five months.[119]

On September 8, the "three wise men" submitted their completed report to French President Jacques Chirac. The preceding day, Bavarian Premier Stoiber, who had demanded an end to the "sanctions" and had demonstratively backed Austria, had received a friendly welcome in Vienna—the first official visit by a high-ranking politician from an EU country since the punitive measures had been passed.[120]

While in the end it was considered a certainty that the "three wise men" would not find Austria culpable, their evaluation of the "nature of the FPÖ" might remain controversial. In the report, the experts recommended the abolition of the "sanction" measures because they *would be* "counterproductive."[121] Even representatives of the Austrian opposition parties had certainly made clear during several foreign visits in April and May that the "sanctions" *were already* "counterproductive" in Austria.[122]

According to the "three wise men" the "sanctions" had, however, raised the sensitivity toward the "common values" of the EU states, and they had done so not only in Austria. In the future, maintaining the "sanctions" would not have a beneficial effect because it would "awaken nationalistic sentiments in Austria." The government received an overall positive evaluation. Its record was "in harmony with common European values." The FPÖ, however, was defined as a right-wing populist party "with radical elements." The report referred to the use of terms that were nationalistic, racist, and hostile to foreigners. FPÖ members of the government in fact no longer use such language, but the party takes no measures against members who continue to employ such terms. Ferrero-Waldner was "not surprised" about the positive contents of the report and was confident about the abolition of the "sanctions." She named the upcoming summit meeting in the middle of October as a possible date for it. The opposition parties greeted the recommendation for the abolition of the "sanctions," but a declaration by the SPÖ and the Green Party stated that Austria could not win back international trust.[123]

Justice Minister Dieter Böhmdorfer was the only Freedom Party member of the government to have been mentioned critically in the report by the "three wise men." He had not sufficiently defended the values of the EU when Haider had made the suggestion of prosecuting members of the opposition ("traitors to Austria"). Böhmdorfer attributed this to "the very skilled propaganda of some participants in public life." He obviously referred to representatives from non-governmental organizations (NGOs). Böhmdorfer said that he had offered additional information that the "three wise men" had not chosen to hear, just as Haider had not been heard by the experts.[124]

The question of an immediate abolition or a limited suspension of the "sanctions" was still not resolved. There was to be a positive signal for Vienna at the EU extraordinary summit on October 13-14 in Biarritz. That was three weeks before the referendum on the Euro in Denmark. For the advocates of the Euro in that country, the measures against Vienna had thus far been catastrophic.[125]

On the very evening the "wise men's report" was presented, the Austrian government demanded a rapid abolition of the "sanctions." If this were not to take place, it would pass a government resolution for a referendum on the "sanctions." This had already long been planned by the FPÖ, and Schüssel had accepted and even defended the idea. Nevertheless, it was controversial both within the country and abroad.[126]

Within the EU, a fear of anti-European demonstrations in Austria resulted from this. In spite of declarations to the contrary, the project of isolating Austria could have contributed to the yielding of the EU 14 and might have caused the appointment of the "three wise men." In any case, the report helped provide the EU 14 with a "way out" without losing face.

The Austrian reaction to the report was predominantly positive. All of the political parties drew the conclusion that the "sanctions" had to be abolished.[127] The FPÖ celebrated the "quasi-acquittal," and Haider said that it was an "honor" to be referred to as a "populist."[128] The opposition pointed out, however, that the FPÖ was not cleared by the report.[129]

The reaction in the EU countries varied. The head of the Italian government, Giuliano Amato, had already made known on the day before the submission of the report that he agreed neither with the "sanctions" nor with Haider. He hoped that a solution could be found "as quickly as possible," since the measures were having a negative effect on relations between the states of the EU.[130]

Intensive telephone diplomacy was carried out during the weekend of September 9 and 10. British Prime Minister Tony Blair, among others, tried to talk Chirac into accepting the recommendation of the "wise men."[131] The prime minister of Luxembourg, Jean-Claude Juncker, had already declared that a large majority of the EU heads of government favored an end to the "sanctions." The Finnish prime minister, Paavo Lipponen, expressed his satisfaction over the report of the "wise men," and hoped for a rapid agreement of the EU 14.[132]

Italy's Foreign Minister Dini and the Greek deputy foreign minister were in favor of the abolition. The British government was ready for it, and the head of the Danish government, Poul Nyrup Rasmussen, was also in favor of an end to the isolation of Austria. However, the main driving forces behind the "sanctions," Berlin and Paris, held back conspicuously and still delayed making a hasty decision. The German government remained silent. Neither Schröder nor Fischer wanted to comment on the "wise men's report." They only said that the report would be examined. The CDU and the FDP spoke of a "foreign policy Waterloo" and a "disgrace" and demanded that the German Federal government apologize for having participated in the "sanctions." Fischer replied in the German parliament, "Like hell I will!" The actions, according to him, had been justified. The report, however, should be "correspondingly brought into action." Germany stood behind the French presidency.[133]

As a result of pressure from the smaller and middle-sized states (Luxembourg, Denmark, Finland, Greece, and Italy) and through the mediation of Great Britain, the "big Europeans" and driving forces behind the "sanctions" (Belgium, Germany, and France) finally had to give in on 11 and 12 September.

On Tuesday, 12 September at 7:00 P.M., the EU 14 announced "the immediate abolition of the sanctions." A contradictory and ambivalent communiqué by the French presidency of the Council of the European Union—a classic compromise formulation on the safeguarding of the unity of the Union—stated that the EU 14 had taken note of the report. The "measures" had proven useful but could now be abolished. It would be "counterproductive" if they were to be applied further. Austria had not violated "European values." The development of the FPÖ, however, was "uncertain." This, along with its "nature," were reasons for "serious concern." A "special vigilance toward this party and its influence on the government" must thus be maintained. This "vigilance" would be commonly practiced. At the end of the communiqué it was stated that the procedures followed by the EU should never again be repeated.[134] The recommendation by the "wise men" for the creation of a control mechanism in similar situations was judged as a "useful contribution to these deliberations," but it was not acted upon concretely.[135]

The Austrian government reacted with relief.[136] Schüssel said that Austria had regained its dignity. President Klestil, who had tried in vain to make contact with Chirac at the U.N. summit in New York, commented in an unusually sharp manner that the passage referring to the "vigilance" toward the FPÖ was dispensable.[137] The president's hectic demeanor was obvious. His embarrassing efforts remained fruitless. Did Klestil have to "provide compensation" to the Austrian public for something?

The USA did not change its position. From the very beginning, Washington acted independently from the EU line and wanted to continue to do so. The official opinion did not change—the FPÖ participation in the government was still "disquieting" and "a cause for concern." Contacts would only be maintained at the highest levels in the case of important "American interests." However, the Austrian efforts at introducing measures for the compensation of forced laborers under the Nazis were positively noted.[138] Canada also decided to completely abolish its "sanctions," which corresponded to the line of the EU 14, but said that it intended to keep "a watchful eye" on the FPÖ.[139] Israel disapproved of the abolition. It kept its diplomatic relations frozen. The ambassador who had been withdrawn in February has not been sent back to Vienna.[140]

VI. Conclusion

In the Waldheim affair, no explicit policy of exclusion, in the sense of an "unfriendly act," was enforced in Europe. However, there may well have been informal arrangements about the refusal to issue invitations to the Austrian president on the part of the twelve EC states. Interestingly enough, the USA, in complete contrast to the Waldheim debate, was far less engaged in the Haider case than the countries of

Europe. There was and is no watch list decision against him. He is also much more difficult to "latch on to" than Waldheim. Haider is not someone who consciously lived through the Nazi period or was a member of the wartime generation. This was a key point in the Waldheim debate. In dealing with the Nazi past, Haider is little more than a "problematic case," having been born five years after the end of the Second World War. However, his ethnocentric position in view of a strict anti-immigration policy (a catchword for hostility toward foreigners) was and is a bone of contention.[141]

Upon reflecting on the weeks and months after 4 February 2000, so magnified by the media, the term *sanctions* proves more and more problematic and, indeed, misleading. Apart from the missing legal basis, the punitive actions by the EU 14 can hardly be designated as sanctions if one compares them to the policies toward Saddam Hussein or Slobodan Milosevic. In the Austrian case they were on the whole "sanctions" of a rather harmless sort. From a legal point of view, sanctions can only be imposed if it can be proved that the state in question has violated or broken a law. These would be the preconditions for such measures, and they were not present in the case of Austria.

The threat of "sanction" measures was possibly based upon a fatal misunderstanding. A "democratically legitimized move to the right"[142] in an EU country was mistaken for a seizing of power by right-wing extremists and totalitarians. There was and is no serious sign of a "Haiderization" of Europe. The French and the Belgians, fearing "Haiderization" of Europe, have overreacted and Europe paid a high price for this mistake: the loss of faith in the EU institutions that allow for a member state to be mistreated in the way Austria was. With the "sanctions," this very improbable political option became a serious threat. A non-topic was made into *the* topic through an unnecessary and overblown debate. A danger, which as such did not exist, was debated and discussed to the point that its existence was believed in. The political isolation of Austria actually strengthened the supporters of the center-right government of the country, if not Haider. The "bilateral measures" could only be abolished by the EU 14 itself. Did they fall into Haider's trap? There is no danger that this provincial politician will achieve much. Rather, the only danger is that he, together with his opponents, make a real mess of things.

The relapse into the rule of stronger nations within the EU has probably caused damage to the Union. The institutions of the EU did not have the final word, but the individual nation states did. The EU

Commission was powerless because the measures had been decided upon and carried out outside of the framework of the EU ("intergovern-mentalization of EU policy through the back door").[143] It partly paralyzed the authorities in Brussels and contributed to great uncertainty among officials in their dealings with Austria.

Actions of mediation by the Commission were rejected by Belgium and France. The result was clearly negative. The "sanction" measures showed that decisions had been made without adequate consideration, that decision makers did not plan enough and reacted spontaneously, and that there was a low level of professionalism in dealing with the problem. For a long while, the EU 14 had no idea how to find their way out of a burdensome dilemma which they had created for themselves and Austria. The appointment of the "three wise men" weakened the position of the Commission, which could have reported on Austria too. With regard to the original intention of preventing the formation of the ÖVP-FPÖ government, the "sanction" measures had already failed on February 4. In this respect, nothing was changed.

In addition, the process of EU integration was weakened in other ways; most importantly, the eastern expansion of the EU was now called into question. In the beginning of September, EU Commissioner for Expansion Matters Günter Verheugen (SPD) spoke about the possibility of a referendum in Germany on the eastern enlargement of the EU.[144] If this suggestion had come from Haider with respect to Austria, it would have been condemned lock, stock, and barrel. After irritation was expressed by Fischer and Prodi, Verheugen immediately backed off, while the FPÖ applauded the attempt by the German Social Democrat.[145]

The discussion about right-wing populism in Europe,[146] which occurred simultaneously to the policy of isolation toward Austria, had no moderating effect upon extremist tendencies in other European states. Neo-Nazi excesses against foreigners increased in Germany, blatant hatred of foreigners was articulated in Spain against Moroccans, and animosity toward foreigners, as well as racism, and brutal antisemitism intensified in France. A nationalist wave threatened to come into existence.

The population of Denmark rejected the introduction of the Euro on September 28 by a majority of 53.1%.[147] The Austria case thus had a devastating effect for the advocates of the European common currency. With the "Austria sanctions," the traditionally Europe-friendly conservatives and liberals carried on a "propagandistic guerilla war" in 2000 which generated strong antipathies against the Union in the population.

The weakness of the Euro and a traditionally Euroskeptic atmosphere in Denmark took care of the rest. In the end, what was decisive was latent nationalism and the fear of the loss of the welfare state.[148] The rejection of the Euro by the Danes might have negative effects on the decisions in Sweden and Great Britain, which until now have not yet joined the monetary union.

The election triumph of the Belgian Vlaams Blok, which received the majority of votes (33 %) in Antwerp and Mechelen, followed on 8 October 2000. The other Belgian parties intensified their *cordon sanitaire* policy, i.e. their total isolation of the Flemish right wingers.[149]

In the debate about a new distribution of power within the Union, which took place immediately before the EU summit in Nice (6-11 December 2000), the Austrian case played a subordinate role.[150] Unanimity was to resolve this debate, which is why the "sanction" measures had to be lifted before the summit conference. However, this unanimity was not long-lasting; the fight for power in the EU soon flared up at full scale.[151]

The Austrian case could have been well suited as an instrument for the demonstration of the EU 14's own power. The relapse to the national "law of the jungle" greatly damaged the Union. This was particularly true when the Austrian government attempted to accuse the Portuguese presidency of the Council of the European Union and the Union itself of pandering to national interests and party politics. At the *Ballhausplatz* one called a spade a spade: fourteen European nation-states had acted as "sovereign" against a union member and thereby attempted to exploit the EU framework—with few prospects for success. In the long run, the institutions of the EU could not be ignored.

The result of the "sanction" measures was also negative for Austria. The international media reported intensively about the "sanctions" of the EU 14 states but disproportionately less about their lifting and the reasons for it. The image of a persecuted Austria was conveyed by the domestic tabloids and led to muddled conspiracy theories and new victim theses.[152]

The pro-European mood among Austrians decreased considerably. In the spring of 2000, only 34% of the Austrian population agreed that their country had benefited from membership in the EU. In the autumn of 1999, that figure was still 45%.[153] In comparison with the referendum on membership in 1994 (66.6%), the level of approval dropped by half.

In addition, the fixation on the "sanctions" issue distorted the Austrian view of the actual conditions in Europe even further. Austria was not as significant for the EU partners as it appeared to be through the EU 14 measures, nor was a realistic assessment of the events in the EU to be expected.[154]

The country had suffered an immeasurable loss of international prestige and even greater damage to its political image in Europe than after the Waldheim debate. If, at that time, the president was labeled a "Nazi," now an entire state was regarded as "Naziland" or "Haiderland." However, according to Günter Bischof Austria's prestige in the U.S. suffered more from Waldheim than from the recent debacle.[155] Bischof further argues that no severe loss of prestige resulted from any of these debates.[156]

With the "sanction" measures, Austrian representatives were excluded from informal consultations, preliminary discussions, and coordination, which are very important for European committee work and which take place before the decisions by the Council. This has to be viewed as a severe political disadvantage.

Austria actually became a "victim"[157] of a new policy by the fourteen EU states. The state was supposed to be systematically isolated within Europe at the bilateral level. This actually succeeded only in the first months. The controversial government only received visits from the heads of state of Kazakhstan, Tajikistan, and Azerbaijan. Thus the joy was all the greater when Stoiber flew to Vienna on an official visit on September 7. Greeted by a red carpet at the airport, he was awarded the "Golden Decoration of the Republic," Austria's highest order, for his support in difficult times.[158]

The lifting of the measures signaled that the EU 14 could carry out a policy that was opposed to the public opinion for only a limited time.[159] In addition, Austria, whose international importance is generally overestimated within the country, clearly exemplified that in this situation self-interests obviously ranked above community interests. According to Albert Rohan, general secretary of the Austrian foreign ministry, the country owed the relatively quick end to the EU 14 measures above all else to its EU membership.[160]

The "sanctions" did not result in the transformation of the FPÖ from a right-wing populist fundamentalist opposition party to a responsible governing party. The process of normalization which had set in when the party began to take over its governing functions, and which was confirmed by the "wise men," was not made any easier. The "sanctions" changed the Haider issue from being an internal Austrian topic to a Europe-wide and worldwide one. In fact, Haider became *persona non grata* throughout the entire world. This situation probably also shattered his dream of ever becoming chancellor. If this was a result of the "sanctions," then the question must be raised as to whether the end justified the means.

There is every reason to believe that the "sanctions" affair of the EU 14 with Austria was a unique event in the history of the Community and will not be repeated. After it became clear that small causes can have large effects, damage control had to take place quickly. The EU summit in Nice was positively assessed in Germany and France (and rightfully so) as an important victory on the path to the eastern expansion of the EU. On the whole, however, the results lagged far behind the expectations for integration policy. As a result of the proposal by Belgium and Austria, a regulated, lawful procedure for Article 7 of the EU Constitution was agreed upon; it determines how the Union[62] and its members should act in the future in cases similar to that in Austria. They are to act with an early warning system, followed by hearings that seek the involvement or agreement of the Commission and the European Parliament; the Council is obliged to regularly examine the reasoning behind its decisions; and the Union needs to consider the question of the proportionality of "sanction" measures. This regulation would at least be a lesson that was drawn from the Austria case. To what degree such an agreement or the Treaty of Nice will be implemented, if at all, is admittedly another story.

Notes

1. I am grateful to the mediAwatch forschungsgruppe Innsbruck, especially Clemens Pig, who provided me with the "Volltexte der ORF-ZIB-Berichterstattung" (transcripts of the Austrian national news) of 1-14 February 2000. I would also like to thank the Minister for Foreign Affairs, Dr. Benita Ferrero-Waldner, for an interesting background talk in Vienna (28 September 2000).

2. Retrieved 2 February 2000 from the World Wide Web: http://www.portugal.ue-2000.pt (homepage of the Portuguese EU Council presidency); see also Waldemar Hummer and Walter Obwexer, "Österreich unter 'EU-Kuratel' (Teil I). Die EU als Wertegemeinschaft: Vom völkerrechtlichen Interventionsverbot zum gemeinschaftsrechtlichen Interventionsgebot," *europablätter* 9 (28 April 2000): 52-58, 54.

3. Joëlle Stolz, "L'Autriche en état de choc après la décision des Quatorze," *Le Monde*, 2 February 2000, 2.

4. Waldemar Hummer, "Vom 'Musterschüler' zum Buhmann. Die EU als 'self contained regime'," *Europäische Rundschau* 28 (2000): 13-20.

5. Michael Gehler, "Richard Coudenhove-Kalergi, Paneuropa und Österreich 1923-1972," *Demokratie und Geschichte. Jahrbuch des Karl von Vogelsang-Instituts zur Erforschung der Geschichte der christlichen Demokratie in Österreich*, ed. Helmut Wohnout, vol. 2 (Vienna: Böhlau, 1998), 143-93.

6. For a controversial debate on this see Michael Gehler, "Der 17. Juli 1989: Bruch oder Kontinuität der österreichischen Integrationspolitik?," *Europäische Integration und Erweiterung. Eine Herausforderung für die Wissenschaften*, ed. Rosita Rindler Schjerve, *Biblioteca Europea* 17 (Napoli: Istituto Italiano per gli Studi Filosofici, 2001): 91-98; Thomas Angerer, "'Alte' und 'neue' Integration. Antwort auf Kritik an der These vom Bruch in der österreichischen Integrationspolitik 1989," in ibid., 67-89; and the reply by Michael Gehler, "Der österreichische EG-Beitrittsantrag vom 17. Juli 1989: Mehr Kontinuität als Diskontinuität! Zur Fortführung einer Historikerkontroverse," in *Europäische Dimensionen der österreichischen Geschichte. 105. Fortbildungstagung des Instituts für Österreichkunde in St. Pölten*, ed. Ernst Bruckmüller, (Vienna: Braumüller, forthcoming).

7. Michael Gehler, "Der 17. Juli 1989: Der EG-Beitrittsantrag. Österreich und die europäische Integration 1945-1995," in *Österreich im 20. Jahrhundert. Vom Zweiten Weltkrieg bis zur Gegenwart*, ed. Michael Gehler and Rolf Steininger, Böhlau Studienbücher, Grundlagen des Studiums, vol. 2 (Vienna: Böhlau, 1997), 515-95.

8. Paul Pasteur, "Freiheitliches Österreich. Vom Nutzen des Erinnerns und Vergessens," *Le Monde diplomatique*, retrieved 17 March 2000 from the World Wide Web: http://monde-diplomatique.de/mtpl/2000/03/17./; Walter Lüthi, "Der Mann der vielen Widersprüche," *Der Bund*, 2 February 2000, 2; Reinhard Olt, "Nicht rechtsextrem, aber seit Kriegsende meistens von der Macht fern gehalten," *Frankfurter Allgemeine Zeitung*, 2 February 2000, 3; Beat Ammann, "Vom 'Wesen' der FPÖ - und Österreichs. Als wär's kein Stück von mir," *Neue Zürcher Zeitung*, 26/27 August 2000, 9.

9. Wolfgang Böhm, "Von der Schildlaus bis zum Euro: FP-Desaster mit Volksmobilisierung," *Die Presse*, 7 July 2000, 6.

10. Kurt Richard Luther and Iain Ogilvie, eds., *Austria and the European Union Presidency: Background and Perspectives* (Keele: The Royal Institute of International Affairs, Keele European Research Center, 1998).

11. Michael Gehler, "Die Affäre Kurt Waldheim. Eine Fallstudie zum Umgang mit der NS-Vergangenheit in den späten achtziger Jahren," in *Österreich im 20. Jahrhundert*, 355-414.

12. Heinrich Schneider, "Die österreichische Neutralität und die europäische Integration," in *Die Neutralen und die europäische Integration 1945-1995. The Neutrals and the European Integration,* ed. Michael Gehler and Rolf Steininger, Institut für Zeitgeschichte an der Universität Innsbruck, Arbeitskreis Europäische Integration, Historische Forschungen, Veröffentlichungen, vol. 3 (Vienna: Böhlau, 2000), 465-96.

13. "Österreichs Erwachen als Paria Europas," *Der Bund*, 2 February 2000, 2; Alexander Cockburn, "Austria - Pariah Among Nations," *The Nation*, 28 February 2000.

14. Joachim Fritz-Vannahme, "Jeder summt seine Melodie. Die Europäer sind sich gar nicht so einig, wie sie mit Haider umgehen sollen," *Die Zeit*, 10 February 2000, 10; Frank Schorkopf, "Verletzt Österreich die Homogenität in der Europäischen Union? Zur Zulässigkeit der 'bilateralen' Sanktionen gegen Österreich," *Deutsches Verwaltungsblatt*, 15 July 2000, 1036-44; Heinrich Schneider, "Österreich in Acht und Bann - ein Schritt zur politisch integrierten 'Wertegemeinschaft'?," *integration* 23 (2000): 120-48.

15. Peter Pernthaler and Peter Hilpold, "Sanktionen als Instrument der Politikkontrolle - der Fall Österreich," *integration* 23 (2000): 105-19; Hummer, "Vom 'Musterschüler' zum Buhmann,'" 19-20; Schorkopf, "Verletzt Österreich die Homogenität in der Europäischen Union?," 1040, 1042-3.

16. Schneider, "Österreich in Acht und Bann," 128; Peter Hort, "Mit der großen Keule gegen die kleine Alpenrepublik. Das wenig durchdachte Vorgehen der Europäischen Union gegen das Mitgliedsland Österreich," *Frankfurter Allgemeine Zeitung*, 2 February 2000, 3.

17. Michael Gehler, "Zur Historisierung der sogenannten Sanktionsfrage," *Die Presse*, 6 July 2000.

18. Günter Bischof and Josef Leidenfrost, eds., *Die bevormundete Nation. Österreich und die Alliierten 1945-1949*, Innsbrucker Forschungen zur Zeitgeschichte, vol. 4 (Innsbruck: Haymon, 1988).

19. Thomas Angerer, "Der 'bevormundete Vormund'. Die französische Besatzungsmacht in Österreich," in *Österreich unter alliierter Besatzung 1945-1955*, ed. Alfred Ablei-tinger, Siegfried Beer, and Eduard Staudinger, Studien zu Politik und Verwaltung, vol. 63, (Vienna: Böhlau, 1998), 159-204.

20. Alfred D. Low, *Die Anschlußbewegung in Österreich und Deutschland 1918-1919, und die Pariser Friedenskonferenz* (Vienna: Braumüller, 1975), 54-81, 82-101.

21. Friedrich Weissensteiner, *Der ungeliebte Staat. Österreich zwischen 1918 und 1938* (Vienna: Österreichischer Bundesverlag, 1990), 117.

22. Gabriele Volsansky, *Pakt auf Zeit. Das Deutsch-österreichische Juli-Abkommen 1936*, Böhlaus Zeitgeschichtliche Bibliothek, vol. 37 (Vienna: Böhlau, 2001).

23. Robert Graham Knight, "Besiegt oder befreit? Eine völkerrechtliche Frage historisch betrachtet," in *Die bevormundete Nation*, 75-91; Robert H. Keyserlingk, *Austria in World War II. An Anglo-American Dilemma* (Kingston: MC Gill Queen's University Press, 1988), 123-56; Günter Bischof, *Austria in the First Cold War, 1945-55. The Leverage of the Weak*, Cold War History Series, General Editor: Saki Dockrill (Basingstoke: Macmillan and St. Martin's Press, 1999), 7-29.

24. See the master work by Gerald Stourzh, *Um Einheit und Freiheit. Staatsvertrag, Neutralität und das Ende der Ost-West-Besetzung Österreichs 1945-55* (Studien zu Politik und Verwaltung, ed. by Christian Brünner, Wolfgang Mantl, and Manfried Welan Vol. 62), fourth completely revised and expanded edition (Vienna: Böhlau, 1998).

25. See Heinrich Payr, *Die schwierige Kunst der Neutralität* (Vienna: Böhlau, 1990), 43-55; see also the contributions by Michael Ruddy, Vladislaw Zubok, Wolfram Kaiser, Erwin A. Schmidl, and the commentary by Wilfried Loth in Gehler and Steininger, eds., *Die Neutralen und die europäische Integration 1945-1995*, 13-83.

26. Bruno Thoß, "Modellfall Österreich? Der österreichische Staatsvertrag und die deutsche Frage 1954/55," in *Zwischen Kaltem Krieg und Entspannung. Sicherheits- und Deutschlandpolitik der Bundesrepublik im Mächtesystem der Jahre 1953-1956*, ed. Bruno Thoß and Hans-Erich Volkmann (Boppard am Rhein: Harald Boldt, 1988), 93-136; Michael Gehler, "'L'unique objectif des Soviétiques est de viser l'Allemagne'. Staatsvertrag und Neutralität 1955 als 'Modell' für Deutschland?," in *Österreich in den Fünfzigern*, ed. Thomas Albrich, Klaus Eisterer, Michael Gehler, and Rolf Steininger, Innsbrucker Forschungen zur Zeitgeschichte, vol. 11 (Innsbruck: Studienverlag, 1995), 259-97; Stourzh, *Um Einheit und Freiheit*, 388-391, 450-485; Michael Gehler, "Österreich und die deutsche Frage 1954/55: Zur 'Modellfall'-Debatte in der interna-tionalen Diplomatie und der bundesdeutschen Öffentlichkeit aus französischer Sicht,"

in 20. *Österreichischer Historikertag 1994 in Bregenz* (Vienna: Verband der österreichischen Historiker und Geschichtsvereine, 1998), 83-134.

27. Michael Gehler, "Facing a range of obstacles: Austria's integration policy 1963-69," in *Crises and Compromises: The European Project 1963-1969,* ed. Wilfried Loth, Veröffentlichungen der Historiker-Verbindungsgruppe bei der Kommission der Europäischen Gemeinschaften/Publications du Groupe de Liaison des Professeurs d'Histoire Contemporaine auprès des Communautés Européennes, vol. 8 (Baden-Baden: Nomos, 2001), 459-87.

28. Bruno Kreisky to Josef Klaus, 24 February 1965. Stiftung Bruno Kreisky Archiv (SBKA, Vienna), BMfAA Schachtel F-Köhl.

29. Rolf Steininger, *Südtirol zwischen Diplomatie und Terror 1947-1969,* Veröffentlichungen des Südtiroler Landesarchivs, vol. 6/3 (Bozen: Athesia, 1999), 533-60.

30. Oliver Rathkolb, "Die Kreisky-Ära 1970-1983," in *Österreich im 20. Jahrhundert,* ed. Steininger and Gehler, vol. 2, 305-53; Michael Gehler and Hubert Sickinger, "Politische Skandale in der Zweiten Republik," in *Österreich 1945-1995, Gesellschaft-Politik-Kultur,* ed. Reinhard Sieder, Heinz Steinert, and Emmerich Tálos, Österreichische Texte zur Gesellschaftskritik, vol. 60 (Vienna: Verlag für Gesellschaftskritik, 1995), 671-83.

31. See Preston, *Enlargement and Integration in the European Union,* 87-109, 131-34.

32. Information provided to the author by University Professor DDDr. Waldemar Hummer, University of Innsbruck, 27 March 1998.

33. Interview with Andreas Khol, 23 April 1998.

34. Ibid.; Vranitzky made clear vis-à-vis Mitterrand, that Austria does not want to enter into the EC as a German state, he represents "den ersten und einzigen österreichischen Staat," quoted by Alfred Missong, "Frankreich-Österreich: Von Klischees zu Verständnis," *Europäische Rundschau* 23 (1995): 135-39.

35. "My opponents always make the same mistake: they get all worked up about things that the people actually want." Jörg Haider, *Dolomiten,* 21 July 2000, 3. On populism see also Helmut Dubiel, "Das Gespenst des Populismus," in idem, *Populismus und Aufklärung* (Frankfurt/Main: Suhrkamp, 1986), 33-50.

36. See André Brigot, "Frankreich und Europa," *Aus Politik und Zeitgeschichte* B 42 (1994): 34-38; Wernhard Möschel, "Europapolitik zwischen deutscher Romantik und gallischer Klarheit," *Aus Politik und Zeitgeschichte* B 3-4 (1995): 10-16.

37. Christian Meier, "Die kranken Ärzte. Europa und Österreich, ein Tollhaus," *Frankfurter Allgemeine Zeitung,* 16 March 2000, 51.

38. Hans Arnold, "Die Europäische Union zwischen Maastricht und Maastricht-Revision," *Aus Politik und Zeitgeschichte* B 3-4 (1995): 3-9.

39. Pernthaler and Hilpold, "Sanktionen als Instrument der Politikkontrolle," 114-16; Gisela Müller-Brandeck-Bocquet, "Der Amsterdamer Vertrag zur Reform der Europäischen Union. Ergebnisse, Fortschritte, Defizite," *Aus Politik und Zeitgeschichte* B 47 (1997): 21-29.

40. Waldemar Hummer and Walter Obwexer, "Österreich unter 'EU-Kuratel.' Teil I. Die EU als Wertegemeinschaft: Vom völkerrechtlichen Interventionsverbot zum gemeinschaftsrechtlichen Interventionsgebot," *europablätter* 9 (28 April 2000): 52-58; und Teil II, *europablätter* 9 (30 June 2000): 93-101; Pernthaler and Hilpold, "Sanktionen als Instrument der Politikkontrolle," 105-19.

41. Schorkopf, "Verletzt Österreich die Homogenität in der Europäischen Union?," 1042-44.

42. Ibid., 1042; Olav Willadsen, "Die bilateralen Österreich-Sanktionen und die Realität. Die Sanktionen sind nicht bilateral, sondern tatsächlich eine EU-Aktion und sie sind rechtswidrig," *Die Presse*, 27 July 2000, 2.

43. Waldemar Hummer, "Art. 6 Abs. 1 EUV am Beispiel Österreichs: Vom völkerrechtlichen 'Interventionsverbot' zum unionsrechtlichen 'Interventionsgebot'?," *Wiener Journal* (März 2000): 16-17.

44. Information provided to the author by Ambassador Dr. Gregor Woschnagg, Austria's permanent representative to the Commission in Brussels, 26 January 2001; report by Günter Schmidt from Brussels in "Zeit im Bild 1," ORF, 1 February 2000; Schneider, "Österreich in Acht und Bann," 129-30; Hannes Gamillscheg, "'Völlig undenkbar, aber genau das, was Klestil und Klima taten.' Laut dänischer Presse suchten der österreichische Bundespräsident und der Bundeskanzler die Hilfe ihrer Kollegen gegen die FPÖ," *Die Presse*, 3 February 2000, 3.

45. Schneider, "Österreich in Acht und Bann," 130.

46. Ibid.

47. Ibid.

48. Gamillscheg, "Völlig undenkbar," 3.

49. "Internationale Verschwörung gegen Österreich?," *Dokumentationsarchiv des Österreichischen Widerstandes Mitteilungen*, April 2000, series 146, 5-7.

50. Information provided to the author by Ambassador Dr. Woschnagg, 26 January 2001.

51. Clemens Schuhmann, "Brüsseler Spitzen: Man schlägt die FPÖ und meint den Vlaams Blok," *Die Presse*, 26 February 2000, 6; Elisabeth Wehrmann, "Die jungen Herren Flanderns. In Belgien drängen die Rechtsradikalen vom Vlaams Blok zur Macht," *Die Zeit*, 15 June 2000, 9.

52. Tony Judt, "Kontra: Die Reaktion der EU ist Heuchelei," *Tages-Anzeiger*, 25 February 2000, 65; "Das uralte Schwanken: Frankreichs ambivalentes Österreich-Bild. 'Wenn Paris nach Wien blickt, schielt es mit einem Auge nach Berlin.' Die Haltung der Elite hat historische, aber auch innen- und europapolitische Gründe. Warum an der Seine so massiv auf die Regierungsbildung an der Donau reagiert wird. Erklärungen des Historikers Thomas Angerer," *Die Presse*, 4 March 2000, 8; "L'affaire Haider divise les droites européennes," *Le Monde*, 3 February 2000, 3; Winfried Didzoleit, Jürgen Hogrefe, Olaf Ihlau, and Walter Mayr, "Sperrfeuer auf den Alpenbunker," *Der Spiegel* 6 (2000): 140-46; see Arnaud Leparmentier, "M. Schröder craint une 'haidérisation' de l'Allemagne en cas d'effondrement de la CDU," *Le Monde*, 4 February 2000, 3.

53. Interview with People's Party Politician Prof. Dr. Andreas Khol, 23 April 1998.

54. Schneider, "Österreich in Acht und Bann," 133; *Der Standard*, 26/27 February 2000, 2.

55. *Der Standard*, 26/27 February 2000, 2; Theo Sommer, "Europa leistet sich aus moralischen Gründen eine große Heuchelei," *Die Zeit*, 10 February 2000, 1. The term "collective populism" was coined by Peter Ludlow, head of the Centre for European Policy Studies in Brussels, see *Dolomiten*, 8 February 2000, 3.

56. "Le Conseil fédéral veut faire confiance au nouveau gouvernement autrichien," *Le Temps*, 5 February 2000, 9; "Bern zirkelt. Der Bundesrat hat auf die neue Rechtsregierung in Österreich reagiert: mit drei hoch diplomatischen Sätzen," *Tages-Anzeiger*, 5

February 2000, 7; *Berner Zeitung*, 5 February 2000, 1; "Österreich als Negativbeispiel für Beitrittswerber. EU gegen Fremdenfeinde in Regierungen," *Der Standard*, 26/27 February 2000, 3; François Modoux, "La Suisse reste coite devant la crise autrichienne," *Le Temps*, 2 February 2000, 2-3.

57. "Brüssel: 'Ski fahren in Österreich ist unmoralisch'," *Kurier*, 3 February 2000, 5.

58. "In der EU verstärkt sich die Debatte über eine Aufhebung der Sanktionen," *Der Standard*, 12 May 2000, 3.

59. Ibid.; Helmut Hetzel, "Wim Kok wird wohl doch zum Telephon greifen müssen," *Die Presse*, 11 September 2000, 6.

60. *Der Standard*, 12 May 2000, 3.

61. *Der Standard*, 26/27 February 2000, 2.

62. Ibid.

63. "Auch USA drohen Österreich," *Dolomiten*, 2 February 2000, 1. Information provided to the author by University Professor Lothar Höbelt, University of Vienna.

64. "Die Ansprüche des Anwalts," *Kurier*, 23 February 2000, 3.

65. Klaus-Peter Schmid, "Ende des Tabus. Auch Österreich will nun NS-Zwangsarbeiter entschädigen," *Die Zeit*, 10 February 2000, 35.

66. *Der Standard*, 12 May 2000, 3.

67. Ibid.

68. "Keine neue Initiative geplant," *Dolomiten*, 11 May 2000, 1; "In der EU verstärkt sich die Debatte über eine Aufhebung der Sanktionen," *Der Standard*, 12 May 2000, 3; "Hilfreiche Geister aus dem Norden," *Die Presse*, 17 June 2000, 6.

69. *Der Standard*, 12 May 2000, 3.

70. "Polnische Stimmen zur neuen Regierung in Österreich. Differenzierte Stellungnahmen," *Neue Zürcher Zeitung*, 5/6 February 2000, 4.

71. *Der Standard*, 12 May 2000, 3; "Die Beneš-Dekrete: eine politische und keine juristische Frage," *Die Presse*, 21 September 2000, 3; Martin David, "Die EU als Wertegemeinschaft? Die 'Maßnahmen' der EU-Staaten gegenüber Österreich und die österreichisch-tschechischen Beziehungen," presentation held at the *Institut pro Mezinárodních Studie* in Prague for a class by Alena Mísková, 27 October 2000, manuscript (31 pp.), 28-30. I am grateful to Dr. David for providing me with his paper.

72. *Der Standard*, 26/27 February 2000, 2; Miklós Haraszti, "Ein Schatten über dem Osten. Über den Widerstand von Österreichs Nachbarn gegen die EU-Sanktionen," *Der Standard*, 11 May 2000, 39.

73. "Die 14 und Österreich/EU-Kandidaten," *Der Standard*, 12 May 2000.

74. "Abwartende Haltung Ungarns gegenüber Wien," *Neue Zürcher Zeitung*, 3 February 2000, 2; *Der Standard*, 26/27 February 2000, 2; Haraszti, "Ein Schatten," 39.

75. Christopher Preston, *Enlargement and Integration in the European Union* (London: Routledge, 1997), 45, 59-61, 85-86, 107-109, 227-34.

76. See the comparative approach by Thomas Angerer, "Exklusivität und Selbstausschließung. Integrationsgeschichtliche Überlegungen zur Erweiterungsfrage am Beispiel Frankreichs und Österreichs, in L'Élargissement de l'Union Européenne," in *Actes du colloque franco-autrichien* organisé les 13 et 14 juin 1997 par l'Institut Culturel Autrichien et l'Institut Pierre-Renouvin, *Revue d'Europe Centrale* 6 (1998): 25-54.

77. See the interview with Thomas Angerer, "Das uralte Schwanken," *Die Presse*, 4 March 2000, 8.

78. "Österreich als Negativbeispiel für Beitrittswerber. EU gegen Fremdenfeinde in Regierungen," *Der Standard*, 26/27 February 2000, 3.

79. See Chapter 1 "Die Entwicklung der EVP-Fraktion des Europäischen Parlaments" of Hans August Lücker, "Von der Parlamentarischen Versammlung bis zur ersten Direktwahl," in *Europa als Auftrag. Die Politik deutscher Christdemokraten im Europäischen Parlament 1957-1997. Von den Römischen Verträgen zur Politischen Union*, ed. Günter Rinsche and Ingo Friedrich (Cologne: Böhlau, 1997), 9-27.

80. Christian Mertens, *Die österreichischen Christdemokraten im Dienste Europas* (Vienna: multi media, 1997), 65-66.

81. Andreas Khol, "Die internationale Parteienzusammenarbeit: Die Beziehungen der Österreichischen Volkspartei zu ihren Schwesterparteien und ihre Mitarbeit in den transnationalen Parteienzusammenschlüssen," in *Die Transformation der österreichischen Gesellschaft und die Alleinregierung Klaus*, ed. Robert Kriechbaumer, Franz Schausberger and Hubert Weinberger, Veröffentlichung der Dr.-Wilfried Haslauer-Bibliothek, Forschungsinstitut für politisch-historische Studien, vol. 1 (Salzburg: ITIV, 1995), 367-400.

82. Alexander Demblin, "Die ÖVP in internationalen Organisationen - EDU, IDU," *Österreichisches Jahrbuch für Politik* 83 (Vienna: Oldenbourg, Verlag für Geschichte und Politik, 1984), 243-55; Schneider, "Österreich in Acht und Bann, " 137.

83. "L'affaire Haider divise les droites européennes, " *Le Monde*, 3 February 2000, 3; *Die Zeit*, 10 February 2000, 10.

84. "Ende für Ausschluß," *Plus* 2 (2000), 9; "Freispruch für ÖVP/EVP-Bericht/EVP warnt Regierung vor Volksbefragung über Sanktionen. Nach dem positiven EVP-Bericht will sich die Bundesregierung erneut bei den EU-Partnern um ein Ende der Sanktionen bemühen," *Die Presse*, 7 June 2000, 1, 6.

85. Interview with University Professor Dr. Lothar Höbelt, University of Vienna, 17 July 2000. See also André Osterhoff, *Die Euro-Rechte. Zur Bedeutung des Europäischen Parlaments bei der Vernetzung der extremen Rechten* (Münster: Unrast, 1997).

86. "Sanktionen: Berlin, Paris hart - EU-Bürger jedoch für Aufhebung. EU-Bevölkerung für Aufhebung der Sanktionen, aber für Beobachtung," *Die Presse*, 10/11/12 June 2000, 1, 7.

87. Schorkopf, "Verletzt Österreich die Homogenität in der Europäischen Union?," 1040-42.

88. Hummer and Obwexer, "Österreich unter 'EU-Kuratel' (Teil I)," 57.

89. Ibid., 57-58.

90. Schneider, "Österreich in Acht und Bann," 127-29; Anton Pelinka, "Österreich und Europa. Zur Isolierung eines Landes," *Europäische Rundschau* 28 (2000): 3-8; Andreas Unterberger, "Intoleranz und Heuchelei. Eine Antwort an Anton Pelinka und 14 europäische Regierungen," in ibid, 21-33.

91. "Wie es dazu kam: Schwedens Moral und Frankreichs Wahl," *Die Presse*, 19 June 2000, 5.

92. Michael Gehler, "'... eine grotesk überzogene Dämonisierung eines Mannes ...' Die Waldheim-Affäre 1986-1992," in *Politische Affären und Skandale*, 614-65.

93. "M. Klestil a-t-il demandé aux Européens d'intervenir?," *Le Monde*, 4 February 2000, 4.

94. "Des sources diplomatiques à Paris, citées par l'AFP, ainsi que le quotidien danois Extra Bladet avaient indiqué que le président Klestil avait 'donné son accord' à Jacques Chirac pour que soient rendues publiques les mesures envisagées par les autres Etats membres afin d'empêcher un accord permettant l'arrivée au gouvernement du parti de Jörg Haider," ibid.; Schneider, "Österreich in Acht und Bann," 128; Didzoleit et al., "Sperrfeuer auf den Alpenbunker," 142; "Sternstunde durch Eitelkeit verpatzt," *Die Presse*, 15 September 2000, 6; "Klestil soll die rasche Veröffentlichung empfohlen haben: Wie es dazu kam: Schwedens Moral und Frankreichs Wahl," *Die Presse*, 19 June 2000, 5.

95. Source known to the author.

96. "Österreichs Zukunft im Herzen Europas. Die Präambel zum Regierungsprogramm von ÖVP und FPÖ," *Neue Zürcher Zeitung*, 5/6 February 2000, 4; Dr. Wolfang Schüssel, Dr. Jörg Haider, "Declaration. Responsibility for Austria - A Future in the Heart of Europe," 3 February 2000, retrieved 5 March 2000 from the World Wide Web: http://www.austria.org/newgovt1.html.

97. See Mitchell G. Ash, "Letter from Vienna: Haider, the FPÖ and Europe," retrieved 29 March 2000 from the World Wide Web: http://www.aics.gorg/IssueBriefs/ash.html.

98. Christoph Kotanko, "Rückzug aus taktischen und persönlichen Gründen. Jörg Haider verkündet Rücktritt als FPÖ-Chef," *Kurier*, 29 February 2000; "Taktischer Rückzug auf Zeit," *Tages-Anzeiger*, 29 February 2000; William Drozdiak, "Haider quits as far-right-leader," *Washington Post*, 29 February 2000; "Taktischer Rückzug," *Frankfurter Rundschau*, 1 March 2000; Michael Völker, "Ein Abschied mit Schmerzen, aber nicht auf Dauer," *Der Standard*, 2 May 2000, 7.

99. *Der Standard*, 26/27 February 2000, 4.

100. Hummer and Obwexer, "Österreich unter 'EU-Kuratel' (Teil II)," 97-99.

101. Richard Mitten, "EU could strengthen Haider's hand in Austria," in Woodrow Wilson International Center for Scholars (WWICS) News, retrieved 5 April 2000 from the World Wide Web: http://wwics.si.edu/NEWS/mitten.htm.

102. "Es gibt keine EU-Sanktionen," *Der Standard*, 20/21 May 2000, 6.

103. Ibid.; Reinhard Olt, "In der Wiener Quarantänestation," *Frankfurter Allgemeine Zeitung*, 20 June 2000; Erich Witzmann, "Der Kitt ist weg," *Die Presse*, 14 September 2000, 2.

104. Hannes Gamillscheg, "Sanktionen verstärken dänische Skepsis. Der Haider-Effekt bringt Dänemarks Euro-Strategie ins Wanken," *Die Presse*, 22 February 2000, 1.

105. Markus Warasin, "Ein erster Durchbruch?," *Dolomiten*, 27 April 2000, 3; Idem, "Viel Lärm um nichts?," ibid., 20 June 2000, 3; Idem, "Union der Nationalstaaten," ibid., 28 June 2000, 3; Idem, "Integrationsstopp?," ibid., 7 July 2000, 3.

106. Markus Warasin, "Scheitert Europäische Union?," *Dolomiten*, 16 May 2000, 3; Stephan Baier, "Im Pulverdampf," ibid., 6 September 2000, 3.

107. Michael Gehler, "Waldheim und die EU 14-Maßnahmen," *Die Presse*, 6 February 2001, 2.

108. Danni Härry, "Die Europäische Union in der Haider-Falle," *Berner Zeitung*, 5 February 2000, 2.

109. "Empörte Österreicher EU-freundlich," *Dolomiten*, 5 April 2000, 2.

110. Jean-Jacques Langendorf, "Le produit d'un système bloqué et corrompu," *Le Temps*, 2 February 2000, 3.

111. Andrew Nagorski, "The Politics of Guilt. Austria's Bigot, Europe's Burden," *Foreign Affairs* 79, no. 3 (May/June 2000): 18-22.

112. "Stichwort: 'Drei Weise'," *Das Parlament*, 28 July/4 August 2000, 6; Stephan Baier, "Minderheitenrechte," *Dolomiten*, 1/2 July 2000, 3; Christoph Pan, "EU-Maßnahmen und Frankreichs Rivalität mit Österreich. Frankreichs Volksgruppenpolitik gehört zu den rückschrittlichsten in ganz Europa," *Die Presse*, 22 September 2000, 2.

113. See "Chronologie der Sanktionen. Bericht der Weisen: Der lange Weg von der Verhängung der Maßnahmen gegen Österreich bis zur Abgabe des Berichts in Paris/Porträts," *Die Presse*, 9 September 2000, 7.

114. Peter Hort, "Ein brüchiger Bann," *Frankfurter Allgemeine Zeitung*, 28 February 2000, 1.

115. *Neue Zürcher Zeitung*, 2 February 2000.

116. Hort, "Ein brüchiger Bann," 1.

117. Schorkopf, "Verletzt Österreich die Homogenität in der Europäischen Union?," 1044.

118. "Haiders rhetorischer Amoklauf," *Dolomiten*, 10 March 2000, 2; *Die Welt*, 14 April 2000, 7.

119. Heinz-Peter Dietrich, "'Drei Weise' aus dem Euroland in der Alpenrepublik. Die Europäische Union läßt die Einhaltung der Menschenrechte in Österreich prüfen," *Das Parlament*, 28 July/4 August 2000, 6.

120. "Demonstrative Rückendeckung für Österreich," *Coburger Tageblatt*, 8 September 2000; "Europa würde Schaden nehmen," *Die Presse*, 8 September 2000, 6.

121. "Der Weisenbericht im Wortlaut. Die 119 Antworten der drei Weisen," retrieved 12 September 2000 from the World Wide Web: http://www.o.../000908-31343/31324txt_story.html; "Schlußfolgerungen: Beibehaltung wäre 'kontraproduktiv'," *Die Presse*, 9 September 2000, 6.

122. "Shuttlepolitik mit guten Beziehungen," *Der Standard*, 12 May 2000, 3.

123. *Die Presse*, 9 September 2000, 4; 12 September 2000, 3.

124. "Weise: Chirac hilft NGOs," *Die Presse*, 21 August 2000, 4; "Weisenrat lehnt Treffen mit Jörg Haider ab," *Die Presse*, 30 August 2000, 1.

125. Hannes Gamillscheg, "Sanktionen verstärken dänische Skepsis. Der Haider-Effekt bringt Dänemarks Euro-Strategie ins Wanken," *Die Presse*, 22 February 2000, 11.

126. Hans Rauscher, "Der Meisterspieler als Getriebener," *Der Standard*, 9 May 2000, 37; see also Peter A. Ulram, "Ein guter Mensch zu sein," *Die Presse*/Spectrum, 29 July 2000, IV; Andreas Khol, "EU-Volksbefragung und die Europäische Verfassung," *Die Presse*/Spectrum, 5 August 2000, X.

127. "Bericht der Weisen: Das mit Spannung erwartete Urteil läßt alle Parteien auf ein Ende der Maßnahmen gegen Österreich hoffen," *Die Presse*, 9 September 2000, 4.

128. "Haider erst selbstkritisch, dann polternd," *Die Presse*, 11 September 2000, 4.

129. "Opposition: Vollen Platz in der EU wiederfinden, Kritik gerechtfertigt," *Die Presse*, 9 September 2000, 4.

130. "Amato für Aufhebung," *Die Dolomiten*, 8 September 2000, 1.

131. "'Es war Zeit, die Maßnahmen zu beenden'. Die britische Regierung übte Druck auf Paris aus," *Die Presse*, 14 September 2000, 9.

132. *Neue Zürcher Zeitung*, 11 September 2000, 3.

133. "Tauziehen um Ende der EU-Sanktionen," *Wiener Zeitung*, 13 September 2000, 1, 5; "Sanktionen aufgehoben," *Der Standard*, 13 September 2000, 1; "Nervenkrieg vor Sanktionsende," *Salzburger Nachrichten*, 13 September 2000, 2.

134. "Das Kommuniqué im Wortlaut," *Die Presse*, 14 September 2000, 6; "Diplomatischer Krimi um das Ende der Sanktionen," *Salzburger Nachrichten*, 13 September 2000, 1.

135. "Die Maßnahmen waren nützlich," *Der Standard*, 13 September 2000, 7.

136. "Wien erwartet rasches Ende der Sanktionen," *Neue Zürcher Zeitung*, 11 September 2000, 3.

137. Andreas Schwarz, "Klestil im Wettlauf um die gute Nachricht," *Die Presse*, 8 September 2000, 3; Eva Male, "Vergebliches Warten auf Chirac in New York: Umarmung, Schulterklopfen, Achselzucken," *Die Presse*, 8 September 2000, 6; *Salzburger Nachrichten*, 13 September 2000, 3.

138. "Sanktionen aufgehoben," *Der Standard*, 13 September 2000, 1; "USA sehen Kurs bestätigt und halten daran fest," *Die Presse*, 14 September 2000, 8.

139. "Kanada behält sich neue Schritte vor," *Die Presse*, 14 September 2000, 8.

140. "Barak bleibt hart und kritisiert EU-Einlenken," *Die Presse*, 14 September 2000, 8.

141. Michael Gehler, "Waldheim und die EU 14-Maßnahmen," *Die Presse*, 6 February 2001, 2.

142. Ammann, "Vom 'Wesen' der FPÖ - und Österreichs," 9; looking to the new Austrian government, Werner A. Perger described this with "postfaschistische[r] Autoritarismus:" see Werner A. Perger, "Schüssel mit zwei Zungen. Österreichs Kanzler provoziert Europa," *Die Zeit*, 8 June 2000, 1.

143. "Kommission verliert Einfluß, Staaten gewinnen an Macht," *Die Presse*, 14 September 2000, 6.

144. Thomas Darnstädt et al., "Offen für den Osten. Mit seinem Vorschlag eines Referendums über die EU-Osterweiterung hat der Brüsseler Kommissar Günter Verheugen eine Debatte um die Angst vor den neuen Mitgliedern eröffnet," *Der Spiegel* 37 (2000): 34-36.

145. Stephan Baier, "Im Pulverdampf," *Die Dolomiten*, 6 September 2000, 3.

146. Uwe Backes, "Extremismus und Populismus von rechts. Ein Vergleich auf europäischer Ebene," *Aus Politik und Zeitgeschichte* B 46-47 (1990): 3-14; and Petra Bauer and Oskar Niedermayer, "Extrem rechtes Potential in den Ländern der Europäischen Gemeinschaft," in ibid., 15-26; Hans-Georg Betz, *Radical Right-Wing Populism in Western Europe* (Basingstoke: The Macmillan Press LTD, 1994); Uwe Backes, "Rechtsextremismus in Deutschland. Ideologien, Organisationen und Strategien," *Aus Politik und Zeitgeschichte* B 9-10 (1998): 27-35; Hans-Georg Betz, "Rechtspopulismus: Ein internationaler Trend?," *Aus und Politik und Zeitgeschichte* B 9-10 (1998): 3-12; Frank Decker, *Parteien unter Druck. Der neue Rechtspopulismus in den westlichen Demokratien* (Opladen: Leske und Budrich, 2000).

147. "Dänemark: Jubel und Katzenjammer beim Volk, das stets verneint," *Die Presse*, 30 September 2000, 3.

148. For this information, I am grateful to Dr. Johnny Laursen, Aarhus University, Denmark, 1 November 2000.

149. "Vlaams Blok bleibt in Quarantäne," *Die Presse*, 10 October 2000, 7.

150. Doris Kraus, "Machtspiel in der EU: Davids gegen Goliaths," *Die Presse*, 15 July 2000, 3; "Biarritz zieht Fronten im brutalen Kampf um die innere Reform der EU. Beim EU-Gipfel in Biarritz gingen die Wogen hoch: Das Tauziehen um die neue Machtverteilung sorgte für emotionale Kontroversen," *Die Presse*, 16 October 2000, 7; "Fortschritte sehen anders aus," *Die Presse*, 13 December 2000, 7; "Schuman und De Gaulle müssen sich in ihren Gräbern umdrehen," *Die Presse*, 20 December 2000, 6.

151. Frankreichs Seiltanz um Macht und Einfluß im Zentrum Europas, *Die Presse*, 21 August 2000, 4.

152. "Österreich auf der Watchlist!/Ganz Österreich steht auf der Watchlist!," in *Neue Kronenzeitung*, 3 February 2000; Hans-Georg Behr, "In Sanktionistan. Die Wiener und die EU-Sanktionen: Keiner kennt sie, aber jeder spürt sie genau," *Frankfurter Allgemeine Zeitung*, 10 June 2000, 46; Josef Feldner, *Freispruch für Österreich* (Graz: Stocker, 2000).

153. "Sanktionen hinterlassen Narben: Österreich nun klar EU-skeptisch," *Die Presse*, 25 July 2000, 6; "Zustimmung zur EU ist in Österreich stark gesunken," *Die Presse*, 27 October 2000, 2.

154. Christian David, "Die Eliánisierung der österreichischen Innenpolitik," *Der Standard*, 24 May 2000, 37.

155. Guenter Bischof, "'Experiencing a Nasty Fall from Grace...' Austria's Image in the U.S. after the Formation of the New ÖVP/FPÖ Government," retrieved 10 July 2000 from the World Wide Web: www.centeraustria.uno.edu (homepage of the Center for Austrian Culture and Commerce at the University of New Orleans).

156. E-Mail from Günter Bischof to the author, 24 January 2001.

157. Pelinka, "Österreich und Europa," 2.

158. "Ein Zeichen gegen den Boykott Österreichs," *Coburger Tageblatt*, 8 September 2000.

159. "Sanktionen: Berlin, Paris hart - EU-Bürger jedoch für Aufhebung/EU-Bevölkerung für Aufhebung der Sanktionen, aber für Beobachtung," *Die Presse*, 10/11/12 June 2000, 1, 7.

160. Albert Rohan, "Das Ende der Sanktionen: eine Bilanz," *Die Presse*, 13 September 2000, 2.

NONTOPICAL ESSAY

Jews and Other Victims:
The 'Jewish Questions' and Discourses of Victimhood in Postwar Austria[1]

Richard Mitten

I

In the Proclamation of the Austrian Second Republic, issued on 27 April 1945, the representatives of the three officially anti-fascist parties established, or reestablished, under the auspices of the Soviet Army—the People's Party (ÖVP),[2] the Socialists (SPÖ) and the Communists (KPÖ)—recalled that owing to the complete political, economic and cultural annexation of the country, the National Socialist Reich government of Adolf Hitler led the people of Austria, whom he had made powerless and without will, into a senseless and hopeless war of conquest, which no Austrian had ever wanted, or had ever been in a position to foresee or approve; [Hitler led them] to fight other peoples, against whom no true Austrian had ever entertained any feelings of hostility or hatred. ...[3]

A few months later, in the autumn of 1945, Artur Rosenberg, a Jewish Austrian Holocaust[4] survivor who had spent the war years in various internment camps, delivered a talk in the Vienna *Konzerthaus* on what he called the "Jewish question" in postwar Austria. In his remarks Rosenberg affirmed that "a part of the Austrian population shares guilt [*trägt mit an der Schuld*] for the horrible atrocities [*Untaten*] that were committed against Austrian Jewry," and also that "Austria has a debt towards the Jews [*an den Juden schuldig geworden*]. Austria must discharge this debt [*diese Schuld tilgen*]." "Today it is the duty," he continued, of all those who hold positions of responsibility for the political community [as a whole] to fight hatred of Jews uncompromisingly, to combat its manifestations [*Auswirkungen*] unflinchingly, and to work for its eradication systematically.

This can happen only if the sense of responsibility for what has happened is brought home to everyone: to those who actively took part, and to those who allowed it to happen by standing off to one side. This moral restitution [*moralische Wiedergutmachung*] is the crucial point. Only from it can any material restitution emerge which has value and durability.[5] Rosenberg's remarks, unheeded at the time,[6] were extraordinarily foresighted, for the political and educational program he advocated seems ambitious even today. What seems noteworthy about his words is first the tension between his statement that a "part" of the Austrian population bore co-responsibility for the Nazi genocide and his view that "Austria" (that is the postwar Austrian state) had thereby incurred a moral "debt" or "guilt"[7] to be discharged towards "Austrian Jewry." This tension has still not been satisfactorily resolved. Second, for Rosenberg the "Jewish question" meant above all confronting and combating anti-Jewish prejudice. "Moral restitution," he argued, was not only an indispensable part of the "Jewish question"; it was perhaps even more important than material compensation.[8]

Yet could Rosenberg and the Austrian Second Republic's founding fathers have been describing the same country?

Alas, they were. For however prescient or insightful, Rosenberg's remarks were also illusory. Just how illusory may be judged from the view expressed years later by the *Israelitische Kultusgemeinde (IKG)* in Vienna about the realities of Austrian politics: "Because of their small number (at the moment approximately 10,000 of previously 200,000)," an *IKG* press release stated, "today [1956] the Jews in Austria are neither a political nor an economic nor a cultural factor. Internal Austrian politics are wholly realistic, and [its politicians] are always looking for possibilities to win voters. Thus the Jews in Austria are not a serious political factor." "The Jews," the *Kultusgemeinde* declared, "are inconvenient for the political parties, since through their very presence they disturb the 'good' relationship to the former or incorrigible National Socialists which all parties seek to cultivate.[9]

Jews in postwar Austria learned quickly that moral appeals of the type advanced by Rosenberg in 1945 had little purchase unless backed by political power of some kind.[10] And while the Austrian government was always sensitive to international criticism of its de-Nazification policies and to reported incidents of anti-Jewish hostility—not least because these criticisms frequently led to some inquiries or complaints from the U.S. occupation authorities—the Jews organized in the *IKG* correctly surmised that their specific interests were to a large extent hostage to Austrian domestic party politics. Linking their political fortunes to one or another political party meant, of course, moderating or even sacrificing some objectives to obtain others, while the absence of any plausible alternative (for those Jews who wished to remain in Austria) not infrequently required the reluctant tolerance of such things as the anti-fascist political parties' ingratiation and even recruitment of former Nazis.

II.

Since the Waldheim affair, I, like many of my colleagues, have been attempting to understand why the presumed historical *legacies* of anti-Semitism and "the specific Austrian contribution to the complex process leading to the ovens of Treblinka and Auschwitz[11] failed to become an equally imposing *burden* of collective moral or historical *responsibility* in, and for, postwar Austria. In particular, I have been interested in how and why the notion of a distinct Jewish suffering under National Socialism became successfully incorporated and dissolved into a more comprehensive category of "pan-Austrian" victimhood.

The explanation used to seem less complicated than it does today. It was tempting to view this process as merely one more example of moral considerations having been sacrificed on the altar of postwar *Realpolitik*. All too often, the historiographical response to the Waldheim affair—and I do not exempt myself from this criticism[12]—has been to view postwar Austrian historical memory as a kind of "archaeology of scandal," or a sort of "genealogy of duplicity" by Austrian postwar ruling elites, played out somewhere between Rosenberg's inspired vision of how the "Jewish question" ought to have been addressed in Austria and the morally rather less edifying record of postwar domestic politics. However, while many critical studies tend to ascribe the Austrian elites' failure to address and answer this "Jewish question" either to cynicism or to remnants of anti-Jewish hostilities[13] I think it more helpful to take account of the very different political and discursive contexts within which the various political actors made their respective choices. Indeed, it seems both anachronistic and inaccurate to view the various invocations of the so-called victim thesis enshrined in the Moscow Declaration simply as a matter of Austrian elites' contriving disingenuous arguments to obfuscate or finesse the delicate political legacy of anti-Semitism, or to evade a clearly recognizable moral responsibility. While the ostensible failure of postwar Austrian elites to deal adequately with the Holocaust has been frequently attributed to a culture of amnesia or repression, the handling of the "Jewish question" in postwar Austria reflects, in my view, a culture of highly politicized remembering, based on adversarial but mutually reinforcing historical narratives. These accounts of twentieth century Austrian history, cast largely as political parables, were plausible enough to satisfy partisan constituencies; they were compatible with the integration of former Nazis into the democratic political culture; and they were not considered so *outré* as to endanger Western Allied support, for the Austrian policies seemed consistent with the aims of de-Nazification and democratic constitutionalism. Only on the basis of such a politicized remembering, I want to argue, could a "Jewish question" of the sort Rosenberg advocated—one which included material restitution and combated both the pre- and post-Nazi legacies of anti-Semitic prejudice—be rather effortlessly appropriated and dissolved into a more comprehensive category of persecution and suffering.

III.

In an essay entitled "The Past is Another Country: Myth and Memory in Postwar Europe," Tony Judt draws attention to the fact that, contrary to prevailing postwar mythology, "most of occupied Europe either collaborated with the occupying German forces (a minority) or accepted with resignation or equanimity the presence and activities of the German forces (a majority)." Recalling among other things the "mass, racially motivated purges" which were "undertaken by freely-elected or newly-liberated national authorities," he also reminds us of the very different moral universe that was Europe immediately after the war.[14] More recently, István Deák has forcefully argued that the complex and comprehensive political and social imbrication under the Nazi occupation makes any simple categorization into collaboration, accommodation, and resistance difficult.[15] It would seem to follow that any conception of collective moral or historical responsibility must run aground on this very imbrication. But acknowledging these insights about the war in Europe implies different things for the postwar histories of different countries. I want to suggest that specific, identifiable memories of the Austrian First Republic, the Austro-fascist corporative state (*Ständestaat*), the Anschluss, and the Nazi dictatorship in Austria engendered what I will call *discourses of victimhood*[16] that blurred clear distinctions between perpetrators, victims, and bystanders.[17]

These discourses of victimhood and of suffering were not identical; in specific contexts they were articulated, if not necessarily internalized, by national government officials, by the three anti-fascist political parties, and, perhaps more surprisingly, by many leaders of the newly reconstituted *Israelitische Kultusgemeinde*. Together these discursive practices about victimhood, which were, significantly, fully consonant with the Western Allies' decidedly realist view of their political priorities in postwar Austria, created and reinforced what I have elsewhere referred to as a *"mémoire volontaire"*.[18] This "explained" why Jews, though acceptable as part of the pan-Austrian community of victims (*Opfergemeinschaft*), possessed no privileged claims within it. The tenacity of these discourses of victimhood, and of the memories they helped support, can best be explained by, first, their perceived authenticity as descriptions of people's remembered experiences and sense of justice, and, second, the fact that these discourses, as it were, had the field to themselves.

It is important to emphasize the *plurality* of these discourses, for this takes the discussion beyond the examination of the putatively disingenuous instrumental utilization of the Moscow Declaration by postwar elites emphasized in recent accounts of postwar Austrian memory.[19] More significantly, these discourses of victimhood seem to have encumbered the formulation of a specific "Jewish question" in Rosenberg's sense, on moral as well as political grounds. Given the external and internal determinants within which a new Austrian democratic identity was constructed, it thus seems less pertinent to inquire why Austrian leaders failed to embrace Rosenberg's vision of the "Jewish question" and Austria's moral responsibility, than what might have led these leaders to pursue such a policy in the first place.

The collapse of the Third Reich left all but the most benighted in Austria in a state of physical and moral debilitation that approximated a *tabula rasa*. Although there is only a limited number of meaningful moral categories, there is a far less limited number of potential bearers of moral beneficence and censure, and these are themselves often interchangeable. Consequently, the so-called victim thesis, I wish to argue, was really a series of mutually reinforcing victim theses. These were offered by political elites to all Austrians not directly implicated under the terms of de-Nazification[20] to give some positive meaning to their experience of the Nazi period. However, they also possessed a salience that was able to draw upon moral categories which are recognizable today, even if the assumptions which underlay them then are today no longer considered tenable.

IV.

One corollary benefit of the attempt to refine the categories of collaboration, accommodation, and resistance, as well as those of perpetrator, victim and bystander as they apply to postwar memory in Austria has been the critical insights it has brought to bear on the concepts of individual and collective accountability.[21] Hostilities towards Jews have existed for as long as there are records of their interaction with other peoples, and incidents of hostile acts carried out against Jews have a history nearly as long.[22] The former have been frequently described as prejudice, while the latter generically by terms such as persecution, discrimination, or, more specifically—indicating the increasing, and increasingly systematic, violence against Jews under the Nazis—as murder, destruction, extermination. If the existence (if not the exact nature) of anti-Jewish *prejudice* is undisputed,[23] the precise causal relationship between anti-Jewish prejudice and active persecution, and between lesser forms of persecution and genocide, has remained contested terrain.[24] Thus, the phrase "the specific *Austrian* contribution" to the Holocaust, which Bukey (representatively) employs, quite apart from the issue of legal continuity, involves certain assumptions about agency and causality, not only between attitude and action, but also between what might be called cultural socialization and the propensities to murder; the phrase further involves assumptions about the moral responsibilities of individuals and about individual and collective accountability.[25] Such assumptions about the involvement of those who "allowed [the genocide] to happen by standing off to one side" (Rosenberg), which are implied but seldom explicitly stated, have been indissolubly linked to notions of collective moral or historical responsibility for Germany and, more recently, for Austria.[26]

The stakes in this debate were indeed rather high. Therefore, the conflicts between the presumed moral injunctions of Holocaust memory and the requirements of Western geopolitics and West German and Austrian domestic politics have ordinarily been resolved by making pragmatic compromises which have etiolated the moral principles associated with Holocaust memory, while maintaining a strategic silence at best, and collusive deception at worst, about the compromises thus made. The demands for justice on the part of a post-Nazi generation have been met with (or even to a certain extent pre-empted by) a combination of exemplary punishments of selected individuals (at Nuremberg), a largely administrative (and exceedingly generous) de-Nazification, and the gradual acceptance of the penitent (West) German notion of collective moral responsibility. This was always a fudge of sorts, but one reason it has remained the preferred mode of engagement is because the moral imperatives which Holocaust remembrance seemed to prescribe conflicted not only with the *realpolitische* imperatives of the cold war, but also with certain principles of Western democratic societies. The willingness of the postwar West German political elite to ultimately assume the material as well as rhetorical burdens of moral responsibility as defined by the Western occupying powers (later military allies)—a kind of rite of passage into the Western alliance—meant that the conceptual fragility of these preferred rhetorical conventions went largely unnoticed, or at least unchallenged. It is, in my view, impossible to fully explain the very different course Austria followed without critically examining the assumptions on which the idea of moral or historical responsibility rests.[27] The study of postwar Austrian discourses of victimhood should, therefore, yield an account not only of what moral or historical responsibility has come to mean, who has acknowledged it (or not) and how; it should also propose a theoretically more transparent and ethically more forthright conception of what moral or historical responsibility might plausibly mean (beyond the pragmatic compromises of the postwar period), who ought to be obliged to assume it, and why.

Clearly, it will not be possible to develop this argument in any great detail in this one essay. Instead, in what follows I wish to outline in broad terms why I believe the notion of discourses of victimhood offers a fruitful framework within which we might debate the problem of postwar Austrian memory.

V.

It is customary, and not without reason, to begin the discussion of the so-called victim thesis with the Third Moscow Declaration of 1 November 1943. This Moscow Declaration, as is well known, held Austria to be "the first free country to fall a victim to Hitlerite aggression," but saddled her with "a responsibility which she cannot evade for participation in the war on the side of Hitlerite Germany."[28] According to what might be called the critical post-Waldheim consensus on postwar Austrian memory, the first clause became the exemplar of a postwar culture of amnesia or repression, while the second, artfully parried by successive postwar governments, was so successfully suppressed that the Allies agreed to leave it out of the 1955 State Treaty.[29]

The principal tenets of the "Austria as Hitler's first victim theory," as Heidemarie Uhl, in a recent essay on Austrian historical memory, describes it, were that "In March 1938 Austria was occupied and annexed by Germany against its will; it was liberated in April/May 1945 by Austrian resistance fighters and the Allies. The years between 1938 and 1945 were described as a period of foreign rule and, as far as Austria's role and participation in the war was concerned, these were portrayed as a period of resistance and persecution, of the nation's fight for its liberation."[30] As Robert Knight has observed, the talismanic quality of the Moscow Declaration gave "Austrian politicians and journalists a useful handle on which to hang their attempt at collective exculpation from the Third Reich."[31] Yet the Moscow Declaration's assigned role in determining either Allied foreign or Austrian domestic policy seems, on my reading, to have been exaggerated. One might accept Uhl's argument that "the founding fathers of the Second Republic" showed little concern with "revealing historical truth" (assuming that one could agree on what "historical truth" was, is, or might be). However, I find that her ancillary claim that "[the founding fathers] follow[ed] the 'dictates of political reason' and accept[ed] the status of victim offered by the Moscow Declaration"[32] overemphasizes the specific domestic determinants of the adoption of the victim thesis and neglects the tutorial role played by the occupying powers, in particular the United States. It also seems to suggest that these leaders would (should?) have perceived a clear and morally more acceptable alternative. In a similar vein, Knight's view that the "success of the Austrian strategy depended less on the choice of words of the three Foreign Ministers than on the polarization of the Cold War which made the West unwilling to undermine the Austrian strategy"[33] is undoubtedly correct as far as it goes. However, I believe it underestimates the extent to which the arguments made in support of the official Austrian victim thesis (the "Austrian strategy" to which Knight refers) were accepted by the Allies themselves, especially the United States, not only prior to the cold war, but even prior to the declaration of the Second Austrian Republic in April 1945.[34]

VI.

As Robert Keyserlingk's authoritative study *Austria in WW II. An Anglo-American Dilemma* has shown, those countries which were to become wartime Allies—Great Britain, the Soviet Union, and the United States—had, for all intents and purposes, and despite later attempts to claim otherwise,[35] all accepted Austria's Anschluss with Germany both *de facto* and *de jure* in the spring of 1938.[36] As a result, for most of the war the *Austrian question* was subsumed under the German question. Although the issue of Austria had been addressed periodically by specialists working for the British Foreign Office as early as 1941, and in the United States State Department soon afterwards,[37] Austria re-emerged as a specific focus of postwar planning only when the Allies began discussing the problems of Germany within postwar Europe with renewed urgency in 1943. However, as Keyserlingk argues, far from expressing a firm Allied political conviction in favor of Austrian independence, the Moscow Declaration of 1943 was *primarily* a psychological warfare propaganda measure designed to weaken the Germans militarily by fomenting resistance in Austria.[38] At the time of the Moscow Declaration and after, both the British Foreign Office and the U.S. State Department favored a "de-annexed" Austria as part of a Danubian confederation. Nevertheless, with the Moscow Declaration the Allies became publicly committed to the restoration of Austria's independence, and the question of Austria became a distinguishable feature of Allied planning that was linked to, but not reducible to, the German question.

Although the Allies—the three signatories of the Moscow Declaration plus the Free French, who later endorsed the statement on Austria[39]—publicly described the Anschluss in 1938 as an aggressive violation of Austrian sovereignty, internally they noted some specific features of the German-Austrian relationship that seemed oddly discrepant with a country that was, according to the Moscow Declaration, to be "liberated from German domination."[40] Indeed, Austria, at that time, seemed to be characterized by its peculiar historical relationship to Germany, the peaceful, even enthusiastic local acceptance of the Anschluss, the absence of an appreciable resistance or even a semblance of a government-in-exile, and the Reich's unhesitant willingness to conscript, and successfully to deploy, Austrian soldiers for the duration of the war. All this made issues such as de-Nazification, restitution, and the elimination of anti-Jewish discrimination, which are most directly related to the question "How was National Socialism to be expunged as an active force from the political and economic life of postwar Germany?,"[41] seem relevant also to the debate on Austria in ways that are inapplicable to Poland, Czechoslovakia, or the "satellite" countries. The equivocation of the Moscow Declaration—Austria was declared both a victim and an accomplice of "Hitlerite Germany"—intimated but could not resolve this difficulty, while the Allied ambivalence deriving from Austria's singular status in wartime Europe beclouded issues of responsibility which appeared unambiguous for Germans in the *Altreich*. Nonetheless, to detach Austria from Germany and to maintain this separation after the war was considered indispensable to the long-term Allied objectives for the postwar world, namely to keep Germany weak and to prevent her from endangering the peace of Europe in the future.

After the uprising against the Germans, which the Moscow Declaration was intended to encourage, failed to materialize, Anglo-American planning bodies began to wonder whether Austrians would even be inclined to take up the Allies' offer of future independence. Yet, because Austrian independence was the agreed Allied policy, wartime planners had little choice but to devote their efforts to elaborating policies that would entice Austrians away from seeking a future Anschluss and, consequently, to make independence a more attractive option.

One of the few firm conclusions of the detailed studies on Austria, carried out by the Council on Foreign Relations, the Royal Institute of International Affairs, and later by the Research and Analysis Branch of the OSS,[42] a conclusion which continued to be widely shared among officials in both the United States and British governments throughout the war, was that during the interwar period Austrians had lacked a firm national consciousness. This deficiency, which these experts believed was traceable to the dire economic situation and geopolitical isolation Austria had faced in the 1920s and 1930s, in large part explained the appeal which the Anschluss to Germany had had for Austrians. It followed that a postwar Austria in any political constellation—save remaining a part of Germany, which the Allies rejected, but including a Danubian confederation, the solution they preferred—could survive only if Austria were provided with the economic and (geo)political security in which such a national consciousness could flourish. Consequently, Anglo-American policy towards post-Nazi *Germany* entailed active Allied encouragement of the *Austrians'* hitherto unsuccessful efforts to develop their own national identity. In this view, only a

functioning, politically and economically successful Danubian confederation, which included a nationally conscious, self-confident Austria,
would be able both to offset Austrians' desire for another Anschluss
with Germany and to act as a counterweight to German influence on the
continent.

However, the Danubian confederation solution to the Austrian
question, which was advocated by Churchill at conference after conference, and whose advantages were argued eloquently and exhaustively
in numerous Foreign Office and State Department papers, was scuttled
by Stalin's equally vehement and long-standing opposition to it.[43] At the
same Moscow Conference in October 1943 that issued the Declaration
on Austria, the three foreign ministers, acting on behalf of their governments, also agreed to set up the European Advisory Commission (EAC),
with its seat in London, as the machinery authorized to discuss and
approve Allied policies for postwar Europe. The procedure in the EAC
was cumbersome and effectively gave any one power a veto over any
policy it opposed.[44] Continued Soviet resistance to a Danubian confederation thus ensured that the reestablishment of a "free and independent
Austria"—what the Moscow Declaration described as the three
governments' "wish"[45]—remained the only agreed Allied policy towards
Austria throughout the war and beyond.

But this presented a major policy dilemma for the U.S. and British
governments. If the Allies were determined to undo the Anschluss in
order to weaken Germany, yet the Danubian confederation were closed
off as a probable option, then the reestablishment of Austrian independence could no longer remain a provisional policy, a mere stage on the
way to the emergence of the preferred confederative solution, but became—willy nilly—the longer term policy aim in itself. In other words,
although both the State Department and the Foreign Office were partial
towards a Danubian confederation, the only policy on Austria that had
been endorsed by all three Allies was that contained in the Moscow
Declaration of 1 November 1943, and this situation was unlikely to
change. Since agencies planning for military government needed to
make decisions which assumed an Allied policy towards Austria, they
would have to base themselves on the Moscow Declaration, in particular
on its findings that Austria had been a victim of Nazi aggression, that
the Anschluss was "null and void," and that Austria should be re-establi-
shed as an independent state after the war. The Declaration contained a
formulation that was intended to encompass the Anglo-American desire
for a Danubian confederation: independence would "open the way for

the Austrian people themselves, as well as those neighboring states which will be faced with similar problems, to find that political and economic security which is the only basis for lasting peace."[46] However, this formulation was, not coincidentally, far too vague to be easily translatable into a policy and conceded the re-establishment of independence as the preliminary stage in any case. As a result, it was of little use to those planning for military government, who needed a policy the army could implement upon arrival. Similarly, the passage in which Austria was reminded "that she has a responsibility which she cannot evade for participation in the war on the side of Hitlerite Germany, and that in the final settlement account will inevitably be taken of her own contribution to her liberation,"[47] was also serviceably elastic. Because both the extent of the contribution Austria would make, as well as the minimum contribution it was expected to make remained indeterminate, this clause could scarcely be used as a basis for effective military government policies either. The analyses prepared in and for the planning agencies in the U.S. and British governments all considered the task of establishing an Austrian national consciousness difficult even under conditions they believed most advantageous to it. How much more difficult would it be to overcome this deficit when the fate to which Austrians would be consigned after the war seemed a great deal like the one Austrians had suffered between 1918 and 1938, a fate, moreover, which the analyses of the Allied planners themselves suggested had made Austrians so susceptible to the Anschluss to begin with?

Given the Allied intention to keep Germany weak (among other things by depriving it of its former acquisitions like Austria), given the conviction among planners in the U.S. government that a suitable Austrian national consciousness was a precondition of Austrian viability (and hence independence in any form), and given the increasing recognition of at least U.S. State Department officials that the preferred Danubian confederation would never overcome Soviet objections, the plans of the United States for Austria came to include the ever more urgent promotion of the development of an Austrian national conscious-ness, whose most important distinguishing feature would be that it was not German. In the context of the Second World War, of course, not being German meant, most importantly, not being Nazi and/or Prussian. The studies on Austria which were undertaken by planners in the State Department, and greatly refined by the R&A Branch of the OSS,[48] acknowledged to a greater or lesser extent the widespread support for the Anschluss idea in post-Habsburg Austria, the integration of many Austrians into the Third Reich, and their identification with it. Yet, these historical analyses also provided plausible explanations for Austrians' susceptibility to these ideas and movements, in a way which would, at least implicitly, tend to diminish the Austrians' share of responsibility for Nazi crimes. They also attempted to identify potential alternative positive sources of Austrian nationalism that the Allied policies might reinforce.

While the proposition that the Austrians, in the period between the collapse of the Habsburg empire and the Anschluss, lacked a strong national consciousness was itself was not entirely original, it acquired a new significance in light of the Moscow Declaration: the explicit Allied commitment to Austrian independence as reflected in the Declaration meant that this particular legacy of Austrian history was no longer simply a factor to be considered in evaluating possible policy options, but rather a weakness to overcome. The R&A Branch studies, taken as a whole, dealt with this problem analytically by identifying the events, structures, and ideas in Austrian history which had been detrimental to the formation of Austrian national consciousness in the past, and by indicating strategies which might counteract or surmount them. The R&A Branch experts, for example, recognized that certain beliefs which Austrians held about their own interwar history and experience under National Socialism—as self-serving and factually contentious as they often were, or perhaps precisely because they were thus—would be highly conducive to the construction of an Austrian national consciousness after the war. Although these R&A Branch specialists were in no doubt about the widespread and deep complicity of Austrians in the Nazi regime, in the context of the extremely negative views the Allies held about the Germans, Austrian distinctiveness acquired a certain normative quality: being different from the Germans meant in most important respects being "better," or at least less dangerous. The planners nonetheless advocated, as a matter of policy, that these usable beliefs be accepted and reinforced, in order to ensure that an Austrian national identity would actually emerge. This highly instrumental perspective, however, followed ineluctably from these analysts' conviction that only a much more deeply felt Austrian national consciousness would be capable of sustaining ideologically an independent Austria, that this Austrian nationalism would have to be largely (re)created, and that it was the task of the U.S. military government to encourage the Austrians in (re)creating it. Thus, not only were the planners fully aware that the version of

Austrian distinctiveness and victimhood which they would buttress
might coincide with a similar notion of Austria's postwar leaders
anxious to escape the reckoning awaiting Germany after the war; this
hoped-for convergence was to become the very key to the policy's
success. "Building up an independent Austrian state," the R&A Branch
paper on the "Revival of Austrian Political and Constitutional Life"
argued, "does not involve only boundary and administrative problems;
the success or failure of this job is closely related to the question of how
far a specific Austrian national consciousness can be created and encouraged."[49]

The victim thesis announced in the Moscow Declaration, which
began life as little more than a psychological warfare measure designed
to weaken Germany, thus became in retrospect a substantive foreign
policy gift offered by the U.S. government to postwar Austrian
governing elites and willingly received by them. Austrian leaders,
naturally, were only too happy to accept this gift, because it dovetailed
with their own political interests and their anti-Nazi convictions. In the
end, it mattered little whether the planners in the United States actually
believed this story of Austrian victimhood, or whether they would
personally have subscribed to the claims they would come to make
indirectly in behalf of Austria's postwar political leadership. It was
sufficient for these planners and policy makers to be convinced that it
was necessary, and justified, to promote this notion of distinctiveness
and victimhood as long as it reinforced the Austrian nationalism they
considered necessary to the success of their policy, and discouraged any
future Austrian desire for an Anschluss.

VII.

The provisional and later the elected governments of postwar
Austria were both interlocutors and representatives of the Austrians,
with responsibilities both to the Austrians themselves and to the Allied
occupying powers.[50] The new government's main tasks were to execute
orders of the Allied Council while consolidating and extending the
sovereignty of the Austrian state and government as much as possible.
This always required negotiations, for the Allied Council, and in
particular the U.S. occupation authority, did not shy away from influen-
cing, or even reversing, Austrian policies with which they had major
differences, as the dispute over the draft de-Nazification law in 1946
illustrates.[51] However, what determined the way in which the Western

Allies exerted pressure on the Austrian government with respect to issues related to the "Jewish question" was not merely the advantage they believed endorsing Austria's victimhood would secure them vis-à-vis the Soviets, nor was it entirely because they were convinced that promoting this victimhood would eradicate future Austrian desire for an Anschluss with Germany. It was also that the Allies had certain conceptions about the nature of National Socialism and Austria's relationship to it, and about the origins and significance of anti-Semitism in Austria, which above all the United States occupation forces had brought with them. And these conceptions, I would argue, implied only the most narrowly circumscribed "Jewish question" and a broadly conceived victim thesis.

In 1944 and 1945, State Department planners produced three studies which bear on the issue of Austria and National Socialism.[52] One idea they contained, and which is relevant to my argument, held Nazism to be the embodiment or fulfillment of a German national essence or character *per se*. If Nazism were in a significant sense equated with a specifically (Prussian) German mind or some other such generalizing concept, it would seem to follow that Austria's relationship to National Socialism could be measured in terms of the extent of this *German* influence on it and in it. This would suggest further that the rooting out of National Socialism from Austria—the objective of all de-Nazification efforts—could be conceived as essentially equivalent to the mere elimination of Pan-Germanism or Pan-Germanist influences from Austria.

The State Department study "Austria: The Internal Political Situation in the Period 1918-1938," traced the early growth of Nazi organizations in Austria explicitly to infiltration from Germany. It concluded that it was these Nazi organizations *alone* which had striven "to further the inter-related causes of Pan-Germanism, anti-Semitism, Anti-Bolshevism, and anti-democracy."[53] The study thus not only decoupled the three latter causes from Austrian Christian Social ideology and policies, but also implicitly established a national-political pole (Pan-Germanism) against which to measure the democratic features of a post-Nazi *qua* post-German Austria. Significantly, the study also clearly saw the Anschluss as a major caesura in the treatment of the Jews, and saw no causal connections between pre-Anschluss anti-Semitism and the post-Anschluss treatment of the Jews.[54]

The June 1944 directive prepared by the Inter-Divisional Committee on Germany, "The Treatment of Austria," which outlined

U.S. military government policy towards Austria, itself argued that the United States, "never having accorded de jure recognition to the union of Austria with the Reich, should favor the prompt restoration of Austria as an independent state."[55] The U.S. government should also "support all appropriate means of fostering the growth of a more pronounced Austrian national feeling along democratic lines," as this, along with a viable economy, would most effectively promote "Austrian revival." What it referred to as an "essential predicate" of the "development of sound democratic self-government" would be the "elimination of the fascist vestiges of the Dollfuss-Schuschnigg regime and the destruction of Nazi authoritarianism." Again there is no mention of anti-Semitism; rather, the focus is on the undemocratic features which the "Dollfuss-Schuschnigg regime" and "Nazi authoritarianism" shared.[56]

To the extent that such studies and directives addressed the issue of National Socialism in Austria, they tended to reduce it to a problem of Pan-Germanist influence, and the elimination of this influence in Austria became the touchstone of how the U.S. would view post-Nazi political culture. If, as the study quoted above suggests, this foreign German element were exclusively or predominantly held responsible for the propagation of anti-Semitic beliefs in pre-Anschluss Austria and for the subsequent persecution of the Jews in the *Ostmark*, there would be scant reason for the occupation authorities to imagine, much less require, that the "Jewish question"—apart from banning discrimination—be addressed independently as an integral part of de-Nazification or as an impediment to a new Austrian democratic political culture.

There is no reason why the assumptions and beliefs contained in such planning documents would carry over directly into the specific policies implemented by the occupying power. However, although the personal and institutional continuities that linked planning with occupation policy remain to be fully traced,[57] it nonetheless seems plausible to argue that the views on matters related to the "Jewish question," such as those expressed in the State Department studies mentioned above, were not restricted to the planning stage, but informed occupation policy itself.[58] This can be illustrated by referring to the Austrian elites' evasion of Austrian responsibility for their complicity in the Nazi genocide and to the problem of postwar anti-Jewish prejudice.

In March 1947, Karl Rankin, the Councilor of Legation of the U.S. occupation authority in Vienna, sent a situation report to Washington which discussed, among other things, a recent opinion poll. According to this poll, 71 percent of those surveyed believed that Austrians did not share in the guilt for World War II, while 15 percent believed that Austrians were "partly to blame." Commenting on this result, Political Officer Martin Herz, who had actually authored the report, wrote revealingly, "Since, as a matter of national policy, we encourage a separate Austrian nationalism, we cannot be surprised, and should in fact find comfort in the fact, that most Austrians deny ever having had anything to do with Germany."[59] Although Herz's report reflected some disappointment at these results, his remarks nonetheless suggest three things clearly: first, that he saw a connection between the attitude of the U.S. occupation authorities and that of the Austrian government on war guilt; second, that these attitudes would be reflected in Austrian public opinion on the question; and third, that the attitude towards Austria's war guilt promoted by the U.S. occupation authorities was based upon the victim thesis endorsed in the Third Moscow Declaration and "The Treatment of Austria" directive.

There was also a convergence of attitudes regarding anti-Jewish prejudice. As we have seen, U.S. government planning documents tended to describe anti-Semitism or the persecution of the Jews as German imports. Of course, the occupation authorities, and particularly Martin Herz, were not unaware of the history of anti-Semitism in Austria, and reported occasionally on the issue. But the view of the U.S. authorities, as expressed by the Political Officer, on the combating of anti-Jewish attitudes—what was described as anti-Semitism—was indulgently pragmatic.

One of the most frequently quoted passages attesting to the cynicism of the postwar Austrian political elites towards anti-Jewish prejudice is the February 1947 article published in the *Wiener Zeitung* entitled "The Fairy Tale of Austrian Anti-Semitism." The author was Theodor Körner, at the time mayor of Vienna, who would later become president of the Austrian Second Republic. Körner took up the cudgels against those spreading the "fairy tale" that "also after the defeat of National Socialism and after the secession from Germany, Austria is still prone to anti-Semitism." "It should be stated once and for all," Körner wrote, "that apart from the violent outrages [*Ausschreitungen*] organized by the Nazis during the period of their rule over Austria, there had never been pogroms against Jews in Vienna." Later in the same article, Körner stated that "Vienna had never witnessed anti-Semitic outrages of the kind found in other countries, even long before the founding of National Socialism was even on the agenda, for the

Viennese is a cosmopolitan and thus from the outset not an anti-Semite. Anti-Semitic tendencies are completely foreign to him now as well. Stories about such things are [either] conscious lies or mindless drivel."[60]

Less frequently quoted, if at all, is the response of the U.S. occupation authorities to this article. Martin Herz wrote: "The repeated denials of anti-Semitism which have recently appeared in the Viennese press are in themselves evidence of the fact that political circles, and to some extent even the broad masses, are aware of the damaging results which the reports about anti-Semitism in Austria are having in foreign countries." Herz does state, *pace* Körner, that "there is no doubt that some anti-Semitism exists in Austria," but he did not consider it "a serious political phenomenon," and certainly not likely to take on "the virulent forms of the Nazi era." At the same time, Herz viewed Körner's article favorably overall, reflecting as it did "the positive attitude toward Jews which the Mayor of Vienna is attempting, with considerable success, to infuse in the city administration."[61]

Herz's response to the remarks made by Leopold Kunschak, an interwar leader of the Christian Social workers' organization, was similar. Kunschak was an undisputed foe of National Socialism who had spent seven years in Nazi concentration camps, was one of three signatories of the Proclamation of the Second Republic, and, after the war, was elected president of the Austrian National Assembly. At a mass meeting in Vienna in 1946, Kunschak announced that "the Polish Jews [should] not come to Austria; we Austrians don't need the others either! ... Austrian industry should not fall into Jewish hands."[62] Asked to explain Kunschak's remark, Leopold Figl, the first elected[63] chancellor of the Second Republic and the leader of Kunschak's People's Party, replied that "Kunschak was not an anti-Semite on racial grounds, but on economic grounds."[64] Figl's explanation completely satisfied the American military, which had made the inquiry: Herz later confirmed that "Kunschak's hands—except for his comparatively innocuous, 'patrician' anti-Semitism—are clean."[65]

To summarize briefly, then, the two basic policies that the U.S. occupation authorities (as well as the Allied Council as a whole) pursued were the clear separation of Austria from Germany and the elimination of the National Socialist spirit from all areas of life. In the implementation of both these broad objectives and their corollaries, both at the national level and in their occupation zone, U.S. occupation authorities exhibited a continuity of assumptions and historical-political judgments about Austria that may be found in background documents dating from 1944 and in policies lasting into the 1950s. These assumptions included: the promotion of not only Austrian independence but Austrian nationalism; the designation of National Socialist policies in Austria—including the persecution and murder of the Jews—largely as German, rather than Germanic, abominations; the emphasis in the analysis of both Nazism and fascism on their undemocratic features; and the virtual absence of a specific policy elaborating the combating of prejudice beyond the abolition of legal discrimination on the basis of race or political belief. All this suggests not merely an acquiescence of the West in "the Austrian strategy" as a result of "the polarization of the Cold War" as Robert Knight has argued,[66] but also, and perhaps more significantly, as a result of a kind of informal connivance in delimiting the contours both of Austrian historical memory and the "Jewish question" within it.

VIII.

Even before the Proclamation of the Second Republic on 27 April 1945, a political consensus of the three anti-fascist parties—the ÖVP, SPÖ, and KPÖ—was emerging which bore a striking resemblance to the political conceptions of the U.S. occupying power I have described earlier. For obvious reasons, the representatives of the KPÖ, and in particular Ernst Fischer, took the lead in the beginning, but their views were soon to be echoed by leaders of the other parties. In the 23 April 1945 issue of *Neues Österreich,* for example, Ernst Fischer wrote representatively of the "*German* war criminals" who had left the Austrians "a pile of rubble." "Industry, agriculture, the transportation system, the most elementary elements of life," Fischer argued, "were ruined with *Prussian* thoroughness [*Gründlichkeit*]."[67]

The same general attitude was also evident in the first descriptions of the Nazi death machinery. "In the Majdanek death camp near Lublin," wrote Fischer, "the German henchmen [*Henker*] murdered more than one and a half million prisoners as if on an assembly line [*am laufenden Band*]." Although the description of the gruesome gassings is both detailed and graphic, the primary victims of Majdanek, namely Jews, were not mentioned: "More than two and a half million people from all countries of Europe, among them several thousand Austrians, were gassed and burned as ordered."[68] This editorial practice was not uniform; for example, the description of transports to Semlin did explicitly mention Jews as the exclusive victims. But these Jews, like their "Austrian" counterparts in Majdanek, were nonetheless also *exclusively* the victims of the "Germans."[69]

At the same time, from the beginning *Neues Österreich* published appeals whose urgent, almost forced quality reads as though their purpose was to convince skeptical Austrian readers to embrace their Austrian nationality. "And one thing more is needed," Ernst Fischer wrote at the end of one such appeal in the 23 April 1945 issue: "That we Austrians awake to a genuine national self-consciousness, that we trust our own strength, as we have failed to do in the past. It is not the number of people and geographical expansion that is decisive, but rather the moral energies of the people."[70] And as if the readership might need reinforcement, the more overt political appeals were augmented by publications with Austrian themes written by acknowledged Austrian literary personalities. Some representative examples are: "Have Courage to be Austria!" by Hermann Bahr, "Austrians through and through," by Anton Wildgans, "Austria's Enemy—Prussia, always Prussia," by Johann Nestroy, "Austria—the Empire of Peace," by Hugo von Hofmannsthal, "Yes, there is an Austria," by Adolf Glaßbrenner, and "To Austria," a poem by Richard von Schaukal.[71] These inspirational pieces were doubtlessly reflective of the known cultural preferences of the paper's editor, Ernst Fischer, whose pronounced anti-Prussianism was evinced in countless speeches, articles, editorials, and pamphlets, and was noted favorably by the U.S. authorities.[72] Nevertheless, these pieces, which emphasized Austria's cultural specificity, and implied its cultural superiority to Germany, read as a kind of literary agitprop.

Although the passages quoted above somewhat exaggerate the tone of the first few days of the Second Republic (it was actually the KPÖ which was consistently most vehemently anti-German in its pronouncements), they do so only slightly. The Declaration of the Second Republic, issued on 27 April, also announced not only that "the overwhelming majority" of the Austrian *Volk* "feels [*empfindet*] democratic and detests Nazi criminality," but also that "the free republic has again emerged from the prison of violent German domination."[73]

If there were few exceptions to the general Germanophobic line of *Neues Österreich* in the first euphoric days of the Second Republic, by 1 May 1945 subtle differences of emphasis in the two major anti-fascist parties' description of their sufferings under National Socialism emerged, adumbrating future parallel discourses of victimhood.

In its declaration, the ÖVP understandably emphasized less its anti-fascist credentials than the political persecution the members of the Christian Social *Lager*—of which the People's Party was the political legatee, if not the official successor party—had undergone at the hands of the Nazis. Tens of thousands of them, the declaration stated, had "suffered years for Austria in prisons and concentration camps." "Thousands and thousands died a bitter death for the beloved *Heimat*."[74] The SPÖ took this opportunity to stake its claim as the quintessential anti-fascist party, while making clear that in its view fascism had not begun with the Anschluss: "For the first time in eleven years," the SPÖ declared, "the working class in that part of Austria which has been liberated from fascism is celebrating the 1st of May in solidarity with the socialist working class of the entire world." Though the statement's allusion to February 1934 would have been clear to any reader who could count, the authors of the declaration apparently found it politic not to mention explicitly who had been responsible for the suppression of the party and working class.[75]

Yet mere allusion quickly yielded to explicit, and vehement, polemics between the coalition partners on the nature and significance of the years 1934-1938. The perceived common *national* interests of Austria prescribed the exaggerated emphasis placed on the alien German character of National Socialism. This view delimited one discourse of victimhood that could act as a bridgehead against the implications of a Rosenberg-style conception of the "Jewish question." Even more important in diluting any notion of a distinctive Jewish suffering under National Socialism, however, was the intense and sharp propaganda battles about Austro-fascism, the Dollfuss and Schuschnigg regimes, and the Anschluss, which leaders of both parties waged from the earliest days of the Second Republic. This debate engendered mutually exclusive discourses of culpability and suffering which would have significant implications for one's view of the "Jewish question."

In the first months of the Allied occupation, Edgar Johnson and Paul Sweet, both experts on Austria who served with the OSS, conducted interviews with several prominent members of the SPÖ, ÖVP, and KPÖ. Of course, one would expect these leaders to present their own parties in the best possible light in such interviews, either in order to curry favor with the U.S. authorities, or to disabuse their interviewers of assumptions these party leaders suspected the U.S. occupiers might harbor—for example, that the Socialists were Soviet puppets, or that the People's Party had insufficiently abjured its "Austro-fascist" past. However, the openness with which these members of a common provisional government attacked their domestic political opponents to a foreign occupying power nonetheless seems quite striking.

Theodor Körner, the Socialist mayor of Vienna, for example, was reported to have stated in the interview: "As for the Volkspartei people, [Körner] says he tries to deal with them in a non-partisan way, but finds it hard to sit down to discuss business with men who put him in jail in 1934." Asked about the progress of de-Nazification in the city government, Körner replied that "he thought it had been well handled. Although more than 5,000 out of a total of 30,000 city employees are reported to be Nazis, Körner says they are little people—'poor devils who had no strength of will. They are not very guilty.'" Of more concern to Körner, the OSS interviewers reported, were "the Volkspartei men from the Dollfuss-Schuschnigg days who now occupy high administrative posts. Most of the bureaucrats in the better positions under Renner have, he says, such backgrounds."[76]

Karl Renner, as the head of the Austrian provisional government, spoke to the OSS on several occasions. Renner, a Socialist, spent the greater part of one long interview explaining his support for the Anschluss in 1938. Renner embedded his personal decision to recommend a "yes" vote on the Anschluss plebiscite held in April 1938 within a broader historical account of the First Republic and Austro-fascism, and severely criticized the policies pursued by the Dollfuss and Schuschnigg governments. "But what the world has never understood," Renner was quoted as saying, "was the way in which the authoritarian regime of Dollfuss and Schuschnigg made the Anschluss inevitable. When Dollfuss compacted with Mussolini to destroy Austrian democracy and set up an authoritarian regime in return for Italian protection against Hitler's Germany, he disassociated himself from the great majority of the Austrian population." The majority of the Austrian intelligentsia after 1918, Renner argued further, "was anti-clerical, as well as anti-Semitic and anti-Habsburg, and resented the clerical trend in Austria before 1933. Thereafter, among other reasons, the intelligentsia swung to anti-clerical Hitlerism because of the clerical aspect of Austrian authoritarianism. The Social Democratic workers were likewise anti-clerical. Long before 1933 they had determined to fight for Austrian democracy if the occasion should ever arise. The Austrian peasant, too, was fundamentally democratic in his point of view." "When, therefore," Renner continued, "Dollfuss, in alliance with Mussolini, carried through his coup d'etat against the will of an overwhelming majority of the people, destroyed the workers' parties, confiscated their property, clapped their mouths shut, and quelled their resistance in blood (February 1934), and when thereafter clerical fascism [*Klerikofaschismus*], in the form of an undemocratic corporative constitution [*Standeordnung* [sic]] was imposed upon the country and furbished with elaborate clerical trappings, it was inevitable that democratic and anti-clerical forces in Austria, having been abandoned by the State, should lose interest in it, if not actually fight it." These forces, which had lost interest, included the Austrian workers who, according to Renner, had concluded "that if Austria could not escape fascism it was better to have the German anti-clerical brand [*die deutsche anti-klerikale Lesart*] than the Italian brand. In this they were joined by the anti-clerical intellectuals, including the foot-loose, security-less elements [*Wirtschaftslosen*] who fell to Hitler and to whom, after the crushing of the workers' movement, the Austrian state virtually granted a monopoly of organized agitation. Without Dollfuss in 1934," Renner emphasized, "it would never have been possible for Hitler, or at least it would not have been so easily possible, to carry out his conquest." Indeed, Renner concluded, "[w]hen the Anschluss came, the workers were powerless to resist had they wanted to. The Austrian state of the moment was, however, by far more hateful to them than Hitler's fascism, which couldn't rob them of more than Dollfuss had already taken, and at least promised them in return bread and work. The workers were determined not to move a finger to preserve this state. They would accept the Hitler Anschluss without objection [*ohne Widerspruch*], passively they would let it occur [*passiv über sich ergehen lassen*]. So it was that a good two-thirds of the people preferred Hitler to Schuschnigg."[77]

On the whole the People's Party politicians interviewed by the OSS gave as good as they got. This is particularly true of Leopold Figl, who had been a leader of the Austrian Farmers League (*Bauernbund*) under Dollfuss and Schuschnigg, and later became chancellor of the Second Republic. While Figl and other leaders of the *Bauernbund*, as Johnson and Sweet noted in their report of the interview, were willing to forgive and forget the fact that the pan-Germanist Agrarian League (*Landbund*) had gone over to the Nazis "virtually intact ... in the illegal period," these leaders nonetheless found it "a good deal more difficult to forgive the Social-Democrats. Figl is furious because Renner and other leading members of his party persist in talking about Dollfuss-fascism in their public speeches." Figl "vigorously denies that such a thing as Dollfuss-fascism ever existed. 'Dollfuss was a real democrat,' he says, and with very slight encouragement he launches into a lengthy, and obviously often-rehearsed recital of how the 'so-called' Dollfuss-fascism came into existence. In his version the Social Democrats in general and Renner in particular get a lacing. 'Those of us who knew Dollfuss,' he says, 'know how deeply he was troubled by the policy which he was forced to pursue.' It was Dollfuss's firm intention, Figl insists, to bring the Austrians back to the ways of democracy."

One of the two "salient points" which Johnson and Sweet emphasized about Figl was his "deep-seated animosity and lack of respect toward the Social-Democratic leaders. Those of them who stayed in Austria are accused of coming to terms, almost to a man, with the Nazis. Not a single one of the Social Democrats in the Renner government ever was sent to [a] concentration camp, Figl says. He laughs about Helmer, his Socialist deputy for Lower Austria, who is so proud because he was arrested for three days after 20 July [1944]. At that time, according to Figl, every Austrian who had held office of a certain grade before 1938 was ordered under automatic arrest and even many functionaries who had been illegal Nazis found themselves temporarily in jail." In the interview Figl was equally scornful of Adolf Schärf, who, before being elected president, had served as vice-chancellor in all three governments Figl headed. According to the OSS report, Figl claimed that Schärf had "kept very quiet during the entire Nazi period, and now this school-masterish bourgeois with the mincing step, who claims to be the friend of the working man, has promoted himself to Herr Sektionschef, the highest rung of the bureaucratic ladder." As for Renner, "[i]t is not seemly," Figl is reported as suggesting, "for a man who compromised with the Nazis to belabor the Christian-Socials because they, for reasons of 'necessity,' had to be a little authoritarian."[78]

The mutual hostility these leaders expressed in private to the OSS about the nature of the Dollfuss and Schuschnigg regimes, the Anschluss, and the political character of their political opponents, became a set piece of postwar Austrian political discourse. Thus the spirit of the *Lagerstrasse* at Dachau, which was frequently invoked as a metaphor for the willingness of the Second Republic's founding fathers to overcome the previous hostilities of the First Republic (because of their common suffering as Austrians under the Nazis at Dachau), seemed most conspicuous by its absence among the leaders of the Socialist Party and People's Party at the beginning of the Second Republic.[79] But while the fact of this contentious partisan debate on the First Republic and its aftermath is well known, its significance for the debate on the "Jewish question" has in my view been largely neglected. Let us look at typical examples of the two sides of this public debate, and see what moral lessons they were thought to provide.

Oskar Pollak wrote in the *Arbeiter-Zeitung* in 1948 :

> There was an Austrian fascism before the German descended on us . . . . There had always been negotiations and attempts at reconciliation between the clerical and Heimwehr fascists on the one hand, and the Nazis on the other before it finally came to a weakly led struggle, a miserable attempt at resistance. The entire history of the Dollfuss and Schuschnigg governments is replete with this vacillation, this lack of clarity, this misery ... We have called those survivors of a betrayal of democracy and two dictatorships who today populate the administration of the Second Republic the surviving servants [*Weiterdienenden*] of fascism. They constitute the problem for the ÖVP. We cannot understand how the leading men of the People's Party, who themselves suffered in the concentration camps of German fascism—and these form the majority of their ministers—can tolerate these people in offices of their own party. But we Socialists understand the deeper reason of this internal conflict of the People's Party and have repeatedly stated it explicitly: it is the fact that [the party] itself historically has fascism in its bones [*im Leibe*].[80]

The ÖVP response to such criticism, taken from a parliamentary debate, ran something like this: "We traveled this road [against Hitler] to the end, and we went this way four years long alone. We, the [so-called] trailblazers, in the days of the seizure of power [*Herrschaftsübernahme*], were then locked up in detention centers, were taken to Dachau and Buchenwald, and your people [Social Democrats] were led around in coaches with flowers. You were received in this way because you had stood aside."[81]

Such passages from both sides could be multiplied nearly endlessly. If for the People's Party the Anschluss represented the violent destruction of their leaders' valiant but ultimately futile attempt to defend Austrian independence from the German Nazis, for the Social Democrats the caesura marking the transition to "fascism" and all it entailed, including surrendering Austria to the Nazis, occurred not in 1938 but in 1934. These emotionally charged debates, which were based on not wholly implausible, if ideologically blinkered, readings of Austrian history in the 1930s, shared an important assumption: whoever had done more either to weaken the Republic's defenses, or to pave the way for the Anschluss, neither was responsible for what followed. The crimes against the Jews were Nazi crimes, the argument went, and those responsible for them—the Germans and traitorous Austrian Nazis—were also responsible for the suffering of the Christian Socials and

Socialists. On these terms, of course, a notion of specific *Austrian* responsibility towards the Jews that would have included these "anti-fascist" leaders was excluded conceptually.

These specific discourses of victimhood also anticipated questions about the relationship between pre-Anschluss anti-Semitism and the persecution of the Jews under Nazi rule, and offered positive arguments that pre-emptively undermined special consideration of Jewish claims. As we saw earlier, ÖVP leaders such as Figl explained away examples of ideological anti-Semitism such as Kunschak's by trivializing it. In doing so they could draw upon the known historical facts—expressed by Martin Herz—that the anti-Semitism of the Christian Socials had been very different from the Nazi persecution, and systematic murder of Jews in Austria. In addition, Figl on occasion offered a more inspirational, if also disingenuous, supplementary account of the persecution of Jews under the Nazis and of residual anti-Semitic prejudice in postwar Austria. "It would be foolish to deny," Figl conceded in a 1947 interview with the *Shanghai Echo,* "that Nazi racial propaganda [had] found an echo among some Austrians." "However," he continued, "when they saw the means by which anti-Semitism was implemented, they were cured. One could safely say that the sympathy with the persecuted Jews eradicated anti-Semitism in Austria. I don't think this question will ever acquire even the slightest significance."[82]

The Social Democrats had two basic arguments, one pan-Austrian, the other specifically Social Democratic, to meet explicit or implicit questions regarding vestiges of anti-Jewish hostility in postwar Austria. Körner's article, cited above, denied the existence of a serious, virulent anti-Semitism in Vienna prior to the Nazi dictatorship; this was because the Viennese had always been a "cosmopolitan [*Weltbürger*]." Social Democratic leaders also advanced the same pan-Austrian arguments offered by their People's Party counterparts, sometimes in nearly identical language. In its 27 March 1946 issue the *Arbeiter-Zeitung* published an article entitled "The Austrian People are not Contaminated" which quoted a statement Karl Renner had made on the subject of anti-Semitism. After reporting Renner's view that Austrian anti-Semitism "had never been aggressive," the paper quoted him, stating, as Figl had, that "[w]hen the Austrians, however, witnessed how the National Socialists behaved towards the Jews, the overwhelming majority of the population rejected Nazi methods and helped wherever they could."[83] More significantly for our purposes, Social Democratic leaders also invoked the suffering of their party's members under the

Austro-fascists to undercut morally any real or potential claims Jews might make for the return of Aryanized property. As Karl Renner argued during a meeting of the cabinet in May 1945:

> It would be entirely incomprehensible that every small Jewish businessman or peddler be compensated for his loss, but that there would be no legal remedy for the losses of an entire class and a movement to which forty-six percent of the population belonged which had the accumulated results of their diligent savings and organizational work simply taken away without punishment and [without] compensation. . . . I could not continue to serve tainted by the fact that I had considered the rights of seven percent of the population sacrosanct, that I had helped enact a special law, but that I had not protected the rights of another, and far greater, part.[84]

IX.

Such attitudes could scarcely have surprised members of the "Jewish Unity" organization (*Jüdische Einigkeit*), who belonged to the Communist Party and were appointed by Ernst Fischer, Communist minister of education and culture in the provisional government established in April 1945, as the provisional leaders of the reconstituted *Israelitische Kultusgemeinde* (IKG). In an editorial for the first issue of the official IKG journal, *Der neue Weg*, founded in January 1946, David Brill, former private secretary to Communist Party leader Johannes Koplenig and provisional head of the IKG since September 1945, minced no words about the nature of Jewish suffering, about the disappointment felt by the Jews then living in Austria, or about the hopes Jewish Austrians entertained for the future.

After recalling that there was no Jew in Austria "whose father, mother, son or daughter, brother or sister was not torn from him in the most monstrous way: gassed, shot, trampled to death or tortured to death in some other way," Brill harshly dismissed the idea proposed by some of the "devout" Jews that the suffering of the Jewish was God's punishment for Jewish sin. Borrowing, somewhat surprisingly, from Christian imagery, Brill argued on the contrary that "this path to Golgotha was unprecedented in the history of humanity." Although Brill admitted that it was impossible to fully make amends (*gutmachen*) for what Jews had suffered, he did demand restitution of the Jews' stolen property, the return of their apartments, etc., which in his view were basic democratic rights. Yet the hopes of the Jews for even these gestures turned out to be deceptive, Brill lamented, for not only have Jews not gotten their property or apartments back, but "Jewish camp survivors [*jüdische*

KZler] are treated as though they were criminals." "If National Socialism murdered the Jews," he stated, "today they are not allowed to live."

However, he went on, "[w]e Jews are determined to stay alive, to demand our rights and to achieve them. We have earned the right [*Berechtigung*] to participate in the reconstruction of our homeland, and whoever tries to prevent this will meet stubborn resistance." "This is our aim, this is our path," Brill concluded, "to fight alongside others as loyal sons of our homeland [*Heimat*] in the [common] front of liberated humanity against any return of the damnable fascism, and to devote our full energies to the reconstruction of our fatherland, which the Nazis have destroyed and shattered."[85]

In the same issue of *Der neue Weg,* Bernhard Braver wrote that "it is the duty of the state to return to the Jews who have suffered loss or injury [*geschädigt*] their lawful rights and to restore [*wieder gutmachen*] their lost or damaged property. No one will be able to understand how a Jew who returns to his home in Austria [*in seine österreichische Heimat zurückkehrt*] from a concentration or labor camp in the east will not be invited to serve as a useful member of society. [*als ein brauchbarer Mensch der Gesellschaft herangezogen wird*]."[86]

If the main outlines of my argument are correct, the probability of Austria's ruling elite being, or feeling, compelled to adopt, even rhetorically, the "duty" for restitution measures called for by Brill and Braver, or even the less costly (in material terms) sense of "responsibility" proposed by Artur Rosenberg, would have been slight. This would be the case even if the Jewish community leadership had never missed an opportunity to demand such expressions of "duty" or "responsibility" from the government. But, as Helga Embacher has shown in some detail,[87] while this leadership continued to lament government inaction on restitution and to attack instances of anti-Jewish hostility in the documents of the IKG and the pages of the Jewish press, it also shifted its political priorities. It sought to have Jewish victims of the Nazi race laws and Aryanizations included in the welfare measures intended for all sufferers of political persecution, and insisted on the right of Jewish Austrians, as Brill had written, "to fight alongside others as loyal sons of our homeland in the [common] front of liberated humanity against any return of the damnable fascism, and to devote our full energies to the reconstruction of our fatherland" (see FN 85). I would like to suggest that some of the views the initial leaders of the "Jewish Unity" and their successors of the Socialist-led "Union of Laboring Jews" (*Bund werktätiger Juden*), who were the predominant force in the IKG leadership from 1948 until the 1980s,[88] came to adopt towards the "Jewish question" in postwar Austria also helped reinforce the notion of pan-Austrian victimhood.

Many of the Jews who first returned to Austria, and even more those who wished to return, had previously been politically active and had repeatedly been victims of political persecution, in many cases prior to the Anschluss. Those in exile, who had no political reasons to come back, and were never invited to return, largely stayed abroad. Moreover, given the suspicion of collaboration hanging over the heads of those who had worked in the *Ältestenrat* (which handled Jewish welfare matters immediately after the war), and given the procedural irregularities which characterized the efforts of the IKG leadership under the direction of Heinrich Schur, it was not surprising that Ernst Fischer, the minister with the portfolio for religious affairs, would wish to replace them by politically reliable leaders such as Brill. Both a kind of political self-selection mechanism and some more conventional political considerations thus led to a disproportionate number of the Jews in the IKG leadership who were politically conscious and determined to rebuild democratic Austria. Consequently, Jewish Austrians who had been victims of racial persecution alone constituted a minority of Jews active in the IKG, and these had no specific organization or representatives to speak for them (though the Communist Party had its own "Action Committee of Jewish Concentration Camp Inmates" (*Aktionskomitee der jüdischen Kzler*) to represent some of their interests). Although Communist leaders of the IKG such as Akim Lewit worked, with some success, to have victims of racial persecution included in relief organizations (such as the *Volkssolidarität*), which had been set up to provide assistance for the politically persecuted only,[89] Jews who had been victims of racial persecution alone were initially largely excluded from decision-making processes and from the welfare provisions of the state. Since both the IKG and the camp inmates organization (*KZ-Verband*) had been called into life by one or more of the three anti-fascist parties, the official representatives of the Jews affiliated with these parties (mainly the KPÖ and SPÖ), became the major voice articulating Jewish demands. Those Jews who had returned to rebuild democratic Austria as convinced Communists or Socialists, however, would be inclined to view Nazi persecution of Jews, horrific as they invariably held it to be, within the Marxist conceptual framework of fascism, which ascribed no particularly analytical—and hence political—significance to the specifically racialist character of the Nazi regime.[90] This ideological and political orientation would necessarily view racial discrimination as one form of suffering but would certainly not consider it more significant than the political persecution that the politically active Jews had undergone. Although it was never abandoned or renounced, the struggle against anti-Jewish hostilities *per se* seems to have assumed a correspondingly lower overall priority.

In any event, the attitude of the left-wing leadership of the IKG was overwhelmingly assimilationist, and it fought massive political battles with the Zionists, who from the beginning had recruited heavily among displaced persons. The conflict in the IKG between the Socialist Union of Laboring Jews and the Zionists (which was most vehement in the 1950s[91]) only increased this tendency, as in the face of this challenge the non-Zionists felt bound to combat the charge of divided loyalty. As Embacher put it, "[a]part from the fear that Jewish nationalism could provoke right-wing radicalism and above all anti-Semitism, the *Bund* considered a Jewish nationalist party a threat to its attempt to be accepted as loyal Austrians with equal rights."[92] Yet even the Zionists in the IKG leadership felt compelled to reassure the Austrian public that they were not "motivated by feelings of revenge," but only wanted "to participate in the reconstruction of the new Austria as Austrians, not as a foreign body."[93] The threat felt by these Jews seems exaggerated, but its presence suggests that the strategy pursued to counter the criticism, even if only pre-emptively, would articulate well with notions of pan-Austrian victimhood.

The history Embacher relates of the early years of the Jews organized in the *Kultusgemeinde* is a sorrowful one. For the leadership, everyday anti-Jewish prejudice might be explained and endured by means of the ideological succor of anti-fascism, while delays in restitution might be rationalized by appeals to the seeming justness of other victims' claims. Rank and file Jews, however, frequently saw their hopes of recognition of their suffering or their just demands simply delayed or dashed. Their response was broadly two-fold. On the one hand, most IKG members shifted their allegiance from the "Jewish Unity" to the Social Democratic "Union of Laboring Jews," as they thought that the SPÖ could offer a better defense against anti-Jewish hostilities, and better access to welfare measures from which they would benefit; however, they were forced to swallow the party's hesitation to organize the return of exiled Jews, its foot dragging in settling restitution claims, and even the involvement of Vienna's Socialist-led municipal council in property transactions which the *Kultusgemeinde* leadership called a "second Aryanization."[94] On the other hand, some leaders of the IKG believed that by portraying themselves as new kinds of Jews who had abandoned old stereotypical characteristics, they would reinforce their claim to be normal Austrian patriots, and thus counteract anti-Jewish prejudice. One particularly graphic example of this is a statement released by the IKG in response to a newspaper article which had been published in connection with a showing of *Oliver Twist,* and which had noted several traditional Jewish stereotypes in the film. "Before the [very] eyes of the Jewish population," the *Kultusgemeinde* wrote, "stands shiningly an entirely different type of Jew, [a Jew] who has proven himself in the fight for freedom. Today's Jew is no longer a Fagin, he is a new type: willing to help rebuild, peaceful, willing to work, and returned to the soil [*zur Scholle zurückgekehrt*]. [The portrayal of] Fagin," the statement concluded, "is thus an insult in several ways."[95]

Views such as these might have been born of disappointment or desperation, or of a perfectly rational political calculation of what might neutralize residual anti-Semitic prejudices among non-Jewish Austrians. But whatever their source, these kinds of arguments were unlikely to suggest compelling reasons for non-Jewish Austrians to embrace a position of special responsibility towards Jewish suffering, for in a sense these Jews were volunteering to dissolve into the pan-Austrian community of victims.

X.

Let me summarize the main points of my argument:

The Western Allies' need to make Austrian independence a success, and their tendency to equate National Socialism with pan-Germanism, led them to promote both Austrian victimhood and Austrian nationalism as the most effective means of killing the idea of the Anschluss. The Allies' primary focus on the anti-democratic features of National Socialism hindered, if it did not preclude, the conceptualization of a "Jewish question" that went beyond the formal prohibition of discrimination.

At the national level, the absence of pressure from this source provided Austrian leaders of the anti-fascist parties with a determinate political space within which they could construct their own national and parochial memories of the recent past. The discourses of victimhood developed by the anti-fascist parties did not, however, have one referent,

but two. Austria's loss of its independence to "Hitlerite aggression"—the first referent—was important, but the second referent—namely the period between 1934 and 1938, centered around the
civil war of February 1934 and Austro-fascism—in fact had more
domestic salience. The respective accounts offered different, but
complementary, moral arguments which undermined, if they did not
vitiate, an Austrian version of collective moral responsibility for Jewish
suffering in the *Ostmark*. The ÖVP mourned its martyr Dollfuss who
had been the first Austrian victim of Nazism, and celebrated Schuschnigg as the last bastion against Hitler and Nazism, while the Socialists
basked in their superior moral stature as the longest-suffering Austrian
victim of fascism. For neither the ÖVP nor the SPÖ, however, would
these discourses of victimhood imply *any* responsibility for the crimes
of the Third Reich, including persecution of the Jews; consequently,
they would not provide any arguments as to why Jews ought to receive
any privileged position in the postwar pan-Austrian community of
victims. This inclusive *Opfergemeinschaft* remained the dominant trope
within postwar Austrian *Vergangenheitsbewältigung* precisely because
there were no perceived incentives to do otherwise, nor any threat of
sanctions for failing to do otherwise.

There is no way to judge the extent to which these discourses of
victimhood actually impinged upon the individual memories of the non-
Jewish Austrian population as a whole. However, it seems highly
plausible to assume that there was a connection between the information
to which individual Austrians had most frequent access in describing
and ascribing meaning to events of the past, and the views they came to
adopt. This applies both to those who had lived through the periods as
well as those who were socialized and educated afterwards. Individual
memory is neither static nor unaffected by political debates or power
relations. One's ability to remember at all is influenced by, among other
things, who sets the terms for moral debate, which premises of a moral
vocabulary are privileged, and the kinds and meanings of rituals that
embody the obligations a given moral lesson was thought to imply.

In determining the specific role that the discourses of victimhood
played in circumscribing the "Jewish question" in postwar Austria,
therefore, we must examine the context in which such discourses, which
help constitute such memories, arise, and how a changed context can
allow previously disadvantaged discourses to acquire more importance,
or can engender new, contrasting discourses. As I have tried to show,
there was neither an obvious incentive for Austrian elites to address the

"Jewish question" as Artur Rosenberg had defined it (though plenty of political and material disincentives!), nor the fear of sanction for not doing so.

And here the contrasting case of Germany is instructive. Anson Rabinbach has described what he termed "Adenauer's genius" in concluding the reparations treaty with Israel and in transposing, as he stated, "the crime against the Jews from a taboo to a politically overloaded symbol of the entire Nazi complex." And it served a dual purpose: "[I]nternationally," he argues, "it demonstrated the Federal Republic of Germany's desire to participate in the community of nations as an independent, militarily strong, post-Nazi state. Domestically, it focused the Nazi past on the singular crime against the Jews, which could be accentuated and pursued in the present, thereby consigning all other questions of the Nazi era—especially the issue of former Nazis—to the periphery."[96] At a more mundane level, Frank Stern has also pointed out that the famous *Persilscheine* were much easier to come by if one made a declaration of support for Jews or produced testimony from former Jewish friends and neighbors.[97] Neither of these conditions applied to Austria in the immediate postwar period, with the results I have described.

Rosenberg's "Die jüdische Frage" generated little contemporary public discussion when it appeared. Which is not to say that the potentially explosive nature of Rosenberg's notion of Austrian collective moral responsibility did not elicit energetic ripostes from those who sensed the political, even ideological challenge it represented. In an article entitled "Land without Jews," published in *Neues Österreich* around the same time the pamphlet containing his talk appeared, Rosenberg accurately anticipated the argument that would be advanced as the alternative to his own approach to the "Jewish question": "There is no Jewish question, they assure us," Rosenberg wrote, referring explicitly to views expressed by ideal typical Austrians to whom he ascribed both "upright character" (*gute Gesinnung*) and "political shrewdness"— "there are only questions which are the same for all Austrians, of whichever confession."[98]

The response Rosenberg predicted was not long in coming. The very next day, Herbert Kohlich, in an *Arbeiter-Zeitung* article entitled "A Jewish Question?," took up Rosenberg's challenge. Kohlich denied the existence of a "Jewish question" in postwar Austria. For Kohlich, the definition contained in the Nuremberg race laws had been consigned to the "scrapheap [*Schindanger*] of world history." Consequently, he

continued, both under Austrian law and according to the views expressed at least occasionally by the *Israelitische Kultusgemeinde* itself, Jews
are "only Austrians of the Jewish faith ... as there are Austrians of the
Catholic or Protestant faith, and also non-religious [*konfessionslos*]
Austrians." It followed, Kohlich argued, in a particularly inapt choice of
words, that a "special treatment" [*Sonderbehandlung*] of any particular
"faith" was excluded. Asking whether "the martyrdom of the Jews justified such a *Sonderbehandlung*" nonetheless, Kohlich replied in the
negative, citing "statistics" according to which Jews (as defined by the
Nuremberg laws) represented "only approximately one-sixth or one-
seventh" of the thirty-four million victims of National Socialism. "Despite Hitler's speeches," Kohlich maintained, it is only "partly true that
the 'Jews' occupied a priority position in the hierarchy of Nazi persecution." Indeed, though the absolute numbers are smaller, the Lidice
massacre and the policies towards the Jews of Galicia are "fundamentally comparable" in terms of the "wild raging [*Wüten*] of the brown
beasts." While Kohlich conceded that there was indeed a "Jewish
question" for those "people of the Jewish faith" who were homeless and
looking for a place to find peace and put down roots, "[f]or us in
Austria, however, for our fellow citizens of the Jewish faith, there can
and may not be a Jewish question!" Kohlich quoted favorably Rosenberg's assertion in his *Neues Österreich* article that "restitution [*Wiedergutmachung*] for those who suffered at the Nazi seizure of power is by
no means a Jewish question. It applies equally to all those who were
politically persecuted." But then he goes on to criticize Rosenberg's
view that the problem of restitution is particularly acute for Jews since,
unlike other victims of National Socialism, they lost nearly everything
they had. Against Rosenberg's rather pragmatic approach Kohlich
argued that while those who had lost their jobs should be reinstated, and
those who had been forced from their apartments should receive
accommodation, this should apply to "every citizen of whatever faith."
Moreover, Kohlich maintained, a "six-room apartment for a couple
without children exceeds the limits of *Wiedergutmachung*." Similarly,
although the confiscation of Nazi goods and the assessment of a special
tax on Nazis would help ensure that those who lost their livelihoods
were able to make a living, in Kohlich's view "the reestablishment of
capitalist property [also] exceeds the limits of *Wiedergutmachung*." He
therefore demanded "Equal rights for all victims of Nazism!" Kohlich
ended with a plea to Rosenberg to quit making "confessional distinctions," for to do otherwise would merely "serve to animate racism in

reverse" [*den Rassismus mit umgekehrten Vorzeichen wieder zu beleben*]."[99]

An abridged version of Rosenberg's talk was also published in the March 1946 issue of the *Österreichische Monatshefte,* the theoretical journal of the People's Party.[100] However, Rosenberg's article was accompanied by a caveat informing the magazine's readers that its editors were publishing this "substantial [*gewichtig*] contribution to the discussion of this many-sided problem," without, however, "identifying with all individual details of the exposition." To my knowledge this was the only instance—at least for the period 1945-1950—in which the *Österreichische Monatshefte* published such an editorial disclaimer.

Though without giving it as much prominence as the Social Democrats, the People's Party's pan-Austrian approach to suffering was expressed in a brief commentary on the question of restitution published in the *Österreichische Monatshefte* a few months after Artur Rosenberg's pamphlet had appeared. The immediate occasion of this short commentary, written by one W.O. (presumably Walter Ost[101]) and published in the June 1946 issue of the *Österreichische Monatshefte,* was Kohlich's article in the *Arbeiter-Zeitung.* Ost found merit in Kohlich's views, and, presumably, in his diction (he repeated Kohlich's usage *Sonderbehandlung*), but he believed that Austrian Jews would not. However, Ost did commend what he claimed (mistakenly) to be Rosenberg's "warning" against acts "from the Jewish side" which might "disturb the work of pacification [*Befriedung*] and understanding. The Jews of Austria," Ost concluded, "will be able to prove to our people as a whole their noble sentiments by demonstrating their moderate behavior."[102]

In his initial talk Artur Rosenberg had closed his remarks with an appeal to Austrians' enlightened self-interest. "If Austria were to set an example for the world by its handling of the Jewish question," he said, "it would elicit an equally determined, just treatment of its own needs and demands."[103] The Austrians did indeed wait nine more years before their "just" demand for full sovereignty was finally granted. But the sad irony is that the delay was neither because of, nor in spite of, their failure to address the "Jewish question" in the way Rosenberg had imagined it. When arguments about collective moral responsibility similar to those Rosenberg had raised in 1946 were articulated by Austrian leaders some forty years later, Rosenberg and his "Jewish question" had long since been forgotten.

Notes

1. Some of the research, as well as much of the thinking, that has gone into the preparation of this essay was done during my stay at the Woodrow Wilson International Center for Scholars, where I was privileged to be a fellow during the academic year 1999-2000. The Wilson Center is the closest thing to scholarly heaven I can imagine, and I would like to take this opportunity to thank the Center and its staff for all the support they provided me while I was there. This essay is a substantially revised version of a paper I delivered in the "work in progress" sessions at the Center. I am grateful to all my colleagues for their astute critical remarks but would particularly like to thank Laura Hein for her detailed and invariably incisive comments on that paper. The version of this essay I submitted to CAS has benefited enormously from the critical attention given it by Oliver Rathkolb, an historian whose vast knowledge of the documentary material dealing with contemporary Austrian history is matched only by the generosity with which he shares it, and by the discernment and acuity of his judgments. I am grateful for it all. I would also like to express my gratitude to John Bunzl, Matti Bunzl, István Deák, Kent Hughes, Tony Judt, Yemile Mizrahi, Anson Rabinbach, Jonathan Steinberg, Kurt Weyland, Robert Wistrich, and Ruth Wodak for helping me clarify individual points which are addressed in the essay.

2. The Austrian People's Party (*Österreichische Volkspartei*, or ÖVP), was founded in April 1945 as a new party whose leaders dissociated it programmatically from the Christian Social Party of the First Republic, and from the Patriotic Front of a period described as either the *Ständestaat* or *Austro-fascism*. The new party professed a commitment to parliamentary democracy and to a more extensive separation between the party and the Roman Catholic Church. Indeed, the ÖVP even renounced claims for the restitution of property of the Patriotic Front that had been seized by the Nazis. Nevertheless, in terms of political leadership, organizational structure, and core constituencies, the Christian Social *Lager* exhibited a remarkable continuity between the First and Second Republics. The Social Democrats frequently reminded many leaders of the ÖVP of their *Austro-fascist* past, and, in the heated debates about the period between 1934 and 1938, the ÖVP defended policies of both Dollfuss and Schuschnigg, as we will see later. Thus, while I do not believe there is any reason to doubt that the ÖVP's professed commitment to parliamentary democracy was sincere, it is important to keep these continuities in mind. See ÖVP party program "Die programmatischen Leitsätze der Österreichischen Volkspartei 1945," in *Österreichische Parteiprogramme 1868-1966*, ed. Klaus Berchtold (Vienna: Verlag für Geschichte und Politik, 1967), 376-79; Robert Kriechbaumer, *Parteiprogramme im Widerstreit der Interessen. Die Programmdiskussion und die Programme von ÖVP und SPÖ 1945-1986*, special volume of the series *Österreichisches Jahrbuch für Politik* (Vienna and Munich: Verlag für Geschichte und Politik and R. Oldenbourg Verlag, 1990), 60-61; and Wolfgang Müller, "Die Österreichische Volkspartei," in *Handbuch des Politischen Systems Österreichs. Die Zweite Republik*, ed. Herbert Dachs, et al. (Vienna: Man'sche Verlags- und Universitätsbuchhandlung GmbH, 1997), 265-85.

3. *Neues Österreich,* 28 April 1945, 1.

4. Although I concede Omer Bartov's point that one's choice of term for what he describes as "the Event" is never innocent, my use of the term *Holocaust* is not consciously intended to carry a specific political message, but rather expresses my acknowledgment of certain linguistic conventions. The arguments advanced here are compatible both with more inclusive as well as more restrictive definitions of the term *Holocaust* or its equivalents. In addition, while I recognize that deciding, as it were, who is a Jew is also not innocent and can be fraught with difficulties, the words *Jew* and *Jewish* comprise, for the purpose of this essay, all those who would have suffered any

disability under the Nuremberg race laws. Even granting this definition, one must still decide whether these Jews in Austria were *Austrian Jews* or *Jewish Austrians*. Though this is also a disputed issue, I believe the usage *Austrian Jews could* be read as conceding—willy nilly—an important but contested point about the compatibility of *Austrian* and *Jewish* which the formulation *Jewish Austrians* does not. Since many Jews who returned to Austria considered their Austrian identity at least as important as their Jewish identity, I have chosen, again for the purpose of this essay, to use the term *Jewish Austrians* except where the specific emphasis requires the other. See Omer Bartov, "Antisemitism, the Holocaust, and Reinterpretations of National Socialism," in *Murder in Our Midst. The Holocaust, Industrial Killing, and Representation* (New York: Oxford University Press, 1996), 53-70.

5. Artur Rosenberg, "Die jüdische Frage," in *Zur Jüdischen Frage. Zwei Reden an das österreichische Volk,* ed. Eduard Ludwig and Artur Rosenberg (Vienna: Verlag Erwin Müller, 1946), 36.

6. Shortly after the war, before taking up a position with the German newspaper *Die Zeit,* Artur Rosenberg, a journalist/writer born in Maribor in 1889, worked for the *Wiener Kurier,* the paper published under the auspices of the U.S. occupation authorities. On Rosenberg see the entry for "Dr. Arthur [sic] Rosenberg" in Fritz Hausjell, ed., *Journalisten gegen Demokratie oder Faschismus. Eine kollektiv-biographische Analyse der beruflichen und politischen Herkunft der österreichischen Tageszeitungsjournalisten am Beginn der Zweiten Republik (1945-1947),* vol. 2 (Frankfurt am Main: Peter Lang, 1989), 790; this entry, however, mistakenly amalgamates the author of "Die jüdische Frage" with the German-born historian of almost the same name. This latter Arthur Rosenberg died in 1943. See Sybille Claus and Beatrix Schmidt, eds., *Biographisches Handbuch der deutschsprachigen Emigration,* vol. I, *Politik, Wirtschaft, Öffentliches Leben,* prepared under the direction of Werner Röder and Herbert A. Strauss and with the assistance of Dieter Marc Schneider and Louise Forsyth (Munich: K. G. Saur, 1980), 612.

7. The ambiguity arises because the German words *Schuld* and *schuldig* can mean both guilt/guilty and debt/indebted.

8. Indeed, as Rosenberg argued in "Land ohne Juden," an article published in March 1946 which addresses the same theme as his talk in the Vienna Konzerthaus, "restitution for those who 'suffered in connection with the National Socialist seizure of power' is definitely not a Jewish question. It affects all those in equal measure who suffered political persecution. However, it has an especially critical affect on the Jews, because there is scarcely a single one of them who did not lose everything—property, job or business, claims and entitlements [*Ansprüche*] and apartments—as a result of the occupation." *Neues Österreich,* 26 March 1946, 1.

9. ISKULT, Pressemitteilung der Israelitischen Kultusgemeinden 67/1956, Beilage; cited in Helga Embacher, "Die innenpolitische Partizipation der Israelistischen Kultusgemeinde in Österreich," in *Schwieriges Erbe. Der Umgang mit Nationalsozialismus und Antisemitismus in Österreich, der DDR und der Bundesrepublik Deutschland,* ed. Werner Bergman, Rainer Erb, and Albert Lichtblau (Frankfurt: Campus, 1995), 322.

10. Yeshayahu Jelinek and Beer Sheva usefully distinguish between "moral pressure" and "effective pressure" when discussing the ability to influence policy on matters pertaining to Jews in Germany. Although they apply it to pressure that was possible to exert from abroad, it seems equally applicable to domestic politics. Clearly, "moral pressure" from whatever source would have an impact on policy only if it became "effective pressure," a point the leadership of the IKG grasped precisely. See Yeshayahu A. Jelinek and Beer Sheva, "Political Acumen, Altruism, Foreign Pressure or Moral

Debt: Konrad Adenauer and the 'Shilumim'," in *Tel Aviver Jahrbuch für Deutsche Ge-schichte*, ed. Shulamit Volkov and Frank Stern (Tel Aviv: Bleicher Verlag, 1990), 89-90.

11. Evan Bukey, "Nazi Rule in Austria," *Austrian History Yearbook* XXIII (1992): 202-33.

12. Richard Mitten, *The Politics of Anti-Semitic Prejudice. The Waldheim Phenomenon in Austria* (Boulder: Westview Press, 1992).

13. See Robert Knight, "Introduction," in *"Ich bin dafür, die Sache in die Länge zu ziehen." Die Wortprotokolle der österreichischen Bundesregierung von 1945 bis 1952 über die Entschädigung der Juden,* ed. Robert Knight (Vienna: Böhlau, 2000 [first published 1988]); Sebastian Meissl, Klaus-Dieter Mulley, and Oliver Rathkolb, eds., *Verdrängte Schuld, verfehlte Sühne. Entnazifizierung in Österreich 1945-1955* (Vienna: Verlag für Gesellschaftskritik, 1986); Gerhard Botz, "Verdrängung, Pflichterfüllung, Geschichtskliterrung: Probleme des 'typischen Österreichers' mit der NS-Vergangen-heit," in *Kontroversen um Österreichs Zeitgeschichte. Verdrängte Vergangenheit, Österreich-Identität, Waldheim und die Historiker,* ed. Gerhard Botz and Gerald Sprengnagel (Frankfurt: Campus, 1994), 89-104; Heidemarie Uhl, "The Politics of Memory: Austria's Perception of the Second World War and the National Socialist Period," in *Contemporary Austrian Studie*s, vol. 5, *Austrian Historical Memory and National Identity,* ed. Günter Bischof and Anton Pelinka (New Brunswick: Transaction Publishers, 1997), 64-94; Brigitte Bailer, "They Were All Victims: The Selective Treatment of the Consequences of National Socialism," in *Austrian Historical Memory and National Identity,* ed. Günter Bischof and Anton Pelinka (New Brunswick: Transaction Publishers, 1997), 103-15; Brigitte Bailer, *Wiedergutmachung kein Thema: Österreich und die Opfer des Nationalsozialismus* (Vienna: Löcker Verlag, 1993); Bruce Pauley, "Austria," in *The World Reacts to the Holocaust,* ed. David S. Wyman (Baltimore: Johns Hopkins University Press, 1996), 473-513; Robert Wistrich, *Austria and the Legacy of the Holocaust,* International Perspectives 44 (New York: American Jewish Committee, 1999).

14. Tony Judt, "The Past is Another Country: Myth and Memory in Postwar Europe," *Daedalus* 121, no. 4 (Fall 1992): 85, 89; reprinted in István Deák, Jan T. Gross, and Tony Judt, eds., *The Politics of Retribution in Europe. World War II and Its Aftermath* (Princeton: Princeton University Press, 2000), 293-323.

15. See István Deák, "A Fatal Compromise? The Debate over Collaboration and Resistance in Hungary," *East European Politics and Societies* 9, no. 2 (Spring 1995): 209-33; István Deák, "Post-World War II Political Justice in a Historical Perspective," in *Keine "Abrechnung": NS-Verbrechen, Justiz und Gesellschaft in Europa nach 1945,* ed. Claudia Kuretsidis-Haider and Winfried R. Garscha (Leipzig: Akademische Verlags-anstalt, 1998), 389-96.

16. Discourse has become a rather inflated concept, and can be used to mean something as specific as spoken language, or something as general as the social process of communication. I have found most useful Jay Lemke's general definition of discourse as "the social activity of making meanings with language and other symbolic systems in some particular kind of situation or setting" and the distinctions he draws between text and discourse:
   "On each occasion when the particular meanings characteristic of these discourses are being made, a specific *text* is produced. Discourses, as social actions more or less governed by social habits, produce texts that will in some ways be alike in their meanings. They may be alike in the content of what they say about topics and subjects. They may be alike in their values, attitudes and stances toward their subjects and audiences. They may be alike in the sequence, structure and form of organization of what

they say. These texts will always also be different as well, each will be in some ways unique. The notions of text and discourse are complementary. When we want to focus on the specifics of an event or occasion, we speak of the text; when we want to look at patterns, commonality, relationships that embrace different texts and occasions, we can speak of discourses."

Discourses of victimhood should be understood as discourses in this Lemkean sense. See Jay L. Lemke, *Textual Politics. Discourse and Social Dynamics* (London: Taylor and Francis, 1995), 6-7. For the notion of "discursive-historical methodology" [*diskurshistorische Methode*] see Ruth Wodak, et al., "Wir sind alle unschuldige Täter!"

17. For concise definitions of these three categories see Raul Hilberg, *Perpetrators, Victims, Bystanders* (London: Lime Tree, 1993), ix-xi.

18. See Richard Mitten, "The Social Democratic 'Mémoire Volontaire' and Coming to Terms with the Legacy of National Socialism in Austria," in *Contemporary Austrian Studies*, vol. 4, *Austro-Corporatism. Past, Present, Future*, ed. Günter Bischof and Anton Pelinka (New Brunswick: Transaction Publishers, 1996), 336-50, emphasis added. This idea is, of course, a gloss on the Proustian notion of *"mémoire involontaire."*

19. See Günter Bischof, "Die Instrumentalisierung der Moskauer Erklärung nach dem 2. Weltkrieg," *Zeitgeschichte* 20, no. 11/12 (November/December 1993): 345-66.

20. The moral vocabulary in postwar Austria was so elastic that the notion of victimhood soon came to embrace even some of the "victims" of de-Nazification and the (largely theoretical) restitution of Jewish property. However, these were clearly viewed as "victims" *despite* their affiliation with National Socialism, which made them markedly different from the discourses of victimhood I am describing.

21. Some preliminary thoughts about these issues are contained in Richard Mitten, "Bitburg, Waldheim, and the Politics of Remembering and Forgetting," in *From World War to Waldheim: Culture and Politics in Austria and the United States*, ed. David Good and Ruth Wodak (New York: Berghahn Publishers, 1999), 51-84.

22. See Leon Poliakov, *Geschichte des Antisemitismus*, translation of *Histoire de l'Antisemitisme* (Worms: Georg Heintz, 1979); Friedrich Heer, *Gottes erste Liebe. Die Juden im Spannungsfeld der Geschichte*, rev. ed. (Frankfurt: Ullstein, 1986 [first published 1967]); Robert S. Wistrich, *Antisemitism. The Longest Hatred* (New York: Pantheon Books, 1991).

23. The classic account of the social psychological phenomenon known as prejudice is Gordon Allport, *The Nature of Prejudice* (Reading, MA: Addison-Wesley Publishing Company, Inc., 1987 [originally published 1954]); see also Elisabeth Young-Bruehl, *The Anatomy of Prejudices* (Cambridge, MA: Harvard University Press, 1996), and the important essay Gavin I. Langmuir, "Toward a Definition of Antisemitism," in *Toward a Definition of anti-Semitism* (Berkeley: University of California Press, 1990), 311-52.

24. The controversy surrounding Daniel Jonah Goldhagen's *Hitler's Willing Executioners* is only the most recent, and most concentrated, of this analytical problem. See Daniel Jonah Goldhagen, *Hitler's Willing Executioners. Ordinary Germans and the Holocaust* (New York: Alfred A. Knopf, 1996). Among the most important critical accounts of the "Goldhagen thesis" are Norman G. Finkelstein and Ruth Bettina Birn, *A Nation on Trial: The Goldhagen Thesis and Historical Truth* (New York: Metropolitan Books, 1998); Christopher R. Browning, "Daniel Goldhagen's Willing Executioners," review of Daniel Jonah Goldhagen, *Hitler's Willing Executioners, History and Memory* 8, no. 1 (Spring/Summer 1996): 88-108; Omer Bartov, "Ordinary Monsters," *The New Republic*, 29 April 1996, 32-8; and Dieter Pohl, "Die Holocaust-Forschung und Goldhagens Thesen," *Vierteljahreshefte für Zeitgeschichte* 45, no. 1 (January 1997): 1-

48. See also the collection Julius H. Schoeps, *Ein Volk von Mördern? Die Dokumentation zur Goldhagen-Kontroverse um die Rolle der Deutschen im Holocaust* (Hamburg: Piper Verlag, 1996).

25. Such beliefs are not of recent vintage. Citing Albert Massiczek's 1963 book *Wieder Nazi?*, Friederike Wilder-Okladek, in her study of the return movement of Austrian Jews after the war, offers a particularly strong version of such views: "The typical Austrian is a racial mixture which is the root of the whole complex situation, much more than the German Nazi whose Germanisation is at least a few generations old. Thus, the Austrian nature of the problem leads to a continuous conflict situation in the would-be Nazi. He is completely incapable of conforming to the laws of 'Germanic racial purity,' feels inferior and develops profound sentiments of inferiority . ... Thus the Austrian forms extreme variations of Nationalist and National-Socialist activity just because he is unable to accept and come to terms with the typical Austrian situation of diversity and his inability to be a 'pure German'." Friederike Wilder-Okladek, *The Return Movement of Jews to Austria After the Second World War, with Special Consideration of the Return from Israel* (The Hague: M. Nijhoff, 1969), 13. See also Wistrich, *Austria and the Legacy*, 1-4, and the two reviews of Goldhagen's work by Günter Bischof and Robert Wistrich, both of which specifically address Goldhagen's neglect of Austrian perpetrators. Günter Bischof, "Die normalen Deutschen als Täter," *Die Furche* 18 (1996): 2; and Robert Wistrich, "Helping Hitler," Antisemitism *Research* 1, no. 1 (1997): 19-25; as well as the thoughtful and subtle remarks on the place of National Socialism in Austrian history in Ernst Hanisch, "Der Ort des Nationalsozialismus in der österreichischen Geschichte," in *NS-Herrschaft in Österreich: Ein Handbuch*, ed. Emmerich Tálos, Ernst Hanisch, and Wolfgang Neugebauer (Vienna: Öbv & hpt VerlagsgmbH, 2000), 11-24.

26. The notion of "moral responsibility" derives from West German Chancellor Konrad Adenauer's statement in the *Bundestag* on 27 September 1951, in which he declared that "Unspeakable crimes have been committed in the name of the German people, which enjoins a moral and material restitution, both for individual damages suffered by Jews as well as for Jewish property for which there are no surviving legal heirs." Excerpts from this speech may be found on the web at http://www.jerusalem-schalom.de/konrad.htm. See also Adenauer's statement made at the beginning of the negotiations on restitution: "Although we do not consider ourselves as Hitler's successors, we do believe that the German people have an enormous moral obligation towards the Jews. We cannot bring the dead back to life, but we want to offer what redress is possible to the living." Quoted in Gustav Jellinek, "Die Geschichte der österreichischen Wiedergutmachung," in *The Jews of Austria: Essays on their Life, History and Destruction*, ed. Josef Fraenkel (London: Valentine, Mitchell and Co. Ltd., 1967), 398. The discussion on Austria exhibits certain parallels not only to the debate on restitution, but also to that inaugurated by the publication of Karl Jaspers's *Die Schuldfrage* in 1946. See Karl Jaspers, *Die Schuldfrage. Für Völkermord gibt es keine Verjährung* (Munich: R. Piper & Co., 1979 [originally published 1946]); Hannah Arendt, *The Jew as Pariah: Jewish Identity and Politics in the Modern Age*, ed. Ron H. Feldman (New York: Grove Press, 1978); Anson Rabinbach, *Between Apocalypse and Enlightenment: Central European Thought in the Shadow of Catastrophe* (Berkeley: University of California Press, 1997).

27. As I argue in "Bitburg, Waldheim, and the Politics of Remembering and Forgetting."

28. "Declaration on Austria," in *Foreign Relations of the United States, 1943*, vol. I (Washington, D.C.: U.S. Government Printing Office, 1963), 516-17 [FRUS].

29. On the negotiations to have the "responsibility" clause removed see Gerald Stourzh, *Geschichte des Staatsvertrages 1945-1955. Österreichs Weg zur Neutralität* (Graz: Styria Verlag, 1985), 167.

30. Heidemarie Uhl, "The Politics of Memory: Austria's Perception of the Second World War and the National Socialist Period," in *Contemporary Austrian Studies*, vol. 5, *Austrian Historical Memory*, ed. Günter Bischof and Anton Pelinka (New Brunswick: Transaction Publishers, 1997), 66.

31. Robert Knight, "'Neutrality,' not Sympathy: Jews in Postwar Austria," in *Austrians and Jews in the Twentieth Century. From Franz Joseph to Waldheim,* ed. Robert S. Wistrich (New York: St. Martin's Press, 1992), 224.

32. Uhl, "The Politics of Memory," 67.

33. Robert Knight, "'Neutrality,' not Sympathy: Jews in Post-War Austria," 224.

34. In a very perceptive essay, Thomas Albrich has also called attention to the extremely circumscribed nature of the "Jewish question" in postwar Austria, but in my view he, too, underestimates the extent to which the Allied predisposition to endorse the notion of Austrian victimhood predated the end of the war, a point I would like to stress. See Thomas Albrich, "'Es gibt keine jüdische Frage'. Zur Aufrechterhaltung des österreichischen Opfermythos," in *Der Umgang mit dem Holocaust. Europa - USA - Israel,* ed. Rolf Steininger, Schriften des Instituts für Zeitgeschichte der Universität Innsbruck und des Jüdischen Museums Hohenems (Vienna: Böhlau, 1994), 147-66.

35. According to the official story of the United States' policy toward Austria, which historians until recently had few grounds to challenge, the United States' endorsement of Austrian victimhood and advocacy of its political independence was above all a matter of simple justice. As State Department official James Riddleberger argued in a note drafted in 1946, summarizing previous U.S. policy on the "Status of Austria": "The attitude of the United States to the military occupation of Austria by Germany and its formal incorporation in the German Reich in 1938 was always guided by this consideration (strong disapproval of Nazi attempts to force Austria into the Reich) and by the well-established policy of the United States towards the acquisition of territory by force. While, as a practical measure, the United States was obligated to take certain administrative measures based upon the situation created by the Anschluss, this government consistently avoided any steps which might be considered *de jure* recognition of the annexation of Austria by Germany." The United States had "accordingly regarded Austria as a country liberated from forcible domination by Nazi Germany and not as an ex-enemy state at war with the United States during the world war." Draft Statement, James Riddelberger to Matthews, General Hilldring and Secretary of State, "Status of Austria," 22 October 1946, quoted in Robert H. Keyserlingk, *Austria in World War II*, (Kingston: McGill-Queen's University Press, 1988), 26.

36. Some of the arguments made in this and the next section draw on my article, Richard Mitten, "The Eyes of the Beholder: Allied Wartime Attitudes and the Delimiting of the 'Jewish Question' for Post-War Austria," *Tel Aviver Jahrbuch Für Deutsche Geschichte* XXIII (1994): 345-70. I would, however, no longer subscribe to all the specific views I expressed in it.

37. In addition to Keyserlingk see also Guy Stanley, "Great Britain and the Austrian Question, 1938-1945," Ph.D. diss. (University of London, 1973), 82-123; Günter Bischof, "Die Planung und Politik der Alliierten 1940-1954," in *Österreich im 20. Jahrhundert. Ein Studienbuch in zwei Bänden,* vol. 2, *Vom Zweiten Weltkrieg bis zur Gegenwart,* ed. Rolf Steininger and Michael Gehler (Vienna: Böhlau, 1997), 107-46; Reinhold Wagnleitner, "Die britische Österreichplannung," in *Österreich und die Sieger: 40 Jahre 2. Republik—Jahre Staatsvertrag,* ed. Anton Pelinka and Rolf Steininger (Vienna: Wilhelm Braumüller, 1986), 67-78.

38. Primarily, but not exclusively. Keyserlingk traces the evolution prior to the Moscow Declaration of Anglo-American thinking about the role of Austria in Europe, and the significance of the third Moscow Declaration (on Austria) itself. His meticulously researched book, together with the more recent account of Günter Bischof, have revised and substantially superseded virtually all previous interpretations about the origins and purposes of this document. While Keyserlingk's account of the origins and immediate significance of the Moscow Declaration on Austria seems to me conclusive, I do dissent from his findings on two points. In my view, the causal connection between the discussions in the planning bodies in and around the State Department (as opposed to, say, the Research and Analysis Branch of the OSS), and the policies the U.S. government eventually adopted towards Austria, was somewhat weaker than Keyserlingk seems to claim. Thus, while the evidence showing the firm commitment of many State Department officials to a policy of confederation involving Austria through the end of the war seems to me compelling, I am less convinced that this remained the policy of the U.S. government itself. Moreover, while Keyserlingk is certainly right to insist on the propagandistic importance of the Declaration itself, it is worth noting that, at least for some in the State Department, the Declaration represented a substantive decision which had important policy implications. For example, Philip E. Mosely, assistant chief of the Division of Political Studies in the State Department, who was part of the U.S. delegation to the Moscow conference, wrote in 1950 about the insistence of Andrei Vishinsky, the Soviet representative to the drafting committee, that a passage be inserted in the Declaration assigning to Austria the "full political and material responsibility for the war." Mosely argued that the British and U.S. representatives in the drafting committee parried Vishinsky's urgings with the argument that such a statement would enable reparations claims to be made against Austria, which would conflict with the characterization of Austria as a victim of Germany and would hamper efforts to re-establish Austria as a free and independent state. In the end, Mosely concluded, the drafting committee settled on the compromise formula contained in the final version, but it seems clear from this that important members of the U.S. and British delegations believed that substantive policy issues were being discussed. See Robert H. Keyserlingk, *Austria in World War II. An Anglo-American Dilemma* (Kingston: McGill-Queen's University Press, 1988), 123-55; Oliver Rathkolb, "Professorenpläne für Österreichs Zukunft," in *Geheimdienstkrieg gegen Deutschland: Subversion, Propaganda und politische Planungen des amerikanischen Geheimdienstes im Zweiten Weltkrieg*, ed. Jürgen Heideking and Christof Mauch (Göttingen: Vandenhoeck & Ruprecht, 1993), 173; Philip E. Mosely, "The Treaty with Austria," *International Organization* 4, no. 2 (May 1950): 227. Another important study which reinforces Keyserlingk's findings on these points, but carries the story into the period of occupation is Günter Bischof, *Austria in the First Cold War, 1945-55: The Leverage of the Weak* (New York: St. Martin's Press, 1999). See also the essays in Alfred Ableitinger, Siegfried Beer, and Eduard G. Staudinger, eds., *Österreich unter alliierter Besatzung 1945-1955* (Vienna: Böhlau, 1998); Siegfried Beer, ed., with Felix Schneider und Johannes Feichtinger, *Die "britische" Steiermark 1945-1955* (Graz: House publisher of the Historische Landes-kommission für Steiermark, 1995); Siegfried Beer, "Target Central Europe: American Intelligence Efforts Regarding Nazi and Early Postwar Austria," Center for Austrian Studies Working Paper 97-1 (Minneapolis, 1997).

39. The Comité Français de la Libération Nationale (French Committee of National Liberation, C.F.L.N.) issued a declaration on 16 November 1943 which endorsed the independence of Austria. See Eva-Marie Csáky, ed., *Der Weg zu Freiheit und Neutralität. Dokumentation zur österreichischen Außenpolitik 1945-1955*, vol. 10, *Schriftenreihe der österreichischen Gesellschaft für Außenpolitik und internationale Beziehungen* (Vienna: Österreichische Gesellschaft für Außenpolitik und internationale Beziehungen, 1980), 34.

40. "Declaration on Austria," in FRUS 1943, vol. 1, 516-17.

41. Walter L. Dorn, "The Debate Over American Occupation Policy in Germany in 1944-1945," *Political Science Quarterly* LXXII, no. 4 (December 1957): 483.

42. On the role of the various planning agencies see Keyserlingk, *Austria in World War II*, 110; Alfons Söllner, ed., *Zur Archäologie der Demokratie in Deutschland: Analysen von politischen Emigranten im amerikanischen Geheimdienst 1943-1945*, vol. I, transl. Sabine Gwinner, Manfred Paul Buddeberg, and Niko Hansen (Frankfurt am Main: Fischer Taschenbuch Verlag, 1986); Lutz Niethammer, *Die Mitläuferfabrik. Die Entnazifizierung am Beispiel Bayerns* (Berlin: J.H.W. Dietz, 1982 [originally published 1972]); Barry M. Katz, *Foreign Intelligence: Research and Analysis in the Office of Strategic Services, 1942-1945* (Cambridge, MA.: Harvard University Press, 1989). On the specific planning for Austria see Oliver Rathkolb, "Professorenpläne."; idem, "'Verfassungs'-Projekte der Alliierten, der Exilanten und der Gründungsväter der Zweiten Republik 1944/1945," in *Justiz und Zeitgeschichte. Symposionsbeiträge*, vol. 2, ed. Erika Weinzierl, Oliver Rathkolb, Rudolf G. Ardelt, and Siegfried Mattl (Vienna: Jugend und Volk, 1995), 877-87; Siegfried Beer, "Target Central Europe."

43. Wilfried Aichinger, "Sowjetische Österreichpolitik 1943-1945," Ph.D. diss. (Vienna: University of Vienna, 1977), 101; and more recently, idem, "Sowjetische Österreichplanung," in *Österreich und die Sieger: 40 Jahre 2. Republik—30 Jahre Staatsvertrag*, ed. Anton Pelinka and Rolf Steininger (Vienna: Wilhelm Braumüller, 1986), 99-108.

44. See Philip E. Mosely, "Dismemberment of Germany. The Allied Negotiations from Yalta to Potsdam," *Foreign Affairs* 28, no. 3 (1950): 580-604; Hans-Günter Kowalski, "Die 'European Advisory Commission' als Instrument alliierter Deutschlandplanung 1943-1945," *Vierteljahrshefte für Zeitgeschichte* 19, no. 3 (July 1971): 261-93.

45. "Declaration on Austria," in FRUS 1943, vol. 1, 516-17.

46. Ibid.

47. Ibid.

48. See "The Implementation under Military Occupation of the Moscow Declaration on Austria," which bears the date 16 August 1944. This paper condensed the findings of several other individual studies made by the R&A Branch on Austria, including "The Administrative Separation of Austria from Germany," "The Elimination of Totalitarian Laws from Austria," "The Revival of Austrian Political and Constitutional Life under Military government," "The Roman Catholic Church in Austrian Political Life," "Labor Movements in Austrian Politics," "Changes in Austria's Social Structure," and "Welfare Problems in Austria." These studies are also located in the U.S. National Archives RG 260/ACA Austria/B870 f Directives, and in RG 59/Microfiche files/OSS R & A Branch Reports.

49. OSS R & A Branch, "The Revival of Austrian Political and Constitutional Life Under Military government," 6 January 1944, 4.

50. In my view still the best overall study which emphasizes this interplay is Manfried Rauchensteiner, *Der Sonderfall. Die Besatzungszeit in Österreich, 1945 bis 1955* (Graz: Verlag Styria, 1979).

51. See Dieter Stiefel, *Entnazifizierung in Österreich* (Vienna: Europaverlag, 1981), 101-24, in particular 106-7. As Stiefel points out, however, within the United States occupation authorities there was a difference of opinion between the Political Section and the Internal Division. The Political Section was in favor of the Austrian de-Nazification law that had been submitted to the Allied Council for approval in August 1946, as they believed this would encourage the democratic process in Austria; the

Internal Division's Public Safety branch opposed the law. The Internal Division won the argument.

52. Advisory Committee on Postwar Foreign Policy, "Germany: National Socialist Education," T-485, 6 May 1944; "Austria: The Internal Political Situation in the Period 1918-1938," T-511, 28 July 1944; NA RG 59: General Records of the Department of State/Records of Harley A. Notter, 1939-45/Records of the Advisory Committee on Postwar Foreign Policy/Lot 60D-224/Box 67; "Austria in European Politics, 1918-1938," 15 December 1945, NA RG 59: General Records of the Department of State/Records of Harley A. Notter, 1939-45/Records of the Advisory Committee on Postwar Foreign Policy/Lot 60D-224/Box 68.

53. "Austria: The Internal Political Situation in the Period 1918-1938," 20-21.

54. "Austria: The Internal Political Situation in the Period 1918-1938," 22-25.

55. "The Treatment of Austria" (JCS 1024), 8 June 1944. NA RG 260: Records of United States Occupation Headquarters, World War II/Records of the Office of Military government for Germany (U.S.) (OMGU.S.)/Policy Records Retained by the Military Advisor to the U.S. Delegate, European Advisory Commission, London ("Subject File"). 1943-45/Cont. 31/Box 21/Folder 12.

56. "The Treatment of Austria," 8-9, 12-13.

57. See Oliver Rathkolb, ed., *Gesellschaft und Politik am Beginn der Zweiten Republik: Vertrauliche Berichte der US-Militäradministration aus Österreich 1945 in englischer Originalfassung* (Vienna: Hermann Böhlaus Nachf. Ges.m.b.H., 1985), 414-21; idem, "Professorenpläne"; idem, "'Verfassungs'-Projekte"; Siegfried Beer, "Target Central Europe."

58. See above all Oliver Rathkolb, "U.S.-Entnazifizierung in Österreich zwischen kontrollierter Revolution und Elitenrestauration (1945-1949)," *Zeitgeschichte* 11, no. 9/10 (June/July 1984): 302-25.

59. Quoted in Reinhold Wagnleitner, ed., *Understanding Austria. The Political Reports and Analyses of Martin F. Herz, Political Officer of the US Legation in Vienna 1945-1948* (Salzburg: Wolfgang Neugebauer Verlag, 1984), 132.

60. Theodor Körner, "Das Märchen Vom Antisemitismus in Wien," *Wiener Zeitung*, 9 February 1947, 3. See also Körner's letter of 17 April 1947 to Leon Kubowitzkei of the World Jewish Congress: "Catholic and Socialist politicians occupy the highest positions in our state; in Vienna the Socialists are in the majority. All these politicians have an international and inter-confessional outlook of which you are certainly not unaware. A party whose founder was Victor Adler and whose most significant leaders included Dr. Otto Bauer, Dr. Robert Danneberg, Hugo Breitner, Prof. Tandler, Dr. Wilhelm Ellen-bogen, and more, all of whom were Jews, is certainly the best guarantee against the resurrection of an anti-Semitic movement." Quoted in Helga Embacher, *Neubeginn ohne Illusionen. Juden in Österreich nach 1945* (Vienna: Picus, 1995), 144. Karl Renner, first president of the Austrian Second Republic, had made a similar argument as early as March 1946, as we shall see below. *Arbeiter-Zeitung*, 26 March 1946, 1.

61. Despatch from Erhardt to Secretary of State, 4 March 1947, in Reinhold Wagnleitner, *Understanding Austria*, 113, 112.

62. *Aufbau*, 16 April 1946, quoted in Oliver Rathkolb, "Zur Kontinuität antisemitischer und rassistischer Vorurteile in Österreich 1945/1950," *Zeitgeschichte* 16, no. 5 (February 1989): 168.

63. Technically, of course, Figl, like all Austrian chancellors, was appointed by the Austrian president, not directly elected.

64. Quoted in Oliver Rathkolb, "Die Wiedererrichtung des auswärtigen Dienstes nach 1945," unpublished manuscript (Vienna, 1988), 13.

65. Memorandum from Martin F. Herz to Political Advisor, U.S.FA, 14 December 1945, in Wagnleitner, *Understanding Austria*, 86. In an interview held in August 1945 with Edgar N. Johnson and Paul R. Sweet of the OSS, Körner emphasized that although Kunschak was in charge of schools, Körner himself, as mayor, was in a "position to exercise decisive influence." Moreover, in their report on an interview they conducted with Kunschak in August 1945, Johnson and Sweet wrote: "Although [Kunschak's] position as grand old man of the Volkspartei is beyond dispute, his views cannot be taken as those of the Party as such; indeed, they are to a substantial degree at variance with those described as official by younger party leaders." There is no evidence that Kunschak was asked, or that he offered, any views on Jews during this interview. Interview Edgar N. Johnson and Paul R. Sweet with Theodor Körner, 20 August 1945, RG 226 XL 15.077, and Interview Edgar N. Johnson and Paul R. Sweet with Leopold Kunschak, 21 August 1945, in Rathkolb, *Gesellschaft und Politik*, 118, 135.

66. Knight, "'Neutrality,' not Sympathy: Jews in Post-War Austria," 224.

67. *Neues Österreich*, 23 April 1945, 1-2, emphasis added.

68. *Neues Österreich*, 25 April 1945, 3.

69. *Neues Österreich*, 25 April 1945, 3. See also "Mehr als 51,000 Nazimorde in Buchenwald," *Neuösterreich*, 29 April 1945, 2.

70. "Mit vereinter Kraft," *Neues Österreich*, 23 April 1945, 1-2.

71. Hermann Bahr, "Habt Mut zu Österreich!," *Neues Österreich*, 23 April 1945, 2; Anton Wildgans, "Oesterreicher durch und durch," *Neues Österreich*, 24 April 1945, 2; Johann Nestroy "Österreichs Feind—immer wieder Preußen," ibid.; Hugo von Hofmannsthal, "Oesterreich—das Reich des Friedens," *Neues Österreich*, 25 April 1945, 2; Adolf Glaßbrenner, "Ja, es gibt ein Land Österreich!," *Neues Österreich*, 26 April 1945, 2; Richard von Schaukal, "An Österreich," *Neues Österreich*, 28 April 1945, 3.

72. Edgar Johnson and Paul Sweet report of their interview with Fischer: "Fischer comes from a family of professional army officers who served under the Habsburgs; his father was colonel in the Austro-Hungarian army. Undoubtedly this family background helps to explain his staunch Austrian patriotism, and it is in this that he differentiates himself most sharply from his old Social-Democrat associates who were by no means free from predilections toward Anschluss. In this feeling about Austria Fischer acknowledges greater kinship with the Christian-Socials, who have long nourished the idea that Austria has a specific culture and destiny of her own and should therefore preserve her independence. In retrospect Fischer says: 'The Christian-Socials were good Austrians, but bad democrats. The Austrian Socialists were good democrats, but bad Austrians.' ... Fischer appeals to his countrymen to school themselves against the illusion that because they speak German they are therefore Germans. Austrian education should emphasize that which is specifically Austrian, and should give to German history and literature no greater attention than that of any of the other important nations." Interview Edgar N. Johnson and Paul R. Sweet with Ernst Fischer, 21 September 1945, RG 226 XL 23.815, in Rathkolb, *Gesellschaft und Politik*, 154. A more systematic presentation of Fischer's views about the specificity of Austrian identity may be found in Ernst Fischer, *Die Entstehung des österreichischen Volkscharakters* (Vienna: "Neues Österreich" Zeitungs- und Verlagsgesellschaft, 1945).

73. *Neues Österreich*, 28 April 1945, 1-2.

74. *Neues Österreich*, 1 May 1945, 1.

75. *Neues Österreich,* 1 May 1945, 1.

76. Interview Edgar N. Johnson and Paul R. Sweet with Theodor Körner, 20 August 1945, RG 226 XL 15.077, in Rathkolb, *Gesellschaft und Politik,* 119.

77. Interview Edgar N. Johnson and Paul R. Sweet with Karl Renner, 15 September 1945, RG 226 XL 23.818, in Rathkolb, *Gesellschaft und Politik,* 124-26. Unlike most others, this interview with Renner contains long excerpts of verbatim quotations.

78. Interview Edgar N. Johnson and Paul R. Sweet with Leopold Figl, 10 September 1945, RG 226 XL 17.718, in Rathkolb, *Gesellschaft und Politik,* 142-5.

79. As Oliver Rathkolb laconically put it, the spirit of the *Lagerstrasse* "did not correspond to the social and political reality of 1945." See Rathkolb, *Gesellschaft und Politik,* 105.

80. *Arbeiter-Zeitung,* 14 January 1948, 1.

81. Frisch, ÖVP, 28th Session, 24 July 1946, p. 606, quoted in Dieter Stiefel, *Entnazifizierung in Österreich* (Vienna: Europa Verlag, 1981), 55.

82. *Shanghai Echo,* quoted in *Der Neue Weg. Jüdisches Organ* 11 (June 1947): 11.

83. *Arbeiter-Zeitung,* 27 March 1946, 1.

84. Karl Renner, "Rede an die Beamtenschaft der Staatskanzlei," 30 April 1945, in Knight, *"Ich bin dafür,"* 83; Richard Mitten, "'Die Sühne... möglichst milde zu gestalten': Die sozialdemokratische 'Bearbeitung' des Nationalsozialismus und des Antisemitismus in Österreich," in *Schwieriges Erbe. Der Umgang mit Nationalsozialismus und Antisemitismus in Österreich, der DDR und der Bundesrepublik Deutschland,* ed. Werner Bergman, Rainer Erb, and Albert Lichtblau (Frankfurt: Campus Verlag, 1994), 21-39.

85. David Brill, "Unser Weg," *Der Neue Weg. Jüdisches Organ* 1-2 (15 January 1946): 2-3.

86. Bernhard Braver, "Die Juden und die Demokratie in Österreich," *Der neue Weg. Jüdisches Organ* 1-2 (15 January 1946): 6.

87. Embacher, *Neubeginn.* This article was completed before the new book by Evelyn Adunka, *Die vierte Gemeinde. Die Geschichte der Wiener Juden von 1945 bis heute* (Vienna: Philo, 2000), reached me. Hence I have not been able to integrate its findings.

88. This essay is concerned primarily with the motivations of the group of Jewish Austrians who formed, or competed for, leadership of the *Israelitische Kultusgemeinde,* not with the Jewish (returnee) population in Vienna as a whole. See, however, the early study Wilder-Okladek, *The Return Movement,* and the more recent investigation of the motivations of postwar Austrian Jewish returnees, Christoph Reinprecht, *Zurückgekehrt: Identität und Bruch in der Biographie Österreichischer Juden* (Vienna: Braumüller, 1992).

89. Lewit's *Jüdisches Aktionskomitee* was only able to have racial victims accepted by the *KZ-Verband* only by redefining racial persecution as political. When on 14 February 1946 the *KZ-Verband* accepted the affiliation, it did so by reasoning that since Jews had been persecuted because of their origins, they had been considered politically unreliable by the Nazi regime; Jews who had been interned for racial reasons thus could claim this additional *political* reason. Embacher, *Neubeginn,* 104-5.

90. On this point see Gerhard Botz, "The Austro-Marxist Interpretation of Fascism," *Journal of Contemporary History* 11, no. 4 (1976): 129-56; Mitten, "The Social Democratic 'Mémoire Volontaire.'"

91. Just how vehement this conflict became may be judged from a 1952 article in the paper *Tribune,* the paper of the Zionist group Misrachi: the task of Misrachi was, the article claimed, "to save Judaism from the grip of assimilation and to lead it back to tradition . ... Nothing will keep us from publicly denouncing the vermin of our people, whether they are among us or outside us, and to fight for their eradication." (This sounds much worse in German: *"das Judentum aus den Armen der Assimilation zu retten und zur Tradition zurückzuführen. ... Nichts wird uns davor zurückhalten, die Schädlinge unseres Volkes, egal ob es sich um äußere oder innere handelt, öffentlich anzuprangern und für ihre Ausmerzung zu kämpfen."* *Tribune,* October 1952, quoted in Embacher, *Neubeginn,* 186.

92. Embacher, *Neubeginn,* 217.

93. *Die Gemeinde,* 30 April 1947, p. 4, cited in Embacher, "Die innenpolitische Partizipation," 327-28.

94. Cited in Embacher, "Die innenpolitische Partizipation," 324.

95. Resolution adopted by the plenary session of the IKG Vorstand 2 March 1949; cited in Embacher, "Die innenpolitische Partizipation," 327.

96. Anson Rabinbach, "The Jewish Question in the German Question," in *Reworking the Past. Hitler, the Holocaust, and the Historians' Debate,* ed. Peter Baldwin (Boston: Beacon Press, 1990), 50. See also Jelinek and Sheva, "Konrad Adenauer and the 'Shilumim'." For a more favorable view of Adenauer's motives see Michael Wolffsohn, *Eternal Guilt? Forty Years of German-Jewish-Israeli Relations,* transl. Douglas Bokovoy (New York: Columbia University Press, 1993), 119-22.

97. Frank Stern, *The Whitewashing of the Yellow Badge. Antisemitism and Philosemitism in Postwar Germany,* transl. William Templar (Oxford: Pergamon Press, 1992). *Persilscheine,* which might be translated as "certificates of cleanliness," were so called in allusion to the laundry detergent Persil. Persilscheine were affidavits or testimonials which former members of the Nazi party secured from Jews or anti-Nazis which attested to these Nazis' good conduct during the war despite their affiliation with the NSDAP. Such "certificates of cleanliness" were important in securing a reduction of or even exemption from the administrative penalties that were imposed on former Nazis under the de-Nazification laws.

98. *Neues Österreich,* 26 March 1946, 1.

99. *Arbeiter-Zeitung,* 27 March 1946, 1-2. The same issue of this newspaper contained "The Austrian People are not Contaminated."

100. Artur Rosenberg, "Die jüdische Frage," *Österreichische Monatshefte* 1, no. 7 (April 1946): 226-28.

101. Walter Ost was the author of the article "Ein Wort über die 'Volksösterreicher'" in an earlier issue of the *Österreichische Monatshefte,* and the short commentary "Zur jüdischen Frage" was one of two short pieces in that volume, as well as in several others during these early years of the journal, which were signed simply "W.O."

102. *Österreichische Monatshefte* 1, no. 9 (June 1946): 397; see also Walter Manoschek, "'Aus der Asche dieses Krieges wieder auferstanden'. Skizzen zum Umgang der Österreichischen Volkspartei mit Nationalsozialismus und Antisemitismus nach 1945," in *Schwieriges Erbe. Der Umgang mit Nationalsozialismus und Antisemitismus in Österreich, der DDR und der Bundesrepublik Deutschland,* ed. Werner Bergman, Rainer Erb, and Albert Lichtblau (Frankfurt: Campus Verlag, 1994), 55. Although Ost's use of the subjunctive, plus the internal evidence in the comment, clearly suggest otherwise, Manoschek inexplicably credits Ost, rather than Kohlich, with the initial usage of the

term *"Sonderbehandlung"* with regard to restitution.
103. Rosenberg, "Die jüdische Frage," 37.

FORUM

World War II Crimes against Jews in Austria and Their Prosecution in Austrian Courts after the War

Günter Bischof

Introduction

These three "Forum" papers were read in the panel *"Persecution and Murder of Austrian Jews in Austrian Postwar Trials"* in Houston, Texas, at the 24th annual meeting of the German Studies Association (6 to 8 October 2000). They deal with crucial aspects of the most sordid and painful chapter in recent Austrian history—the persecution and extermination of Austrian Jews as well as the wholesale expropriation ("Aryanization") of their property. However, the three scholars take their investigations beyond the perpetration of war crimes by Austrians and also trace the postwar Austrian prosecution of these perpetrators before courts of law. These papers lucidly outline Austrians' descent into barbarism during the war and the difficult reestablishment of the rule of law and civilization after the war in the second Austrian Republic. It is this transition from war to peace that makes these perspectives unique.

In the ongoing and heated debate over Austrians' role and contribution to the final solution, these papers make a strong case that it was considerable. It is well established by now that the "Vienna model" of expropriation of Jewish property through "Aryanization" and the forced emigration of the Jewish community after the Anschluss encouraged and *radicalized* anti-Jewish policies in the *Altreich* during the course of 1938, culminating in the infamous November progrom ("*Reichskristallnacht*"). The Nazi bureaucracies, springing up like mushrooms in the *Ostmark* in March 1938, quickly developed a "conveyor belt system" (Garscha) for the persecution, expropriation, and forced mass emigration of Jews, which by 1941 began to culminate in deportation and mass murder. This "successful" Viennese model was then also exported and practiced in Berlin, Prague, and Paris (and other occupied territories), often with Austrian NS-bureaucrats from Adolf Eichmann's entourage in the lead. In a similar fashion, the Austrian Nazi bureaucrats who learned their skills by implementing the euthanasia killing program in the *Ostmark* in Castle Hartheim in 1941, went on to "bigger and better" careers in the "final solution" extermination programs in the East. Maybe the strongest and most disturbing evidence for how many "willing executioners" (Goldhagen) Hitler gathered in Austria can be found in Polaschek's paper. Hundreds of Austrians participated in the dehumanization and massacring of Jews in the final weeks of the war in April/May 1945. In one case, ordinary Styrian Nazis took Jews as personal slaves, hid with them in the mountains outside of Graz, and killed them weeks *after* the war had ended! Here a murderous mentality way beyond the call of duty and Nazi orders was on display in the final days of the "Danube and Alpine *Gaue*" that scholarship has hardly begun to explain so far.

Yet these papers only constitute the tip of the iceberg of the vast research field of specifics of the discrimination and persecution of Jews and other "forgotten victims of National Socialism" (R. Steininger) in the *Ostmark* during World War II. In the fall semester of 2000 Dieter Stiefel organized a "ring lecture series" at the University of Vienna on "the political economy of the Holocaust" in Austria and Germany. While the "economics of discrimination" practiced against some 200,000 Austrian Jews (92 percent of which lived in Vienna) enriched numerous Austrian individuals and corporations, it also hurt the Austrian economy as a whole considerably. Case studies on "Aryanization," banks, insurance companies, forced labor and art theft demonstrate this rich web of discriminatory practices which resulted in personal enrichment for many Austrian Nazis. The Nazis themselves valued "Aryanized" Jewish property at more than 2 billion *Reichsmark* (in today's currency well over 100 billion Schillings). But the Jews did not only lose their property, jobs, means of livelihood, and basic humanity—eventually their lives were taken. They were pushed into ghetto conditions in Vienna and some 20,000 among them were compelled to be forced laborers, particularly in Austrian construction companies. Wolf Gruner's new book shows how Hermann Göring's program of *modernizing* the *Ostmark's* economy for maximizing its contributions to the German war economy was also furthered by Jewish forced labor (next to much larger numbers of Eastern European and POW forced labor). Doron Rabinovici's new book shows how the Nazis forced the Jewish community to willy-nilly cooperate with its economic policies through the *Judenräte*. Undoubtedly, the various historical commissions working in Austria today on these various aspects of the "economics of discrimination," persecution, and extermination of the Jews will make the picture even clearer in the years to come.

As has been noted above, the process of "Aryanization" seems to have been a specifically Austrian contribution to the radicalization of Nazi persecution policies vis-à-vis Jews. In the escalating Nazi terror against Jews it constituted a crucial way station to the final solution. In his essay in the Stiefel volume, Gerhard Botz has refined this role of Nazi "Aryanization" policies: It progressed from the "wild Aryaniza-tions" after the Anschluss in the spring of 1938, to the "legal Aryaniza-tions" and the beginning of forced mass emigration in the summer of that year; it proceeded to the November pogrom, the completion of forced "Aryanizations," and the "ghettoization" of Jews in Vienna in 1939/40; and it finally resulted in the deportations beginning in 1941. While the Loitfellner essay in this "Forum" deals with the statistics of the "Aryanization" process in Vienna, Garscha adumbrates the specifics of the deportations from Vienna to the East. Readers interested in the twisted process of restitution of Jewish property after the war should start with Brigitte Bailer's essay (in the Stiefel volume) and continue with Irene Etzersdorfer's case studies in *Arisiert*. The former posits the jungle of legal obstacles put up by the state and the latter the "Aryani-zers'" personal skullduggery resisting lawful restitutions after the war. After more than fifty years of fitful Austrian procrastination on speedy restitution, the matter has only recently reached a point of closure with the Austro-American agreement of January 2001 to set up a special Austrian restitution fund for "Aryanized" Jewish property.

The most compelling and fine-tuned psychological portrait of postwar Austria's disinterest in and resistance to restitution of "Aryani-zed" Jewish property can be found in Anna Mitgutsch's fascinating novel *Haus der Kindheit*. Her protagonist's family is forced to emigrate from an unnamed Austrian provincial town before the war. He grows up in New York City and returns many years after the war to repossess the house of his childhood. In part he fights for the restitution of this house as a tribute to his mother, who never adapted to life in the "big apple" and who kept inhabiting it in her mind's eye, refusing to mentally relinquish the house and her comfortable middle-class life style in prewar Austria to the robber-"Aryanizer." Unlike most victims of failed restitution attempts, Mitgutsch's protagonist has the patience and grit to wait out the painfully slow legal process of seeing his family's property returned (only after the death of the "Aryanizer" in his house). He moves into the house and remodels it but eventually returns to New York, his real home, after he realizes his alienation from provincial Austria. He no longer belongs here, as Jewish life—with so little of it left after the war—had been dying a slow death in postwar Austria. It is the loss of this vital Jewish community which Austria has never recovered from after the war.

Ironically, historians have only in the past few years started to unearth one of the most useful sources for research on Austrian perpetrators (including "Aryanizers") during World War II, namely postwar *court records*. Here it becomes obvious that the *"Volksgerichtsbarkeit"* (special people's courts), set up still in 1945 by the Provisional Renner Government, made a valiant effort to persecute the worst Austrian Nazi war criminals after the war. Particularly the perpetrators of heinous crimes committed against Jews in the final weeks and days of the war were prosecuted vigorously in 1945/46 as Polaschek shows in his essay. British and American pressure for thorough investigations and their setting up of separate military courts further contributed to this effort. Yet both this judicial persecution of war criminals and the larger effort of "de-Nazification" in Austria began to abate by 1948. Both the growing distance from the horrors of the war and the international political realignment of the occupation powers present in Austria as a result of the cold war contributed to this growing disinterest in prosecuting war criminals and ferreting out Nazis from the body politic. Once the occupation powers exited from Austria after the signing and ratifying of the Austrian Treaty in the fall of 1955, the people's courts were terminated and the effort to prosecute Austrian war criminals—particularly those who had contributed so much to the final solution—quickly petered out. Garscha's brief case study of the saga of Franz Novak's serendipitous journey through the Austrian courts during the 1960s and 1970s speaks volumes about the lack of commitment by the post-occupation Austrian courts to bring Nazi war criminals to justice. A similar case study could be made about the Austrian courts and the Austrian Nazi doctor Heinrich Gross. The fact is that while the judicial prosecution of Austrian Nazi war criminals was vigorous during the first third of the postwar Austrian occupation, it became lackadaisical when Austria regained her full sovereignty and the occupation powers no longer looked over Austrian shoulders.

Winfried Garscha and Claudia Kuretsidis-Haider of the *Dokumentationsarchiv des Österreichischen Widerstandes* have been the leading impresarios in this effort of recouping the treasure trove of the postwar court records as a valuable historical source for the World War II history of Austrian perpetrators. They have done valuable spadework in court records themselves and in collecting these in valuable data bases and thus making them more available to a larger community of scholars. They have inspired a younger generation of scholars such as Sabine Loitfellner to delve into these records. They have organized international conferences and workshops to study the postwar trials of Nazi war criminals from a comparative European perspective. Indeed, it is true that "all [European] countries had great difficulty in mastering this time through the judicial process" (D. Stiefel in Stiefel, p. 23). The new volume *The Politics of Retribution in Europe*, which grew out of a conference organized by the Vienna *Institut für die Wissenschaften vom Menschen*, clearly proves this. Garscha and Kuretsidis-Haider have also organized a working group in Vienna to systematically collect and make accessible to researchers all these postwar court records relating to Nazi war crimes. It is safe to say that the research agenda and fine-tuning of scholarly inquiry suggested by the essays in this "Forum" surely will become much richer in years to come. This research ought to one day answer definitively the contentious question of what exactly the extent of the Austrian contribution to the final solution was.

Suggested Further Readings:

Deák, István, Jan T. Gross, and Tony Judt, eds. *The Politics of Retribution in Europe: World War II and Its Aftermath* (Princeton: Princeton University Press, 2000).

Etzersdorfer, Irene. *Arisiert: Eine Spurensuche im gesellschaftlichen Untergrund der Republik* (Vienna: Kremayr & Scheriau, 1995).

Gruner, Wolf. *Zwangsarbeit und Verfolgung: Österreichische Juden im NS-Staat 1938-45,* Der Nationalsozialismus und seine Folgen, vol. 1 (Innsbruck: Studienverlag, 2000).

Kuretsidis-Haider, Claudia and Winfried R. Garscha, eds.. *Keine "Abrechnung": NS-Verbrechen, Justiz und Gesellschaft in Europa nach 1945* (Leipzig: Akademische Verlagsanstalt, 1998).

Mitgutsch, Anna. *Haus der Kindheit* (Munich: Luchterhand, 2000).

Rabinovici, Doron. *Instanz der Ohnmacht: Wien 1938-1945. Der Weg zum Judenrat* (Frankfurt a. M.: Jüdischer Verlag, 2000).

Steininger, Rolf, ed.. *Vergessene Opfer des Nationalsozialismus* (Innsbruck: Studienverlag, 2000).

Stiefel, Dieter, ed.. *Die politische Ökonomie des Holocaust: Zur wirtschaftlichen Logik von Verfolgung und "Wiedergutmachung"* (Vienna: Verlag für Gesellschaft und Politik - R. Oldenbourg, 2001).

Tálos, Emmerich, Ernst Hanisch, Wolfgang Neubgebauer, and Reinhard Sieder, eds.. *NS-Herrschaft in Österreich: Ein Handbuch* (Vienna: öbv & hpt, 2000).

The Aryanization of 1938-1939 in Vienna and the People's Court Trials After 1945

Sabine Loitfellner

Aryanization and the Persecution
of Jews in Austria

In March 1938 the National Socialist expropriation of Jewish property began in Austria. At the time the majority of Austrian Jews lived in Vienna. Their dispossession offered numerous economic and social benefits to the so-called *Volksgenossen* and can be seen as a National Socialist compensation politics; this has been shown, among others, by Gerhard Botz who conducted extensive research on the National Socialist housing policies in Vienna.[1]

Immediately after the Anschluss, Jewish companies were expropriated by overzealous party members who had temporarily put themselves in charge of the Aryanization process (*"kommissarische Verwalter"*). About 33,000 Jewish companies and 70,000 apartments were expropriated from Jews during the *Aryanization* process in Vienna. Since such arbitrary and uncontrolled Aryanizations were common practice during the annexation period, the party leadership had to intervene. In April 1938 the Aryanization of companies became subject to party approval. For this purpose the "Property Distribution Authority" (*Vermögensverkehrsstelle*) was established as the central authority for Aryanization and was incorporated into the department of commerce and labor.[2] Only the economically most important Aryanizations were implemented by the *Austrian Control Bank for Industry and Trade* or other Austrian banks.[3]

This frenzy of Jewish expropriation reached such great extents that new means and agencies had to be established for its implementation, as for example the "Authority for the Distribution of Jewish Removal Goods" of the Gestapo (*Verwaltungsstelle für jüdisches Umzugsgut der Gestapo* or *Vugesta*).[4] This office carried out the confiscation and the sale of the properties and goods left behind by the emigrated Jews. Later the *Vugesta* seized also the property of the deported Viennese Jews.

It should be stressed that the process of *"Entjudung,"* i.e. the elimination of Jews from the Austrian economy, was carried out much faster and more effectively than in the *Altreich*. In 1938 alone more measures were implemented in Austria than in Germany. For this reason, as Susanne Heim and Götz Aly have pointed out, Austria can be referred to as a "model" for future Nazi action in the Third Reich.[5]

In Austria to this day numerous business careers are still based on Jewish estates expropriated after the Anschluss. After 1945 the Republic of Austria showed little interest in returning this stolen property. On the one hand the Austrian government still held some latent anti-Semitic attitudes—as Robert Knight has shown in his book.[6] On the other hand there were economic concerns: for example, if postwar Austria returned Aryanized property too eagerly, the young and poor Second Austrian Republic would encounter great financial trouble. This is documented in a recently published book about the "Austrian department of property protection and economic planning" (*Österreichisches Ministerium für Vermögenssicherung und Wirtschaftsplanung*) and how it dealt with the seized Jewish properties.[7] Austria's economic problems of the immediate postwar era were used as an excuse to assume what was called "economic reasoning" (*wirtschaftliche Vernunft*) and a "moderate attitude" regarding the property claims of Jewish survivors and their descendants.

Because of the prolonged inability of the Austrian Republic to clear up these sweeping seizures of Jewish estates, an acute need for addressing this issue has existed until today. Only in October 1998 was a committee of Austrian historians assigned to research the Aryanization of Jewish estate during the NS-era as well as the property claims after 1945.

However, it is a little known fact that between 1945 and 1955 Austria attempted to legally prosecute the perpetrators of Aryanization crimes in a particular form of postwar justice, the so-called people's courts (*Volksgerichte*). The author of this essay was among the first to point to the importance of the criminal prosecution of Aryanization crimes at the people's court in Vienna.[8]

A Summary of the Research on
Postwar Justice in Austria

The prosecution of Nazi crimes in Austria is usually viewed from the perspective of the few trials of the 1960s and 1970s, with their rare convictions of Nazi war criminals.[9] In fact, 136,829 cases of suspected Nazi crimes were taken to Austrian people's courts between 1945 and 1955. This fact was never widely known among the Austrian public and has not been much researched so far. The Austrian judiciary, however, has always recognized the importance of the people's court files. Upon termination of the people's court jurisdiction the entirety of the files was classified as historically valid and was thus protected from the usual process of sorting out and destroying old court files.

The first publication in this field, a statistical treatise with an—albeit incomplete—listing of the most important people's court trials, was published by Karl Marschall and commissioned by the Federal Ministry of Justice in the year 1977.[10] In general, only a small circle of critical Austrian researchers discusses the legal aspect of the de-Nazification after 1945. One reason for this lack of research has been the absence of specialized research institutions in this field. Another reason is the public disapproval of this attempt to come to terms with the past through the instruments of justice. To fill the lack of research in this field and to scientifically document the pertaining trial-files, a research institution with special emphasis on Austrian postwar justice was established in 1998 (*Zentrale österreichische Forschungsstelle Nachkriegsjustiz*).

Special Courts and Laws for the Prosecution
of Nazi Crimes

In postwar Austria some special laws for the judicial prosecution of Nazi crimes were put on the books. First, the constitutional law about the prohibition of the NSDAP and other Nazi organizations (*Verbotsgesetz*) of 8 May 1945, controlled the de-Nazification process and introduced the people's court jurisdiction.[11] Second, the War Criminals Act (*Kriegsverbrechergesetz*) of 26 June 1945 applied to "war crimes and other National Socialist atrocities."[12] It became the legal instrument for persecuting and punishing of individual Nazi perpetrators. As the well-known Austrian professor for criminal law Winfried Platzgummer has emphasized, the War Criminals Act was especially tailored to investigate NS-tyranny.[13]

For the prosecution of crimes that violated the *Verbotsgesetz* and the War Criminals Act a special form of jurisdiction was created: the people's courts (*Volksgerichte*). This term, ironically, is reminiscent of the *Volksgerichtshof*, the court of justice of the Nazi regime. The historian Ernst Hanisch has called this a "symbolic re-definition."[14] Winfried Garscha and Claudia Kuretsidis-Haider have argued that calling these courts *people's courts* also suggests an indication for retaliation.[15]

The people's courts were located in the following Austrian provincial capitals:

*   in Vienna for the Soviet zone of occupation (Lower Austria, Burgenland, Upper Austria north of the Danube) and for Vienna itself;
*   in Graz (incl. two branch senates in Leoben and Klagenfurt) for the British zone of occupation (Styria, Carinthia, and Eastern Tyrol);
*   in Linz for the American zone of occupation (Upper Austria south of the Danube and Salzburg);
*   and in Innsbruck for the French zone of occupation (Northern Tyrol and Vorarlberg).

The largest people's court handling the highest number of cases and prosecuting the most serious perpetrators was the one in Vienna.

In the discourse about the prosecution of Nazi war crimes it becomes evident that the specific social and political situation of post-war Austria strongly determined how the country has been confronting National Socialism in general. The myth of Austria as "Hitler's first victim" influenced the way the de-Nazification process was handled. However, it should also be mentioned that an anti-fascist spirit undoubtedly pervaded the Austrian parties in 1945. Immediately after the war, when the memory of the war was still strong and the population was confronted with the war crimes, the Nazi regime was clearly regarded as a reign of terror. Nevertheless, the government of Austria still assumed the role of the helpless, deceived victim. This was evident, for example, in the declaration of independence on 27 April 1945. This key document reflected the same ambivalence that came to characterize the half-hearted prosecution of NS perpetrators, as Brigitte Bailer has argued.[16] Only *the Germans* were blamed for the Nazi crimes and, except for a few black sheep, *the Austrians* had supposedly stayed clean during the Nazi terror.

Changes in domestic politics and in the international arena in 1948-1949 influenced people's court jurisdiction. Both the number of new trials and of verdicts decreased. After 1948 the number of acquittals was higher than the number of convictions.[17] Dieter Stiefel writes in his acclaimed work about de-Nazification in Austria: "In general one can note that the severity of the sentencing decreased as time passed after the war and the Nazi regime."[18]

Now amnesties enabled the vast majority of Austrian Nazi *fellow travelers* to be re-integrated into Austrian society. In the course of the 1949 Austrian election campaign and the fight of the major parties for the votes of former Nazis, the attorney general reduced the people's courts' jurisdiction. The attorney general—who directly reported to the Ministry of Justice—had influence on the procedural law of the trials. Here it became evident that coming to terms with the past was not only a question of social climate, but also an expression of political intention.

With the signing of the State Treaty in 1955 the foreign policy contest of the people's courts also became obsolete. For the prosecution of Nazi crimes this entailed a gradual return to the regular Austrian jurisdictions. In 1957 the War Criminals Act was annulled during another NS-amnesty. From that time on the crime of *improper enrichment* (*missbräuchliche Bereicherung*, §6 of the War Criminals Act), on which the prosecution of Aryanization perpetrators depended, could only be pursued through the regular penal law.

Aspects of the Legal Prosecution of Aryanization Crimes before the People's Court in Vienna, 1945 - 1955

An editorial of the newspaper *Neues Österreich* of July 1945 clearly reflects Viennese public opinion about crimes of Aryanization at the time: "Remember what happened after 1938 when the Nazi hordes, led by the *Unkulturträger* [those without culture] of the Reich, plundered thousands of apartments in Vienna. ... The entire Hitler gang haggled and bargained for old furniture, paintings, and rugs. ... And yet another virtue of our community was badly harmed—our sense of justice and our morals." The editorial continues, "In defense of the inhabitants of Vienna it must be said that the majority of our population kept away from those dirty means of enrichment."[19] It is obvious who was made responsible for the Aryanizations during the NS era: the "Hitler gang in the Reich." Considering this prevailing opinion about the *honorable* people of Vienna, one wonders what could have been expected in terms of a serious prosecution of Aryanization crimes?

With this question in mind I conducted a statistical analysis of the initial trials and proceedings at the people's court in Vienna. The analysis is based on a digitalized database of the file card index of the Vienna people's court. This database, a project of the Central Austrian Research Institute for Postwar Justice is currently subjected to a revision and further methodical analysis. The long-term goal of the project is to create a comprehensive database for the history of Nazi war crimes and their prosecution in the Second Austrian Republic and to make it available to future historical research.

The people's court proceedings were filed in a separate card index at the regional criminal court of Vienna. This file card index, which has been kept at the Viennese regional court, offers the only access to the files of the people's court proceedings. Using this index is quite difficult because it is not in alphabetic but in phonetic order. As a rule the file cards carry the following information:

- family name
- first name (with a few exceptions)
- academic title
- date of birth (with a few exceptions),
- the trial and court identification numbers
- the articles which initiated proceedings—i.e. articles of the *Verbotsgesetz* and of the War Criminals Act, but also articles of the penal code.

Most articles of the War Criminals Act—such as war crimes (§1), maltreatment (§3), or the breach of human dignity (§4)—regulate very different crimes: atrocities against Jews, against forced laborers, and against victims of the NS euthanasia programs. However, §6 of the War Criminal Act—*improper enrichment*—almost always refers to the crime of Aryanization. Because instances of *improper enrichment* were noted on the file index cards, the subsequent analysis was conducted without having to inspect the entire files of the people's court proceedings. The assumption is that most Austrian Aryanization crimes were handled by the Vienna people's court since it was here that most Jewish property was seized in the course of Nazi Aryanizations.

As this research of the people's court proceedings is still at its beginning, it has not yet been possible to carry out a complete analysis of all trials, sentences, and suspended proceedings. These first interpretations of a small sample of Aryanization crimes are only a first step into this completely unexplored research terrain. It must be mentioned that even if a complete study of Aryanizations becomes available, the exact number of Aryanization perpetrators will always remain uncertain. After all, only those culprits of *improper enrichment* were prosecuted who had been reported to the police. The number of Aryanization perpetrators who were not reported seems to be considerable.

According to §6 of the War Criminals Act, those guilty of *improper enrichment* "appropriated foreign possessions for themselves and others or harmed property of somebody else with the intention of gaining disproportionate pecuniary advantages for themselves or for others, through the exploitation of the Nazi seizure of power or generally of National Socialist institutions and measures ..."[20] The sentence for this crime was one to five years of imprisonment; if the perpetrator's enrichment had been considerable or the damage to the victim severe, a prison sentence of five to ten years was imposed. Thus §6 of the War Criminals Act determined that only the crime of *improper enrichment* was punishable. The mere appropriation of Jewish property in any other way (i.e. if the appropriator acted as *trustee* or *customer*) was not criminal. Although acts of Aryanization were often accompanied by acts of improper, personal enrichment, these could not be prosecuted unless they were unambiguously proven. This circumstance might have been responsible for the fact that many perpetrators of Aryanization were not prosecuted after the war and many proceedings were suspended.

To figure out how much the people's court of Vienna was occupied with crimes of Aryanization, I compared the number of perpetrators prosecuted for *improper enrichment* with the total number of perpetrators tried at the people's court: Of a total of 38,674 prosecuted for Nazi war crimes, 5,914, i.e.15.3 percent, were accused of *improper enrichment*. This opens up new perspectives in research about the punishment of Aryanization crimes. In the above mentioned survey conducted by the department of justice in the 1970s, Karl Marschall found that the percentage of sentences for *improper enrichment* at all four Austrian people's courts was 2.2 percent.[21] However, this percentage of Aryanization crimes reflects only the year 1947, when most sentences were pronounced. Comparing these results—2.2 percent of sentences versus 15 percent of Aryanization proceedings—indicates that indeed only a small part of the proceedings against culprits of Aryanization ended with a sentence. Nevertheless, it shows that the people's court spent a considerable amount of time prosecuting Aryanization crimes.

Most of these investigative proceedings against probable *"Ariseure"* (aryanizers) were suspended early. An analysis of more than six hundred court files conducted by the Documentation Center of Austrian Resistance and the Central Austrian Research Institute of Postwar Justice supports this assumption. In any case, the high number of proceedings against *improper enrichment* has remained unknown until recently and points to the gigantic scale of Aryanization crimes in the *Ostmark* of the Third Reich. Investigation proceedings against probable *"Ariseure"* might have been stopped prematurely. The question about when the pretrial hearings against suspected culprits of Aryanization were initiated is interesting in so far as the prosecution of National Socialist crimes generally decreased in 1948-1949. 80 percent of the total 7,304 proceedings based on §6 of the War Criminals Act were conducted at the Vienna people's court between 1945 and 1948.

It is also important to know about the other crimes committed by those accused of Aryanization since this helps to shed light on the perpetrators and the circumstances under which Aryanizations happened in the Nazi era. Of the total number of those accused of Aryanization (5,914) nearly 70 percent (4,102) were suspected of having committed at least one additional NS war crime. This investigation demonstrated a clear connection between Aryanization crimes and crimes violating the *Verbotsgesetz*. In fact, 31.4 percent (1,857) of all *Ariseure* were considered *illegal* National Socialists and were tried at the people's court of Vienna for this formal offense against §10 of the *Verbotsgesetz* (illegal affiliation with a Nazi organization before 1938). However, many *Volksgenossen* joined the NSDAP or other Nazi organizations only after the Anschluss in March 1938 and were not prosecuted under §10. One can assume that most NSDAP members—illegally before March 1938 or legally after the Anschluss—were involved in Aryanization crimes. An even bigger part of those accused of Aryanization, indeed 2,192 or 37.06 percent, were also indicted for a break of §11 of the *Verbotsgesetz*. They had either committed crimes *"aus besonders verwerflicher Gesinnung"* (for their particularly abominable convictions), or they were specific higher functionaries within NS-organizations.

Examining the cases of *improper enrichment* and other violations of the War Criminals Act has shown that numerous culprits of Aryanization also committed crimes against humanity and human dignity out of political spite or by taking advantage of their power (§4 of the War Criminals Act). 21.15 percent or 1,252 perpetrators were accused of this crime. Also the crime of torture and torment (§3 of the War Criminal Act) often was committed hand in hand with the crime of *improper enrichment*: 15.08 percent or 892 suspects were accused of having tortured or severely abused other human beings in the act of *improper enrichment*. Finally, 15 percent of all suspects of Aryanization crimes were also prosecuted for §7 of the War Criminals Act (denunciation). Considering that so many Austrian *Volksgenossen* participated actively and unscrupulously in the expropriation of Jews and the deprivation of their rights, the connection between crimes of *improper enrichment* and crimes such as torture, torment, violation of human dignity and denunciation is not surprising. In numerous people's court proceedings against suspects of Aryanization some offenses against the Austrian penal code (theft, blackmail, fraud, robbery, abuse of authority) were also tried.

The analysis of the people's court proceedings can be extended to include sex-specific interpretations or the age structure of the *Ariseure*. These results could then be taken into consideration for sociological and/or social-historical research. The investigation of the proceedings at the people's court in Vienna between 1945 and 1955, as conducted by the author, produced informative results, even though a detailed representation of all proceedings including their verdicts was not possible. The investigation has clarified when the proceedings against those accused of Aryanization were initiated and how far they progressed. Moreover, it has clearly shown that with the increasing tendency of repressing and playing down the Nazi crimes, they were attributed less and less importance. In addition, some useful information about the culprits or Aryanization could be gathered: They took advantage of the extreme predicament of Jewish citizens and enriched themselves with Jewish property by consciously and violently enforcing National Socialist tyranny.

Only a small fraction of the *Ariseure* was convicted—mostly due to the fact that the charge of *personal enrichment* had to be proven unambiguously. Furthermore, the fact of having participated in the Aryanization process was soon considered to be a *"Kavaliersdelikt"* (minor infringement) and was played down by blaming the Jews themselves ("the Jews are responsible for everything being taken from them"). That sufficient postwar material restitution of Jewish property did not occur might therefore be strongly linked to insufficient judicial prosecution of the crimes of Aryanization. This seems to be the case for the period after 1948. This hypothesis is the result of the first steps into a new research area. To strengthen it a complete analysis of the people's court verdicts executed, together with an intense file study, would be required, especially since specific treatment of the Jewish victims can be viewed from the available judicial files.

Notes

1. Gerhard Botz, *Wohnungspolitik und Judendeportation in Wien 1938-1945. Zur Funktion des Antisemitismus als Ersatz nationalsozialistischer Sozialpolitik* (Vienna: Geyer, 1975).

2. Helmut Genschel, *Die Verdrängung der Juden aus der Wirtschaft* (Berlin: 1965), 137-49.

3. Hans Witek, "Arisierungen in Wien. Aspekte nationalsozialistischer Enteignungspolitik 1938-1940," in *NS-Herrschaft in Österreich 1938-1945,* ed. Emmerich Talos, Ernst Hanisch, and Wolfgang Neugebauer (Vienna: OEBV & HPT, 1988), 209.

4. Herbert Rosenkranz, *Verfolgung und Selbstbehauptung. Die Juden in Österreich 1938 - 1945* (Vienna: Herold, 1978), 231.

5. Götz Aly and Susanne Heim, *Vordenker der Vernichtung. Auschwitz und die deutschen Pläne für eine europäische Ordnung* (Hamburg: Hoffmann & Campe, 1991), 33-43.

6. Robert Knight, *"Ich bin dafür, die Sache in die Länge zu ziehen." Wortprotokolle der österreichischen Bundesregierung von 1945-1952 über die Entschädigung der Juden* (Frankfurt: Athenaeum, 1988). For a more subtle analysis, see also Richard Mitten's essay in this volume, pp. 223-70.

7. Peter Böhmer, *Wer konnte, griff zu. Arisierte Güter und NS-Vermögen im Krauland-Ministerium (1945-1949)* (Vienna: Böhlau, 1999).

8. Sabine Loitfellner, "Arisierungen während der NS-Zeit und ihre justizielle Ahndung vor dem Volksgericht Wien 1945-1955. Voraussetzungen – Analyse – Auswirkungen," Master thesis, University of Vienna, 2000.

9. Winfried Garscha and Claudia Kuretsidis-Haider, *Die Verfahren vor dem Volksgericht Wien (1945-1955) als Geschichtsquelle. Eine Projektbeschreibung* (Vienna: Dokumentationsarchiv des österreichischen Widerstandes, 1993), 8.

10. Karl Marschall, *Volksgerichtsbarkeit und Verfolgung von nationalsozialistischen Gewaltverbrechen in Österreich (1945-1972). Eine Dokumentation* (Vienna: Bundesministerium für Justiz, 1977).

11. *Federal Law Gazette*, no. 25 (1947).

12. *Federal Law Gazette*, no. 198 (1947).

13. Winfried Platzgummer, "Die Bewältigung des Nationalsozialismus durch das Strafrecht nach 1945," in *Nationalsozialismus und Recht. Rechtsetzung und Rechtswissenschaft in Österreich unter der NS-Herrschaft,* ed. Ulrike Davy (Vienna: Orac, 1990), 216.

14. Ernst Hanisch, *Der lange Schatten des Staates* (Vienna: Ueberreuther 1994), 423.

15. Garscha, Kuretsidis-Haider, *Die Verfahren vor dem Volksgericht Wien,* 94.

16. Brigitte Bailer, *Wiedergutmachung kein Thema. Österreich und die Opfer des Nationalsozialismus* (Vienna: Löcker, 1993).

17. Garscha, Kuretsidis-Haider, *Die Verfahren vor dem Volksgericht Wien*, 86.

18. Dieter Stiefel, "Der Prozess der Entnazifizierung in Österreich/" in *Politische Säuberung in Europa. Die Abrechnung mit Faschismus und Kollaboration nach dem Zweiten Weltkrieg*, ed. Klaus-Dietmar Henke and Hans Woller, (Munich: dtv, 1991), 141.

19. Editorial, *Neues Österreich*, 8 July 1945, 1; on this issue, see also the Mitten essay in this volume.

20. *Federal Law Gazette*, no. 198 (1947).

21. Marschall, *Volksgerichtsbarkeit*, 41.

Holocaust on Trial:
The Deportation of the Viennese Jews between 1941 and 1942 and the Austrian Judiciary After 1945

Winfried R. Garscha

On 25 October 2000 the Holocaust memorial for 65,000 murdered Austrian Jews was unveiled on the Judenplatz in central Vienna. Close to the monument a branch office of the Jewish Museum was opened, where it is possible to access the database of Austrian Holocaust victims, compiled by the Documentation Center of Austrian Resistance (*Dokumentationsarchiv des österreichischen Widerstandes, DöW*).

The public discussion about the monument and its location omitted two places which might have been more appropriate than the Judenplatz, but are not as centrally located: the former Palais Rothschild, near the Southern Train Station, where the Nazis had installed the Central Authority for Jewish Emigration (*Zentralstelle für jüdische Auswanderung*); and the Aspang Station, located in a remote part of Vienna's third district. At the *Zentralstelle* the deportations were conceived, from the Aspang Station they started; their destination was the ghettoes and the extermination sites in the East.

The first of a total of forty-five deportation trains was assembled on 15 February 1941 at the post platform in the freight train part of the Aspang Station. The train with 996 deportees left Vienna for Pulawy, a town in the Lublin district of the General Government for the Occupied Areas of Poland (*Generalgouvernement*), from where the deportees were transferred to the ghetto of Opole Lubelskie. In the three years preceding their transport to Poland, these Jews had gradually been turned out of their apartments in Vienna and were billeted in so-called Jewish houses situated in Leopoldstadt, the second district of Vienna. Those appointed for deportation had to report to one of the two assembly camps which the Nazis had established in Leopoldstadt. The little Polish town of Opole housed more than seven thousand Jews at that time. Two thousand more arrived from Vienna in the second half of February 1942, who had to be accommodated in the already overcrowded dwellings (eleven days after the first transport a second train with 1,049 deportees had left Vienna for Opole). The outbreak of diseases was inevitable; within a short time more than 1,500 people died. In March 1942 the liquidation of the ghetto began. Polish Jews were transferred to the extermination camp of Belzec, but at the same time other Jews from Poland and Slovakia were brought to Opole. In May 1942 a transport of two thousand men, women, and children left Opole for the extermination camp Sobibor. In October 1942 the ghetto was evacuated. Five hundred people were immediately shot; of the remaining eight thousand, those able to work were brought to the nearby labor camp Poniatowa. They were ill-treated, beaten, and, in many instances, killed by Ukrainian auxiliary troops, the so-called Travniki men, or by SS men when the labor camp was evacuated in November 1943. Those who had remained in the ghetto of Opole were murdered later in the extermination camp of Sobibor.

It should be mentioned that ordinary policemen escorted the deportation transports from the Aspang Station to their destination, whether one of the ghettoes like Theresienstadt, the extermination camp Sobibor, or the pits around the estate of Maly Trostinetz near Minsk, where the deportees were shot upon arrival.

The forty-five deportation trains were dispatched from the Aspang Station within a period of less than two years, between 15 February 1941 and 9 October 1942. Their destinations were ghettoes and camps in Bohemia, Poland, Belorussia, and the Baltic states. The trains transported between 990 and 1,000 Jews each; only the trains to the Theresienstadt ghetto were crammed with up to 1,300 people. In this manner more than 45,000 Jews were deported from Vienna in less than two years. Add to this the two transports of around 1,500 Viennese Jews to Nisko on the San river in October 1939 and several small scale transports of altogether 2,000 people to Theresienstadt and Auschwitz in the years 1943 and 1944, and the number of Jews deported directly from Vienna totals 48,593, according to October 2000 figures; we know of only 2,098 survivors. In addition more than 16,000 Austrian Jews were deported from other countries and several hundred committed suicide before they could be deported. In the course of the *DöW* project "registration by names," the names and presumable dates and locations of the death of around 60,000 Austrian Jews have been confirmed so far.

Carrying out the deportation transports was a task for which it was necessary to navigate the maze of Nazi regulations and prove one's competence. Adolf Eichmann, a native German who had grown up in Austria, showed exceptional initiative in this endeavor. Already in the spring of 1938 he united all authorities involved in the expulsion of the Jewish population of Vienna into a central authority, the already mentioned Central Authority for Jewish Emigration. The purpose of this insistence on bureaucratic efficiency was to induce as many Jews as possible to emigrate "deliberately" in as short a time as possible and to deprive them of as much money as possible. This "Viennese model," described by Hans Safrian in his book about the *Eichmann Men*,[1] worked so well that it was copied in Berlin and, after the occupation of Czechoslovakia, also in Prague.

After February 1941, after the failure of the so-called Madagascar plan, those Viennese Jews whose emigration had been impossible were deported to the conquered territories in the East. The deportations were carried out by the well functioning bureaucracy of the Central Authority for Jewish Emigration. In spring 1941 the killing of these people was still out of the question, but from the fall of 1941 it became clear that, in the end, deportation meant extermination. Yet that was an issue the Gestapo functionaries were not interested in; they *were* interested, however, in the furniture, linen, and other goods the deportees had had to leave behind. The Gestapo created a special authority for the distribution of these Jewish "removal goods" (*Verwaltungsstelle für jüdisches Umzugsgut der Gestapo*, better known as *Vugesta*).[2] Even before this, a similar institution had been founded, the Property Distribution Authority (*Vermögensverkehrsstelle*), which had jurisdiction over the so-called Aryanization process. The functionaries of this authority had no perso-nal contact with the Jews, but they were strongly involved in the deportations: If a deportee still possessed any assets—and this applied to around 25% of all cases—the Central Authority for Jewish Emigra-tion addressed itself to the Property Distribution Authority which then asked the Gestapo to declare this Jew an *enemy of the people*. By this act also the deportee's assets formally became *enemy* and were forfeited to the state. Lists of these confiscation decisions were published periodi-cally in the Viennese edition of the *Völkischer Beobachter*, the official Nazi party newspaper. The Viennese Gestapo issued more than ten thousand confiscation decisions, all of them personally signed by Dr. Karl Ebner, deputy chief of the Gestapo.

Adolf Eichmann's fate is well known. But what has become of the *Eichmann Men* after 1945, and how did the Austrian judiciary avenge their crimes?[3]

Eichmann's right hand man was Alois Brunner. Between 1941 and 1942, when the big deportation transports were dispatched, he was head of the Central Authority for Jewish Emigration. He was feared by the deportees as a brutal thug. His superiors at the Reich Central Security Office (*Reichssicherheitshauptamt*) found his performance in Vienna—the deportation of 7/8 of all Jews still living there—so satisfactory that they dispatched him and his staff to Greece, from where Brunner sent 46,000 Greek Jews to Auschwitz. After the deportation of the Greek Jews between February and June 1943, he continued his *work* in France and Slovakia.

After the war Alois Brunner managed to flee to Syria. 1954 he was sentenced to death in absentia by two French courts. In Austria his trial had been pending since 1947. Because the accused could not be found, the proceedings were suspended in accordance with §412 of the Austrian code of criminal procedure until he could be arrested. This is the normal procedure in such cases—especially if, as in the case of Brunner, the location of the accused is suspected by the authorities, but an extradition is not likely to occur. On 23 January 1960, however, there was an unexpected turn of events. The Viennese prosecuting attorney submitted a statement to the court declaring that, according to §109, code of criminal procedure, the prosecution did not see any more reason for prosecuting Alois Brunner.[4] After such a statement the court was requi-red to abandon the proceedings against the suspect. The only possible way to reopen abandoned proceedings is to introduce completely new evidence which—as the code of criminal procedure runs—"appears to make a conviction of the suspect likely" (§352). Already in the early postwar era, police and the examining magistrates had collected sufficient evidence that Brunner was involved in the killing of 130,000 to 140,000 men, women, and children. Nobody expected that fifteen years after the war further documents or witnesses would emerge. Therefore the abandonment of the proceedings could have been the first step in enabling Alois Brunner to come home as a free man. We do not know who pulled the strings in this—at the very least—*astonishing* action of the judiciary. The prosecuting attorneys were bound by the instructions of the department of justice. The minister at that time was the Social Democratic lawyer Otto Tschadek, who, in the years before, had not seemed to be excessively zealous in prosecuting Nazi crimes.

But before the silent pardoning of Alois Brunner could take place, Adolf Eichmann was caught in Argentina. During his trial in Jerusalem, evidence emerged which made a conviction of Brunner likely. On 8 June 1961 the proceedings were reopened, but because Brunner remained inaccessible for the Austrian judiciary at his hiding place in Damascus, the proceedings were interrupted once again in 1962 according to §412 of the code of criminal procedure (and have been suspended since).

Alois Brunner had a namesake, Anton Brunner, who—in order to avoid confusion with his superior—was called "Brunner II." It was Anton Brunner who robbed the Jews of their last belongings before their deportation. In September 1945 the prosecuting attorney instituted preliminary proceedings against him before the Viennese people's court according to §3 and §4 of the War Criminals Act (torment, assault and battery, and violation of human dignity) for the countless infringements he had committed against the deportees in the assembly camps of Leopoldstadt between 1941 and 1942. For his participation in the deportations, the prosecution extended the indictment later also to §5a of the War Criminals Act. This paragraph made the "expulsion of people from their home country" a punishable offense and imposed the death penalty to those perpetrators who played a *leading role* in the execution of this crime. After his one-week trial before the Viennese people's court, Anton Brunner was sentenced to death on 10 May 1946 and was hanged two weeks later.

At the same time that the preliminary proceeding against Anton Brunner took place, a proceeding against the temporary commandant of the Theresienstadt ghetto, Siegfried Seidl, started. Seidl, among others, was responsible for the transfer of Viennese Jews from Theresienstadt to the extermination camps. He was sentenced to death on 3 October 1946 by the Viennese people's court and was executed on 4 February 1947.

Another deputy of Alois Brunner, Ernst Girzick, was temporarily assigned to Theresienstadt. Girzick's office in Prague was the Central Authority for the Settlement of the Jewish Question in Bohemia and Moravia (*Zentralstelle für die Regelung der Judenfrage in Böhmen und Mähren*), where he organized the deportation of Jews from the *protectorate* to the death camps in the East before he was detached to Hungary. There he assisted in sending more than a half million Jews to the gas chambers of Auschwitz-Birkenau between March and December 1944. The proceedings against Girzick before the Viennese people's court dragged on for two years, until 3 September 1948. According to §5a of the War Criminals Act, he should have received the death penalty for his leading role in the deportation process but in fall 1948 no more death sentences were imposed.

It is fairly certain that Girzick also profited from the fact that the Austrian people's courts normally did not summon foreign witnesses and used foreign evidence only in exceptional cases. Therefore, crimes committed outside of Austria were punished, if at all, more leniently than crimes committed in Austria. Girzick was sentenced to fifteen years in prison; five years later he was paroled.

Of course, members of the Gestapo administration took a significant part in implementing the deportations. Gestapo chief Franz Josef Huber, a native German, managed to cover up his tracks after 1945 and even became *de-Nazified* in his home town of Nuremberg. His already mentioned deputy, Dr. Karl Ebner, was a Viennese police officer. In a very calculated manner, Ebner took early precautions. After the German defeat at Stalingrad, he helped certain prominent Gestapo prisoners (including several Jews), whom he expected to be useful to him after the war. The reward did not fail to materialize: As a result of the positive testimony of several former Gestapo prisoners, the prosecuting attorney abandoned the proceedings for §5a (expulsion from the home country) in October 1948. It is difficult to understand how a man who had signed ten thousand confiscation papers that claimed the assets of deportees for the Nazis could convince the prosecution that he had played no major role in the deportation of Viennese Jews. Nevertheless, on 11 December 1948 Ebner was sentenced to twenty years for the other crimes that he had committed during the war.

A well-known functionary in the so-called Jewish division (*Juden-referat*) of the Viennese Gestapo headquarters was Johann Rixinger. He was prosecuted for participation in deportations, torment, as well as assault and battery, and Aryanization. On 11 October 1947 the Viennese people's court sentenced him to ten years in prison.

One of the commandants of the two Leopoldstadt assembly camps, Alfred Slawik, was charged not only with participation in the deportations but also with Aryanization and torment, as well as assault and battery in Vienna, Budapest, Slovakia, and Bavaria. Despite the long list of offenses, he got off with only five years, probably because of the late date of his conviction, 20 September 1949. The preliminary proceedings against another Leopoldstadt commandant, Ernst Brückler, were instituted in 1951. The middle of the cold war was not the right time for a fair trial. The prosecution was not able to produce sufficient evidence, and in October 1955 the proceedings were abandoned.

Those who did not torment the deportees but only robbed them of their property could expect a lenient judiciary. Although several preliminary proceedings against functionaries of the *Vugesta*, the authority for the distribution for Jewish goods, were instituted, only few of them ended with a verdict. And I have never heard of proceedings against any one of the many policemen who *only did their duty* when they escorted the deportation transports.

All perpetrators involved in deportation proceedings had a good chance for impunity if they had not been sentenced by December 1955 when the people's courts were abolished. And those who were not prosecuted by the mid-1970s had no reason to fear any legal action against them: The last conviction for a Nazi crime in Austria occurred in 1972; the last trial was completed in 1975.

Only one single deportation case was brought before a jury after the abolishment of the people's courts: the case of Eichmann's transportation officer, Franz Novak. His proceedings were also triggered by the Eichmann trial in Jerusalem, where Novak's name was mentioned several times. Although this case was linked to the extermination of the Hungarian Jews in 1944 rather than to the deportation of the Viennese Jews between 1941 and 1942, I would like to discuss these proceedings here because they show—better than any other case—the lack of understanding among much of the Austrian judiciary for the scope of Nazi atrocities. Granted, in many trials the verdict of the jurors was far more scandalous than in the four trials against Novak. The peculiarity of the Novak case is that it highlights the fact that one cannot blame only the men and women of the jury for the blatant inefficiency in prosecuting Nazi crimes but must find fault with the Austrian judicial system of the 1960s as well.

Franz Novak, who had managed to disappear after the war, was arrested in 1961 on a charge of murder. As the prosecuting attorney formulated in several documents, Novak committed murder by "organizing the transport of Jews from several countries of Europe to concentration camps in the occupied territories in the East and handing the deportees over to the organs of those camps in order to treat them according to the purpose of the Final Solution."[5]

Novak himself could claim to have participated only indirectly in the extermination machinery. More than fifteen years after the war this *distant participation* (as the judicial term went in the Austrian criminal code of that time) was already under the statute of limitation. It was the achievement of the Viennese prosecuting attorneys to bring Novak to court nevertheless. They discovered the clue, i.e. the policemen escorting the deportations: "[By] providing for custody and police escort of the deportees to the concentration camps, [Novak] intentionally caused these policemen to actively participate in the murder of the deportees."[6] Because the policemen had been directly under Novak's command, the attorneys could prosecute Novak for *immediate participation* in murder, which was not yet a statute-barred crime.

But the judges of the Viennese district court had a different point of view. On 26 February 1963 a council of three judges (*Ratskammer*) rejected the charge and abandoned the legal proceedings, because the prosecution could not produce any evidence that Novak had personally killed a Jew. The prosecution appealed, and the Viennese provincial high court annulled the decision of the district court. But the district court dismissed the claims of the prosecution to supply the charge and of the Jewish community to join the case against Novak as a private litigant. Nevertheless, on 30 June 1964 Novak was indicted not only for murder but also for *public violence by malicious acts and omissions* because he used insufficient railroad equipment for the deportation transports. The punishment was life imprisonment if a perpetrator could foresee that such malicious acts and omissions might cause the death of human beings. For crimes which are punished with life imprisonment the Austrian criminal code does not provide a statute of limitation.

After a main trial of twenty-one days the eight jurors' verdict on public violence was *guilty* (5 to 3), and the court sentenced Novak to eight years in prison. The prosecution appealed; the defense attorney appealed to nullify the verdict. The verdict on participation in murder was *not guilty* (8 to 0).[7]

On 15 December 1965 the Supreme Court accepted the nullity appeal and overruled the judgement. The men and women of the jury understood the message of the Supreme Court in their own way. On 6 October 1966, after a second main trial which dealt only with Novak's implementation of the deportation transports, the majority of the jury agreed that Novak had committed public violence, but their verdict was *not guilty* because they conceded that he had the obligation to obey orders. After the acquittal the court awarded him compensation for the detention period pending trial. The prosecution challenged the judgement and appealed to have it nullified. On 12 February 1968 the Supreme Court overruled the acquittal. During the third main trial, in

December 1969, the German expert witness Wolfgang Scheffler testified concerning the problem of superior orders and crimes of obedience. This time the jurors unanimously declared Novak guilty of public violence (verdict of 18 December 1969), and the court sentenced Novak to nine years in prison. But the jurors had not answered an additional question of the court: whether the defendant had wrongly assumed that he had to obey superior orders (imaginary necessity); this would have been a lawful excuse for his crimes. Therefore, the attorney general (the supreme prosecuting authority in Austria) appealed the decision. Cross appeals came from the prosecuting and the defense attorneys. On 8 March 1971 the Supreme Court followed the appeal of the attorney general and ordered a new trial, which was held between 20 March and 13 April 1972 before a Viennese jury. The verdict was *guilty* (polling result: 7 to 1). The jurors agreed that in 1944, both in Vienna and Hungary, Novak had maliciously and knowingly implemented the "Final Solution of the Jewish Question"; he had endangered human lives and jeopardized the health and safety of many Jewish men, women, and children by organizing their transports from Hungary; he had ordered the transport of these human beings in overcrowded freight cars without sufficient food and drinking water, and had thus caused the death of a very high number of Jews.[8]

The sentence of the Viennese district court on 13 April 1972 was seven years imprisonment. Both the appeal of the prosecuting attorney and the nullity appeal of the defense attorney were dismissed by the Supreme Court. On 18 October 1974 Novak was paroled, and in 1978 he was pardoned.

As the course of the Novak proceedings shows, in the beginning of the 1960s not only several jurors but also some judges accepted Novak's pretended ignorance of the fate of the deportees. When, in his first trial, he was asked by the presiding judge whether he had never thought about the fact that the destination of those trains was a well-known concentration camp, he answered: "For me Auschwitz was a heavily frequented train station."[9]

Notes

1. Hans Safrian, *Die Eichmann-Männer* (Vienna: Europaverlag, 1993); see also the revised paperback edition *Eichmann und seine Gehilfen* (Frankfurt/Main: Fischer Taschenbuch Verlag, 1997).

2. See also the contribution of Sabine Loitfellner in this issue.

3. The information about the legal proceedings derives from articles about trials in the newspaper clip collection of the *DöW*, copies of indictments, judgements and other parts of the trial records in the file collection of the *DöW*, and the databases of the Austrian Postwar Justice Research Institute (*Zentrale österreichische Forschungsstelle Nachkriegsjustiz*).

4. § 109 Code of criminal procedure runs as follows: "The examining magistrate has to abandon the preliminary proceeding as soon as the prosecutor withdraws the instruction for criminal prosecution, or applies for nolle prosequi, or declares that he does not find any more reason for a criminal prosecution of the suspect."

5. Quoted from the indictment of 30 June 1964, printed in Kurt Pätzold and Erika Schwarz, *Auschwitz war für mich nur ein Bahnhof* (Berlin: Metropol, 1994), 159-60.

6. Ibid.

7. The information about jury polling results and appeals is printed in Karl Marschall, *Volksgerichtsbarkeit und Verfolgung von nationalsozialistischen Gewaltverbrechen in Österreich*, 2nd ed. (Vienna: Justizministerium, 1987), 150-56.

8. Pätzold and Schwarz, *Auschwitz*, 174.

9. Ibid., 161.

Austrian and British Trials Over Massacres of Jews at the End of World War II

Martin F. Polaschek

1. The Crimes

Beginning in the summer of 1944, Hungarian Jews were carried off to today's Austria as forced laborers. Many of them were assigned to the building of the Nazi defense line on the Hungarian border (*Südostwall*).[1] Those laborers, some of whom had already done forced labor for the Hungarian army, were in a very bad condition. Hard work and the resultant weakness had caused diseases, especially epidemic typhus. For the Nazis they had lost their "worth" as workers, so many of them were murdered.[2] For example, in March 1945 in Rechnitz, then part of the *Reichsgau* Styria, participants of a social gathering killed 180 Jews during one night. The next day eighteen Jews had to bury the bodies; after that, they were killed, too.[3]

Many more crimes were committed when the front-line approached the *Ostmark* in late March 1945.[4] The work camps were closed, and the Jews were brought to the concentration camp Mauthausen; those who seemed too weak to survive the transport were killed. That happened, for instance, in the camp of Engerau near Bratislava/Slovakia. More than two thousand Hungarian Jews had dug up entrenchments there, and about four hundred of them died working. When the Soviet troops approached, the camp was vacated. A special detachment shot those who were sick or unfit to march (about one hundred people); the others were forced to walk to the Danube port at Deutsch-Altenburg. During that march another one hundred Jews were killed. The rest were shipped to Mauthausen; on the week-long journey more prisoners died.[5]

Comparable crimes were committed in other places, too. For example near Persenbeug 223 Jews were murdered by unknown members of the SS at the beginning of May.[6] The prisoners were not only killed in the vacated camps, but also on the way to Mauthausen.

They had to walk and were not allowed to take the main roads, which were used by the army; their march on the side roads was rough and exhausting.[7] The escorts killed the weak and footsore prisoners, but also relatively healthy ones arbitrarily. Such atrocities happened on many such transports ("death marches") in Styria, Lower and Upper Austria,[8] and in many other regions at the Eastern front of the Third Reich.[9]

The cruelest crime of all was committed on the Präbichl, a Styrian mountain pass. Early in April 1945, members of the local SA fired their guns randomly at the passing prisoners; more than two hundred of them lost their lives. Another atrocious crime was the following: Late in April 1945, a group of members of the SA and of the *Volkssturm* retreated into the mountains northwest of Graz, the capital of Styria. Nine Jewish men had to come with them as personal slaves. Despite the surrender of the German *Wehrmacht* and the fall of the Nazi regime, the group stayed in their mountain camp until late May when they decided to vacate their hiding-place. The nine Jews were executed, although the war had already ended weeks ago (!). We will return to both these crimes and the British and Austrian proceedings concerning them at the end of this paper.

2. The Perpetrators: "Following Orders"

The above mentioned crimes were committed in today's Austria and to some extent in full view of the public. Although in many cases there were no eyewitnesses, the large groups of marching people and the dead bodies left behind did not go unnoticed. The escorts, in most cases members of the SS or SA, were assisted by local units of the *Volkssturm* or the *Gendarmerie* (local police). Many of the crimes were committed by escorts, who joined the transport just for a short time and often did not even belong to the NSDAP, the SS, or the SA. That these men, who had no reason to commit such random crimes, became murderers, is particularly frightening.

In the people's courts (*Volksgerichte*) most defendants pleaded not guilty; in cases with overwhelming evidence, the defendants argued that they had been obliged to follow orders.[10] The men who had given the orders and, in most cases, not actually performed the crime blamed their execution-style murders on ignorance, incompetence, or superior orders. It was especially the *Kreisleiter* (regional leaders) who made the case for only *following orders*, and who were paid special attention to by the Austrian and British courts. In the first years after the war, the punishment of the former Nazi elite met with the approval of Austrian public opinion, but that was soon to change. Even if their initial punishment had been quite severe, many of those convicted by Austrian as well as British courts were later granted amnesty or were released on probation. Some people even disapproved of the harsh punishment of those who had *simply* given the orders. In the court records, one can find many letters of support and requests for grace.

For example, in November 1947 Anton Rutte, *Kreisleiter* of Feldbach, was sentenced to death by a British general court for ordering the murder of Hungarian-Jewish forced laborers. The British commander in chief, however, reduced the verdict to fifteen years imprisonment.[11] A few months before the sentence, the local branch of the Austrian People's Party (ÖVP) had handed the Austrian judicial authorities a so-called "political certificate" for Rutte. This document attested that it was only in the last days of war that he had "lost his head" and "made a not so good impression." Furthermore, it stressed that Rutte had never maliciously harmed anyone and was said to be of decent character.[12]

3. The Courts

The prosecution of war criminals fell under the jurisdiction of the Austrian people's courts (*Volksgerichte*) as well as special military courts of the Allied occupation powers. Some important research has already been presented concerning British and U.S. military justice in the Austrian occupation period, but we still know very little about the French and Soviet tribunals. However, given the location of the crimes (eastern or northeastern Austria) and the origin of the victims (above all Hungarian Jews), neither the French nor the Soviets might have been very interested in prosecuting those crimes.[13]

The American courts in Austria did not claim jurisdiction over such crimes, either, because no U.S. citizens or other Allied subjects were involved.[14] The only Allied power that was prepared to conduct proceedings against perpetrators of massacres at Jews were the British. We will later return to their motives.

3.1. The Austrian People's Courts

The principal legal ground for the Austrian *Volksgericht* proceedings was the War Criminals Act (*Kriegsverbrechergesetz*) of 26

June 1945.[15] This defined offenses against the civilian population of countries occupied by German troops ("crimes against humanity").[16] Executing higher orders was no reason for exculpation. If crimes involved the death of humans, it was to be punished by death. The same applied to the person who had given the order. In addition to the War Criminals Act, the *Verbotsgesetz* (outlawing of all Nazi organizations in Austria) of 8 May 1945,[17] and the regulations of the Austrian penal code concerning murder had to be observed.[18] So-called people's courts (*Volksgerichte*) were established at the provincial courts and were staffed by two career judges and three lay judges. The procedure of the court was to obey the Austrian rules of *normal* criminal procedure, but without the legal remedies applicable to such procedures (e.g. appeal). In some cases a review of a verdict by the Austrian Supreme Court was granted.[19]

Soon after the end of the war, the Austrian authorities started prosecuting war crimes, but with some restrictions. The Western Allies permitted the application of the War Criminals Act in their zones only at the beginning of 1946, while the people's courts in the Soviet zone had already begun their task in the summer of 1945. The occupation forces could intervene in the proceedings at any time—they had the power to move them to their own authorities or decide whether an Austrian court was allowed to conduct a trial at all.[20] These restrictions also concerned the investigating authorities, who were under the direct control of the Allies.

This is not the place to investigate the activities of the people's courts in detail. It should only be noted here that the people's courts passed some 13,600 verdicts, 7,300 of which concerned violent crimes (including cases dealing with informers and "Aryanization"). Forty-three people were sentenced to death (thirty actually executed), twenty-nine were imprisoned for life.[21] Most of these severe verdicts applied to massacres of Jewish forced laborers in the final weeks of the war.

3.2. The British Courts

The British occupation authorities established their own military courts in their zone to deal with war crimes. They doubted that the Austrian courts, which had just started their activities and were understaffed and overworked, would be able to handle such large and complex trials. Additionally, the British were afraid that the high number of natives involved in the cases could influence the Austrian judges. Besides, the political character of the trials had to be considered, too, for they offered the possibility of *reckoning* with the Nazi regime. For this reason, the perpetrators who had given orders to commit murders or had acted in the background were punished as severely or even harder than those men executing the orders[22].

The British military government contemplated the alternative of establishing an international military tribunal like in Nuremberg or a British court martial ("Royal Warrant Military Court"). However, both types of procedure seemed too complicated and a rather bad example for the Austrian legal system. Therefore, the British decided to transfer war crime cases under the jurisdiction of the courts of the military government. These courts had already been established early in the occupation with the first decree of the British military government to punish "persons, who had offended the orders of the military government or the Austrian law."[23] Three different types of courts might apply according to the gravity of the crime. Grave crimes and "atrocities" (i.e. "war" crimes committed by Germans against Germans or citizens of (former) confederates, e.g. Hungary) fell under the jurisdiction of "general courts," consisting of three army officers of whom at least the chairman had to have legal expertise.[24] Verdicts required confirmation by the British commander in chief in Austria. The military government courts could apply English as well as Austrian law (in some cases even German law).[25] The rules of procedure were based on English law, although some adjustments were made to the continental law system. The English law system was supposed to stand as an example to the Austrian legal authorities for the rule of law and democratic jurisdiction.

Austrian authorities had to give support to these British judicial proceedings. Because of the demarcation lines, the British could not investigate in the Soviet sector, where some of the crimes had been committed only months earlier. Thus, they availed themselves of the Austrian *Gendarmerie*. The trials took place in Austrian court buildings, and those found guilty served their punishment in Austrian prisons. In November 1951 the last thirty-five prisoners of the British were entrusted to the Austrian authorities.[26]

The first investigations were executed by military security authorities, but in December 1946 a separate unit was charged with this task.[27] However, already half a year later, the British military government decided to cede all unresolved cases of war crimes against Jews to Austrian jurisdiction; the last British trial dealing with Nazi war crimes before a general British military court took place in November 1947. By this time, the Austrian courts had proven that they were capable of dealing with complex war crime cases. At any rate, the British courts had only been able to relieve the Austrian legal authorities partially; in some cases, they had even caused delays and handicapped Austrian investigations[28].

To get an impression of the byzantine legal situation at the time, we will take a closer look at the proceedings concerning the massacre of Jews in Strem in the Austrian province of Burgenland. Three courts were involved—both the people's courts of Vienna and of Graz, as well as the British general court. In autumn 1945 two perpetrators charged with war crimes were committed to pre-trial detention in Graz; one of them was soon transferred to a British internment camp because he had previously been the local leader of the NSDAP. The fact that the crime had been committed in the Soviet zone made the investigations even more difficult. The Styrian *Gendarmerie* (as well as the British investigators) were not allowed to enter the Soviet zone; asking their colleagues in the Burgenland for help with the investigations was quite complicated. In addition, the people's court in Vienna initiated its own investigations because the crime scene now lay in its jurisdiction. Thus, some of the suspects were transferred from Graz to Vienna. After some months, the case was moved back to Graz and now came under the jurisdiction of the British military government. In November 1947, when the already mentioned investigative unit was disbanded, the British transferred the case back to the people's court of Graz. Given all these legal maneuvers and jurisdictions the case became more and more chaotic; one of the main suspects, for example, was imprisoned in Vienna until June 1947, although the case had already been transferred to Graz.[29]

Finally, in August 1948 two trials took place at the people's court in Graz. The verdicts were not particularly harsh, but the courts had tried to assess the defendants' different grades of guilt. The main perpetrators received several years of imprisonment, one was sentenced to death, but not executed. Some members of the *Hitlerjugend*, who had been very young when the crimes were committed, were acquitted or were sentenced to only a few years of imprisonment.[30]

What did the British courts accomplish? Between April 1946 and August 1948, the general courts pronounced about one hundred verdicts in about twenty trials. Fifty-three defendants were sentenced to death, forty-two were executed.[31] In Styria, fourteen trials were held concerning the murders of Hungarian Jews; thirty death penalties were

pronounced, twenty-four executions implemented.[32] However, it is hard
to compare the numbers of British and Austrian trials: The people's
courts had to deal with a large number of offenses besides violent
crimes. Prosecutions had to be started, although it was often uncertain
whether an indictment could be drawn up, after the perpetrators were on
the run. It actually seems as if the British courts only laid charges in
rather clear cases—at least the statistics do not reveal information about
discontinued proceedings or prosecutions against unknown perpetrators.
While in the first years the British imposed rather severe sentences—this
applies also to most Austrian *Volksgericht* trials—verdicts became
increasingly milder after 1948. In the last section, we will take a look at
some important Austrian and British cases.

4. Some Important Cases

Earlier in this paper the ghastly murder by several members of the
SA and the *Volkssturm* of nine Jewish men a few weeks after the end of
the war was mentioned.[33] Soon after the massacre about a dozen of the
presumed perpetrators could be arrested; but the leader of the group,
who had ordered the execution, had disappeared.[34] In August 1946 two
defendants were sentenced to death and executed, one man received
twelve years imprisonment, and another, who had been under eighteen
years old at the time of the offense, was sentenced to seven years
imprisonment.[35]

In June 1962, sixteen years later, the leader of the group and a second defendant finally stood trial in a regular court (the people's courts
had been dissolved in 1955). For lack of evidence the second defendant
could not be charged with active participation in the murders, so he just
received a three-year term of imprisonment.[36] The leader was condemned for inducing the others to the crime and was sentenced to seven
years imprisonment. However, the Supreme Court reversed the
judgement in November 1962 and remanded the matter to the court. In
a second trial (with different judges), the defendant was scandalously
found innocent on 6 March 1963![37]

During the first years after the end of the war some Austrian perpetrators received severe sentences. For example, between August 1945
and July 1954 twenty-one men, most of them members of the Viennese
SA, were put on trial in six different "Engerau-trials."[38] Their crime, the
murder of numerous Jews during the evacuation of the camp in Engerau
near today's Austrian-Slovakian border, has already been mentioned.

Nine defendants were sentenced to death and executed, one was sentenced to life imprisonment and others were jailed for several years; only one man was acquitted.

In these proceedings—to briefly digress to some methodical questions—the problem of the historical value of judicial sources shows up clearly. Case records are the only written testimony of the Engerau camp with its approximately six hundred victimized inmates. When reading these court documents today, one must bear in mind that their purpose was legal investigation and not historical documentation. They contain only the information gathered to charge the perpetrators of the Engerau crimes.[39] Additional information of interest to historians today but not pertaining to the actual crimes was not recorded since it was not considered important for the preparation of the case.[40] On the other hand, the records contain numerous details referring to the perpetrators (reports of the investigators, personal testimonies, etc.), which we do not find in that extent in British or American files, due to the different procedural law.

Finally, I would like to mention the best-known British trial, the so-called "first Eisenerz murder trial" of April 1946,[41] dealing with the aforementioned massacre against Hungarian Jews on the Präbichl pass in Styria.[42] At the time the newspapers called the trial "little Nuremberg,"[43] for there were eighteen defendants and it lasted four weeks.

Although the indictment rested only on indirect evidence, it was proven that the principal defendant Otto Christandl, the *Kreisleiter* of Leoben, had organized the transport of the Jews in his district and that his orders had resulted in the massacre. Both, the men who had given the orders and those who had shown a lust for murder, were condemned to death and executed.[44] Those who had followed the orders with reluctance received ten years imprisonment; some were acquitted.[45] Some parts of the population criticized the conviction of those instigators who had given orders and not stained their hands with blood, particularly in the communities of the executed.[46]

5. Summary

The British and Austrian war crimes trials are an important source to learn about the fate of Hungarian Jewish slave laborers during the final stage of the Nazi regime in the *Ostmark*. As legal documents they are especially important in comparing Austrian and Anglo-American criminal and procedural law and their specific applications. These legal cases often provide the only historical documentation of the heinous crimes committed on Austrian soil in the final weeks of the war by Austrian Nazis. The more time that had lapsed since the end of the war, the more the verdicts became lenient and the less often Austrian public opinion accepted severe convictions. This process reached its culmination in the 1960s with some scandalous acquittals by grand juries. In this respect, the trials are a mirror of Austrian postwar society, which after the termination of the *Volksgerichte* increasingly repressed the war crimes of Austrian Nazi perpetrators.

Notes

1. See Leopold Banny, *Schild im Osten: Der Südostwall zwischen Donau und Untersteiermark 1944/45* (Lackenbach: Eigenverlag, 1985), 60; Hermann Hagspiel, *Die Ostmark: Österreich im Großdeutschen Reich 1938 bis 1945* (Vienna: Braumüller, 1995), 252-54; Franz Timischl, *Fürstenfeld und Umgebung von 1930 bis 1950: Ein zeitgeschichtliches Forschungsprojekt der Volkshochschule Fürstenfeld* (Fürstenfeld: Landesverband der Steirischen Volkshochschulen, 1994), 191.

2. Eleonore Lappin, "Ungarisch-jüdische Zwangsarbeiter in Österreich 1944/45," in *Studien zur Geschichte der Juden in Österreich,* ed. Martha Keil and Eleonore Lappin (Bodenheim: Philo, 1997), 152-3.

3. Eva Holpfer, "Der Umgang der burgenländischen Nachkriegsgesellschaft mit NS-Verbrechen bis 1955: Am Beispiel der wegen der Massaker von Deutsch-Schützen und Rechnitz geführten Volksgerichtsprozesse," Thesis, Vienna University, 1998, 35ff; Szabolcs Szita, *Verschleppt, verhungert, vernichtet: Die Deportation von ungarischen Juden auf das Gebiet des annektierten Österreich 1944-1945* (Vienna: Werner Eichbauer, 1999), 204-5. Soon after the end of the war, a few of the perpetrators were put on trial, but most of them have not been disclosed to this day. This could be attributed to the fear of the inhabitants of Rechnitz, who remember the murder of two chief witnesses in 1946; see Eva Holpfer, "Das Massaker an ungarischen Juden in Rechnitz als Beispiel für den Umgang der politischen Parteien mit der NS-Vergangenheit in den ersten Nachkriegsjahren," in *Keine "Abrechnung": NS-Verbrechen, Justiz und Gesellschaft in Europa nach 1945,* ed. Claudia Kuretsidis-Haider and Winfried R. Garscha (Leipzig: Akademische Verlagsanstalt, 1998), 425-9.

4. See Felix Schneider, "Die militärischen Operationen in der Steiermark. März bis Mai 1945," *Graz 1945, Historisches Jahrbuch der Stadt Graz* 25 (1994): 17.

5. Claudia Kuretsidis-Haider, "Justizakten als historische Quelle am Beispiel der 'Engerau-Prozesse': Über einige Probleme bei der Suche und Auswertung von Volksgerichtsakten," in *Österreichischer Zeitgeschichtetag 1995: Österreich - 50 Jahre Zweite Republik,* ed. Rudolf G. Ardelt and Christian Gerbel (Innsbruck: StudienVerlag, 1996), 338; Szita, *Verschleppt,* 197-8.

6. Lappin, "Ungarisch-jüdische Zwangsarbeiter," 147; Dokumentationsarchiv des Österreichischen Widerstandes, ed., *Widerstand und Verfolgung in Niederösterreich 1934-1945: Eine Dokumentation,* vol. 3 (Vienna: Österreichischer Bundesverlag, Jugend und Volk, 1987), 396-7.

7. Hans Marsalek, *Die Geschichte des Konzentrationslagers Mauthausen: Dokumentation,* 2nd ed. (Vienna: Österreichische Lagergemeinschaft Mauthausen, 1980), 285.

8. Günther Burczik, "Nur net dran rührn! Auf den Spuren der Todesmärsche ungarischer Juden durch Österreich nach Mauthausen im April 1945," in *Studien zur Geschichte der Juden in Österreich*, ed. Martha Keil and Eleonore Lappin (Bodenheim: Philo, 1997), 169-204; Lappin, "Ungarisch-jüdische Zwangsarbeiter," 156ff; Marsalek, *Die Geschichte*, 287.

9. See Martin Gilbert, Endlösung: *Die Vertreibung und Vernichtung der Juden. Ein Atlas* (Reinbeck bei Hamburg: Rowohlt Taschenbuch Verlag, 1982), 208-35.

10. See Lappin, "Ungarisch-jüdische Zwangsarbeiter," 153-4.

11. Eleonore Lappin, "Die Ahndung von NS-Gewaltverbrechen im Zuge der Todesmärsche ungarischer Juden durch die Steiermark," in *Keine "Abrechnung"*, ed. Kuretsidis–Haider and Garscha, 41 (footnote 41).

12. Landesgericht für Strafsachen (LGS), Vr 2482/47-11, Provincial Archives of Styria, Graz. Martin F. Polaschek, *Im Namen der Republik Österreich! Die Volksgerichte in der Steiermark 1945 bis 1955* (Graz: Eigenverlag des Steiermärkischen Landesarchivs, 1998), 92-94. Such certificates were written in many cases, not only by the ÖVP, the Austrian People's Party, but also by the SPÖ, the Socialist Party, and KPÖ, the Communist Party of Austria, as well as private persons.

13. Winfried R. Garscha and Claudia Kuretsidis-Haider, *Die Nachkriegsjustiz als nicht-bürokratische Form der Entnazifizierung: Österreichische Justizakten im europäischen Vergleich, Überlegungen zum strafprozessualen Entstehungszusammenhang und zu den Verwertungsmöglichkeiten für die historische Forschung* (Vienna: Eigenverlag des Dokumentationsarchivs des Österreichischen Widerstandes, 1995), 26-27; for Soviet trials against war criminals see Nikita V. Petrov, "Verurteilungen deutscher und österreichischer Kriegsverbrecher in der Sowjetunion 1943-1952," in *Der Krieg gegen die Sowjetunion 1941-1945*, ed. Stefan Karner and Gerald Schöpfer (Graz: Leykam, 1998), 49-78.

14. Kurt K. Tweraser, "Military Justice as an Instrument of American Occupation Policy in Austria 1945-1950: From Total Control to Limited Tutelage," *Austrian History Yearbook* 24 (1993): 153-78; Kurt Tweraser, "Amerikanische Kriegsverbrecherprozesse in Salzburg: Anmerkungen zur justiellen Verfolgung von Kriegsverbrechern in der amerikanischen Besatzungszone in Österreich, 1945-1955," in *Keine "Abrechnung"*, ed. Kuretsidis-Haider and Garscha, 66-101.

15. *Staatsgesetzblatt* Nr. 32/1945; Winfried R. Garscha and Claudia Kuretsidis-Haider, "Justice and Nazi-crimes in Austria 1945-1955 between Self-Purge and Allied Control," *1945: Consequences and Sequels of the Second World War*, Bulletin of the International Committee for the History of the Second World War, no. 27/28 (1995): 249-50.

16. Sect. 1, subs. 1, War Criminals Act. This also applied to crimes committed against Hungarian Jews, for they were citizens of a country that was no longer a confederate of Nazi Germany, but occupied by German troops; see for instance People's Court Graz against Franz Isker, opinion of the court, LGS Graz, Vr 6791/47-55, Provincial Archives of Styria, Graz.

17. *Staatsgesetzblatt* Nr. 13/1945; Gernot D. Hasiba, "Das NS-Verbotsgesetz im Spannungsfeld von Rechtsakzeptanz und Rechtsstaatlichkeit," in *Festschrift zum 80. Geburtstag von Hermann Baltl*, ed. Kurt Ebert (Vienna: Verlag Österreich, 1998), 165-80.

18. Sect. 134, Austrian Penal Code, and following sect.; Theofried Allinger-Csollich, "Das geltende Strafrecht," *Juristische Blätter* 68 (1946): 33-37.

19. Martin F. Polaschek, "Nachkriegsprozesse gegen Kriegsverbrecher in der Steiermark," in *Der Krieg gegen die Sowjetunion 1941-1945*, ed. Stefan Karner and Gerald Schöpfer (Graz: Leykam, 1998), 92-93.

20. Polaschek, *Im Namen der Republik Österreich*, 18.

21. Further details, e.g. the different kinds of imprisonment and secondary punishments, cannot be dealt with in the framework of this essay.

22. Eleonore Lappin, "Prozesse der britischen Militärgerichte wegen nationalsozialistischen Gewaltverbrechen an ungarisch-jüdischen Zwangsarbeitern," in *Österreichischer Zeitgeschichtetag 1995: Österreich - 50 Jahre Zweite Republik*, ed. Rudolf G. Ardelt and Christian Gerbel (Innsbruck: StudienVerlag, 1996), 346.

23. Decree no. 1, Art. XI, printed in *Verordnungs- und Amtsblatt für das Land Steiermark*, 31 August 1945, 68; also Art. II of the ordinance Nr. 100 of the military government Austria, in *Verordnungs- und Amtsblatt für das Land Steiermark*, 29 January 1946, 21. See in general Gustav Kafka, "Probleme der alliierten Militärgerichtsbarkeit," *Österreichische Juristen-Zeitung* 1 (1946): 229-31.

24. Siegfried Beer, "Aspekte der (politischen) Militärgerichtsbarkeit der Briten in der Steiermark, 1945-50," in *Österreichischer Zeitgeschichtetag 1995*, 326.

25. See ordinance no. 103, specifying the Austrian acts approved by the British early in 1946; in *Verordnungs- und Amtsblatt für das Land Steiermark*, 4 March 1946, 73.

26. Lappin, "Die Ahndung," 42.

27. Siegfried Beer, "Die Briten und der Wiederaufbau des steirischen Justizwesens in der Steiermark 1945-1950," in *Die "britische" Steiermark 1945-1955*, ed. Siegfried Beer (Graz: Selbstverlag der Historischen Landeskommission für Steiermark, 1995), 122; Siegfried Beer, "Aspekte der britischen Militärgerichtsbarkeit in Österreich 1945-1950," in *Keine "Abrechnung"*, ed. Kuretsidis-Haider and Garscha, 60-61.

28. Lappin, "Die Ahndung," 40.

29. Ibid., 45-46.

30. Polaschek, *Im Namen der Republik Österreich*, 163-8.

31. See Lappin, "Prozesse," 345-350; Beer, "Aspekte der (politischen) Militärgerichtsbarkeit," 329-30, with a specification of the sentences of death, imposed by British general courts.

32. Beer, "Briten," 132-3; and Beer, "Aspekte der britischen Militärgerichtsbarkeit," 62.

33. The record LGS Graz, Vr 832/45, could not be found in the Provincial Archives. The description of the case is following Wolfgang Muchitsch, "Das Volksgericht Graz 1946-55," in *Die "britische" Steiermark 1945-1955*, ed. Beer, 152; Karl Marschall, *Volksgerichtsbarkeit und Verfolgung von nationalsozialistischen Gewaltverbrechen in Österreich*, 2nd ed. (Vienna: Bundesministerium für Justiz, 1987), 74-76; and various newspaper articles.

34. *Neue Zeit*, 11 May 1946, 3.

35. An abridged version of the verdict is printed in *Verordnungs- und Amtsblatt für das Land Steiermark*, 26 October 1946, 367; see also Marschall, *Volksgerichtsbarkeit*, 74-76; and Polaschek, *Im Namen der Republik Österreich*, 158-9.

36. For more examples see Heimo Halbrainer and Thomas Karny, *Geleugnete Verantwortung: Der "Henker von Theresienstadt" vor Gericht* (Grünbach: Edition Geschichte der Heimat, 1996), 52-95; Marschall, *Volksgerichtsbarkeit*, 183-5.

37. Halbrainer and Karny, *Geleugnete Verantwortung*, 56-60.

38. Kuretsidis-Haider, "Justizakten," 338-340; Claudia Kuretsidis-Haider, "Die Volks-gerichtsbarkeit als Form der politischen Säuberung in Österreich," in *Keine "Abrechnung"*, ed. Kuretsidis-Haider and Garscha, 20-21.

39. Henry Friedlander, "Der deutsche Strafprozeßakt als historische Quelle," in *Keine "Abrechnung"*, ed. Kuretsidis-Haider and Garscha, 280-4.

40. Kuretsidis-Haider, "Justizakten," 338.

41. In October 1946 two trials dealing with the same massacre, followed; see, for instance, *Wahrheit*, 17 October 1946, 3; *Neue Zeit*, 19 October 1946, 3; *Wahrheit*, 23 October 1946, 3, and *Neue Zeit*, 24 October 1946, 3.

42. Burczik, "Nur net dran rühm," 169; Benedikt Friedman, *"Iwan, hau die Juden!" Die Todesmärsche ungarischer Juden durch Österreich nach Mauthausen im April 1945* (St. Pölten: Eigenverlag des Instituts für Geschichte der Juden in Österreich, 1989), 18-31; Hans Jürgen Rabko, "Die letzten Tage der Menschheit," in *Zwischen den Fronten: Die Region Eisenerz von 1938-1945* (Leoben: Institut für Strukturforschung und Er-wachsenenbildung der AK-Steiermark, 2000), 60-75.

43. *Neue Zeit*, 2 April 1946, 1.

44. *Wahrheit*, 30 April 1946, 1-2; *Wahrheit*, 22 June 1946, 1.

45. *Wiener Zeitung*, 25 April 1946, 3; Lappin, "Prozesse," 347.

46. Lappin, "Die Ahndung," 41; *Wahrheit*, 30 April 1946, 2.

REVIEW ESSAYS

The State of Intelligence Studies in Austria—Breaking Ground

Siegfried Beer

Albert Pethö, *Agenten für den Doppeladler.*
Österreichs Geheimer Dienst im Weltkrieg
(Graz: Leopold Stocker Verlag, 1998)

Gerald Steinacher, *Südtirol und die Geheimdienste,*
Innsbrucker Forschungen zur Zeitgeschichte 15
(Innsbruck: Studienverlag, 2000)

Over the last quarter of a century a new sub-discipline has emerged in the world of academia: intelligence studies.[1] Paradoxically, in Austria hardly anyone has noticed this, despite some valiant attempts to spread the word through different means: through the publication of several scholarly articles on intelligence-related aspects of Austrian history over the last decade or so;[2] through small conferences on intelligence issues (the first one in Vienna in 1998, the second one in Graz in 1999);[3] and through the teaching of intelligence courses at university level, foremost at the Karl-Franzens-Universität Graz.[4] Intelligence specialists, not only in the historical, but also in the military, political, social, and judicial fields, have been speaking of a veritable academic intelligence revolution—particularly in the Anglo-American world— that started in the mid-1970s and followed the revolutionary effects of the systematic information-gathering by governments and private institutions since the beginning of the 20th century. This scholarly intelligence revolution has been *based on* a proliferation of secondary and documentary literature; professional associations devoted to the study of intelligence have been founded, as, for example, the Netherlands' Intelligence Studies

Association (NISA) in 1992 or Germany´s International Intelligence History Study Group (IIHSG) in 1994; scholarly intelligence journals have started to appear in numerous sub-fields: historically oriented periodicals like the *International Journal of Intelligence and Counter-intelligence* (USA) and the quarterly *Intelligence and National Security* (Great Britain), both initiated in 1986, or the recently-founded *Journal of Intelligence History* (Germany);[5] last but not least courses on various intelligence topics have been taught in a wide range of academic institutions, not restricted to the English-speaking world.[6]

Though spying has been called the second-oldest profession, it was not until the latter part of the 19th century that the leading powers of the world started to organize military intelligence departments within their military service branches. For the hegemonic powers of the last two centuries, Great Britain and the United States, naval intelligence was initially of primary concern, while army intelligence was secondary; diplomatic, and finally economic intelligence, came last. The establishment of naval and army branches of military intelligence in several countries in the 1880s and 1890s was followed by the creation of separate civilian intelligence organizations in the 20th century. The British Secret Intelligence Service (SIS), also known as MI6, for example, dates back to 1909.[7] Paradoxically, today's only remaining superpower was a late-comer to civilian intelligence; it was not until July 1941, less than half a year before the dramatic and traumatic Japanese attack on Pearl Harbor, that President Franklin D. Roosevelt put the Office of the Coordinator of Intelligence (COI) into place by executive order. The Central Intelligence Agency (CIA), founded by President Harry S. Truman in 1947, traces its roots back to these comparatively late and conspicuously humble beginnings.[8]

Not surprisingly, it was the three major global conflicts of the 20th century, The First World War, the Second World War, and the cold war, which have first hastened, then strengthened, and finally entrenched the role of intelligence in modern warfare. Governmental elites became aware of its necessity and began to allocate resources to this type of activity. Furthermore, not only the major, but also the minor powers in the international systems have consistently participated in systematic intelligence gathering and at times even in subversive intelligence activities, and that not only in war time. Although the great powers directed their endeavors in intelligence gathering mainly against each other, they also impacted—and to no small degree—the minor players in the international arena, particularly those situated in geopolitical regions of interest to the major powers.

The Republic of Austria, even in its dramatically diminished size and starkly reduced political influence after 1918, was such a traditionally embattled and important territory for the intelligence organizations of major and minor European powers. There is a wide consensus about the fact that, between 1918 and 1989, the small state of Austria was extremely exposed, both politically and militarily, to, first, the voraciousness of the great fascist powers and, then, the ideological struggles of the cold war protagonists. And there is no indication that Austria has since the collapse of communism in Eastern Europe and the demise of the Soviet Union become significantly less important to the intelligence needs of the former four occupational powers of 1945 to 1955, or, for that matter, to her neighbors in Central Europe. Vienna is still one of the undisputed intelligence capitals of Europe.

In addition to this outside interest in Austria, the country itself has a traditionally intensive tendency to political involvement in intelligence-related issues.[9] There may even be a significant bent in the Austrian (political) character for the secretive and irregular side of politics. This would comply with the sagacious observation of a top American diplomat who was stationed in Vienna and Salzburg in the late 1940s and who, in a letter to the State Department, commented on the "fantastic intelligence saturation of Austria," speculating that every fourth inhabitant of the city of Salzburg spied for some domestic or foreign intelligence service.[10] This ratio would even have exceeded the degree of spying in the "*Spitzelsystem*" of the Nazis in Germany and Austria, or later of the Stasi in East Germany. Needless to say, Austria, from the era of Metternich onwards, has had a rich and pervasive tradition of state surveillance and state-organized intelligence gathering, as it has also had its share of spectacular cases of espionage from Alfred Redl to Felix Bloch, to mention only the better-known espionage stories of this century.[11]

Thus, there can be no doubt that the general intelligence revolution of the 20th century has had a substantial impact on Austria. Yet, as mentioned before, serious and methodical research in or even general academic attention to intelligence studies has not yet become established in Austria.

However, a modest step towards the gradual integration of intelligence issues into the larger context of historical studies has, at last, been made, even in Austria. A number of Austrian historians have taken up the challenge of tackling issues in which intelligence plays a central role, and several academics in non-historical fields have also concerned themselves with questions of historical or current importance in the area of state surveillance, military counter-espionage, or Austrian involvement in the larger intelligence community. They can be quickly enumerated. The historians are, listed alphabetically: Thomas Albrich, Siegfried Beer, Walter Blasi, Edda Engelke, Michael Gehler, Gerhard Jagschitz, Stefan Karner, Arnold Kopeczek, Albert Pethö, Oliver Rathkolb, Felix Schneider, and Gerald Steinacher.[12] Fortunately, there are also several non-Austrian specialists who have made significant contributions to the field of Austrian intelligence history, among them, again alphabetically: Ralph W. Brown III, James T. Carafano, Hans Rudolf Fuhrer, Barry McLoughlin, Timothy J. Naftali, Kevin C. Ruffner, and D.C. Watt.[13]

So far practically all monographs on espionage in Austria, except the two books under review, have been written by journalists or practitioners of the intelligence trade. The following journalists deserve recognition of their works: Manfred Fuchs, Harald Irnberger, Kid Möchel, and Hans Wolker.[14] Relevant contributions about Austrian intelligence by former practitioners of the trade have been made by T.H. Bagley, Blake Baker, Peer de Silva, Wilhelm Höttl, William Hood, Erwin Kemper, James V. Milano, and, most recently, Michael Sika.[15]

In the other social sciences even fewer specialists have so far contributed to an understanding of secretive and subversive phenomena in Austrian society, past or present; those who have published in this field are mostly judicial experts and political scientists.[16] The dearth of non-historical intelligence specialists is the more surprising as the question of the role and legitimacy of the current intelligence organizations in Austria has surfaced again and again over the last few years. Successive governments have tried to find a political consensus on modern legislation with which the *Staatspolizeilicher Dienst* (*Stapo- political police*) and the two military intelligence organizations, the *Heeresnachrichtenamt* (*HnaA*) for foreign military intelligence and the *Abwehramt* (*AbwA*) for military security, can perform their challenging tasks under close scrutiny of the Austrian parliament and without infringing on the citizens' rights.

The intelligence studies community, as it has emerged since the early 1980s, basically brings together seven groups which can be differentiated by their specific focuses: historians, military scientists, political scientists, juridical experts, practitioner-scholars, journalists/

laymen, and freelance writers. In this community the historians have clearly achieved pre-eminence. Also, most experts are still from the English-speaking world. In my opinion, the leading historians are, in alphabetical order: Richard J. Aldrich, Christopher Andrew, F.H. Hinsley, Rhodri Jeffrys-Jones, David Stafford, and D.C. Watt from the "British school";[17] Wesley Wark, a Canadian;[18] and H. Bradford Butterfield, Ernest May, Timothy J. Naftali, John Prados, Bradley F. Smith, and Robin Winks from American academia.[19] Among American political scientists the following intelligence scholars stand out: Roy Godson, Loch K. Johnson, and Jeffery T. Richelson.[20] A listing of outstanding non-Anglo-American experts of intelligence history must include Jürgen Heideking, Wolfgang Krieger, Christof Mauch, and Michael Wala from Germany, as well as Bob de Graaff and Cees Wiebes from the Netherlands.[21] This list could be extended with individual historians from France, Italy, Norway, Sweden, and Switzerland. Regrettably, Austrian historians have not yet entered the international arena of intelligence studies in force.

There is, however, new promise. Recently two monographic studies by younger Austrian historians have been published; both exhibit a broad foundation in archival sources and good empirical evidence. They are both impressive case studies, primarily on military matters, and can generally be characterized as significant contributions to the historical eras which they address. However, both works also exemplify some of the typical weaknesses and drawbacks which have plagued so many monographic attempts at chronicling the impact of intelligence and intelligence organizations on particular historical events or periods. Both authors have difficulty defining the larger context which the agents or agencies of intelligence have touched, influenced, or even dominated. This has proved to be the ultimate challenge for contributions to intelligence history in the military, diplomatic, and even economic fields. Both studies are impressively rich in texture, documentation, and historical detail. This may in part be explained by the fact that both have originally been submitted as doctoral dissertations, Albert Pethö's at the University of Vienna, and Gerald Steinacher's at the University of Innsbruck.

Pethö's book of altogether 448 pages provides 1247 footnotes which refer to sources mainly in Austrian archives, while Steinacher's tome of 350 pages contains 1045 endnotes quoting documents in Austrian depositories as well as in foreign archives of Italy, England, Germany, Switzerland, and the United States. This richness of sources in both books, mostly emanating from intelligence units, represents a significant breakthrough in the context of Austrian historiography. At the same time, they both cannot quite hide their origins as doctoral theses in that they each cater to archival detail at the cost of analytical conviction. While these monographs share several strengths as well as weaknesses, they do differ substantially in their approach to the respective topics. Therefore each should be examined according to its own merits.

The title of Albert Pethö's work is somewhat misleading: *Agenten für den Doppeladler.Österreichs Geheimer Dienst im Weltkrieg*, meaning literally "Agents for the Double Eagle: Austria-Hungary's Secret Service in the World War." From this title the reader must inevitably expect the emphasis of the book to lie on the four-year period of World War I. However, only one fifth of the entire text deals with the experiences, feats, and losses of the various military intelligence units during this war, while most of the coverage pertains to the pre-war period from the turn of the century to the outbreak of hostilities in August 1914. This emphasis seems to be linked to the availability of sources, as most of the war time documents were annihilated by the various military intelligence branches toward the end of, and after, the war. Laudably, Pethö also devotes a good portion of his book to the historical genesis of the intelligence functions brought about by the Habsburg military establishment. He thus accounts for the phenomenon that despite a relative military backwardness and even unpreparedness for war, the major services managed to develop a better-than-average intelligence potential for the imperial leadership, both military and governmental. The Austro-Hungarian monarchy could avail itself of an innovative and surprisingly proficient signals service called *Radiohorchdienst* which, at least partly, managed to compensate for inferior field effectiveness and lack of troop strength. Furthermore, Austro-Hungarian agents successfully penetrated almost all corners of the hostile world—from the Vatican and Italy, to Switzerland, France, Russia, and even the deserts of Arabia and the Levant. These Habsburg agents, serving the army and the navy, came from all social and professional backgrounds and, as a rule, showed a great sense of duty and devotion to the imperial cause. The war was eventually lost not because of, but despite their efforts. As one would expect, the treachery of Alfred Redl receives also adequate coverage in Pethö's book though it is not analyzed in terms of concrete damage to the war effort as a whole.

The strength of this book lies in its minute depiction of the system and methods of information gathering, as well as of the aggressive and subversive measures against enemy forces and the various shortcomings and/or failures of concrete intelligence units. Its unmistakable weaknesses lie in the lack of cohesiveness in the narrative, in an obvious reluctance to analyze the impact of what is often minutely described and, above all, in the failure of placing these intelligence efforts into the larger context of the monarchy's increasing military, political, and social disintegration which had started long before the war was ignited. Juxtaposing evidence from home and "enemy" archives would probably have sharpened the eye for relevancy and dispensable detail. Nevertheless, Pethö manages to provide a fascinating panorama of a well-orchestrated array of intelligence activities abroad and of a meticulous counter-espionage effort at home. His study can provide the basis for smaller, bi-lateral case studies and for an examination of the changes that occur when an empire service is turned into a republican military intelligence apparatus. The author is to be commended for a frank admission of the deficiencies of his own study in a remarkable post-script. Some of the editorial slips are well-compensated for by the addition of a glossary and a largely reliable index of names, as well as the inclusion of sixty-nine illustrations and a short appendix of maps and facsimile documents. In any case, Pethö must be acknowledged for a contribution upon which further efforts to erect a structure of Austrian intelligence studies can rely.

With his book *Südtirol und die Geheimdienste 1943-1945* (Intelligence Operations in South Tyrol, 1943-1945), originally submitted as an ambitious dissertation at the University of Innsbruck, the young Tyrolean historian and archivist Gerald Steinacher tackles some difficult, yet important questions: How was the postwar situation of South Tyrol influenced or even pre-determined by the activities of the local and regional resistance, first to Mussolini's *fascist rule* and then to Hitler's military occupation? And how crucial were the activities of the various Allied intelligence services in the *Operationszone Alpenvorland*, i.e. in the provinces of Bolzano/Bozen, Trento/Trient and Belluno, during the last two years of World War II? Although the formerly heated and controversial issue of South Tyrol has been much appeased since Austria joined the European Union in 1995, Steinacher's book clearly has the potential to stir both Austria and Italy to re-examine the historical evidence surrounding the last turbulent months of the war and the early chaotic weeks after the surrender of the German Armed Forces in early May 1945.[22]

Steinacher has assembled an impressive fabric of hitherto unknown documentation about the main protagonists in the military and intelligence struggles in Northern Italy, researched in the National Archives (NA) of the United States in College Park, Maryland and in the Public Record Office (PRO) in London/Kew. Moreover, the author has ploughed through several state and private archives in Italy, Germany, Austria, and Switzerland. While the lack of Russian documentation is due to the Soviet absence from the region, the lack of French sources may have the effect of distorting the over-all Allied impact on the further evolution of the South Tyrol question in international politics. The strong emphasis on Anglo-American documentation can easily be explained: The records of the American intelligence organization OSS (Office of Strategic Services) in Record Group 226 at the National Archives have gradually and continually been opened since 1983 and have now reached a degree of accessibility of well over 90%; this archival availability is unparalleled. Although the archives of the former East-German *Staatssicherheit* (*Stasi*) have been entirely opened to research since the collapse of the German Democratic Republic, extensive parts of the *Stasi*-archives have been annihilated during the last weeks and months of this expansive security apparatus, particularly the records of the foreign intelligence branch, the *Hauptverwaltung Aufklärung* (*HVA*). This has not happened to any of the records of the OSS and of its short-time successor, the SSU (Strategic Services Unit). Furthermore, ample documentation exists on the work of the various U.S. military intelligence units which had been at work in Northern Italy during the war and during the period of the Allied military occupation and administration of Italy. It must be added here, however, that the author appears not to have consulted some of these records, particularly those of the American Counter Intelligence Corps (CIC), in the research for his book.

The British case concerning access to intelligence documentation is quite different still. The British government has long maintained a policy of silence and restriction on the more sensitive areas of diplomacy and military engagement in anything even faintly related to British intelligence endeavors abroad. To this day not a single document pertaining to the activities of the most important British foreign intelligence organization, the Secret Intelligence Service (SIS), has been released for historical research. Only recently London has started to open the door for general research into other secret operations before 1945, but ever so selectively. Thus, a carefully chosen array of archival holdings of the domestic Security Service MI5 has been made available at the Public Record Office; more significantly in the context of the topic under review, the fragmentary holdings of the British war-time SOE, the Special Operations Executive, has been open to research since the mid-1990s.[23] Gerald Steinacher is one of the first researchers on Central European issues to make extensive use of these. If the important academic sub-discipline called intelligence studies is to take root in countries like Austria, Italy, the Czech Republic, and other new democracies in Eastern Europe, we need more studies of the quality and archival density of Steinacher's on South Tyrol.

Recent years have seen the rise of several substantive studies on the South Tyrol question, mainly produced and published, though not exclusively, in the Austrian Tyrol proper.[24] Steinacher has therefore been able to build on a well-documented corpus on the dramatic developments of this central European region. However, studies of the intelligence activities of the various secret and subversive organizations and agents both during the war and in the immediate postwar period constitute an important dimension which has been missing so far. This is why the emphasis of this book lies on hitherto largely unknown organizations, operations, occurrences, and individual agents, who worked more or less successfully for their respective causes. The author has managed to question and even destroy many a myth and legend, as, for example, that of the chief of the *Comitato Liberazione Nazionale* (*CLN*) in Bozen, Bruno de Angelis, who was said to have conspired for the securing of the Brenner border for the new democratic Italian state. Steinacher, however, proves conclusively that the OSS/Italy, which was dominated by Italo-Americans with close connections to the Italian *Servizio Informazioni Militari* (*SIM*), was totally geared towards the re-establishment of the *status quo ante* in Northern Italy. No conspiracy on the part of the CLNAI (Comitato Liberazione Nazionale Alta Italia) was therefore needed in order to achieve that goal.

The loosely formulated and mainly historically motivated reservations of the OSS analysts in Washington towards the official, restorative line of the American State Department had little impact on the OSS men in the field who saw the Austrians not only as victims but also as collaborators of the Nazi revolution. Interestingly, the consistent initiative in the question of South Tyrol lay with the British, both in the field and at the center of British diplomacy and politics in London.

Steinacher also unearthed a hitherto totally ignored or unknown Austrian resistance group by the name of *Patria*, closely connected to the South Tyrolean *Andreas-Hofer-Bund* (*AHB*), which had established close ties to the Austrian-German section of the SOE in Berne, and which also managed to get a good measure of support from the Swiss. *Patria's* activities were not restricted to exile politics; it organized resistance activities in most parts of Austria and also in South Tyrol; by March 1945 it had managed to get the support of the French and British intelligence services and finally even of the British government. Its Swiss branch was led by Wilhelm Bruckner, an Austrian patriot with pro-monarchist but also anti-American leanings. He personally enjoyed the respect and support of the French and British. However, the Americans put their money on Fritz Molden's *Provisorisches Österreichisches Nationalkomitee* (*POEN*) and the *O5* resistance network. The OSS-operative Fritz Molden managed to secure the attention and support not only of the Americans—even into the postwar era in Austria—but also of Karl Gruber, the provisional governor of Tyrol and later Austrian foreign minister, who facilitated Molden's entry into the political, diplomatic, and press elites of the new Austria. Hans Egartner (*AHB*) and Wilhelm Bruckner (*Patria*), on the other hand, fell by the wayside of postwar Austrian history as both their resistance organizations became not only marginalized but soon fell into disrepute and, as in the case of *Patria*, total oblivion in the new Austria.[25] And South Tyrol quickly became enmeshed in the maelstrom of the emerging cold war.[26] Steinacher traces and illustrates the tragedy which befell the Austrian patriots Egartner and Bruckner. Both were to *become personae non gratae*, the one in South Tyrol, the other in Switzerland. Steinacher should be commended for recovering the contributions of these resistance fighters hitherto ignored by historical resistance analysis in Austria. Steinacher's research also suggests that the traditional tale of the Austrian resistance, particularly its contacts to Allied intelligence organizations, might have to be newly investigated and possibly rewritten. It appears, furthermore, that the elaborate accounts of the Molden brothers have provided a highly selective analysis of Austrian resistance at best.[27]

Though Steinacher's book contains many a relevant historical story and detail (not the least in its documentary section), it also suffers from inaccuracies and careless editing. Just a few examples must suffice. The records of the Allied Commission for Austria (ACA) are grouped in FO 1020 not FO 371, which is the General Correspondence Series at the

PRO (p. 337). By the same token, John McCaffery was chief of the Central European Section at SOE Berne, not director of a British wartime intelligence organization (p. 13); and the OSS operation GREENUP in which Fred Mayer was to play an important part was not operative until late February 1945 and therefore could not have been in contact with the Ötztal partisans at the end of 1944 (p. 118).[28] However, these and other inaccuracies cannot detract from the value and significance of this monographic study which respresents a major step towards putting the new historical sub-discipline of intelligence studies on the map in Austria.

It is to be hoped that more interest can be stirred among the young generation of historians of contemporary history for the genuine contributions and insights that can be deduced from the difficult but rewarding research of the role and influence of intelligence organizations and their work in wartime and peace.

Notes

1. For an earlier attempt to address some of the issues presented here see Siegfried Beer, "Intelligence Studies: The Case of Austria," in *A Flourishing Craft: Teaching Intelligence Studies*, ed. Russell G. Swenson, Occasional Papers Number Five (Washington, DC: Joint Military Intelligence College, 1999), 143-53.

2. See for example Siegfried Beer, "Von der russischen zur britischen Besetzung der Steiermark. Berichte des amerikanischen Geheimdienstes OSS aus dem Jahre 1945," *Blätter für Heimatkunde* 59 (1985): 103-20; idem "ARCEL, CASSIA, REDBIRD. Die Widerstandsgruppe Maier-Messner und der amerikanische Kriegsgeheimdienst OSS in Bern, Istanbul und Algier 1943/44," in *Jahrbuch 1993* (Vienna: Dokumentationsarchiv des österreichischen Widerstandes, 1993), 75-100; idem, "Early CIA Reports on Austria, 1947-1949," *Contemporary Austrian Studies,* vol. 5, *Austrian Historical Memory and National Identity,* ed. Günter Bischof and Anton Pelinka (1997): 247-88; and idem, "Research and Analysis about Austria, 1941-1949: American Intelligence Studies on the Reconstruction of Central Europe," *Wiener Beiträge zur Geschichte der Neuzeit* 24 (2000): 192-210.

3. Several papers delivered at these symposia have now been published in Erwin A. Schmidl, ed., *Österreich im Frühen Kalten Krieg 1945-1958. Spione, Partisanen, Kriegspläne* (Vienna: Böhlau, 2000). Both conferences were favorably reviewed by the media. See *Die Presse,* 27 December 1999 ("Wien als ein Tummelplatz der Agenten – Mythos und Wirklichkeit").

4. Among the topics covered by the author over the years are the lecture courses on "Intelligence in War and Peace" (1994), the "The CIA and KGB in the Cold War "(1998), and "The Stasi in the System of the SED-State" (2001). For a discussion of the state of intelligence teaching over the last decade, cf. Judith M. Fontaine, *Teaching Intelligence in the 1990s. A Survey of College and University Courses on the Subject of Intelligence* (Washington, DC: National Intelligence Study Center, 1992).

5. An annotated bibliography of such intelligence journals lists roughly150 publication, see Hayden B. Peake, *The Reader's Guide to Intelligence Periodicals* (Washington, DC: National Intelligence Center, 1992).

6. See Meredith Hindley, "Teaching Intelligence Project," *Intelligence and National Security* 15 (Spring 2000): 191-218.

7. Initially called Secret Service Bureau, it developed within a year into a home department responsible for counter-espionage (later MI5) and then into a foreign intelligence department, the forerunner of MI6. See Christopher Andrew, *Secret Service: The Making of the British Intelligence Community* (London: Heinemann, 1985).

8. For a brief overview of the beginnings of civilian intelligence in the United States see Siegfried Beer, *Target Central Europe: American Intelligence Efforts Regarding Nazi and Early Postwar Austria, 1941-1947*, Working Papers in Austrian Studies 97.1 (Minneapolis: Center for Austrian Studies, 1997), 1f.

9. See Siegfried Beer, "Von Alfred Redl zum 'Dritten Mann'. Österreich und ÖsterreicherInnen im internationalen Geheimdienstwesen, 1918-1949," *Geschichte und Gegenwart* 16 (1997): 3-25.

10. Secret and personal letter from Coburn Kidd to Francis Williams, 7 October 1950, in National Archives (NA), Record Group (RG) 43, Lot M-88, Box 7, cited by Günter Bischof in *Contemporary Austrian Studies* 5 (1997), 12. This particular issue of CAS also included a ground-breaking Forum discussion entitled "Toward a History of Austrian Intelligence Studies"; CAS has continued to treat intelligence studies seriously, while, for example, the oldest Austrian contemporary history journal, *Zeitgeschichte,* has yet to discover the increasing importance of that new historical sub-discipline.

11. There are plenty of other cases which have not yet made their way into the national history books. Let me just mention some of the names connected to these cases: Theodor Maly, Arnold Deutsch, Hede Massing, Peter Smolka, and Gustav Hochenbichler.

12. The following are selected examples of their work: Thomas Albrich, *Exodus durch Österreich. Die jüdischen Flüchtlinge 1945-1948*, Innsbrucker Forschungen zur Zeitgeschichte 1 (Innsbruck: Haymon, 1987); Edda Engelke, "Zum Thema Spionage gegen die Sowjetunion," in *Österreich im Frühen Kalten Krieg,* 119-35; Michael Gehler, ed., *Verspielte Selbstbestimmung? Die Südtirolfrage 1945/46 in US-Geheimdienstberichten und österreichischen Akten. Eine Dokumentation* (Innsbruck: Universitätsverlag Wagner, 1996); Stefan Karner, ed., *Geheime Akten des KGB. "Margarita Ottilinger"* (Graz: Leykam, 1992); and Oliver Rathkolb, ed., *Gesellschaft und Politik am Beginn der Zweiten Republik. Vertrauliche Berichte der US-Militäradministration aus Österreich 1945 in englischer Originalfassung* (Wien: Böhlau, 1985).

13. Examples of their works are: Ralph W. Brown, "Stalin Tells Us that War is Inevitable': What American Military Intelligence in Austria Learned from Soviet Defectors, 1946-1948," unpublished paper, 1995; James T. Carafano, "'Waltzing into the Cold War'. US Army Intelligence for Postwar Austria, 1944-1948," *Contemporary Austrian Studies,* vol. 7, *The Vranitzky Era in Austria,* ed. Günter Bischof, Anton Pelinka, and Ferdinand Karlhofer (1999): 165-89; and Timothy Naftali, "Creating the Myth of the Alpenfestung: Allied Intelligence and the Collapse of the Nazi-State," *Contemporary Austrian Studies* 5 (1997): 203-46.

14. Manfred Fuchs, *Der österreichische Geheimdienst. Das zweitälteste Gewerbe der Welt* (Vienna: Ueberreuter, 1993); Harald Irnberger, *Nelkenstrauß ruft Praterstern. Am Beispiel Österreich: Funktion und Arbeitsweise geheimer Nachrichtendienste in einem neutralen Staat* (Vienna: Promedia, 1983); Kid Möchel, *Der geheime Krieg der Agenten. Spionagedrehscheibe Wien* (Hamburg: Rasch und Röhring, 1997); and Hans Wolker,

Schatten über Österreich. Das Bundesheer und seine geheimen Dienste (Vienna: Promedia, 1993).

15. Peer de Silva, *Sub Rosa: The CIA and the uses of Intelligence* (New York: Times Books, 1978); Wilhelm Höttl, *Einsatz für das Reich. Im Auslandsgeheimdienst des Dritten Reiches* (Koblenz: S. Bubblies, 1997); William Hood, *Mole: The True Story of the First Russian Intelligence Officer Recruited by the CIA* (New York: Ballantine Books, 1982; 2nd ed.: Random House, 1993); Erwin Kemper, *Verrat an Österreich* (Vienna: Zeitschriftenbuch, 1996); James V. Milano, *Soldiers, Spies, and the Ratline. America's Undeclared War against the Soviets* (Washington, DC: Brassey's, 1995) and Michael Sika, *Mein Protokoll. Innenansichten einer Republik* (St. Pölten: NP Buchverlag, 2000).

16. Among these the following must be mentioned: Benjamin and Ulrike Davy, Robert Fuchs, Walter Hauptmann, Markus Purkart, Ingrid Schätz and Helmut Widder. Examples of their contributions are: Benjamin and Ulrike Davy, eds., *Gezähmte Polizeigewalt? Aufgaben und Neuordnung der Sicherheitspolizei in Österreich* (Vienna: Manz, 1991); Markus Purkart, "Staatspolizei, Heeresnachrichtenamt und Abwehramt. Die österreichischen Geheimdienste aus der Perspektive parlamentarischer Transparenz und Kontrolle. Eine politikwissenschaftliche Analyse zur österreichischen Demokratie," M.A. thesis, Universität Wien, 1998; and Helmut Widder, "Die parlamentarische Kontrolle von Staatspolizei und militärischen Nachrichtendiensten in Österreich," in *Für Staat und Recht. Festschrift für Herbert Schambeck*, ed. Johannes Hengstschläger (Berlin: Duncker&Humblot, 1994), 647-61.

17. For reasons of space I restrict myself to just one of their contributions respectively: Richard J. Aldrich, *Espionage, Security and Intelligence in Britain 1945-1970* (Manchester: Manchester University Press, 1998); Christopher Andrew, *For the President's Eyes Only. Secret Intelligence and the Presidency from Washington to Bush* (New York: HarperCollins, 1995); F.H. Hinsley et al., *British Intelligence in the Second World War*, 6 vols. (London: Her Majesty's Stationary Office, 1984 ff.); Rhodri Jeffrys-Jones, *The CIA and American Democracy* (New Haven: Yale University Press, 1989); David Stafford, *Secret Agent. The True Story of the Special Operations Executive* (London: BBC Worldwide Limited, 2000); and D.C. Watt, *How War Came. The Immediate Origins of the Second World War* (New York: Pantheon Books, 1989).

18. Wesley Wark, *The Ultimate Enemy. British Intelligence and Nazi Germany 1933-1939* (Ithaca: Cornell University Press, 1985).

19. H. Bradfield Westerfield, ed., *Inside CIA's Private World* (New Haven: Yale University Press, 1995); Ernest R. May, ed., *Knowing One's Enemies: Intelligence Assessment before the Two World Wars* (Princeton: Princeton University Press, 1986); Timothy Naftali and Aleksandr Fursenko, *"A Hell of a Gamble": The Secret History of the Cuban Missile Crisis* (New York: W.W. Norton&Co, 1998); John Prados, *Presidents' Secret Wars: CIA and Pentagon Covert Operations since World War II* (New York: William Morrow, 1986); Bradley F. Smith, *Sharing Secrets with Stalin. How the Allies Traded Intelligence 1941-1945* (Lawrence: University Press of Kansas, 1996); and Robin Winks, *Cloak and Gown: Scholars in America's Secret War, 1939-1961* (New York: William Morrow, 1987).

20. The following books are representative of their work: Roy Godson, ed., *Comparing Foreign Intelligence. The U.S., the U.S.S.R., the U.K. and the Third World* (McLean: Pergamon, 1988); Loch K. Johnson, *Secret Agencies. U.S. Intelligence in a Hostile World* (New Haven: Yale University Press, 1996); and Jeffery T. Richelson, *A Century of Spies. Intelligence in the Twentieth Century* (New York: Oxford University Press, 1995).

21. Among their contributions are: Jürgen Heideking and Christof Mauch, eds., *American Intelligence and the German Resistance to Hitler. A Documentary History* (Boulder: Westview Press, 1996); Wolfgang Krieger and Jürgen Weber, eds., *Spionage für den Frieden? Nachrichtendienste in Deutschland während des Kalten Krieges* (Munich: Olzog Verlag, 1997); Christof Mauch, *Schattenkrieg gegen Hitler. Das Dritte Reich im Visier der amerikanischen Geheimdienste 1941 bis 1945* (Stuttgart: Deutsche Verlags-Anstalt, 1999); and Gerard Aalders and Cees Wiebes, *The Art of Cloaking* (Amsterdam: Amsterdam University Press, 1995).

22. See Hans Heiss and Gustav Pfeifer, eds., *Südtirol – Stunde Null? Kriegsende 1945-46*, Veröffentlichungen des Südtiroler Landesarchivs 10 (Innsbruck: Studienverlag, 2000).

23. See *SOE Operations in Western Europe. A Guide to the Newly Released Records in the Public Record Office* (London/Kew: Public Record Office, 1998).

24. Among these publications the following are perhaps the most important: Rolf Steininger, *Los von Rom? Die Südtirolfrage 1945/46 und das Gruber-De Gaspari Abkommen,* Innsbrucker Forschungen zur Zeitgeschichte 2 (Innsbruck: Haymon, 1987); Hans Woller, ed., *Italien und die Großmächte 1943-1949,* Schriftenreihe der Vierteljahrshefte für Zeitgeschichte 57 (München: 1988); Rolf Steininger, *Südtirol im 20. Jahrhundert. Vom Leben und Überleben einer Minderheit* (Innsbruck: Studienverlag, 1997); Margareth Lun, "Der Zusammenbruch 1945. Das Vorspiel zum Ende in Italien," *Der Schlern* 68 (1994): 507-19; and Eva Pfanzelter, "Südtirol wird amerikanisch: Der Einmarsch und die Etablierung der Militärregierung im Mai 1945" *Zeitgeschichte* 27 (2000): 348-65.

25. This state of affairs is well reflected in the existing, mainly autobiographically motivated literature on this episode in Austrian history. See Fritz Molden, *Fepolinski und Waschlapski auf dem berstenden Stern. Bericht einer unruhigen Jugend* (Vienna: Molden, 1976): idem, *Die Feuer in der Nacht. Opfer und Sinn des österreichischen Widerstandes 1938-1945* (Vienna: Amalthea, 1988).

26. See Rolf Steininger, "Die Südtirolfrage," *Archiv für Sozialgeschichte* 40 (2000): 209.

27. See Otto Molden, *Der Ruf des Gewissens. Der österreichische Freiheitskampf 1938-1945* (Vienna: Herold, 1958); and idem, *Odyssee meines Lebens und die Gründung Europas in Alpbach* (Vienna: Amalthea, 2001).

28. See Gerald Schwab, *OSS Agents in Hitler's Heartland. Destination Innsbruck* (Westport: Praeger, 1996).

1968 in Austria

Alexandra Friedrich

Historical events are usually associated with specific dates, their actors, their participants, their origins, their short-term and long-term influences, and so on. Especially an episode's consequences for the future determine whether it deserves to be categorized as *historical fact* and hence become part of general knowledge, or whether it will be obliterated from people's memory. *Historical facts* generally produce a huge body of contemporary literature. They nonetheless profit from anniversaries that revive the public's memory and stimulate its interest in the event. Historians in particular take advantage of such anniversaries by addressing the thus generated demand for additional studies with newer, fresher, and better researched analyses.

In 1998 an important anniversary was celebrated: the thirtieth recurrence of the frequently mythologized year *1968* and the so-called *1968 movement*. This year represents not a single incident but a variety of events: the Vietnam War reached a preliminary peak with 540,000 Americans fighting in Southeast Asia; at the beginning of the year the Tet Offensive proved that the North Vietnamese enemy was nowhere close to giving up; the worldwide protest against the war grew and became a uniting factor in the various national student movements; the general readiness for violence increased as demonstrated by the assassinations of Martin Luther King Jr. and Robert F. Kennedy, the shooting of Rudi Dutschke, the Democratic national convention in Chicago, and the Soviet invasion of Czechoslovakia, ending the Prague Spring; extraparliamentary oppositions, demanding manifold political and social reforms, gained more and more public attention; and the youth, mostly students, experimented with new forms of life-style, including free sexuality, drugs, alternative music and clothing (*Hippie-culture*).[1]

The thirtieth anniversary of 1968 has once again sparked the general public's interest in the elusive events and developments associated with this year. Many historians and other social scientists all over the world answered their respective society's reawakened desire for new interpretations producing numerous books and articles on either the overall 1968 movement or particular aspects of it, and conducting national, regional, or local analyses, as well as comparative studies. The *nineteen-sixty-eighters* themselves also continued to add their personal recollections to the steadily growing historiography of this topic.[2]

Austria's scholarly and societal interest in 1968 and its consequences, however, seems to differ from that of other countries. Whereas, for example, German and American historians generated a considerable amount of studies dealing with various aspects of 1968, hardly any Austrian contributions appeared in the year of its thirtieth anniversary. Fritz Keller published his most comprehensive study on the 1968 movement in Austria already in 1983, the fifteenth anniversary, and revised it for the movement's twentieth anniversary in 1988. What are the reasons for this phenomenon? Lack of general interest? Lack of a story to tell? Lack of sources? This essay intends to answer some of these questions and to propose additional research areas.[3]

Looking at the list of Austrian publications on 1968 in the past twenty years, it is conceivable to conclude that everything of interest for the general public and scholars alike has already been said and written down. Looking closer at the variety of the examined topics, however, reveals considerable gaps in the literature. Although the universities promoted studies that analyzed the movement's theoretical background, its contribution to Austria's cultural development, or its regional and local occurrence, the *published* Austrian literature on 1968 still lacks these approaches. The debates in other countries on the origins and consequences of 1968 for their respective societies failed to encourage Austrian scholars to put their country's 1968 experience into a European or international context. To this day, no Austrian study compares Austria's 1968 movement with that of other countries, although Ingo Juchler demonstrated in his excellent book *Die Studentenbewegungen in den Vereinigten Staaten und der Bundesrepublik Deutschland der sechziger Jahre* how much historians and social scientists can profit from such a comparative method.

In *Die zahme Revolution*, one of the few Austrian publications on the occasion of the 1968 movement's thirtieth anniversary, Paulus Ebner and Karl Vocelka recognized these shortcomings in the Austrian literature and promised to address some of them. "For the first time the 'Austrian 1968' will be introduced here as comprehensively as possible: from the basic requirements in the economic wonderland to the developments of the pop culture to the huge demonstrations and happenings (keyword 'orgy in *Hörsaal* I' [lecture hall I])." The authors also left no doubt about their premise: "The 68ers had hardly any real success in the political or economic realm, but rather in the social-political and cultural ones. *There* it came to the revolutions in 1968 that still form our everyday life; *there* those social freedoms and cultural standards developed without which Austria would look different today."[4]

Ebner and Vocelka's study fulfills its promise of extensively describing the Austrian 1968 movement in its various manifestations. The authors briefly summarize Austria's post-World War II economic and political situation, outline the student revolt in other parts of the world, and introduce the reader to the precursors of the Austrian 1968, the period between 1965 and 1967. The year 1968 is dealt with in detail: Ebner and Vocelka familiarize the reader with the agenda of the political parties, analyze the media, the catholic church, and popular and high culture, and follow the student protest inside and outside the universities. They devote, for example, almost a whole chapter to the notorious incident in *Hörsaal I* on 7 June 1968—the teach-in on *art and revolution*—and its consequences. The authors also look quickly at the student movement in 1969 before they end with a devastating conclusion:

> Compared with the ideals of the year 1968 the social reality of the year 1998 is disastrous: nobody talks of Marxism anymore, even the term socialism seems to have been discredited since 1989. Capitalism has triumphed everywhere and now reveals its true face in Europe as well. And that has, after all, nothing to do with "social market economy," but rather with a complete flexibility to the disadvantage of the employees, with the maximization of profits at all costs ("shareholder value"), and with the weakening of unions on all levels—not even "conservative" values such as Sunday rest or the family will be protected.[5]

Although the book is relatively short (216 pages of text plus bibliography and index), it clearly proves that 1968 in Austria was more than a "hot quarter of an hour," as the title of Keller's 1983 treatise indicated. Hence lack of a story cannot be the reason for the comparatively neglected treatment of 1968 in Austrian literature. Neither can lack of sources explain this phenomenon. Although Ebner and Vocelka provide merely occasional notes, the topic's age and therefore the availability of potential interview partners as well as the bibliography of published sources at the end of the book—albeit rather short—confirm the wealth of existing material.

Yet Ebner and Vocelka's study also shows that more in-depth analyses are needed. Certain aspects of the Austrian 1968 movement deserve a closer examination than they receive in this book. The interesting, though cursory chapter on Austria's political parties during 1968 and their reaction to the student protest, particularly that of the Austrian Socialist Party (SPÖ), raises more questions than it answers. Bruno Kreisky, since 1967 the party's new chairman and initially the hope of the party's left wing, and his role in delimiting the SPÖ from the student movement and the New Left require more detail and analysis than can be presented on three pages. The same holds true for the treatment of the Catholic church's reaction to the social environment of 1968. Although Ebner and Vocelka describe the split within the Austrian Catholic church between conservatives and progressives, particularly regarding the controversial anti-baby pill, they fail to put this development within its wider international context. The influence of the liberation theology on the Austrian clergy as well as on the religious segment of the student protesters and the Catholic fraternities lacks proper examination in this book. It provides ample material for a study in its own right.[6]

Ebner and Vocelka's *Die zahme Revolution* clearly demonstrates the need for more comparative analyses. Although the authors frequently refer to the importance of the West German model for the Austrian student protest, their work does not present a systematic comparison between the two movements. The West German student protest had one of its origins in the young generation's inquiry about its parent generation's involvement in the Third Reich and questioned the Federal Republic's general mastering of its Nazi past. The Austrian students dealt with similar issues, as the notorious case of university professor Taras Borodajkewycz testifies to. Borodajkewycz escaped de-Nazification, taught at the Austrian Economics University in Vienna, and continually propagated his anti-Semitic tirades. In the early 1960s an increasing number of students at the university voiced their outrage at his behavior, demanded Borodajkewycz's dismissal, and finally managed to have him removed. Was the questioning of the past an overall generation problem and did it equally influence the West German and Austrian students? Did the West German experience spread across the borders and make the Austrians more sensitive to the topic? What other common issues did the two movements share? Where did they diverge? These questions still require more research.[7]

Ebner and Vocelka's study also neglects to put the Austrian 1968 experience into its wider international context. Although the authors provide a brief excursion into the protest movements of other European countries and the United States, they do not trace the impact of these movements on Austria. Did France's unique experience of temporary solidarity between students and workers influence the initial support by the Association of Austria's Socialist Students (*VSStÖ*) of striking *Elin* plant workers in April 1968? How did the American protest against the Vietnam War contribute to the formation of the Austrian social-democratic Indochina committee and shape its actions? It remains yet to be researched how Austria's 1968 compares to France's or Italy's or the United States'.[8]

After more than thirty years Austrian scholars researching the 1968 movement, both in Austria as well as in other countries, are able to profit from the topic's international historiography. Using a theoretical framework or investigating socio-economic and socio-political phenomena, and thus following the models of some earlier Austrian studies—mostly dissertations and theses—and of many international publications, would greatly enrich the presently theory-poor Austrian literature on this topic. Whereas some aspects of the worldwide 1968 movement, such as the American civil rights conflict, might be less relevant for Austria's 1968 experience, others might prove more appropriate. By putting the Austrian experience into its international context, it might also be possible to discover some purely *Austrian* facet of the 1968 movement that would contribute to and enrich the topic's international historiography.

Let's look at some issues of the international 1968 historiography that Austrian scholars thus far have paid only minor attention to. The recent German literature on 1968, for example, poses some interesting questions whose answers might be different when put into the Austrian context. Was the 1968 movement really a *revolutionary* movement or simply a *revolt*? If it was a revolution, was it a *political, economic* or *cultural* one? Ebner and Vocelka do not explain how they arrive at their chosen terminology—*revolution*. They denounce the existence of a political or economic revolution but do not doubt that *revolutions* took place in Austria's social and cultural environment. Venanz Schubert, on the other hand, devotes a whole chapter in his book *1968. 30 Jahre da-*

nach to the ambivalence of the year 1968. According to him, the decision to call the movement associated with this year a *revolution* is a subjective one and depends on the individual's personal perception. He deems it still too early to arrive at a final evaluation. Peter von Becker does not share Schubert's caution. In "Mythos, Heldenlied, Verwünschungsarie. 30 Jahre nach der Kulturrevolte 1968," he declares that "[1968] was most of all: *no revolution*. 1968 was a cultural revolt." Von Becker nevertheless admits that this cultural revolt succeeded in changing the political culture of Europe and, more concretely, that of the United States because it had its origins in the political sphere. Even if Schubert and von Becker cannot offer a universally valid definition to determine whether the 1968 movement qualifies to be called a revolution or not, the question certainly deserves to be further researched, also in the Austrian context. Where did the Austrian 1968 movement have its origins? Can its influence on Austria's contemporary political culture and society help determine whether Austria really experienced *revolutions*, as Ebner and Vocelka claim, or whether 1968 in Austria was merely a revolt?[9]

Another issue that has not been sufficiently dealt with in the Austrian 1968 historiography is the definition of *1968*. Most publications on 1968 do not analyze exclusively this year but take it as synonymous for the protest and youth movement that swept through all continents at various points throughout the 1960s and early 1970s. Ebner and Vocelka, for example, focus their study on explaining the reactions of various components of Austria's society to the 1968 movement and thereby describe how Austria experienced 1968. A clear definition of what the movement is or encompasses is missing.[10]

For comparative studies the explanation of the term's meaning is essential. Without reducing *1968* or *the 1968 movement* to commonly accepted elements no meaningful comparison of 1968 in different countries is possible. Hans Günter Hockerts, for example, reduces 1968 to three variables that render the movement international: a) the high political mobilization of young people around the world; b) the international or global character of the movement; c) the non-exclusive focus on university reforms. He also considers the anti-colonialism movement a common aspect of the international 1968. Ingo-Juchler likewise defined Third World liberation movements and theories as integral parts of the world wide 1968 movement and studied their influence on the West German and American student movements. The protest against the Vietnam War as *the* unifying element of the international 1968 movement is another useful category for comparisons between various *national* 1968 movements. Thus far Austrian scholars refrained from pursuing such an approach to the analysis of Austria's 1968. Studying the common phenomena within various *national* 1968 movement, however, contributes to a more accurate description of what the overall 1968 movement was. Together with the strictly national characteristics of Austria's 1968, such comparisons would contribute to a comprehensive definition of the Austrian movement.[11]

Regional and local studies of the Austrian 1968 movement serve the same purpose. Karl Stocker demonstrated in his micro-analysis of the Styrian 1968 movement that it reached all parts of Austria, despite the fact that Vienna was its center. Ewald Hiebl accomplished the same result with his thesis on the student movement in Salzburg. Austria's 1968 will not be complete unless more studies like these examine how the 1968 movement affected the provinces, how they reacted, who participated, and how the *Bundesländer* helped shape a distinctly Austrian 1968. Such micro-histories are also necessary to determine the long-time effect of the 1968 movement in Austria.[12]

Because of its diversity and elusiveness, the 1968 movement needs to be approached from and analyzed within various theoretical frameworks. In 1983 Joachim Giller already looked at the 1968 movement as a *new social movement*, as did Hiebl almost ten years later. The latter specifically examined the Salzburg student movement's actions and explored its themes as pertinent analytical categories for the study of *new social movements*. In order to learn more about the origins or the character of the 1968 movement it is helpful to determine which elements make 1968 a *new social movement* and whether such an international protest movement could have been caused by a mere generational change and concurrently shifting values, regardless of the specifics of the 1960s (Vietnam War, anti-colonialism, civil rights conflict).[13]

Lack of a story to tell or lack of sources do not explain the few publications in Austria on 1968 on the occasion of its thirtieth anniversary. Is thus the lack of general interest in the topic to blame? Are Ebner and Vocelka right when they conclude that "thirty years later, we have repressed the movement of the year 1968 itself or have transfigured it—depending on one's own position. For us ... the studying of this year shows most of all how far Austrian society has moved away from the thinking, the problems, and also from the ideals of this time"?[14] Did the social-cultural successes of the 1968 revolt become so integrated into the present life-style that nobody feels the need to trace their origins? Or are the political and economic failures of the 1968 movement so visible and ubiquitous in today's political culture that nobody deems it necessary to recount what might have happened? Ebner and Vocelka's book as well as the comparable historiography in other countries unmistakably demonstrate—at least to this author—that Austria's 1968 deserves more scholarly and general attention and still offers many untouched areas that await to be researched.

Notes

1. At the beginning of 2001—although not an anniversary of 1968—the German public also shows an intensified interest in the events of 1968 and their aftermath because of Foreign Minister Joschka Fischer's allegedly *militant* past as a revolutionary during the 1970s. It remains to be seen whether this affair will spur a renewed wave of scholarly and popular literature. See, for example, Ekkehart Krippendorff, "Es war einmal die Revolution. Die zweite Gründung der Bundesrepublik fand auf der Strasse statt—ein 68-er erinnert sich," *Süddeutsche Zeitung*, 16 January 2001; and Ulrich K. Preuss, "Geschichte auf krummen Wegen. '1968'—oder: Die schwierige und widerspruchsvolle Geburt der liberalen Demokratie aus dem Geist der Rebellion," *Ibid.*, 3 March 2001.

2. See for example Philipp Gassert and Pavel A. Richter, eds., *1968 in West Germany: A Guide to Sources and Literature of the Extra-Parliamentary Opposition* (Washington, DC: German Historical Institute, 1998); Carole Fink, Philipp Gassert, and Detlef Junker, eds., *1968: The World Transformed* (Washington, DC: German Historical Institute and Cambridge University Press, 1998); Ingrid Gilcher-Holtey, ed., *1968: Vom Ereignis zum Gegenstand der Geschichtswissenschaft* (Göttingen: Vandenhoeck & Ruprecht, 1998); Christiane Landgrebe and Jörg Plath, eds., *'68 und die Folgen. Ein unvollständiges Lexikon* (Berlin: Argon, 1998); Tilman Fichter and Siegward Lönnendonker, *Macht und Ohnmacht der Studenten. Kleine Geschichte des SDS* (Hamburg: Rotbuch Verlag, 1998); Wolfgang Kraushaar, *Neunzehnhundertachtundsechzig (1968). Das Jahr, das alles verändert hat* (Munich: Piper, 1998); and Hans Heiss, "Bewegte Gesellschaft: Südtirol 1968," *Geschichte und Region/Storia e regione* 7 (1998): 57-100. The earlier anniversary literature on 1968 includes, for example, Franz Schneider, ed., *Dienstjubiläum einer Revolte. '1968' und 25 Jahre* (Mainz: Hase und Köhler, 1993); Ulrich Chaussy, *Die drei Leben des Rudi Dutschke. Eine Biographie* (Berlin: Links Verlag, 1993); Werner Kohn et al., *In Bamberg war der Teufel los* (Bamberg: Collibri-Verlag, 1993); idem, *In der Provinz. 1968* (Berlin: Nishen, 1988); Tom Hayden, *Reunion: A Memoir* (New York: Random House, 1988); Ronald Fraser, ed., *1968: A Student Generation in Revolt: An International Oral History* (New York: Pantheon Books, 1988); David Caute, *The Year of the Barricades: A Journey Through 1968* (New York: Harper & Row, 1988); David Farber, *Chicago '68* (Chicago: University of Chicago Press, 1988); Richard N. Goodwin, *Remembering America: A Voice from the Sixties* (Boston: Little, Brown & Co., 1988); Antoine Artous, ed., *Retours sur Mai* (Montreuil: La Brèche-Pec, 1988); Laurent Joffrin, *Mai 68: Histoire des événements* (Paris: Seuil, 1988); Geneviève Dreyfus-Armand and Laurent Gervereau, eds., *Mai 68: Les mouvements étudiants en France et dans le monde* (Nanterre: BDIC, 1988); Angelo Quattrocchi, *E quel maggio fu: rivoluzione* (Turin: Nautilus, 1988); Claus Leggewie, "1968: Ein Laboratorium der postindustriellen Gesellschaft: Über die Tradition der antiautoritären Revolte seit den 60er Jahren," *Aus Politik und Zeitgeschichte* B20/88 (13 May 1988): 3-15; Tobias Mündemann, *Die 68er ... und was aus ihnen geworden ist* (Munich: Heyne, 1988); Tilman Fichter, *SDS und*

SPD. Parteilichkeit jenseits der Partei (Opladen: Westdeutscher Verlag, 1988); Bernd Rabehl, *Am Ende der Utopie. Die politische Geschichte der Freien Universität Berlin* (Berlin: Argon, 1988); Lothar Baier et al., *Die Früchte der Revolte. Über die Veränderung der politischen Kultur durch die Studentenbewegung* (Berlin: Wagenbach, 1988). This listing of *anniversary literature* does not include the publications on the year 1968 that appeared in-between anniversaries, such as Siegward Lönnendonker, Bernd Rabehl, and Jochen Staadt, *Die antiautoritäre Revolte* (Wiesbaden: Westdeutscher Verlag, 2001); Wolfgang Kraushaar, *Neunzehnhundertachtundsechzig (1968) als Mythos, Chiffre und Zäsur* (Hamburg: Hamburger Ed., 2000); Ingo Juchler's comparative study, *Die Studentenbewegungen in den Vereinigten Staaten und der Bundesrepublik Deutschland der sechziger Jahre. Eine Untersuchung hinsichtlich ihrer Beeinflussung durch Befreiungsbewegungen und –theorien aus der Dritten Welt* (Berlin: Dunker & Humbolt, 1996); David Burner, *Making Peace with the 60s* (Princeton, NJ: Princeton University Press, 1996); Gretchen Dutschke's biography *Wir hatten ein barbarisches, schönes Leben. Rudi Dutschke* (Cologne: Kiepenheuer & Witsch, 1996); or David Fraser et al., ed., *The Sixties: From Memory to History* (Chapel Hill: University of North Carolina Press, 1994).

3. Among the few books and articles on 1968 that were published in Austria in 1998 are Paulus Ebner and Karl Vocelka, *Die zahme Revolution. '68 und was davon blieb* (Vienna: Ueberreuter, 1998); Bärbel Danneberg and Robert Schindel, eds., *Die 68er. Eine Generation und ihr Erbe* (Vienna: Döcker, 1998); Kurt Tozzer and Günther Kallinger, *"Marschmusik für Glockenspiel." 1968: Österreich am Randes des Krieges* (St. Pölten, Austria: NP-Buchverlag, 1998); Peter Huemer, "Was blieb? Was war es? War was?" *Die Presse*, 18/19 April 1998; and Holger Rust, "Ach, Ihr Achtundsechziger!" *Trend* 3 (1998): 132-4, 137. Earlier Austrian publications include Rolf Schwendter, "Das Jahr 1968. War es eine kulturelle Zäsur?" in *Österreich 1945-1995. Gesellschaft, Politik, Kultur*, ed. Reinhard Sieder, Heinz Steinert, and Emmerich Tálos (Vienna: Verlag für Gesellschaftskritik, 1995), 166-75; Karl Stocker, "'Wir wollten alles ganz anders machen.' Die 68er Bewegung in der österreichischen Provinz. Ein Fallbeispiel," in ibid., 176-85; Christian Werner, "Para-Mächte: Von der Subversion zur politischen Kompetenz. Der studentische Befreiungsversuch der 60er Jahre und seine Fortführung durch die neuen sozialen Bewegungen im Paradigma der Transformation auf Basis der Selbstbestimmung. Ein Paradigmenvergleich," M.A. thesis, University of Vienna, 1993; Ewald Hiebl, "Kein ruhiges Plätzchen. Studentenbewegung in Salzburg 1965-1975," M.A. thesis, University of Salzburg, 1991; Maria-Rita Pacher, "Österreich 1968—Studentenbewegung in Wechselwirkung mit künstlerischen Entwicklungen," M.A. thesis, University of Graz, 1988; Wilhelm Pevny, *Die vergessenen Ziele. Wollen sich die 68er davonstehlen?* (Vienna: Europaverlag, 1988); Elisabeth Welzig, *Die 68er. Karrieren einer rebellischen Generation* (Vienna: Böhlau, 1985); Joachim Giller, "Soziale Bewegung und Wertwandel in Österreich. Von der 'Studentenbewegung' zu den 'Grünen' und 'Alternativen'," Ph.D. diss., University of Vienna, 1983; Fritz Keller, *Wien, Mai 1968—Eine heiße Viertelstunde* (Vienna: Junius, 1983); and Hildegard Weiss, "Eine Analyse ideologischer Konzepte der 'Studentenbewegung' (1966-1971)," Ph.D. diss., University of Vienna, 1974.

4. Ebner and Vocelka, *Die zahme Revolution*, 10 [emphasis in the original]. All translations from German sources are by the author, unless indicated otherwise.

5. Ibid., 214.

6. Ibid., 79-83, 106-17. Juchler's study *Die Studentenbewegungen* serves as a good model for analyzing the influence of the ideology of liberation movements on the student protest in the western world, although Juchler focuses more on Third World movements than on liberation theology.

7. For frequent references to the West German movement see Ebner and Vocelka, *Die zahme Revolution*, 145-49. On Borodajkewycz see ibid., 59-64. Ebner and Vocelka nevertheless claim that "Austria's NS-past was no topic for the student movement in Austria;" ibid., 149. In his M.A. thesis "Kein ruhiges Plätzchen" Ewald Hiebl, however, documents the Salzburg students' discussion of fascism and their handling of neo-Nazism and Austria's Nazi past, albeit without comparing it to the West German situation; Hiebl, "Kein ruhiges Plätzchen," 157-61. In their introduction to *Österreich 1945-1995* Reinhard Sieder, Heinz Steinert, and Emmerich Tálos also argue that the question "What were you in Hitler's Reich?" was often pondered but rarely posed by many members of the Austrian student movement; "Wirtschaft, Gesellschaft und Politik in der Zweiten Republik," in *Österreich 1945-1995*, 20-21.

8. Ebner and Vocelka, *Die zahme Revolution*, 26-58, 65-66, 151-55.

9. Ibid., 10; Venanz Schubert, "Die Ambivalenz von 1968. Einführung," in *1968. 30 Jahre danach*, ed. idem (St. Ottilien: EOS Verlag, 1999), 8; and Peter von Becker, "Mythos, Heldenlied, Verwünschungsarie," in *'68 und die Folgen*, 10 [emphasis added]. Reinhard Sieder, Heinz Steinert, and Emmerich Tálos define the Austrian 1968 movement as "culturally revolutionary;" see "Wirtschaft, Gesellschaft und Politik in der Zweiten Republik," in *Österreich 1945-1995*, 21. In his essay "Das Jahr 1968. War es eine kulturelle Zäsur?" Rolf Schwendter does not deal with the revolutionary character of the movement but questions whether this year even functioned as a cultural caesura in Austria. He arrives at the conclusion that the year itself does not qualify as a break but that the overall 1968 movement certainly influenced Austria's cultural scene; see Schwendter, "Das Jahr 1968. War es eine kulturelle Zäsur?" in *Österreich 1945-1995*, 166-67.

10. Ebner and Vocelka, *Die zahme Revolution*. Kurt Tozzer and Günther Kallinger, for example, chose to examine the Soviet invasion of Czechoslovakia as their contribution to Austria's literature on 1968; see *"Marschmusik für Glockenspiel."*

11. Hans Günter Hockerts, "'1968' als weltweite Bewegung," in *1968. 30 Jahre danach*, 14-15, 22, 29; and Juchler, *Die Studentenbewegungen*.

12. Stocker, "'Wir wollten alles ganz anders machen,' in *Österreich 1945-1995*, 176-85; and Hiebl, "Kein ruhiges Plätzchen." Elisabeth Welzig already traced the careers of some prominent 1968ers in *Die 68er. Karrieren einer rebellischen Generation*, and Ebner and Vocelka looked at Austria's contemporary political culture to deplore the failed success of the 1968 movement in Austria. Thus far no book-length study exists that examines the consequences of 1968 on Austria's social and cultural development along the lines of Hermann Lübbe's essay "1968. Zur kulturellen und politischen Wirkungsgeschichte in Deutschland" in *1968. 30 Jahre danach*, 185-208. Bärbel Danneberg's *Die 68er. Eine Generation und ihr Erbe* comes closest to filling this gap but still leaves room for further detailed analyses.

13. Giller, "Soziale Bewegung und Wertwandel in Österreich;" and Hiebl, "Kein ruhiges Plätzchen," 2-15, particularly 13. See also Ronald Inglehart, *Culture Shift in Advanced Industrial Society* (Princeton, NJ: Princeton University Press, 1990); and idem, *The Silent Revolution: Changing Values and Political Styles Among Western Publics* (Princeton, NJ: Princeton University Press, 1977). A study of 1968 within the framework of its ideological influences, i.e. Marxism, Maoism, the Critical School, etc., is also missing from the Austrian 1968 literature.

14. Ebner and Vocelka, *Die zahme Revolution*, 216.

BOOK REVIEWS

Evan B. Bukey: *Hitler's Austria: Popular Sentiment in the Nazi Era, 1938-1945* (Chapel Hill & London: The University of North Carolina Press, 1999)

Ernst Hanisch

The years 1938-45 were long omitted from Austrian history and relegated to the history of Germany. It was not until external pressure was applied during the Waldheim Affair (1986-87) that political leaders began integrating these years into Austrian history. Indeed, historians had gotten a much earlier start in demolishing the victim myth, but it was not until 1988 that the first book was published in which Austrian historians and social scientists analyzed the entire Nazi era in Austria. Regional studies had made important preparatory scholarship available, but the attitudes of the people toward National Socialism, war, and Hitler remained rather vague in the works that have appeared so far.

This important book, *Hitler's Austria*, by an American expert on Austria has now filled this gap. It is divided into three sections: the historical path leading to the *Großdeutschen Reich*, the period between the Anschluss and war, and the effect of Hitler's war on the Austrian people. It focuses particularly on the Nazi movement, the working class, Austrian Catholicism, the rural peasantry, and, above all, the radical persecution of the Jews that prefigured subsequent events in the *Altreich*.

From a wealth of previously unknown archival sources, Bukey has put together a fair, conscientiously multifaceted, though unsparingly frank picture of the Austrian people during the period of Nazi rule. He unambiguously refutes the hypothesis that has been put forward by many scholars according to which Austrians were indeed enthused by the Anschluss but quickly became disillusioned and discovered their hidden, anti-Prussian, Austrian consciousness. This old view is replaced by a new one whereby the majority supported the Anschluss system and the German war effort to the bitter end. Bukey's arguments concerning Austrian overrepresentation among the perpetrators on the German side are plausible and supported by the research of others. The exact figures that the author cites—Austrians made up only 8% of the population of the *Großdeutschen Reich* but 14% of all SS men and 40% of the "perpetrators" involved in killing operations (p. 43)—should, however, be used only with the greatest care, since, even to this day, we do not know the total number of "perpetrators."

It is a bitter experience to read that the Austrian population supported the elimination of the Jews, whether through forced emigration or deportation to concentration camps, that many shamelessly enriched themselves and most looked away with a complete lack of interest. Nevertheless, the question of what the Austrians knew about the Holocaust remains open.

Bukey does not fail to mention the examples of modernization that Nazi rule brought to many aspects of life, and which are a prominent part of recollections to this day. But he does not isolate them; rather, he fits them into an overall picture that also includes countless expressions of dissatisfaction and discontent that the author documents with numerous quotations from original sources. The contradictory findings—consent and rebelliousness—lead the study to the impressive formulation: "many individuals held splitminded views, looking in opposite directions at the same time" (XI). That hardly distinguished the *Ostmark* from the *Altreich*. But the central question remains: were the demonstrable Austria-tendencies of the period 1938-45 a form of particularism like in Bavaria and southern Germany, or did they already constitute the nucleus of an Austrian national consciousness? Only a methodologically more rigorous comparison can clear this question up.

Evan Bukey spent many years doing laborious research on primary sources to produce this work, finally battling severe illness in order to complete it. Scholars of Austrian history and the Austrian public owe him a debt of gratitude. In concrete terms, that means that a German translation ought to be published without delay.

Thomas Angerer and Jacques Le Rider, eds., *Ein Frühling, dem kein Sommer folgte. Französisch-österreichische Kulturtransfers seit 1945* (Vienna: Böhlau, 1999)

Friedrich Koja and Otto Pfersmann, eds., *Frankreich – Österreich. Wechselseitige Wahrnehmung und wechselseitiger Einfluss seit 1918* (Vienna: Böhlau, 1994)

Kurt Tweraser

In the last decade the cultural dimension of international relations has become an accepted part of the historical discipline in Austria. The two books under review are vivid examples of the attempt to conceptualize international relations as an intercultural enterprise. The Koja-Pfersmann volume successfully demonstrates that the more conventional political and economic aspects of French-Austrian relations have been underpinned by manifold cultural connections. The Angerer-Le Rider volume focuses more narrowly on how scholars and officials have conceptualized and evaluated the process of culture transfer between France and Austria. Both books competently show that French-Austrian relations cannot be fully understood without taking into account the weight of cultural influences. Both volumes can be interpreted as examples of the workings of culture in international relations involving "the sharing and transmitting of ... dreams and aspirations ... within and across national boundaries."[1]

The essays in the Koja-Pfersmann volume originated in a 1993 symposium in Vienna dealing with a number of significant themes on the complex relationship between France and Austria in the 20th century. Some of the contributions give an overview, others report the results of more recent research. The historical overview is provided by Felix Kreissler, best known as the author of the massive treatise *Der Österreicher und seine Nation* in which he dissected the traumatic

Austrian identity crises the country has undergone through the
centuries.[2] In his wide-ranging essay Kreissler differentiates between
official history and what he calls a "parallel history." He compares the
former to a conflictive, tempestuous, and warlike series of "belches," the
latter to a lasting, often unruly and subversive moment which shows a
rising curve of cultural and scientific achievement over time (p. 31). It
is, in Kreissler's view, the parallel cultural and not the official history,
which best expresses the affinities between France and Austria. The
carriers of parallel history are the creators of literature and music, the
sculptors, the painters, the scientists, and the philosophers.

The other chapters of the volume spell out the details of official and
parallel history. Thus, Pierre Béhar delivers an erudite commentary on
the image of Austria in French historiography since 1918. He, too,
concludes that the overwhelmingly positive elements of Franco-Austrian
relations lay in the realm of culture, whereas in the realm of politics an
older austrophobic tradition clashes with a younger austrophile tradition.
Two contributions deal with the judicial field, in particular the Austrian
innovation of empowering a constitutional court to rescind unconstitu-
tional laws which served as a model for the French judicial reform of
1958. Three essays explore philosophical issues such as the problematic
history of the French reception of logical positivism developed in the
Vienna Circle, the flawed French reception of Hans Kelsen's *Pure
Theory of Law*, and the reception of Austrian philosophical currents in
France. These essays convincingly demonstrate the extent to which the
internationalization of philosophy and philosophers has been hampered
by the existence of national boundaries. Four essays deal with the
mutual reception of literature and art, giving rise to images of France
and Austria not always congruent with a semblance of reality. They
range from an analysis of the image of France in contemporary Austrian
literature to the influence of French painting in the Austrian art world.
Especially rewarding is Gerald Stieg's discussion of a radical turn in the
French image of Austria from effusive idyll to unbridled nightmare in
the wake of the Waldheim affair. The principal Austrian witnesses for
the French press about this affair were Thomas Bernhard and Elfriede
Jelinek.

For the student of more conventional international relations,
especially for those whose interest lie in the politics of occupations, the
volume provides two very informative essays. Nicole Piétri delivers a
commentary on Austrian foreign policy vis-à-vis the other successor
states of the Habsburg empire as seen by the French foreign office. In a

brilliant piece Thomas Angerer reconstructs the basic principles underlying the French-Austrian political relationships since 1938/45. He points to the *Anschlusstrauma* as the essential constant factor of French policy toward Austria. French and Austrian foreign policy can be understood only if one takes the relation of both countries with Germany into account. Because its policy of containment of Germany in the interwar period failed, France sought a better working solution for weakening Germany after World War II, namely by way of an engaged positive policy vis-à-vis Austria. This policy provided for Austria a stable and satisfying existence under the protection of the Great Powers and avoided the economic, political, and military isolation which might have tempted the Austrians to turn toward Germany again for salvation. Consequently, France, as one of the four occupying powers, displayed an extraordinarily positive and enlightened attitude toward the two essentials of Austrian foreign policy: preservation of the unity of the country and conclusion of a state treaty. These French endeavors, welcome to the Austrians while often annoying to the Americans, were part of the French policy of obstructionism in the development of the West German state. With the ironic phrase of the *"bevormundete Vormund,"* Angerer captures the French role of a "tutor" in the Austrian context and a "tutored" party in the American-German context.[3]

France was unwilling to face the loss of its role as a world power. The desire to *rentrer dans le rang* of the Great Powers dominated the French approach to the Austrian question as well. France subscribed to the positive aspects of the Moscow Declaration and insisted successfully on a French seat in the European Advisory Commission and on the establishment of occupation zones in Germany and Austria. Liberated Austria was to be treated as a *pays ami*. The French came as friends eager to lead their Austrian charges back into the fold of European culture after a deplorable flirtation with Nazi barbarism. *Désintoxication* from things German and *désolidarisation* vis-à-vis Germany were the mottos for the strong engagement of France in Austria. However, the French occupation of Austria was also dominated by the tension between the desire to conduct great power politics and the lack of adequate means for it. Thus, the emphasis of the French in Austria centered on the relatively cheap cultural politics.

The second book under review deals with French-Austrian cultural transfers since 1945. In a succinct introduction Angerer sketches the theoretical and methodological framework for cultural transfers in general. He objects to interpreting cultural transfers as cultural imperialism and emphasizes the selective and adaptive capacities of those who import a foreign culture as well as the heterogeneous character of both the sending and the receiving "national cultures." Instead of cultural imperialism, he advocates the more neutral and unemotional concept of cultural transfer. His major hypothesis is that the senders and the recipients of cultural messages are not passive like a radio but are actively engaged in domesticating the foreign messages and objects: *"Transfer transformiert, Übertragungen ergeben auch übertragene Bedeutungen"* (p.15). In contrast to the cultural imperialism in which foreign wares are considered a danger to national identity (*Überfremdung*), Angerer regards them as constituent parts of identity: *"Das andere verliert seine Befremdlichkeit, erhält gleichsam ein Heimatrecht"* (p.16). Angerer's defiance of cultural imperialism, a favorite topic for cold war revisionists, puts him in the company of a rather heterogeneous group of scholars such the Austrian specialist on "Americanization," Reinhold Wagnleitner.[4] In consonance with other "cultural transferists," Angerer interprets the spread of other cultures as a continuous process of negotiations among national groups, deconstructs the notion of cultural imperialism, and substitutes cultural transfer as a more refined and therefore more useful analytical tool. Whether the concept of cultural transfer can be emptied of evaluative overtones remains, however, doubtful. Values have a way of showing up in the most unlikely of places and concepts usually carry their own ideological baggage under the guise of a value free science.

The various contributions to the volume focus on cultural transfers mostly from France to Austria. These include language, the so-called high culture (paintings, theatre, literature, science), but also previously neglected or undervalued art forms such as film and chanson. French cultural diplomacy is loosely defined and encompasses: schools in which French is taught, publishing houses which specialize in French authors, record shops which sell French chansons, university institutes and libraries which specialize in Romance instruction and publications, and even "cultural" vacations in France. In some of the essays cultural "mediators" and "multipliers" come to the center of attention such as Eugène Susini. Touched upon are the image of France entertained by prominent Austrians, the image of France in Austrian schoolbooks and among Austrian tourists; the futile attempt to have French as the first foreign language rather than English; the history of the Lycée Français de Vienne; the reception of modern French culture in Graz, of French theatre on Viennese stages, of French participation in the Alpach Forum.

The impact of French cultural politics on Austria was relatively strong during the period of occupation, but stagnated after its termination, hence the title of the book.

In the final chapter Angerer deftly, but cautiously, summarizes the various contributions in what he terms a bit too modestly "Versuch einer Zusammenschau." His conclusions reflect the ambiguity inherent in the intercultural enterprise. On the one hand, he agrees with the Salzburg cultural historian Georg Schmid that in the Austrian perspective Latin Europe, including France, has been, by and large, invisible.[5] Primarily because of the language barrier, methodological innovations arrived via Germany and/or the United States with all the changes and distortions that cultural detours cause. On the other hand, Angerer correctly discerns a trend towards the relativization of bilateral cultural relations in favor of multilateral and supranational relations, which, so he hopes, might result in an intercultural history, *"die über den bilateralen Rahmen hinausgeht und der Pluralität von Kulturtransfers besser gerecht wird"* (p. 337). The final question seems to be: What will Europeanization and/or globalization do to national identity? So far cultural nationalism and international culture have coexisted, however uneasily. Whether people will adjust to entertaining double or even triple loyalties remains to be seen.

Notes

1. Akira Iriye, "Culture and International History," in *Explaining the History of American Foreign Relations*, ed. Michael J. Hogan and Thomas G. Paterson (New York: Cambridge University Press, 1991), 214–5.

2. Felix Kreissler, *Der Österreicher und seine Nation: Ein Lernprozess mit Hindernissen* (Vienna: Böhlau, 1984).

3. Thomas Angerer, "Der 'bevormundete Vormund': Die französische Besatzungsmacht in Österreich," in *Österreich unter alliierter Besatzung 1945 – 1955*, ed. Alfred Ableitinger, Siegfried Beer, and Eduard G. Staudinger (Vienna: Böhlau, 1998), 159 – 204.

4. Reinhold Wagnleitner, *Coca-Colonisation und Kalter Krieg. Die Kulturmission der U.S.A. in Österreich nach dem Zweiten Weltkrieg* (Vienna: Verlag für Gesellschaftskritik, 1991).

5. Georg Schmid, "Zur Geschichte asymmetrischer Kulturbeziehungen am Beispiel des französischen und österreichischen Films," *Zeitgeschichte* 15 (1987/88): 27 – 36.

Erwin Schmidl: *Österreich im Frühen Kalten Krieg*
1945-1958: Spione. Partisanen Kriegspläne
(Vienna: Böhlau, 2000)

Klaus Larres

It is the major aim of this interesting book to demonstrate that even during the early years of the East-West conflict, small and neutral Austria was an active rather than a mere passive player in international affairs. Although the book's nine articles cover very different aspects of the repercussion of international Cold War policy on Austria between 1945 and 1958, the editor has succeeded admirably in integrating the different articles into a coherent whole. Thus, the book enables the reader to gain a very good overview of the role of Austria in western Cold War planning and execution. Although in any book consisting of articles from a number of different authors the quality and style of the individual pieces tend to vary, the overall quality of the individual chapters is very high. Some of the most important articles are discussed in the following.

The book's opening chapter, written by Günter Bischof, consists of a succinct historiographical account of the developing scholarly interpretations of the Cold War. The chapter thus sets the following chapters into context by covering important conceptual areas which are of crucial importance for the scholarly study of the Cold War. For example, Bischof provides a good overview of the increasing 'institutionalization' of Cold War Studies (as is the case particularly in the USA), reviews the long-standing debates about Cold War 'traditionalism', 'revisionism' and 'post-revisionism', and, in view of the more recent development, adds an enlightening section on 'post-Postrevisionism'. Subsequently, the author summarizes the debate over the periodization of the cold War although here he is a little economical with adding his own thoughts. Moreover, one other aspect has been a little neglected. Since 1990, an increasing number of authors move towards viewing the entire East-West conflict as one 'long' Cold War (from 1945-1990) with different phases of intensity. Thus, international Cold War studies may soon do away with the controversial and not always very satisfying differentiation between a first and a second Cold War which was largely based on the work of International Relations scholar Fred Halliday. Bischofs final section on the Cold War in Austrian historiography is highly illuminating and is an excellent introduction to the field for anyone not mainly concerned with Austrian affairs.

The subsequent three chapters largely deal with the role of the USA in post-war Austria; in particular, the work of the American intelligence services in Austria is examined in great detail. Of particular interest is Siegfried Beer's illuminating account. Beer rightly complains about the still insufficient scholarly access to the relevant archival material in both Vienna and Washington. He points out that in public mythology the CIA, which reports to the National Security Council, is the dominant American intelligence organ, although 85 per cent of the budget for the intelligence community goes to the Department of Defence's National Security Agency and the relatively unknown National Reconnaissance Office. Yet, the CIA is responsible for the co-ordination of the various American intelligence services and this probably explains why in the public mind the CIA is regarded as the American intelligence organ par *excellence*. Beer analyses the development of the various American intelligence organisations during the Second World War in Austria, especially the role of the OSS, before assessing the three main successor organisations to the OSS and also the various military intelligence organs. Of particular interest, however, is the author's thorough analysis of the CIA's activities in Austria in the immediate aftermath of the Second World War. In contrast to earlier studies, Beer comes to the conclusion that despite some initial organisational problems, due to the active support of many Austrians, the CIA and other American in-telligence organs assumed an ever growing importance in the country during the early Cold War years. The crucial time in this connection was the year 1948 when the Berlin crisis and the coup in Prague commenced the East-West conflict proper. Instead of continuing to pursue Nazi criminals, the CIA now focused on fighting the Soviet Union and even began to accept the services of former Nazis for western intelligence purposes.

Arnold Kopeczek's article largely confirms Beer's conclusions. Kopeczek writes that during as well as after the period of occupation the co-operation between the Austrian police organs and western intelligence was very high. Not only did the Austrian authorities tolerate the activities of the various western intelligence organisations but they also actively collaborated by exchanging information and acting on their behalf. On the whole Kopeczek concludes that the clear anti-Communist direction of the Austrian security and intelligence organs contributed to the stabilization of the country and thus to the successful western integration of Austria. In particular, the author credits Interior Minister Franz Olah and his para-military organisation, the CIA financed "*Sport-, Wander- und Geselligkeitsverein*", for convincing the Americans of the firm western orientation of Austria. The cache's of arms, ammunition and explosives found in 1996 were meant to be used by Olah's organisation in case of a coup by the Austrian Communist Party or for fighting off the actitivites of partisans to prepare a Soviet invasion. However, wether this would have been successful is more than doubtful. The author's praise for Olah's peculiar group appears to be somewhat exaggerated.

Edda Engelke's chapter is a moving account of the fate of Austrians in the Soviet zone who were active in espionage activities on behalf of the western powers. Often arrested in dubious circumstances and, after a brief court hearing, sent to far-away camps in remote areas of the Soviet Union many Austrians were thus severely punished for their disloyalty to the Soviet occupation power. While this chapter does not really add to our overall knowledge of the structure of the intelligence operations of the four powers in post-war Austria, with her chapter Engelke contributes the 'human dimension' which is often missing from scholarly accounts. It is heart-breaking to read about the men and women who perished in the Soviet camps for often very minor offences or were isolated in very harsh conditions without the right to write to their families. While some of the Austrians who survived these conditions were allowed to return to their home country in the course of the post-Stalin thaw in mid-1953, most were returned to Austria after the signing of the State Treaty in 1955.

One of the most interesting chapters in the book is the article by the editor, Erwin A. Schmidl. He analyses in great detail the allied plannings for a 'Vienna airlift' in case of a Soviet blockade on the model of the Berlin blockade in 1948-49. The author makes clear that during the early Cold War allied contingency planning for West Germany/West Berlin and Austria cannot be viewed in isolation. Preparations for building an airport in the Viennese suburb of Simmering were made and food and other provisions for almost three months were organized.

Aptly, the whole effort was called Operation 'Squirrel Cage'. Once the war in Korea had been resolved the likelihood of another blockade of Berlin or Vienna however appeared to be increasingly remote and the stockpiles were run down. Early in 1955 the final provisions of canned horse meat were sold as dog feed. The chapter's initial sections are also very valuable as they provide a convenient overview of allied war planning in the late 1940s and discuss the genuine fear, once the Berlin crisis had erupted, that a Soviet attempted coup in Austria might be imminent.

While scholars tend to pay most attention to American and British policies and military contingency planning, the view and activities of the French occupation power, admittedly the smallest and weakest of the 'Big Four', are often somewhat neglected. Bruno Koppensteiner's article successfully closes this gap in the literature. The author discusses the plans of the commander of the French zone, General Béthouart, to make a Soviet invasion of Austria impossible by erecting a vast complex system of defensive barriers. After all, the prevention of a Soviet invasion appeared to be even more important for France and its position in Western Europe than for Britain and the US. Moreover, Paris never failed to consider its Austrian policy without taking the crucial German question into consideration. Koppensteiner concludes his interesting though somewhat long article that France was seriously considering to intervene militarily to uphold Austrian independence if Moscow appeared to threaten it or if there was another tendency for an Austrian-German *Anschluss*. Although French documents are still largely unavailable, it is clear that the French defensive barriers were part of a comprehensive military plan to prevent the Soviet Union's invasion of central and western Europe. In fact, they were meant to balance France's military weakness and make the French position in Austria stronger than it was when considering that after mid May 1946 there were merely 7,000 French troops based in Austria. This contrasted poorly with the 50,000 troops maintained by Britain and the USA and the 250,000 Soviet troops stationed in Austria.

Walter Blasi considers the Lebanon crisis of 1958 when tension arose between Austria and the United States regarding the right for American planes to overfly Austrian territory in order to take the shortest route to the crisis area in the Middle East. As had happened in the past, Austrian authorities tended to give their verbal agreement to American requests for crossing Austrian airspace without much ado. Yet, shortly before a planned visit by Chancellor Raab to Moscow, the

Lebanon crisis provided the Soviet Union with an opportunity to ask Austria to show a more balanced understanding of the meaning of Austrian neutrality. After all, during the Hungarian crisis of 1956 Austria had firmly sided with the West. However, Raab's concessions to the Soviet Union and his decision not to grant permission for any more American flights through Austrain air space arose the suspicion in Washington that Austria was gradually moving into the Soviet orbit. Still, when the United States requested permission in September/October 1958 to return its planes from the Middle East to the US via Austrian air space, Austria once again gave in to Washington. Although the author believes that it was the Soviet Union who benefitted from the episode as Moscow could criticize Austria's 'peculiar neutrality' and for a while undermine the good relationship between Washington and Vienna, a different interpretation is also possible. After all, the episode helped Austria to demonstrate that its neutrality was largely confined to military neutrality. As far as politics was concerned it became clear that Austria attempted to uphold a careful balance between East and West but in the last resort would also side with the United States.

Erwin Schmidl has succeeded in putting together a very useful and stimulating book which substantially adds to our knowledge about Austria's role during the early Cold War.

ANNUAL REVIEW

Survey of Austrian Politics Austria 2000

Reinhold Gärtner

FPÖ-ÖVP-Government: The Causa Prima
The Reactions
The Report by Ahtisaari, Frowein and Oreja
Elections in Styria and Burgenland
Echoes of Watergate?
The Catastrophe of Kaprun

FPÖ-ÖVP-Government: The Causa Prima

The main political topic in 2000 was the establishment of the FPÖ-ÖVP government in February. After the elections of 3 October 1999, the SPÖ was still the strongest political party, followed by the FPÖ and the ÖVP. During the election campaign in 1999, ÖVP Party Chairman Wolfgang Schüssel realized that his party would not be in the government again if it finished third in the elections. Finally, the FPÖ gained 26.91 percent of the votes—and so did the ÖVP. The two parties thus gained the same amount of seats (both 52). However, the small difference of 415 votes—1,244,087 for the FPÖ and 1,243,672 for the ÖVP—became a decisive factor.

After fruitless negotiations between the SPÖ and the ÖVP about a continuation of their coalition, the FPÖ and the ÖVP formed the new government President Klestil accepted it only after a rearrangement of the list of FPÖ ministers Hilmar Kabas and Thomas Prinzhorn, who had been responsible for the FPÖ's xenophobic election campaign, were not accepted as ministers.

While some aspects of this government-building process were not remarkable, others were:

- It was not remarkable that the new chancellor was a member of the ÖVP rather than the SPÖ. This ended a 30-year dominance of SPÖ in Austrian governments (1970-2000).

- It was not remarkable that the second and the third strongest parties formed a government, and that the strongest party went into opposition.
- It was remarkable, though, that the chancellor was appointed by the third strongest party rather than the second strongest.
- It was remarkable, too, that neither the chairman (Haider) nor the top candidate (Prinzhorn) of the stronger party in government were actually members of the government.
- It was remarkable that a right wing populist party, which has a very undistinguished attitude towards Nazism, was represented in government—for the first time in recent (EU-) European history.
- It was also remarkable that the government of an EU-member state had to write a preamble to its inaugural speech. This preamble explicitly stated what one should be able to expect of a European government: the condemnation of Nazism and the disapproval of all forms of racism and xenophobia.

The New Austrian Government

		Replaced by
Chancellor	Wolfgang Schüssel (ÖVP)	
Vice-Chancellor	Susanne Riess-Passer (FPÖ)	
• Public Sector and Sports	Susanne Riess-Passer (FPÖ)	
• Agriculture, Environment, and Water	Wilhelm Molterer (ÖVP)	
• Defense	Herbert Scheibner (FPÖ)	
• Economy and Labor	Martin Bartenstein (ÖVP)	
• Education and Culture	Elisabeth Gehrer (ÖVP)	
• Finance	Karl-Heinz Grasser (FPÖ)	
• Foreign Affairs	Benita Ferrero-Waldner (ÖVP)	
• Interior	Ernst Strasser (ÖVP)	
• Justice	Michael Krüger (FPÖ)	Dieter Böhmdorfer (FPÖ)
• Social Security and Generations	Elisabeth Sickl (FPÖ)	Herbert Haupt (FPÖ)
• Traffic, Innovation, and Technology	Michael Schmidt (FPÖ)	Monika Forstinger (FPÖ)
• State Secretaries		
• Office of the Chancellor	Franz Morak (ÖVP)	
• Social Security and Generations	Reinhart Waneck (FPÖ)	
• Economy and Labor	Mares Rossmann (FPÖ)	
• Finance	Alfred Finz (ÖVP)	

The Reactions

What followed the Austrian formation of government were many reactions from other countries. The other fourteen EU-member states implemented bilateral measures in which they urged to minimize relations with Austria and not to support Austrian candidates for international jobs. The United States and Canada supported these bilateral measures; Israel withdrew its ambassador from Vienna.

Throughout the first half of the year 2000, these bilateral measures—often referred to as "sanctions" in Austria—were the main topic of Austrian politics. Especially the FPÖ and the ÖVP regarded them as unjustified and consequently created the enemy "EU-14." Sooner or later, most of Austria's media adopted this strategy, and the voices arguing in favor of the bilateral measures were largely ignored. The official Austria presented itself in a bizarre mixture of populism and the stereotypes of "The Sound of Music." At the EU summit in Feira (Portugal) Austria tried to promote itself with Sachertorte, beer, and wine; the foreign minister pointed out that Sachertorte was not poisonous and that it was as nice as the Austrians.

Critics were called *Vernaderer* (slanderers) and the governor of Carinthia, Jörg Haider, began to sue them. Alarmingly, this idea was supported by the minister of justice, Dieter Böhmdorfer.

The main problem was (and still is) the FPÖ. The quotations of Jörg Haider are legendary (e.g. calling extermination camps *Straflager*; calling former Waffen-SS members honorary people who stuck to their convictions and principles; or praising Nazi employment policy), and many other FPÖ members added their shocking remarks. Here is just one example: Ernest Windholz, the senior FPÖ official in Lower Austria, opened a party meeting with the phrase "Unsere Ehre heißt Treue" ("Our honor is called loyalty"), the former motto of the SS.

The official Austria remained reluctant to take the criticism seriously and clung to its strategy of "we (the innocent Austria) against them (the unjust others)." Finally, in July, the president of the European Court for Human Rights asked Martti Ahtisaari, Jochen Frowein, and Marcelino Oreja to "deliver, on the basis of thorough extermination, a report covering

- the Austrian Government's commitment to the common European values, in particular concerning the rights of minorities, refugees and immigrants;
- the evolution of the political nature of the FPÖ. ...

Based on the conclusions of this report the XIV will re-examine their bilateral relations with the Austrian Government."[1]

The Report of Ahtisaari, Frowein, and Oreja

On September 8, Ahtisaari, Frowein, and Oreja, the "three wise men," presented their report. Not surprisingly, the Austrian government got off lightly, and not surprisingly, too, the FPÖ was criticized seriously (though in a very diplomatic way). The main points were: [...]

a) The continuous use of ambiguous language by leading members of the FPÖ

   • 88: In fact, it seems to have become a typical phenomenon in Austrian politics that representatives of the FPÖ use very ambiguous language. High level officials of the FPÖ have over a long period of time used statements that can be interpreted to be xenophobic or even racist. The language used is seen by many observers to carry nationalist undertones, sometimes even undertones close to characteristic National Socialist expressions, or to trivialize the history of that period.

   • 89: The FPÖ has reportedly not taken any action against its members who have used xenophobic statements in public; it has neither condemned nor suppressed those statements, nor clearly apologized for them. When confronted with these statements the authors will deny that any National Socialist intention or even character really existed.

   • 90: There are, unfortunately, several political groupings using similar language in Europe. The FPÖ has, however, become the second strongest party in Austria and has been, since February 2000, a coalition partner in the Austrian Federal Government. We are of the opinion that a governmental party must be under much heavier scrutiny as far as its language and statements are concerned than opposition parties. ...

   • 92: The FPÖ has been described as a "right wing populist party with extremist expressions." This description is, according to our judgment, still applicable after the party joined the Federal Government. This must give rise to concern, since Governments are the organs of the European states which have to direct responsibility to implement their positive obligations concerning the protection and promotion of human rights, democracy, and the suppression of any kind of ethnic or racial discrimination.

b)   Attacks on the freedom of criticism

*   93: One of the most problematic features concerning important members of the FPÖ are attempts to silence or to even criminalize political opponents if they criticize the Austrian Government. The frequent use of libel procedures against individuals who have criticized the FPÖ or the statements of its political leaders should also be seen in this context.

*   94: The possibility of using provision in the Criminal Code for deputies who criticise [sic] the Government was mentioned in a press conference by the Landeshauptmann (Prime Minister) of Carinthia in presence of the Federal Minister of Justice. When the opposition parties introduced formal parliamentary questioning, the Minister of Justice insisted on the freedom of opinion of those submitting such as proposal. ...

*   5: We are of the opinion that such a position by a Minister in the Federal Government is not in line with his obligations as an organ of the state under the constitutional structure of the European Union as confirmed by Art. 6 of the Union Treaty. ...

*   96: It must also be stressed that propositions of that sort may easily create a chilling effect for those who want to criticise [sic] the Government.

c)   The use of libel procedures by the FPÖ

*   97: The chilling effect just mentioned is apparently strengthened by what has been described to us as a strategy to use the courts to suppress criticism wherever that criticism is expressed in strong terms. FPÖ politicians have used the courts continuously during the recent years. At the present time, according to information given to us, there is a peak in the number of court cases brought by politicians of the FPÖ.[2]

Elections to the State Diet in Styria and Burgenland

In October 15 and December 3 respectively the state diets of Styria and Burgenland were elected. The Styrian election took place as scheduled; the Burgenland election was a new election due to the so-called Bank Burgenland Scandal. In 2000, Bank Burgenland had to face liabilities of bankruptcies which amounted to 4 billion Schillings (290 million Euro). Thus the ÖVP/FPÖ government called for new elections in 2000 (instead of 2001).

In Styria, the elections presented a landslide victory for governor Waltraud Klasnic (ÖVP): the ÖVP received 47.3 percent—11 percent more than in the 1995 elections. The SPÖ lost votes, and so did the FPÖ. The Greens were the second winner with 5.6 percent (+1.3 percent).

State Diet Elections in Styria

	2000 percent	2000 seats	1995 percent	1995* seats
ÖVP	47.3 (+11)	27	36.2	21
SPÖ	32.3 (-3.6)	19	35.9	21
FPÖ	12.4 (-4.3)	7	17.1	10
Grüne	5.6 (+1.3)	3	4.3	2

* 2 seats for LIF (Liberales Forum)

In Styria, the FPÖ—for the first time in state diet elections since 1986—had to face a serious loss. This triggered nervous reactions from the FPÖ, including Jörg Haider's threat of new national elections.

In Burgenland, the election results were slightly different. The SPÖ and the Greens gained votes; the ÖVP and, again, the FPÖ lost.

State Diet Elections in Burgenland

	2000 percent	2000 seats	1996 percent	1996 seats
SPÖ	46.6 (+2.1)	17	44.5	17
ÖVP	35.3 (-0.8)	13	36.1	14
FPÖ	12.6 (-1.9)	4	14.5	5
Grüne	5.5 (+3)	2	2.5	0

Echoes of Watergate?

"Sinister allegations have surfaced in Austria of a Watergate-style dirty tricks campaign conducted by Jörg Haider's right-wing populist

Freedom Party against opponents with the help of rogue police officers", writes *The Independent* on 28 October 2000. A senior policeman had confessed that for years the Freedom Party had been paying certain police officers for illegally extracting information from police sources. According to media reports, as many as sixty-seven FPÖ officials, including Haider, are under investigation by the state prosecutor. Officials from the prosecutor's office have raided the homes of leading Freedom Party members, including the home of Hilmar Kabas, the Viennese FPÖ leader.

Already in December 1997, Haider had boasted to journalists that he could gain certain information for himself at any time.

The case is still under investigation.

The Catastrophe of Kaprun

On November 11 a cable car to the glacier of Kitzsteinhorn caught fire. 155 skiers, many of them teenagers and young children, were killed in the inferno. It was the most serious accident in the Austrian Alps to date.

Economic Data

In 2000 on average 3,133,000 people were employed; 194,000 were unemployed; the rate of unemployment was 5.8%.

The GNP was at 2,712 billion Schillings (197 billion Euro) in 1999; inflation at 2.6 % (2000). Exports amounted to 951 billion Schillings (64 billion Euro), imports to 1,022 billion Schillings (74.3 billion Euro).

According to the Maastricht criteria the public deficit was at 32.5 billion Schillings (2.36 billion Euro; 1.15% of the GNP) and the public debt was 1,782 billion Schillings (129.5 billion Euro; 62.88% of GNP).

Notes

1. "Report by Martti Ahtisaari, Jochen Frowein, Marcelino Oreja," Paris, 8 September 2000," see http://www.virtual-institute.de/de/Bericht-EU/report.pdf.

2. Ibid.

List of Authors

Thomas Angerer, Associate Professor of Modern History, University of Vienna

Siegfried Beer, Professor of Modern History, University of Graz

Hans-Georg Betz, Professor of Political Science, Centre for German and European Studies, York University, Canada

Günter Bischof, Professor of History and Executive Director, Center Austria, University of New Orleans

Gerda Falkner, *Max Planck Institut für Gesellschaftsforschung*, Cologne, Germany

Alexandra Friedrich, Independent Scholar, Munich, Germany

Winfried Garscha, Senior Associate, *Dokumentationsarchiv des Österreichischen Widerstandes*, Vienna

Reinhold Gärtner, Associate Professor of Political Science, University of Innsbruck, and Secretary *Gesellschaft für Politische Aufklärung*

Michael Gehler, Professor of Contemporary History and Coordinator, Working Group of European Integration, University of Innsbruck

Ernst Hanisch, Professor of Modern History, University of Salzburg

Michael Huelshoff, Associate Professor of Political Science, University of New Orleans

Klaus Larres, Reader in Politics and Jean Monnet Chair for European Foreign and Security Policy at the Queen's University of Belfast

Jacques Le Rider, Professor of German, University of Paris VIII (Sorbonne)

Sabine Loitfellner, Researcher, *Dokumentationsarchiv des Österreichischen Widerstandes*, Vienna

Walter Manoschek, Professor of Political Science, University of Vienna

Richard Mitten, Director of International Office, Trinity College

Heinrich Neisser, Jean Monnet Professor, Department of Political Science, University of Innsbruck

Anton Pelinka, Professor of Political Science, University of Innsbruck, Director, *Institut für Konfliktforschung*, Vienna

Martin Polaschek, Professor of Law, University of Graz

Johannes Pollak, Austrian Academy of Sciences, Vienna

Sonja Puntscher Riekmann, Austrian Academy of Scienes, Vienna, and Humboldt University, Berlin, Germany

Kurt Tweraser, Professor Emeritus of Political Science, University of Arkansas, Fayetteville

10 Years of *Contemporary Austrian Studies*

Günter Bischof and Anton Pelinka, Editors
Ellen Palli, Production Editor

Transaction Publishers, New Brunswick (N.J.) and London (U.K)

Volume 1 (1993)
Austria in the New Europe

Volume 2 (1994)
The Kreisky Era in Austria
Oliver Rathkolb, Guest Editor

Volume 3 (1995)
Austria in the Nineteen Fifties
Rolf Steininger, Guest Editor

Volume 4 (1996)
Austro-Corporatism: Past –
Present – Future

Volume 5 (1997)
Austrian Historical Memory &
National Identity

Volume 6 (1998)
Women in Austria
Erika Thurner, Guest Editor

Volume 7 (1999)
The Vranitzky Era in Austria
Ferdinand Karlhofer, Guest
Editor

Volume 8 (2000)
The Marshal Plan in Austria
Dieter Stiefel, Guest Editor

Volume 9 (2001)
Neutrality in Austria
Ruth Wodak, Guest Editor

Volume 10 (2002)
Austria and the EU
Michael Gehler, Guest Editor

.

For Product Safety Concerns and Information please contact our EU
representative GPSR@taylorandfrancis.com
Taylor & Francis Verlag GmbH, Kaufingerstraße 24, 80331 München, Germany

www.ingramcontent.com/pod-product-compliance
Lightning Source LLC
Chambersburg PA
CBHW020333270326
41926CB00007B/168